# TEILHARD IN THE 21ST CENTURY

# Teilhard
## in the 21st Century

*The Emerging Spirit of Earth*

Arthur Fabel
Donald St. John
Editors

ORBIS BOOKS

Maryknoll, New York 10545

Founded in 1970, Orbis Books endeavors to publish works that enlighten the mind, nourish the spirit, and challenge the conscience. The publishing arm of the Maryknoll Fathers and Brothers, Orbis seeks to explore the global dimensions of the Christian faith and mission, to invite dialogue with diverse cultures and religious traditions, and to serve the cause of reconciliation and peace. The books published reflect the views of their authors and do not represent the official position of the Maryknoll Society. To learn more about Maryknoll and Orbis Books, please visit our website at www.maryknoll.org.

Library of Congress Cataloging-in-Publication Data

Teilhard in the 21st century : the emerging spirit of earth / Arthur
Fabel, Donald St. John, editors.
    p. cm.
  Includes bibliographical references and index.
  ISBN 1-57075-507-8
  1. Teilhard de Chardin, Pierre. I. Title: Teilhard in the
twenty-first century. II. Fabel, Arthur. III. St. John, Donald P.
(Donald Patrick), 1941- IV. Title.
  B2430.T374T425 2003
  194—dc22

                                          2003010718

# Contents

# Introducing
# the American Teilhard Association
# and *Teilhard Studies*

## THE ASSOCIATION

The American Teilhard Association, established in 1967, is dedicated to achieving the following objectives:

1. A future worthy of the planet Earth in the full splendor of its evolutionary emergence.

2. A future worthy of the human community as the expression and fulfillment of Earth's evolution process.

3. A future worthy of the generations that will succeed us.

Guided by the writings of Pierre Teilhard de Chardin, the association seeks to bring an encompassing perspective to this task of shaping the well-being of the Earth community at a time when so many crises threaten it. Teilhard's vision of the sequential evolution of the universe from its origin to the human phenomenon can provide a firm and inspiring basis upon which to proceed. Now for the first time, humanity is converging toward a new multiform planetary civilization that needs to be understood and facilitated.

The American Teilhard Association publishes the *Teilhard Perspective* newsletter along with *Teilhard Studies* twice a year. The association's annual meeting is held in the spring in New York City. Annual membership is $30. For membership or further information, please contact The American Teilhard Association, c/o The Spirituality Institute, Iona College, 715 North Ave., New Rochelle, NY 10801.

Visit the American Teilhard Association website at **www.teilhard.cjb.net**.

## TEILHARD STUDIES

For twenty-five years the American Teilhard Association has published a semiannual series of short studies concerned with the future of humanity in light of the thought of Pierre Teilhard de Chardin (1881–1955). In the *Teilhard Studies* series, a consistent attempt has been made to expand the Teilhardian vista into many relevant areas. The volume you hold, *Teilhard in the 21st Century,* is a representative selection of the *Studies*. A complete list of studies follows.

These issues of *Teilhard Studies* are available for $4.50 each from President of the American Teilhard Association, John Grim, Department of Religion, Bucknell University, Lewisburg, PA 17837.

# Acknowledgments

A multi-author volume whose contents span a quarter century and which springs from the entire *Teilhard Studies* series and its host American Teilhard Association would be possible only through the efforts of many dedicated individuals.

Thomas Berry served for many years as president of the Association, during which time he initiated the *Teilhard Studies*. He participated in the original 1964 meeting at Fordham University to discuss a Teilhard society and gave it a much-needed home in the 1980s and 1990s at the Riverdale Center for Religious Research in New York City. Thomas has made a significant advance by providing Teilhard's thought with a necessary ecological dimension, as conveyed by his articles in this volume. He remains a mentor and inspiration to everyone engaged in the great work of achieving a sacred Earth community.

Ewert Cousins, a professor of theology at Fordham University, has also been a president of the Association. Similarly involved from the 1960s, Dr. Cousins has taught many courses on Teilhard and has introduced a generation of students to an integral global spirituality much of which was rooted in Teilhard's work. A recent paper is included in the Teilhardian bibliography.

Original planning for the book was done in consultation with Brian Swimme in Berkeley, California. Dr. Swimme's evocative telling of the cosmic genesis story through video imagery, lyrical writings, and many workshops has uniquely communicated this vital vision.

The American Teilhard Association is unusual among such groups by having the same people stay on the job indefinitely. Both the *Teilhard Studies* and its *Teilhard Perspective* newsletter have benefited from only one publisher, Harry Buck. Now an emeritus professor of religion from Wilson College in Chambersburg, Pennsylvania, Harry has patiently transformed diverse materials and manuscripts into professional documents.

Special recognition is further merited for Donald Gray, the first editor of the *Teilhard Studies*. Professor Gray, whose own study and biographical note are within, established the academic quality of the series and its range of subjects through the initial ten issues.

The late Winifred McCullough likewise edited the *Teilhard Perspective* for some nineteen years until 1996. Winifred's international travel and network of friends made this semiannual publication a reliable source of everything Teilhardian.

For many years now John Grim has been the president of the Association and Mary Evelyn Tucker, vice president. They have effectively guided its course and growth, and they conceived the initial idea for this collection. John and Mary Evelyn have provided vigorous leadership for efforts to achieve religious resources for environmental responsibility through many conferences, a book series, and a popular website, each noted within.

And finally our compliments to a remarkable publisher, Orbis Books. Its editor-in-chief, Bill Burrows, recognized the currency and value of an anthology of selected studies, which he artfully guided through to this comprehensive edition. Many thanks also to Catherine Costello, production manager at Orbis Books, and to The HK Scriptorium, Inc., for copyediting, typesetting, and indexing.

# Contributors and Editors

**EULALIO BALTAZAR** has a degree in agriculture from the University of the Philippines and a doctorate in philosophy from Georgetown University with a dissertation on Teilhard. Dr. Baltazar is Professor of Philosophy at the University of the District of Columbia, which serves many inner-city students. Among his works are *Teilhard and the Supernatural* (1966) and *God in Process* (1970).

**THOMAS BERRY** is Professor Emeritus of the History of Religions at Fordham University, a program that he founded along with the Riverdale Center for Religious Research. He is past president of the American Teilhard Association (1972–1985). Among his works are *The Dream of the Earth* (1988), *The Great Work* (1999), and *The Universe Story* (with Brian Swimme; 1992).

**KATHLEEN DUFFY, S.S.J.,** received her Ph.D. in physics from Drexel University and currently she is Professor of Physics at Chestnut Hill College. Formerly, she has taught physics at Drexel University, Bryn Mawr College, Ateneo de Manila University, and the University of the Philippines. Dr. Duffy has published research in atomic physics and chaos theory in journals such as *Physics Review Letters* and *Journal of Chemical Physics*.

**ARTHUR FABEL** has recently retired as an engineer and writer in the field of materials and environmental technology. He was the editor of the *Teilhard Studies* from 1983 to 1993 and is presently editor of the *Teilhard Perspective* newsletter of the American Teilhard Association. Fabel has published articles in *Cross Currents, Journal of Evolutionary and Social Systems,* and *Environmental Ethics.*

**JOSEPH A. GRAU** was Professor of Religious Studies at Sacred Heart University, Fairfield, Connecticut, and has passed away since making his contribution to *Teilhard Studies.* He held a doctorate in moral theology from the Catholic University of America and is the author of *Morality and the Human Future in the Thought of Teilhard de Chardin* (1976). Dr. Grau served as the executive director of the Justice and Peace Center in Milwaukee and also taught at St. Mary's College and Marquette University.

**DONALD P. GRAY** is Professor of Religious Studies at Manhattan College and was the original editor of the *Teilhard Studies* series and past vice president of the American Teilhard Association. His doctoral thesis at Fordham University was published as *The One and the Many: Teilhard de Chardin's Vision of Unity* (1969).

**JOHN GRIM** is a professor in the religion department at Bucknell University, Lewisburg, Pennsylvania. His doctoral work was on Ojibway shamanism under the mentorship of Thomas Berry and was published as *The Shaman.* Grim conducts field studies among the Apsaaloke/Crow peoples of Montana and the Swy-ahl-puh/Kettle Falls peoples of Washington state. Since 1985 he has been the president of the American Teilhard Association. With Mary Evelyn Tucker he is the co-coordinator of the Forum on Religion and Ecology. He is also the editor of *Indigenous Traditions and Ecology* (2000).

JOHN F. HAUGHT received his Ph.D. from Catholic University of America and currently is Healy Distinguished Professor of Theology at Georgetown University. He served as chair of the Georgetown Department of Theology from 1990 to 1995. His teaching and research interests focus especially on issues in science and religion, cosmology and theology, and religion and ecology. Haught is the author of many books and articles, and his latest work is *Deeper Than Darwin* (2003).

THOMAS M. KING, S.J., has been teaching courses on Teilhard since 1968 when he joined the theology department at Georgetown University. Among his works is *Teilhard de Chardin* (1988) written for The Way of the Christian Mystics series. Fr. King has a master's degree in education from Fordham University, a doctorate in sacred theology from the University of Strasbourg, and an S.T.L. degree from Woodstock.

URSULA KING is Professor Emerita in Theology and Religious Studies and senior research fellow at the University of Bristol, England. A prolific author, Dr. King has written or edited several current works about Teilhard published by Orbis Books: *Spirit of Fire: The Life and Vision of Teilhard de Chardin* (1996), *Pierre Teilhard de Chardin: Writings* (1998), and *Christ in All Things: Exploring Spirituality with Teilhard de Chardin* (2000).

ELEANOR RAE has a Ph.D. in contemporary systematic theology from Fordham University. She is the author of *Women, the Earth, the Divine* published by Orbis Books (1994). Most recently, her article on "The Holy Spirit and Process Theology" was published in *Christianity and Ecology* in the Harvard World Religions and Ecology series. Rae has spoken widely in the United States and abroad on subjects such as the Holy Spirit and an Earth-centered spirituality.

WILLIAM E. REES received his Ph.D. in population ecology from the University of Toronto and has taught at the University of British Columbia's School of Community and Regional Planning (SCARP) since 1969. He founded SCARP's program in environment and resource planning and from 1994 to 1999 served as director of the school. Rees's teaching and research focuses on the public policy and planning implications of global environmental trends and the necessary ecological conditions for sustainable socioeconomic development. Much of this work is in the realm of human ecology and ecological economics, where he is best known for inventing the concept of the "ecological footprint." Rees is a founding member and recent past president of the Canadian Society for Ecological Economics. He is also a co-investigator in the Global Integrity Project, aimed at defining the ecological and political requirements for biodiversity preservation.

**DONALD ST. JOHN** is coeditor of this volume and has been editor of *Teilhard Studies* for the past ten years. He is a professor in the department of religion at Moravian College, Bethlehem, Pennsylvania, and earned his doctorate at Fordham University with Thomas Berry. St. John has authored articles on ecological spirituality, Native American religions, and Thomas Merton. He is the coauthor of *Teilhard Study* no. 37: Merton and Ecology.

**BRIAN SWIMME** earned his Ph.D. from the University of Oregon with research on gravitational systems. Brian coauthored with Thomas Berry *The Universe Story* (1992) and produced the acclaimed video series *Canticle to the Cosmos* and *Earth's Imagination*. In 1998 Orbis Books published his book *The Hidden Heart of the Cosmos*. Swimme is presently on the graduate faculty of the California Institute of Integral Studies.

**MARY EVELYN TUCKER** received her Ph.D. from Columbia University and is a professor of religion at Bucknell University. Her most recent book is *Worldly Wonder: Religions Enter their Ecological Phase* (2003). Since 1979 Tucker has served as vice-president of the American Teilhard Association. With John Grim she is the co-coordinator of the Forum on Religion and Ecology and editor of the ten-volume Harvard series on Religions of the World and Ecology. They have also constructed a comprehensive website on religion and ecology based at the Harvard University Center for the Environment at http//:environment.harvard.edu/religion.

# Introduction

JOHN GRIM and MARY EVELYN TUCKER

At the beginning of the twenty-first century, as mechanistic models of the cosmos lose their explanatory power, the organic relationship of emergent matter and consciousness continues to challenge human understanding. Despite the limits of his vision and the historical constraints of his knowledge, the thought of Pierre Teilhard de Chardin (1881–1955), French Jesuit and paleontologist, still reflects one of the most inspired examinations of these evolutionary questions. Teilhard's significance extends into current discussions regarding the relationship of religion and science, religion and evolution, and spirit and matter.

During the twentieth century, religious and secular thinkers have pondered the relationship of human consciousness to material reality. Religious thinkers have often framed their inquiry in terms of divine and human interactions—that is, religious revelations in which a divine mediation is seen as having broken into the separated worlds of the human and created matter. Consciousness is imaged as having been extended from the divine realm to the human as if God reached across space to impart psychic vitality to the languid body of Adam.

Secular humanistic thinkers have emphasized a second, or human, mediation by highlighting the significance of personal interactions with other humans. Human agency is considered primary; divine agency is discounted. In this anthropocentric perspective matter often occupies a subservient, secondary position in which the nonhuman life-world is seen largely as of service to or use by humans. This has been further extended by the empirical sciences, where consciousness appears as an emergent phenomenon having come from nothing but inert, nonconscious matter that composes the known universe.

Teilhard took a different approach from either of these predominantly traditional religious or secular emphases. He offered a more holistic vision by situating consciousness as integral to the emerging universe. Teilhard proposed that the increasing complexity and consciousness of humans is directly related to the evolution of the universe. This complexity-consciousness, for Teilhard, is an emergent property of matter itself. Highlighting planetary developments and using the phrase "the spirit of the Earth," he focused on the quantum of matter that successively evolves into the layered envelopes encircling the planet. Following scientific categories he labeled these layers the lithosphere of rock, the hydrosphere of water, and the biosphere of life. This subsequently evolves, he proposed, into the consciousness humankind now displays in the thought sphere or noosphere surrounding the globe. Unwilling to separate matter and spirit, he understood

1

these linked spheres as different but interrelated perspectives on the same emergent reality. For Teilhard, the plural, diverse matter of the universe in the process of evolutionary change is ultimately pulled forward by the unifying dynamics of spirit.

Teilhard dedicated his life work to fostering an active realization by humans of their evolutionary roles in relation to emergent matter-spirit. This he framed as the challenge of *seeing*, namely, cultivating mindfulness to imagine an organically developing universe. To assist this seeing Teilhard articulated a phenomenology of the involution of matter, a metaphysics of union with spirit, and a mysticism of centration of person.[1] This introduction will begin by describing the challenge of "seeing" and will investigate the nature of Teilhard's phenomenology, metaphysics, and mysticism. We will conclude by highlighting some of the contributions and the limitations of Teilhard's thought.

## TEILHARD'S LIFE QUESTION: SEEING

Born into a Catholic family in the Auvergne region of southern France, Teilhard entered the Jesuit religious order, where he was encouraged to study early life forms, or paleontology. It is not surprising that his readings in evolutionary biology and his field studies of fossils brought him to question the traditional Genesis cosmology of the Bible. The Genesis story of creation in seven days did not correspond to Teilhard's understanding of an emerging universe that had changed over time. The challenge, as Teilhard saw it, was to bring Christianity and evolution into a mutually enhancing relationship with each other. The path to this rapport was first to wake up to the dimensions of time that evolution opened up: "For our age, to have become conscious of evolution means something very different from and much more than having discovered one further fact. . . . It means (as happens with a child when he acquires the sense of perspective) that we have become alive to a new dimension."[2]

Teilhard thus struggled to extend contemporary science beyond an analytical investigation into the world to become a means of seeing the depth dimensions of space and time in the evolutionary process. In so doing his efforts became entangled in the Modernist controversy. This involved an ongoing conflict from the late nineteenth century into the first two decades of the twentieth century between the Vatican and various modern ideas that were perceived as threatening to orthodox Catholic thinking. This included, in particular, the Darwinian theory of evolution and critical methods for interpreting the Bible. Caught in these tensions, Teilhard struggled throughout his life to remain loyal to the teachings of the Catholic Church at the same time as he articulated an unfolding vision of what he saw as a vast creative universe.

At the very outset of his major work, *The Human Phenomenon,* Teilhard spoke of the challenge for humans to see into the deep unity of evolution:

Seeing. One could say that the whole of life lies in seeing—if not ultimately, at least essentially. To be more is to be more united—and this sums up and is the very conclusion of the work to follow. But unity grows, and we will affirm this again, only if it is supported by an increase of consciousness of vision. That is probably why the history of the living world can be reduced to the elaboration of ever more perfect eyes at the heart of a cosmos where it is always possible to discern more. Are not the perfection of an animal and the supremacy of the thinking being measured by the penetration and power of synthesis of their glance? To try to see more and to see better is not, therefore, just a fantasy, curiosity, or a luxury. See or perish. This is the situation imposed on every element of the universe by the mysterious gift of existence. And thus, to a higher degree, this is the human condition.[3]

For Teilhard a central problem in seeing the unity of evolution was a perceived separation between matter and spirit. This was evident in the mechanistic, Cartesian science of his day, which viewed matter as dead and inert, and in dualistic religious worldviews, which saw God as transcendent and apart from matter. He sought to reunite affirmation of the world of matter with an affirmation of the divine manifest in evolution. Thus, in one of his most striking statements Teilhard put forward an apologetic, or defense, of his personal belief that boldly proclaims his faith in the world.[4] He writes:

> If, as the result of some interior revolution, I were to lose in succession my faith in Christ, my faith in a personal God, and my faith in spirit, I feel that I should continue *to believe* invincibly *in the world*. The world (its value, its infallibility and its goodness)—that, when all is said and done, is the first, the last, and the only thing in which I believe. It is by this faith that I live. And it is to this faith, I feel, that at the moment of death, rising above all doubts, I shall surrender myself.[5]

Teilhard argued that the scientific investigation of evolution, rather than leading away from Christianity, would actually lead one toward a profound sense of a Cosmic Christ in the universe, whom he saw as drawing evolution toward a greater personalization and deepening of the spirit.[6] The separation of spirit from matter so prevalent in both science and religion missed this deep unitive quality of the universe.

As science since Darwin has revealed, the universe is a cosmogenesis, namely, in a state of continual development over time. This is in contrast to an unchanging creation as presented in the Bible or degeneration from a once perfected cosmos as in Neoplatonism. Evolution displays dynamic, self-organizing processes from the atom to the galaxies. Thus atoms eventually form into cells that evolve into multicellular organisms and eventually into higher forms of life. This is what Teilhard implies when he notes that with greater complexity of life comes greater consciousness until self-reflection emerges in humans.

Disintegration, change, and suffering are, for Teilhard, inevitable dimensions of the evolutionary process in which the plurality of matter resists unity with spirit.[7] Progress to higher states of complexity and consciousness seems to require a deficit as the flow of energy decays to unusable entropy. In the individual person, suffering has a redemptive function as part of the larger transformations related to creative, universe processes.

As individuals "see" into the unity of evolution they will come to realize how they are participating in larger evolutionary dynamics and thus contributing to the flourishing of the Earth community. For Teilhard the ultimate human adventure is to bind one's energies with evolution and to unite one's personhood with that animating center that is drawing forward all of creation.


## PHENOMENOLOGY:
## THE SIGNIFICANCE OF COMPLEXITY-CONSCIOUSNESS

Teilhard attempts his fullest telling of the story of evolutionary processes in *The Human Phenomenon,* which was completed in 1940. This comprehensive synthesis first appeared in English in 1959, and a new translation was published forty years later in 1999. In this work Teilhard suggests that any consideration of physical mass in the world entailed at least "three infinites." The first two "infinites" were the realms of the infinitely large and the infinitely small. While scientific studies emphasized cosmos and atom (the large and the small), Teilhard proposed a third axis of biological complexity that provided a link to consciousness. This axial law of complexity-consciousness for Teilhard moves through matter and acts as its basis for organization. The evolution of matter in this perspective proceeds as an involuting or inward-turning progression that moves from a simple cellular stage toward greater complexity and conscious reflection. From particles and molecules to atoms, from single cells to multicellular organisms, from plants and trees to invertebrates and vertebrates, evolution displays a movement toward more complex organisms and toward greater sentience.

Teilhard accepts the idea of initial creation in the great flaring forth of the primal fireball. However, he clearly could not accept a biblical literalist view of a completed seven-day creation in the form presented in Genesis. The facts of science contradict such an explanation of the appearance of life. Moreover, it was his understanding of evolutionary time and his explanation of evil as resulting from the energy and entropy flows of life's progression that brought him into conflict with the Church.[8]

From Teilhard's perspective all of matter is evolving toward higher forms of complexity-consciousness. Matter, then, could not be regarded as simply evil in the gnostic sense, or as emanations from a higher consciousness into lower worlds of intelligence and form as in Neoplatonism. Instead, matter is inexorably associated with spirit, in which both work as a vital instrument for the growth of consciousness. This process culminates in the personalizing force of hominization—that is, the conscious reflection of the universe in the human.

In *The Human Phenomenon,* Teilhard posits three qualities of matter: plurality, unity, and energy.[9] Plurality implies an endless degradation or breaking apart, a downward movement of things. Thus, there is in the universe an infinite possibility for differentiation. Unity arises in relation to plurality in that the different volumes of matter are coextensive and bound to one another. Paradoxically, union differentiates into increasingly identifiable entities. Energy resides in the dynamic interaction of things, the power of bonding. It indicates an upward movement, a power of building up. While complexity-consciousness is an emergent property, Teilhard also saw that the cosmos is being held together and drawn forward from above or ahead.

Teilhard emphasizes the wholeness of all of matter rather than its fragmentation. It is exactly that vision of wholeness in evolutionary processes that he strives to outline in *The Human Phenomenon*. He sees matter as differentiated by plurality, as an interconnected whole by unity, and as a quantum infused by energy.[10] An essential principle of this total system is the second law of thermodynamics, which specifies the dissipation and the loss of usable energy. This basic dialectic is at the root of the entire evolutionary process whereby entropy or dissipation is an inevitable corollary of forward movement.

In explaining the internal and external dimensions of spirit-matter Teilhard spoke of the psychic and physical dimension of things. His justification for such a view lies in inductive observation in which human consciousness is situated not as an evolutionary aberration or addendum but as the defining emergent quality of matter itself. He asserts:

> Indisputably, deep within ourselves, through a rent or tear, an "interior" appears at the heart of beings. This is enough to establish the existence of this interior in some degree or other everywhere forever in nature. Since the stuff of the universe has an internal face at one point in itself, its structure is necessarily *bifacial*; that is, in every region of time and space, as well, for example, as being granular, *coextensive with its outside, everything has an inside.*[11]

For Teilhard, then, evolution is both a psychic and a physical process; matter has its within and its without. Teilhard describes two kinds of energy as involved in evolution, namely, *tangential* and *radial*. Tangential is "that which links an element with all others of the same order as itself in the universe." Radial energy is that which draws the element "toward ever greater complexity and centricity, in other words, forwards."[12] Teilhard observes that there are self-organizing principles or tendencies evident in matter that result in more intricate systems:

> Left long enough to itself, under the prolonged and universal play of chance, matter manifests the property of arranging itself in more and more complex groupings and at the same time, in ever deepening layers of consciousness; this double and combined movement of physical unfolding and psychic interiorisation (or centration) once started, continuing, accelerating and growing to its utmost extent.[13]

He suggests, then, that the evolution of spirit and matter are two phases of a single process: "Spiritual perfection (or conscious 'centricity') and material synthesis (or complexity) are merely the two connected faces or parts of a single phenomenon."[14]

Teilhard thus saw the deep weave of matter and spirit from the early formation of the universe to the emergence of life on Earth and into the appearance of the human. Matter is in a state of complex development that passes through certain critical phases of transformation. The first of these phases is that of granulation, in which matter gives birth to constituent atoms and molecules are formed. Eventually, mega-molecules arise and, finally, the first cells. In all of this, Teilhard assumes vast spans of time as opposed to the seven-day creation story of Genesis. While Teilhard would clearly not have known the most current estimate for the age of the Earth, namely, some 13.7 billion years, he was abreast of the latest thinking of his scientific colleagues on many issues regarding evolutionary theory.

The thresholds of the evolutionary process as outlined by Teilhard are, first, *cosmogenesis*—the rise of the mineral and inorganic world. The second is *biogenesis* in which organic life appears. Gradually, there is an increase in cephalization (development of a more complex nervous system) and cerebration (more complex brain) until *anthropogenesis* is reached. This third phase implies the birth of thought in humans and for the first time evolution is able to reflect upon itself. Humans become the heirs of the evolutionary process capable of determining its further progression or retrogression. This is an awesome responsibility, and much of Teilhard's later work explicates how humans can most effectively participate in the ongoing creativity of evolutionary processes.

The importance of greater personalization, or "hominization," of the individual and the species joins the cosmological and ethical dimensions in Teilhard's thought. The florescence of humans around the planet has resulted in natural processes being adapted into the human realm or noosphere. For example, hominization of natural selection now results in humans deciding, in many instances, which forms of life will survive in fragile ecosystems. As Brian Swimme notes, another natural process, neotony, or the observed characteristic of an extended juvenile stage among mammals that encourages play, is hominized into an extended youth among humans manifested in such social expressions as celebrations and sports.[15]

At our present stage of evolution humans join with the interior pull of complexity-consciousness resulting in an affection that draws forward all of evolution. Thus a greater spiritualization of the universe is generated, which he calls the transforming power of love, the amorization of things. By the increase of amorization and personalization in the individual, there arises a collective spirit of human consciousness encompassing the globe that Teilhard terms *noogenesis*. The final threshold is when evolution moves toward its highest form of personalization and spiritualization in the Cosmic Christ of the universe. Having come to that which has been drawing evolution forward through all its millennia of movement, spirit-matter simultaneously arrives at the end that was its beginning—its Omega point.

The implications, then, of Teilhard's evolutionary thought for human action can be summarized as follows:

The essential phenomenon in the material world is life (because life is interiorized).

The essential phenomenon in the living world is the human (because humans are reflective). . . .

The essential phenomenon of humans is gradual totalization of humankind (in which individuals super-reflect upon themselves).[16]

Within this perspective the human plays a vital part in the evolutionary process through deepened reflection, increased socialization, and broadened planetization. This is because the human is that being in whom evolution becomes conscious of itself and looks back on the unfolding universe process.

The collective consciousness and action of humans now emerging in the noosphere were something that Teilhard realized had enormous potential for creating a global community. Thus, Teilhard saw a need for increased unification, centration, and spiritualization. By unification, he means the need to overcome the divisive limits of political, economic, and cultural boundaries. By centration, he means the intensification of reflexive consciousness—embracing our place in the unfolding universe. By spiritualization, he means an increase in the upward impulse of evolutionary processes that create a zest for life in the human. In all of this he sees the vital importance of the activation of human energy so as to participate more fully in the creative dynamics of evolution. Human creativity recognizes the need for a passionate dedication to meaningful work and productive research along with the renewing dimension of the arts and culture.

As the human currently makes itself felt on every part of the planet, the challenge now is to learn how to enter appropriately into the planetary dimension of the universe story. As Thomas Berry has suggested in drawing Teilhard's thought forward, this requires new roles for the human—ones that enhance human-Earth relations rather than contribute to the deterioration of the life systems of the planet. Because humans are increasingly taking over the biological factors that determine their growth as a species, they are capable of modifying or creating their own selves. As we become a planetary species by our physical presence and environmental impact, we need also to become a planetary species by our expansion of comprehensive compassion to all life forms.

## Metaphysics:
## The Dynamics of Union

Teilhard realized that his speculations regarding the inherent nature and direction of the universe were preliminary.[17] Yet what he sought was a "universe-of-thought" that would increasingly build toward a unified center of coherence and convergence. Thought, as a form of animate motion, carries forth complexity-consciousness. In this sense Teilhard argued that "the moving body is physically engendered by the motion which animates it."[18] By analogy, the Omega point is that which allures as well as is the culmination of the evolutionary process.[19]

Such an animating and alluring center, Teilhard recognizes, is not directly apprehensible to humans, but its existence can be postulated from three points.

The first is the *irreversibility* of the evolutionary process—once put into motion, it cannot be halted. Furthermore, there must be a supreme focus toward which all is moving, or else a collapse would occur. The second point is *polarity*. This implies that a movement forward necessitates a stabilizing center influencing the heart of the evolutionary vortex. This center is independent but active enough to cause a complex centering of the various cosmic layers. The final principle is of *unanimity*. Here, he suggests that there exists an energy of sympathy or love that draws things together, center to center. However, the existence of such a love would be lost if focused on an impersonal collective. Thus, there must exist a personalizing focus—"If love is to be born and to become firmly established, it must have an individualized heart and an individualized face."[20]

Teilhard calls this the "metaphysics of union," for he claims that the most primordial notion of being suggests a union.[21] He describes the active form of being as uniting oneself or uniting with others in friendship, in marriage, in collaboration. The passive form he sees as the state of being united or unified by another. He then describes the successive phases of union. The first is that God in his triune nature contains his own self-oppositions. Thus God exists only by uniting himself. Second, at the opposite pole of the self-sufficient First Cause (God) there exists the multiple of matter. This is the passive potentiality of diverse matter yearning for union with the divine pole of Being. Finally, the creative act of God takes on a significant meaning—creation reflects the creator. The emergence of increasing complexity in matter and the participatory reflection of humans is an echo to the deepest personalization toward which the divine moves. "To create is to unite"; thus by the very act of creation the divine becomes immersed in the multiple. This implies that the scope of the incarnation extends through all creation.[22]

## MYSTICISM:
### THE CENTERING OF PERSON IN EVOLUTION

The challenge for Teilhard of integrating his religious and scientific commitments placed him in a personal crucible that forged a creative, unitive vision. Traditional mysticism in the world's religions, as he understood this interior experience, demanded a dematerialization and a transcendent leap into the divine. Teilhard achieved a radical reconceptualization of the mystical journey as an entry into evolution, discovering there an immanental communion with the divine.

As a stretcher-bearer during World War I, he had intuited the inherent directions of this call when he wrote, "There is a communion with God, and a communion with the earth, and a communion with God through the earth."[23] Eventually, Teilhard came to realize that human participation in this communion experience brought one into the depths of mystery. As Teilhard expressed it, "I see in the World a mysterious product of completion and fulfillment for the Absolute Being himself."[24] The process of communion is for Teilhard the centration and convergence of cosmic, planetary, and divine energies in the human.

Teilhard defines mysticism as "the need, the science and the art of attaining the Universal and the Spiritual at the same time and each through the other."[25] To become one with a larger whole through multiplicity was the goal of his mysticism. He sees mysticism as a yearning of the human soul toward the cosmic sense evident in many of the world's religions.[26] Teilhard understands mystical union as the deepest interiority that leads to a cosmic sense of being pulled forward into the whole without losing the personal. For Teilhard, this union is found at the heart of all art, poetry, and religion.

Teilhard sees the mysticism that is needed for the future as the synthesis of the two powerful currents—namely, that of evolution and that of human love. "To love evolution" is to be involved in a process in which one's particular love is universalized, becomes dynamic, and is synthesized. As with all mystical visions a paradoxical challenge unfolds in trying to relate the particular character of human love to the sense of an all-embracing divine love. Teilhard extends this challenge to love without hesitation into the larger human family, but also into an increasingly expanding awareness of spirit and matter throughout nature and the cosmos. By universalized, then, Teilhard means "the Real is charged with Divine Presence."[27] This mystical experience reaches back to those earlier experiences Teilhard understood as "communion." He wrote:

> As the mystics felt instinctively, everything becomes physically and literally lovable in God; and God in return becomes intelligible and lovable in everything around us. . . . as one single river, the world filled by God appears to our enlightened eyes as simply a setting in which universal communion can be attained.[28]

This view embodies not simply an anthropocentric or human-centered love, but a love for the world at large. Teilhard's mysticism is activated, for example, in scientific investigation and social commitment to research as well as in comprehensive compassion for all life. Mysticism is something other than simply passively enjoying the fruits of contemplation of a transcendent or abstract divinity. For Teilhard, love is always synthesized in the personal. Here lies the point of convergence of the world for Teilhard—the center in which all spiritual energy lies. By means of this personalizing force at the heart of the universe and of the individual, all human activities become an expression of love. It is in this sense he conjectures that "every activity is amorized."[29]

For Teilhard the mystical path leads to a sense of evolution in which individual personalization converges from the meridians of overwhelming plurality toward a powerful intuition of the whole. This whole, for Teilhard, is the Divine Milieu within which we live, and breathe, and have our becoming.

## CONTRIBUTIONS AND LIMITATIONS IN TEILHARD'S THOUGHT

Teilhard's particular legacy for the twenty-first century includes a vastly deepened sense of an evolutionary universe that can be understood as not simply an unchanging cosmos but an unfolding cosmogenesis. This dynamic emergent universe can now be viewed as one that is intricately connected: from the great flaring forth of the original fireball and the first hydrogen and helium atoms to the appearance of life in the original replicating cells and the gradual development of the myriad life forms. Teilhard shows us again and again how this process is at once unified and diversified.[30]

The legacy of Teilhard's vision of cosmogenesis affirms the extraordinary interrelationship and interconnection of the whole. Teilhard describes the irreversible flow of increasing complexity in cosmic evolution from atoms to humans. He thus provides empirically documented evidence for seeing the profound relationality between and among all parts of the universe.

This interconnectivity changes forever the role of the human. We can no longer see ourselves as an addendum or something "created" apart from the whole. We are, rather, that being in whom the universe reflects back upon itself in conscious self-awareness. The deepening of interiority in the mind-and-heart of the human gives us cause for celebration and participation in the all-embracing processes of universe emergence.[31] The implications for a greatly enlarged ecological consciousness are clear.

Such a perspective leads to a subtle but pervasive sense for Teilhard that the universe is threaded throughout with mystery and meaning. This is in distinct contrast to those who would suggest (often dogmatically) that the universe is essentially meaningless, that evolution is a completely random process, and that human emergence is a result of pure chance. For Teilhard, however, the evolving universe is not one he would describe as due to "intelligent design." Rather, evolution for Teilhard is dependent on an intricate blending of the forces of natural selection and chance mutation, on the one hand, along with increasing complexity and consciousness, on the other. This does not lead automatically to a teleological universe, but one nonetheless that holds out to the human both a larger sense of purpose and promise.

This promise at the heart of an innately self-organizing evolutionary process is also the lure toward which the process is drawn.[32] With this insight Teilhard provides a context for situating human action. This context of hope he felt was indispensable for humans to participate with a larger sense of meaning in society, politics, and economics as well as in education, research, and the arts. A primary concern for Teilhard was the activation of human energy that lends zest to life. The existentialist despair that pervaded Europe between the two world wars was something he wished to avoid. The spirit of the human needed to be understood as joined with the spirit of Earth for the flourishing of both humans and Earth.

In the face of enormous odds from a conservative religious opposition and from a materialist scientific perspective, Teilhard provided the human community with novel ways of understanding creation apart from the static cosmos pictured in the Genesis story. He dramatically shifted Christian theological agendas from an exclusively redemptive focus on the historical person of Jesus of Nazareth toward one cognizant of the dynamic picture of creation given by the evolutionary sciences. His sense of the Cosmic Christ embedded within creation and drawing it forward constitutes a creative reading of the epistles of Paul and the early Christian Church Fathers. As Thomas Berry suggests, his perspective moves from a preoccupation with redemption to a concern for creation, namely, an understanding of the universe at large (cosmology) and of Earth in particular (ecology). This is because his comprehensive incarnational spirituality affirms an increasingly centered, personalized universe radiating a numinous interiority. Teilhard struggled to understand this "within of things" in light of his scientific work and came to profound reflections on the mystical character of science itself in exploring the universe that are among his most original contributions.

Some limitations of Teilhard's thought might be noted along with his contributions.[33] Teilhard inherited the modern faith in progress and in human ingenuity that was a particular legacy of the French Enlightenment. This accounts for his optimism with regard to the human capacity to "build the Earth." There is a tendency toward an overstated anthropocentrism in his description of the human as the culmination of universe evolution. This led to his overemphasis on scientific discoveries and technological achievements as signs of progressive evolution. In this sense, Teilhard's eloquent reflections on scientific research as a mode of contemplation make us aware that he inadvertently affirmed applied science without considering its implications for disrupting Earth processes. For example, he appears unwilling or unable to consider the implications of nuclear waste and pollution when he wrote about the marvels of nuclear power in the late 1940s and early 1950s. Likewise, with regard to genetic engineering, Teilhard seemed unaware of the potentially deleterious consequences of intrusion into the genetic patterning of matter itself. As a corrective to this overly optimistic faith in science and technology to create a better future, many of the essays here suggest that our current environmental challenges call for engaged ecological sciences and alternative technologies that promote flourishing life on the planet.

Despite his eloquent expression of a communion with Earth, Teilhard had no developed ecological understanding of what we call "bioregions," or local ecosystems and watersheds. Profoundly committed to a vision of cosmic interdependence, he was in some ways unable fully to appreciate that vision unfolding in the particularity of fluorescence of life on Earth. His Christian sensibilities often led him to collapse the diversity of life into a plurality of matter brought to higher convergence in the Cosmic Christ. For example, his Mass on the World in the *Hymn of the Universe* is a striking cosmic liturgy that celebrates matter as the vehicle of the holy. It thus can be appreciated for its advancement in Christian thinking. Yet what language of sacrifice might Teilhard have expressed had he thought of the current assault of extractive economies on the planet and the scale of global demands for limitless consumer goods? In addition to human achievements through science and technology he might have considered particular ecosystems and life forms as part of the creative diversity of evolution that are valuable in themselves.

Like most people of his time, Teilhard was also limited by his understanding of the world's religions. For example, he discusses Hinduism largely through the lens of Upanishadic monism. This limited understanding did not adequately consider the rich varieties of regional, philosophical, or devotional Hinduism. In addition, Teilhard had little understanding of Confucianism, Daoism, or Chinese

Buddhism even though he spent several decades living in China. Finally, he had a stereotypical Western view of indigenous traditions as "static and exhausted."[34] Teilhard, on the other hand, positioned Christianity as the vehicle for a rich spirituality that would foster and direct the evolutionary process. Thus, he privileged Christianity as a major axis of evolution.

Despite these limitations, what emerges in any consideration of the life and thought of Teilhard is an appreciation of his grace under pressure, his steadfast commitment to a vision that challenged many of his deepest values, and his efforts to align a life of science with his religious journey. He has provided us with one of the few intellectual and affective syntheses that draw on science and religion in such profound and novel ways. His vision of universe emergence and of the role of the human in that emergence stands as one of the lasting testimonies of twentieth-century thought.

## SUMMARY

Teilhard's sweeping evolutionary perspective provides a context for understanding the human in a universe far larger and more complex than we had imagined. Teilhard saw that the evolutionary perspective requires a shift in thinking and in moral commitment. Realizing that we are participating in an unfolding, changing, developing universe, he understood that the human mirrors a dynamic cosmogenesis, not simply a static cosmos. A primary question for Teilhard was how to valorize human action and inspire the zest for life amidst inevitable human suffering and the travail of natural disasters, as set within a picture of evolutionary space and time as indifferent to life.

Teilhard presents evolution as a dynamic process in which the psychic character of physical matter evolves into greater complexity and consciousness. He posits an ever-present unifying center drawing forward a creative process. Teilhard was aware of the mystical character of his vision of reality, and he groped for the language that would accord with his deep commitment to Catholicism. Simultaneously, he sought a language that would also speak to nonbelievers. Personhood appealed to him as a metaphor that satisfied his concern lest he be misunderstood as advocating a monistic pantheism or favoring the impersonalizing tendencies of certain political ideologies. In his view, mystical union was not a collapse of the individual into a cosmic void. Rather, human participation in the evolutionary process was, for Teilhard, a centration of person in the cosmic turn toward increasingly complex organization and conscious indwelling. For these profound insights into evolutionary dynamics and our particular role in them we are indebted to Teilhard. His legacy is taken up in this book from a variety of disciplines, which is testimony to an enduring influence nearly half a century after his death. This volume also celebrates the twenty-fifth anniversary of the beginning of the *Teilhard Studies* with *The New Story* by Thomas Berry. This seminal piece marks a significant expansion of the Teilhardian view of the universe story as an all-inclusive communion of subjects.

# PART ONE

# TEILHARD

## HIS LIFE AND THOUGHT

To introduce the achievements of Pierre Teilhard de Chardin we begin with a biographical essay by Bucknell University historians of religion John Grim and Mary Evelyn Tucker. They summarize and bring into relief the most important dimensions of Teilhard's extraordinary life journey from youth in the bioregion of Auvergne, France, to worldwide travels embracing scientific research and spiritual exploration. Grim and Tucker provide a succinct introduction to Teilhard's life and thought.

In "A New Creation Story: The Creative Spirituality of Teilhard de Chardin," Manhattan College professor of religious studies and former *Teilhard Studies* editor Donald Gray situates Teilhard as not only a scientist, philosopher, theologian, and metaphysician but also a narrator of grand evolutionary vision, moving beyond a limited Darwinism.

Next Thomas King, S.J., the distinguished Georgetown professor of theology, in "Teilhard's Unity of Knowledge," conveys an expansive view of evolution to emphasize its systemic qualities of coherence and convergence. While mainstream science focuses on the tangential "without" of things, Teilhard, according to King, saw their internal unity, a radial "within," a ramifying spirit.

Teilhard's life was blessed with many colleagues and friends. He corresponded with several over long periods, often expressing his deepest insights in those letters. Ursula King's insightful chapter brings into relief the rich exchange that took place between Teilhard and the American sculptor Lucile Swan, who lived in Peking during the war years and frequently joined Teilhard for afternoon tea. Their correspondence is later collected in King's book *The Letters of Teilhard de Chardin and Lucile Swan* (1992), and its highlights are presented in our volume in an essay by the same title.

The final chapter of Part 1 is by the cultural historian Thomas Berry, "Teilhard in the Ecological Age." Berry underscores both the still-important contributions and the limitations of Teilhard's thought. He articulates and extends Teilhard's conceptions of evolution, the rise of consciousness, a shift in emphasis from redemption to creation, the activation of human energy, and the scientific project so they may better accommodate and serve our contemporary need for a more comprehensive ecological vision.

13

# 1

# Teilhard de Chardin

## *A Short Biography*

### JOHN GRIM and MARY EVELYN TUCKER

> There is a communion with God,
> and a communion with the earth, and
> a communion with God through the earth.
> —Pierre Teilhard de Chardin[1]

These lines, which conclude Pierre Teilhard de Chardin's essay "The Cosmic Life," provide an appropriate starting point for a consideration of his life. They are of special interest because Teilhard wrote them in 1916 during his initial duty as a stretcher-bearer in World War I. In many ways they are an early indication of his later work. Yet the communion experiences emphasized here take us back to his early childhood in the south of France and ahead to his years of travel and scientific research. Throughout Teilhard's seventy-four years, then, his experience of the divine and his insight into the role of the human in the evolutionary process emerge as his dominant concerns. In this brief biography of Teilhard three periods will be distinguished: the formative years, the years of travel, and the final years in New York.

### THE FORMATIVE YEARS

Pierre Teilhard de Chardin was born on May 1, 1881, to Emmanuel and Berthe-Adele Teilhard de Chardin. While both of his parental lineages were distinguished, it is noteworthy that his mother was the great-grandniece of François-Marie Arouet, more popularly known as Voltaire. Pierre was the fourth of the couple's eleven children and was born at the family estate of Sarcenat near the twin cities of Clermont-Ferrand in the ancient province of Auvergne. The long-extinct volcanic peaks of Auvergne and the forested preserves of this south-

---

First published in *Teilhard Studies* no. 11 (spring 1984).

ern province left an indelible mark on Teilhard. He remarks in his spiritual autobiography, *The Heart of Matter:*

> Auvergne moulded me. . . . Auvergne served me both as museum of nat-
> ural history and as wildlife preserve. Sarcenat in Auvergne gave me my
> first taste of the joys of discovery . . . to Auvergne I owe my most precious
> possessions: a collection of pebbles and rocks still to be found there, where
> I lived.[2]

Drawn to the natural world, Teilhard developed his unusual powers of observation. This youthful skill was especially fostered by his father, who maintained
an avid interest in natural science. Yet Teilhard's earliest memory of childhood
was not of the flora and fauna of Auvergne or the seasonal family houses but of
a striking realization of life's frailty and the difficulty of finding any abiding reality. He recollects:

> A memory? My very first! I was five or six. My mother had snipped a few
> of my curls. I picked one up and held it close to the fire. The hair was burnt
> up in a fraction of a second. A terrible grief assailed me; I had learnt that I
> was perishable. . . . What used to grieve me when I was a child? This inse-
> curity of things. And what used I to love? My genie of iron! With a plow
> hitch I believed myself, at seven years, rich with a treasure incorruptible,
> everlasting. And then it turned out that what I possessed was just a bit of
> iron that rusted. At this discovery I threw myself on the lawn and shed the
> bitterest tears of my existence![3]

It was but a short step for Teilhard to move from his "gods of iron" to those
of stone. Auvergne gave forth a surprising variety of stones: amethyst, citrine,
and chalcedony, just to name a few, with which to augment his youthful search
for a permanent reality. Undoubtedly his sensitive nature was nurtured also by his
mother's steadfast piety. Teilhard's reflection on his mother's influence is striking:

> A spark had to fall upon me, to make the fire blaze out. And, without a
> doubt, it was through my mother that it came to me, sprung from the stream
> of Christian mysticism, to light up and kindle my childish soul. It was
> through that spark that "My universe," still but *half*-personalized, was to
> become amorised, and so achieve its full centration.[4]

This early piety was well established so that when he entered Notre Dame de
Mongre near Villefranche-sur-Saone, thirty miles north of Lyons, at twelve years
of age, his quiet, diligent nature was already well formed. During his five years
at this boarding school Teilhard exchanged his security in stones for a Christian
piety largely influenced by Thomas à Kempis's *Imitation of Christ.* Near the time
of his graduation he wrote his parents indicating that he wanted to become a
Jesuit.

Teilhard's training as a Jesuit provided him with the thoughtful stimulation to continue his devotion both to scientific investigation of the Earth and to cultivation of a life of prayer. He entered the Jesuit novitiate at Aix-en-Provence in 1899. Here he further developed the ascetic piety that he had learned in his reading at Mongre. It was also at Aix-en-Provence that he began his friendship with Auguste Valensin, who had already studied philosophy with Maurice Blondel. In 1901, owing to an anticlerical movement in the French Republic, the Jesuits and other religious orders were expelled from France. The Aix-en-Provence novitiate, which had moved in 1900 to Paris, was transferred in 1902 to the English island of Jersey. Prior to the move to Jersey, however, on March 26, 1902, Pierre took his first vows in the Society of Jesus. At this time the security of Teilhard's religious life, apart from the political situation in France, was painfully disturbed by the gradual sickness that incapacitated his younger sister, Marguerite-Marie, and by the sudden illness of his oldest brother, Alberic.

Alberic's death in September 1902 came as Pierre and his fellow Jesuits were quietly leaving Paris for Jersey. The death of this formerly successful, buoyant brother, followed in 1904 by the death of Louise, his youngest sister, caused Teilhard momentarily to turn away from concern for things of this world. Indeed, he indicates that but for Paul Trossard, his former novice master, who encouraged him to follow science as a legitimate way to God, he would have discontinued those studies in favor of theology.

From Jersey, Pierre was sent in 1905 to do his teaching internship at the Jesuit college of St. Francis in Cairo, Egypt. For the next three years Teilhard's naturalist inclinations were developed through prolonged forays into the countryside near Cairo studying the existing flora and fauna and also the fossils of Egypt's past. While Teilhard carried on his teaching assignments assiduously, he also made time for extensive collecting of fossils and for correspondence with naturalists in Egypt and France. His collected *Letters from Egypt* reveal a person with keen observational powers. In 1907 Teilhard published his first article, "A Week in Fayoum." He also learned in 1907 that due to his finds of shark teeth in Fayoum and in the quarries around Cairo a new species named *Teilhardia* and three new varieties of shark had been presented to the Geological Society of France by his French correspondent, Monsieur Prieur.

From Cairo, Pierre returned to England to complete his theological studies at Ore Place in Hastings. During the years 1908 to 1912 Teilhard lived the rigorously disciplined life of a Jesuit scholastic. Yet the close relation he maintained with his family is evident in the depth of feeling expressed at the death in 1911 of his elder sister, Françoise, in China. This sister, who was the only other family member in religious life, had become a Little Sister of the Poor and had worked among the impoverished of Shanghai. For Teilhard her death was particularly poignant because of the selfless dedication of her life.

His letters during this period at Hastings indicate that the demands of his theological studies left little time for geological explorations of the chalk cliffs of Hastings or the clay of nearby Weald. Yet his letters also reveal his enthusiasm for both of these types of study. In summary, three different but interrelated developments occurred during this period that significantly affected the future course of Teilhard's life: the reading of Henri Bergson's *Creative Evolution,* the anti-Modernist attack by Pope Pius X, and his discovery of a fossil tooth in the region of Hastings.

In reading Henri Bergson's newly published *Creative Evolution,* Teilhard encountered a thinker who dissolved the Aristotelian dualism of matter and spirit in favor of a movement through time of an evolving universe. Teilhard also found the word *evolution* in Bergson. He connected the very sound of the word, as he says, "with the extraordinary density and intensity with which the English land-scape then appeared to me—especially at sunset—when the Sussex woods seemed to be laden with all the fossil life that I was exploring, from one quarry to another, in the soil of the Weald."[5] From Bergson, then, Teilhard received the vision of ongoing evolution. For Bergson, evolution was continually expanding, a "Tide of Life" undirected by an ultimate purpose. Teilhard would eventually disagree with Bergson with respect to the direction of the universe. Later he put forward his own interpretation of the evolutionary process based on the inter-vening years of fieldwork.

In 1903, before Pierre went to Egypt, Pius X succeeded Leo XIII as pope. The forward-looking momentum of Leo was abandoned by the conservative Italian curia in favor of retrenchment and attacks on a spectrum of ideas labeled "mod-ernism" in the encyclical *Pascendi* (1907) and the decrees of *Lamentabili* (1907). Among the many new works eventually placed on the Index of Forbidden Works was Henri Bergson's *Creative Evolution,* although it was not yet suspect when Teilhard read it at Hastings. It is in this ecclesiastical milieu that Teilhard endeav-ored to articulate his emerging vision of the spiritual quality of the universe.

It was also during his years at Hastings that Teilhard and other Jesuits met Charles Dawson, an amateur paleontologist. Because of Pierre's years of col-lecting in Cairo, he had acquired a growing interest in fossils and prehistoric life, but he was not an accomplished paleontologist, nor did his studies allow him the time to develop the skills needed to accurately date or determine prehistoric fos-sils. In his very limited association with Dawson, Teilhard discovered in one of the diggings the fossil tooth that caused his name to become known to the scien-tific community. Moreover, Teilhard's enthusiasm for the scientific study of pre-historic human life now crystallized as a possible direction after his ordination in August 1911.

Between 1912 and 1915 Teilhard continued his studies in paleontology. But because of his initiative in meeting Marcellin Boule at the Museum of Natural History and in taking courses at this Paris museum and at the Institut Catholique with Georges Boussac, Teilhard now began to develop that expertise in the geology of the Eocene Period that earned him a doctorate in 1922. In addition, Pierre also joined such accomplished paleontologists as the Abbé Henri Breuil, Father Hugo Obermaier, Jean Boussac, and others in their excavations in the Aurignacian-period caves of southern France, in the phosphorite fossil fields of Belgium, and in the fossil-rich sands of the French Alps. While Teilhard was developing a promising scientific career he also renewed his acquaintance in Paris with his cousin Marguerite Teilhard Chambon. Through Marguerite, Teil-hard entered into a social milieu in which he could exchange ideas and receive critical comment from several perspectives. In these surroundings Teilhard developed his thought until the outbreak of World War I in 1914.

When the war came in August, Teilhard returned to Paris to help Boule store museum pieces, to assist Marguerite in turning the girls' school she headed into a hospital, and to prepare for his own eventual induction. August was a disastrous month for the French army; the German forces executed the Schlieffen Plan so successfully that by the end of the month they were about thirty miles from Paris. In September the French rallied at the Marne and Parisians breathed easier. Because Teilhard's induction was delayed, Teilhard's Jesuit superiors decided to send him back to Hastings for his tertianship, the year before final vows. Two months later word came that his younger brother Gonzague had been killed in battle near Soissons. Shortly after this Teilhard received orders to report for duty in a newly formed regiment from Auvergne. After visiting his parents and his invalid sister Guiguite at Sarcenat, he began his assignment as a stretcher-bearer with the North African Zouaves in January 1915.

The powerful impact of the war on Teilhard is recorded in his letters to his cousin Marguerite, now collected in *The Making of a Mind*. They give us an intimate picture of Teilhard's initial enthusiasm as a "soldier-priest," his humility in bearing a stretcher while others bore arms, his exhaustion after the brutal battles at Ypres and Verdun, his heroism in rescuing his comrades of the Fourth Mixed Regiment, and his unfolding mystical vision centered on seeing the world evolve even in the midst of war. In these letters are many of the seminal ideas that Teilhard would develop in his later years. For example during a break in the fierce fighting at the battle of Verdun in 1916 Teilhard wrote the following to his cousin Marguerite:

I don't know what sort of monument the country will later put up on Froideterre hill to commemorate the great battle. There's only one that would be appropriate: a great figure of Christ. Only the image of the crucified can sum up, express and relieve all the horror, and beauty, all the hope and deep mystery in such an avalanche of conflict and sorrows. As I looked at this scene of bitter toil, I felt completely overcome by the thought that I had the honour of standing at one of the two or three spots on which, at this very moment, the whole life of the universe surges and ebbs—places of pain, but it is there that a great future (this I believe more and more) is taking shape.[6]

Through these nearly four years of bloody trench fighting Teilhard's regiment fought in some of the most brutal battles at the Marne and Ypres in 1915, Nieuport in 1916, Verdun in 1917, and Chateau Thierry in 1918. Teilhard himself was active in every engagement of the regiment, for which he was awarded the Chevalier de la Legion d'Honneur in 1921. Throughout his correspondence he wrote that despite this turmoil he felt there was a purpose and a direction to life more hidden and mysterious than history generally reveals to us. This larger meaning, Teilhard discovered, was often revealed in the heat of battle. In one of several articles written during the war, Pierre expressed the paradoxical wish experienced by soldiers on leave for the tension of the front lines. He indicated this article in one of his letters saying:

> I'm still in the same quiet billets. Our future continues to be pretty vague, both as to when and what it *will* be. What the future imposes on our present existence is not exactly a feeling of depression; it's rather a sort of seriousness, of detachment, of a broadening, too, of outlook. This feeling, of course, borders on a sort of sadness (the sadness that accompanies every fundamental change); but it leads also to a sort of higher joy. I'd call it "Nostalgia for the Front." The reasons, *I* believe, come down to this; the front cannot but attract us because it *is,* in one way, the *extreme boundary* between what one is already aware of, and what *is* still in process of formation. Not only does one see there things that you experience nowhere else, but one also sees emerge from within one an underlying stream of clarity, energy, and freedom that is to be found hardly anywhere else in ordinary life—and the new form that the *soul then takes on is* that of the individual living the quasi-collective life of all men, fulfilling a function far higher than that of the individual, and becoming fully conscious of this new state. It goes without saying that at the front you no longer look on things in the same way as you do in the rear; if you did, the sights you see and the life you lead would be more than you could bear. This exaltation is accompanied by a certain pain. Nevertheless it *is* indeed an exaltation. And that's why one likes the front in spite of everything, and misses it.[7]

Teilhard's powers of articulation are evident in these lines. Moreover, his efforts to express his growing vision of life during the occasional furloughs also brought him a foretaste of the later ecclesiastical reception of his work. For although Teilhard was given permission to take final vows in the Society of Jesus in May 1918, his writings from the battlefield puzzled his Jesuit superiors, especially his rethinking of such topics as evolution and original sin. Gradually Teilhard realized that the great need of the church was, as he says, "to present dogma in a more real, more universal, way—a more 'cosmogonic' way."[8] These realizations often gave Teilhard the sense of "being reckoned with the orthodox and yet feeling for the heterodox."[9] He was convinced that if he had indeed seen something, as he felt he had, then that seeing would shine forth despite obstacles. As he says in a letter of 1919, "What makes me easier in my mind at this juncture, is that the rather hazardous schematic points in my teaching are in fact of only secondary importance to me. It's not nearly so much ideas that I want to propagate as a spirit: and a spirit can animate all external presentations."[10]

After his demobilization on March 10, 1919, Teilhard returned to Jersey for a recuperative period and preparatory studies for concluding his doctoral degree in geology at the Sorbonne, for the Jesuit provincial of Lyon had given his permission for Teilhard to continue his studies in natural science. During this period at Jersey, Teilhard wrote his profoundly prayerful piece on "The Spiritual Power of Matter."

After returning to Paris, Teilhard continued his studies with Marcellin Boule in the phosphorite fossils of the Lower Eocene period in France. Extensive field trips took him to Belgium, where he also began to address student clubs on the significance of evolution in relation to current French theology. By the fall of 1920, Teilhard had secured a post in geology at the Institute Catholique and was lecturing to student audiences, who knew him as an active promoter of evolutionary thought.

The conservative reaction in the Catholic Church initiated by the curia of Pius X had abated at the pope's death in 1914. But the new pope, Benedict XV, renewed the attack on evolution, on "new theology," and on a broad spectrum of perceived errors considered threatening by the Vatican curia. The climate in ecclesiastical circles toward the type of work that Teilhard was doing gradually convinced him that work in the field would not only help his career but would also quiet the controversy in which he and other French thinkers were involved. The opportunity for fieldwork in China had been open to Teilhard as early as 1919 by an invitation from the Jesuit scientist Emile Licent, who had undertaken paleontological work in the environs of Peking. On April 1, 1923, Teilhard set sail from Marseille bound for China. Little did he know that this "short trip" would initiate the many years of travel to follow.

## THE YEARS OF TRAVEL

Teilhard's first period in China was spent in Tientsin, a coastal city some eighty miles from Peking, where Emile Licent had built his museum and housed the fossils he had collected in China since his arrival in 1914. The two French Jesuits were a contrast in types. Licent, a northerner, was unconventional in dress, taciturn, and very independent in his work. He was primarily interested in collecting fossils rather than interpreting their significance. Teilhard, on the other hand, was more urbane; he enjoyed conversational society in which he could relate his geological knowledge to a wider scientific and interpretive sphere. Almost immediately after his arrival, Teilhard made himself familiar with Licent's collection and, at the latter's urging, gave a report to the Geological Society of China. In June 1923 Teilhard and Licent undertook an expedition into the Ordos desert west of Peking near the border with Inner Mongolia. This expedition, and successive ones during the 1920s with Emile Licent, gave Teilhard invaluable information on Paleolithic remains in China. Teilhard's correspondence during this period gives penetrating observations on Mongolian peoples, landscapes, vegetation, and animals of the region.

Teilhard's major interest during these years of travel was primarily in the natural terrain. Although he interacted with innumerable ethnic groups, he rarely entered into their cultures more than was necessary for expediting his business or satisfying a general interest. One of the ironies of his career is that the Confucian tradition and its concern for realization of the cosmic identity of heaven, Earth, and humanity remained outside of Teilhard's concerns. Similarly tribal peoples and their Earth-centered spiritualities were regarded by Teilhard as simply an earlier stage in the evolutionary development of the Christian revelation.

Teilhard returned to Paris in September 1924 and resumed teaching at the Institut Catholique. But the intellectual climate in European Catholicism had not changed significantly. Pius XI, who became pope in 1922, had allowed free rein to the conservative factions. It was in this hostile climate that a copy of a paper that Teilhard had delivered in Belgium made its way to Rome. A month after he returned from China, Teilhard was ordered to appear before his provincial superior to sign a statement repudiating his ideas on original sin. Teilhard's old friend Auguste Valensin was teaching theology in Lyon, and Teilhard sought his counsel regarding the statement of repudiation. In a meeting of the three Jesuits, the superior agreed to send to Rome a revised version of Teilhard's earlier paper and his response to the statement of repudiation.

In the interim before receiving Rome's reply to his revisions, Teilhard continued his classes at the Institut. Those students who recalled the classes remembered the dynamic quality with which the young professor delivered his penetrating analysis of *homo faber.* According to Teilhard, the human as tool-maker and user of fire represents a significant moment in the development of human consciousness or hominization of the species. It is in this period that Teilhard began to use the term of Edward Suess, "biosphere," or Earth-layer of living things, in his geological schema. Teilhard then expanded the concept to include the Earth-layer of thinking beings, which he called the "noosphere" from the Greek word *nous* meaning "mind." While his lectures were filled to capacity, his influence had so disturbed a bloc of conservative French bishops that they reported him to Vatican officials, who in turn put pressure on the Jesuits to silence him.

The Jesuit superior general of this period was Vladimir Ledochowski, a former Austrian military officer, who sided openly with the conservative faction in the Vatican. Thus, in 1925 Teilhard was again ordered to sign a statement repudiating his controversial theories and to remove himself from France after the semester's courses.

Teilhard's associates at the museum, Marcellin Boule and Abbé Breuil, recommended that he leave the Jesuits and become a diocesan priest. His friend Auguste Valensin and others recommended signing the statement and interpreting that act as a gesture of fidelity to the Jesuit order rather than one of intellectual assent to the curia's demands. Valensin argued that the correctness of Teilhard's spirit was ultimately heaven's business. After a week's retreat and reflection on the Ignatian *Exercises,* Teilhard signed the document in July 1925. It was the same week as the Scopes "Monkey Trial" in Tennessee, which contested the validity of evolution.

In the spring of the following year Teilhard boarded a steamship bound for the Far East. The second period in Tientsin with Licent was marked by a number of significant developments. First, the visits of the crown prince and princess of Sweden and later of Alfred Lacroix from the Paris Museum of Natural History gave Teilhard new status in Peking and marked his gradual movement from Tientsin into the more sophisticated scientific circles of Peking. Here American, Swedish, and British teams had begun work at a rich site called Chou-kou-tien. Teilhard joined their work, contributing his knowledge of Chinese geological formations and tool-making activities among prehistoric humans in China. With Licent, Teilhard also undertook a significant expedition north of Peking to Dalai-Nor. Finally, in an effort to state his views in a manner acceptable to his superiors Teilhard wrote *The Divine Milieu*. This mystical treatise was dedicated to those who love the world; it articulated his vision of the human as "matter at its most incendiary stage."

Meanwhile Teilhard had been in correspondence with his superiors, who finally allowed him to return to France in August 1927. But even before Teilhard reached Marseille a new attack was made on his thought as a result of the publication in a Paris journal of a series of his lectures. While Teilhard edited and rewrote *The Divine Milieu* in Paris, he was impatient for a direct confrontation with his critics. Finally in June 1928 the assistant to the Jesuit superior general arrived in Paris to tell Teilhard that all his theological work must end and that he was to confine himself to scientific work. In this oppressive atmosphere Teilhard was forced to return to China in November 1928.

For the next eleven years Teilhard continued this exile in China, returning to France only for five brief visits. These visits were to see his family and friends, who distributed copies of his articles, and to give occasional talks to those student clubs in Belgium and Paris who continued to provide a forum for his ideas. These years were also very rich in geological expeditions for Teilhard. In 1929, Teilhard traveled in Somaliland and Ethiopia before returning to China. He played a major role in the finding and interpretation of "Peking Man" at Chou-kou-tien in 1929-1930. In 1930 he joined Ray Chapman Andrew's Central Mongolian Expedition at the invitation of the American Museum of Natural History. The following year he made a trip across America, which inspired him to write *The Spirit of the Earth*. From May 1931 to February 1932 he traveled into Central Asia with the famous Yellow Expedition sponsored by the Citroen automobile company. In 1934, with George Barbour he traveled up the Yangtze River and into the mountainous regions of Szechuan. A year later he joined the Yale-Cambridge expedition under Helmut de Terra in India and afterwards von Koenigswald's expedition in Java. In 1937 he was awarded the Gregor Mendel medal at a conference in Philadelphia for his scientific accomplishments. That same year he went with the Harvard-Carnegie Expedition to Burma and then to Java with Helmut de Terra. As a result of this extensive fieldwork, Teilhard became recognized as one of the foremost geologists of the Earth's terrain. This notoriety, in addition to his original theories on human evolution, made him a valuable presence for the French government in intellectual circles east and west. His professional accomplishments are even more noteworthy when one recalls the profound tragedies that he experienced in the years between 1932 and 1936 when his father, mother, younger brother, Victor, and his beloved sister, Guiguite, all died during his absence.

The final years of exile in China, 1939 to 1946, roughly correspond to the years of World War II and the disintegration of central control in Chinese republican politics. During this period, Teilhard and a fellow Jesuit and friend, Pierre Leroy, set up the Institute of Geobiology in Peking to protect the collection of Emile Licent and to provide a laboratory for their ongoing classification and interpretation of fossils. The most significant accomplishment of this period, however, was the completion of *The Human Phenomenon* in May of 1940. An important contribution of this work is the creative manner in which it situates the emergence of the human as the unifying theme of the evolutionary process. *The Human Phenomenon* in its presentation of the fourfold sequence of the evolutionary process (galactic evolution, Earth evolution, life evolution, and consciousness evolution) establishes what might almost be considered a new literary genre.

With the war's end Teilhard received permission to return to France, where he engaged in a variety of activities. He published numerous articles in the Jesuit journal *Etudes*. He reworked *The Human Phenomenon* and sent a copy of it to Rome requesting permission for publication, a permission never granted in his lifetime. He was also asked to stand as a candidate for the prehistory chair at the Sorbonne's Collège de France soon to be vacated by his longtime friend, Abbé Henri Breuil. By May of 1947 Teilhard had exhausted himself in the attempt to restate his position and to deal with the expectations of his sympathetic readers. His exhaustion caused a heart attack on June 1, 1947. For Teilhard this illness meant a postponement in joining a University of California expedition to Africa sponsored by the Viking Fund of the Wenner-Gren Foundation in New York. Teilhard had looked forward to the trip as an interlude before the confrontation with Rome over *The Human Phenomenon* and the teaching position at the Sorbonne. While recovering from this illness, Teilhard was honored by the French Ministry of Foreign Affairs for his scientific and intellectual achievements and was promoted to the rank of officer in the Legion of Honor.

In October 1948, Teilhard traveled to the United States. At this time he was invited to give a series of lectures at Columbia University, but permission was refused by the local Jesuit superior. Suddenly, in July 1948, Teilhard received an invitation to come to Rome to discuss the controversies surrounding his thought. Gradually Teilhard realized that the future of his work depended on this encounter, and he prepared himself, as he said, "to stroke the tiger's whiskers."

Rome in 1948 was a city just beginning its recovery from the war's devastation. The Vatican curia was also beginning its reorganization; for Pius XII, who had assumed the pontificate in March 1939, had been in relative isolation during the war years. In the late 1940s he developed his plans for the holy year of 1950. As a former Vatican diplomat, Pius XII continued the curia's conservative stance with a more sophisticated and more intellectual effort.

When Teilhard came to Rome, he stayed at the Jesuit residence in Vatican City. After several meetings with the Jesuit general, Father Janssens, Teilhard realized that he would never be allowed to publish his work during his lifetime and, furthermore, that he would not be granted permission to accept the position at the Collège de France. Those who spoke with Teilhard when he returned to Paris could sense the frustration that enveloped him as he groped to understand the forces against which he was so powerless. During the next two years Teilhard traveled extensively in England, Africa, and the United States, trying to determine an appropriate place to live now that China was no longer open. In December 1951 he accepted a research position with the Wenner-Gren Foundation in New York.

## THE FINAL YEARS IN NEW YORK

Teilhard's decision to live in New York was approved by his Jesuit superiors and this resolved his uncertainty with regard to a place of residence. He lived in the following years with the Jesuit fathers at St. Ignatius Church on Park Avenue and walked both to his office at the Wenner-Gren Foundation and to the apartment of his self-appointed secretary and friend, Rhoda de Terra. Teilhard's correspondence with Father Pierre Leroy during these final years, published in English as *Letters from My Friend,* are remarkable in their lack of bitterness and for their single-minded scientific focus.

In 1954 Teilhard visited France for the last time. He and his friend Leroy drove south together to the caves at Lascaux. Prior to visiting Lascaux they stopped at Sarcenat together with Mrs. de Terra, who had joined them. Wordlessly they walked through the rooms until they came to Teilhard's mother's room and her chair. Only then did Teilhard speak, saying half to himself, "This is the room where I was born." Hoping to spend his final years in his native country, Teilhard applied once more to his superiors for permission to return to France permanently. He was politely refused and encouraged to return to America.

Pierre Teilhard de Chardin died on Easter Sunday, April 10, 1955, at six o'clock in the evening. His funeral on Easter Monday was attended by a few friends. Father Leroy and the ministering priest from St. Ignatius accompanied his body some sixty miles upstate from New York City, where he was buried at St. Andrews-on-Hudson, then the Jesuit novitiate.

Teilhard's life, with its simple, quiet ending, unfolds like the tree of life in his own description—slowly, seemingly half opened at points yet bearing within it an enduring dignity. As he wrote of the tree of life:

Before attempting to probe the secret of its life, let us take a good look at it. For from a merely external contemplation of it, there is a lesson and a force to be drawn from it: *the sense of its testimony.*[11]

# 2

# A New Creation Story

## The Creative Spirituality
## of Teilhard de Chardin

### DONALD P. GRAY

When *The Phenomenon of Man* first appeared, it caused confusion. It was difficult to know precisely how the book was to be read and, hence, how it was to be interpreted and understood. Is it, as Teilhard himself maintained in his preface, "a scientific treatise"? Scientists will discover much scientific material there, but in the end they will find it impossible to accept this as a scientific text. Is it, even though Teilhard himself passionately denied it, "a work on metaphysics" or "a sort of theological essay"? Philosophers and theologians have been reluctant to acknowledge it as belonging legitimately to their own fields of specialization. Scientific, philosophical, and theological elements are woven together in this book, but no one of these familiar categories is entirely appropriate.

Is Teilhard a scientist, a philosopher, or a theologian? In some measure he took up each one of these roles, but no one of them leads us into the heart of the matter. Essentially he is a storyteller and a masterful one at that. This is the source of his attraction. He has a strange but spellbinding story to tell, one that awakens wonder and bewilderment. This story of cosmic history, this new creation epic, possesses the power to transform consciousness, to enable us to see for the first time. It possesses spiritual power, the power to release energy, the power to open up a new spiritual path and a new creative spirituality. But it is time to come to the story, a story of life and of death, of union and of separation, of gain and of loss—a story of the universe and of the man who saw it afresh.

### I

In their biographical study of Teilhard, Ellen and Mary Lukas have provided us with an unusually compelling image of the man and his life story drawn from the legends of his native Auvergne:

First published in *Teilhard Studies* no. 2 (spring 1979).

In that slim literature of the marvelous which does exist, one single theme recurs with curious frequency. It is the story of the Innocent Seeker who leaves his land and all he has to look for the Secret at the Heart of Reality—the Magus who seeks the Single Truth behind the veil of multiple illusion . . . . Because the Auvergnat folklorists were plain men, they knew that there must be some coherence between rock and flower and beast. Because they were patient and hardy, they had always believed that, with industry and determination, the secret of their relationship could be uncovered. But because they were realists, they knew that such things must be paid for, often dearly. In all their tales, therefore, the Searcher-Protagonist who finds what he is looking for is wounded in the conquest. He inevitably ends either by abandoning the Power of the Secret he has so dearly won, or by being forced to walk alone to the end of his life, without being able to communicate it to another living soul.[1]

Pierre Teilhard de Chardin was both a seeker and a seer. He found in the realm of vision what he had long been seeking: indestructible meaning. The spirituality of Teilhard is the spirituality of a visionary. That is both its appeal, because we find ourselves fascinated by the wise man and his wisdom, and its peril, because our ordinary modes of consciousness are ill-adapted to understanding visionary utterance. The first commandment of such a spiritual way is "Thou shalt learn to see," for seeing is everything. Or if it is not exactly everything, it is foundational for everything else.[2] "Nothing here below is *profane* for those who know how to see."[3] But within the context of such an illuminative way it is precisely the journey from blindness to sight, from ignorance to knowledge, from foolishness to wisdom that appears forbidding. The seer, the one who has already attained to insight, must, therefore, offer himself as spiritual guide to provide support for the way even if he must pay a terrible price as a result of incomprehension. Teilhard, in fact, paid a terrible price, in exile and isolation, for his eagerness to play the guide's role. Only after his death was it possible to hear his invitation to "Come and see."[4] And even then the incomprehension continued.

What is it that sends the visionary in quest of his vision in the first place? Perhaps that is a psychic mystery that can never be unraveled sufficiently or satisfactorily. We may hazard the guess that in Teilhard's case it had something to do with an especially acute sense of the disjointedness and incoherence existing between the two traditions he deeply loved: the Christian tradition and the scientific tradition. Both of these traditions represented earnest truth seeking; both were ways of knowing reality. Yet both seemed increasingly to diverge, giving rise to distressingly diverse, even opposed interpretations of the world. These were the available ways of seeing, but they were apparently unable to see the same processes at work. Some better vantage point beyond them both, yet incorporative of them both, must be discovered. From that unfamiliar vantage point everything might become clear, everything might fall into place. But how to arrive there?

Teilhard had inherited two creation stories, apparently irreconcilable. The first, recounted in the Book of Genesis, located the creation in the distant past, at the beginning of all things. It was a story about the Creator God and his all-powerful Word, which brought the world into being within the compass of a week. This was the religious myth, the religious story, about creation. It provided a backdrop for other stories: the fall of humanity, the redemption through the Son of God, the sending of the Spirit, the coming into being of the church, and finally the second coming of the Risen One and the end of the world. The creation story was thus understood as a prologue to the redemption story, the actual heart of the religious storytelling tradition for Christians.

In the nineteenth century, however, another creation story arose, an evolutionary account associated with the work of Charles Darwin. In this story creation has become a lengthy process extending over millions of years and involving the elaboration of myriad life forms. At a late stage of the process the human being appears in conjunction with the evolutionary history of the higher primates. The struggle for survival and the subsequent survivability of the fittest are offered as an explanatory hypothesis to make some sense of this dynamic movement within the biosphere. This later, scientific story is, of course, unable to accommodate God-talk, and so a new creation story arises without explicit mention of or relationship to the sphere of the sacred. This story, while undergoing various modifications and qualifications since the time of Darwin, has largely established its credibility among cultured people. It was accepted as essentially accurate, as far as it went, by Teilhard.

But it did not go nearly far enough in his judgment. It left out of account the whole inward history of the creation, the history of consciousness, as he called it. It did not see deeply enough into things, for accompanying the history of complexifying matter is a concomitant history of inwardness, the capacity for consciousness and relatedness. That history is not over; it continues with man through the elaboration of new cultural forms which make possible new levels of consciousness and relatedness. Creation has been reconceived by Teilhard in the light of the evolutionary account as an unfinished process. Creation continues, and creation also has a history. Salvation history must now be comprehended within the context of a creation history. The world is no longer cosmos, an ordered whole within which human history is set; the world is cosmogenesis, creative process. This means, then, that the creatures, and especially human beings, are provided with a new role in the new creation story being put together by Teilhard. They are co-creators, co-operators, in the forward advance of consciousness. They have become the partners of God in bringing the world into being and guiding it to completion.

Christian spirituality is now required to take a new turn as a result of this new way of seeing things. A new sacral story is demanded by the conjunction of the old religious story and the new scientific story. Christian spirituality has to be reenvisioned as a creative spirituality oriented toward cooperative participation in the divine creative work. Traditional spiritualities, formulated to deal redemptively with the fallenness and sin of humanity, need now to take up a new emphasis designed to activate human creative energy in the service of the divine creative opus: evolving consciousness. The redemptive factor is not thereby ignored—it is simply relocated to a new place, for there will always be a need to remove those resistances standing in the way of creative process and growth, those infidelities to the divine creative invitation.

## II

For Teilhard, the cosmogenetic process has both purpose and meaning because it is moving toward an ultimate goal, which he terms Omega. In this respect his version of the creation story once again diverges from the Darwinian account by incorporating eschatological elements from the Christian tradition. It is only at the end that the creation will attain completeness. Teilhard presents the already long history of complexification (matter) and consciousness (spirit) as evidence of the purposeful patterning present in the evolutionary movement and as proof of final meaningfulness. The evidence is ambiguous, however. Not only may it be read in different ways depending on one's standpoint, but it seems in the last analysis threatened by what Teilhard termed the "death-barrier."[5] If everything ends in death, then there is no abiding indestructible completion toward which to aim. Hence, as far as Teilhard is concerned, there is no cogent reason to aim at all. On the transcending of the death-barrier (and the viability of affirming absolute cosmic meaning) hinges the very possibility of a spirituality of creative action.

Teilhard's concern with the death-barrier is movingly articulated in a letter written in 1934 at the time of the death of his friend and colleague Davidson Black:

> Today I am deeply aware of the call to rescue the world from the blackness of its materialism. You already know that Dr. Black has died. The apparent absurdity of that untimely end, the noble but blind acceptance of this tragedy by his friends here, the complete absence of "light" on the poor body lying in that cold room at the Peiping Union Medical College—all these lent a leaden quality to my sadness, and revolted my spirit.
>
> Either there is an escape from death—somewhere—for an individual's thought, for his self-consciousness, or else the world is a hideous mistake. And if it is, then there is no use in our going on. But, since the uselessness of going on is an idea intolerable to everyone, the alternative must be to believe. To awaken this belief shall be, now more than ever, my task, I swear it. I have sworn it on the mortal remains of Davy, that more than brother of mine.[6]

It is not simply the death of the individual that needs to find a resolution, however. The cosmos itself seems likewise destined to end in a meaningless energy equilibrium as the result of the principle of entropy.[7] This possibility is signaled near the beginning of the argument of *The Phenomenon of Man* where Teilhard is discussing the modern scientific perspective on the world's ultimate demise: "A rocket rising in the wake of time's arrow, that only bursts to be extinguished; an eddy rising on the bosom of a descending current—such then must be our picture of the world. So says science: and I believe in science: but up to now has science ever troubled to look at the world other than from without?"[8]

From the point of view of the within of things, what other scenarios might become available as alternatives to this seemingly inevitable conclusion of the modern scientific creation story? First of all, it should be pointed out that the traditional apocalyptic scenario seems incompatible with the new Teilhardian creation story in spite of the fact that it does involve meaningful finality. This finality, however, is not logically linked to the cooperative creativity of the creatures since it is believed within apocalyptic thought that the end can occur at any time through direct divine intervention without particular attention to the stage of development of the creative process itself. What is needed, then, is an end that appropriately climaxes the "immense journey" of cosmogenesis and necessarily requires the active participation of the creatures, particularly man. The prior development of the world to maturity thus becomes the indispensable condition for the appearance of the kingdom of God at the end of time.[9] Such is the logic of the new creation story as reconstructed by Teilhard.

What then is the nature of this end, and how does it effectively resolve the problem of death, thereby establishing the needed context of meaning for creative action? As the completion of a process of rising and expanding consciousness this end must represent maximal attainment of consciousness. As the completion of a process of human convergence involving both increased socialization and heightened personalization, this end must represent a final intensity of both community and personal fulfillment. As the completion of a process of divine and human creative interaction, this end must represent final divine–human communion "when God will be all in all" (1 Cor. 15:28).[10] In short, this end must represent a final communion of all things in God and of God in all things—what the biblical tradition pointed toward under the symbol of the kingdom of God to come. If communion is the end, then the creation of communion represents the way to the end. A creative spirituality will also be a unitive (or communitive) spirituality, for through the building of community the end is also being constructed, that new thing that has never before existed. The unification of the human community in view of the end, therefore, becomes the single most urgent priority of such a spiritual way. And the basis of this future unification is love-energy, the unitive energy that binds the human community together at the same time that it enables and supports personalization. In the power of love union differentiates.[11]

An effective contemporary spirituality must do two things, according to Teilhard. On the one hand, it must illumine; it must be generative of vision and new consciousness. It must show the way by providing light for the journey. On the other hand, it must evoke energy, energy for action and energy for communion. Vision and energy are intimately interconnected, for vision is productive of energy, both ethical and affective energy. Without vision, energy dissipates and is finally wasted, according to the principle of entropy in human affairs. But vision of itself is not enough, however indispensable. Marxism is a visionary movement, but for Teilhard the Marxist vision is incapable of either transcending the death-barrier or activating the love-energy required to attain Omega.[12]

Only God is able to guarantee immortality for the person and the community alike; only God, himself a loving and present personal Center, is able to activate a love capable of embracing the entire human community as well as the cosmos itself. These are precisely the divine functions within the Teilhardian cosmology: the guaranteeing of meaning and the activating of love-energy. God is source of meaning through his Word and source of energy through his Spirit, the source of both light and life. Teilhard's vision clearly resides upon the foundation of a trusting and hopeful faith nurtured within the Christian tradition.

In the process of retelling the creation story in the light of evolution, Teilhard has also transformed the meaning of death in the light of the Christian tradition. In the new Teilhardian creation story, death no longer presents itself as the menace of nonbeing, imperiling meaning and action. Through the alchemy of vision it has been transmuted into "the final stage of growth."[13] For both the individual and the community death may now be appropriated as the event of ecstatic emergence onto a higher level of being, the point of self-transcending migration into God. In death another evolutionary threshold is crossed—for the last time. Death, the enemy from outside the process, has found its place in cosmogenesis. It too has a meaning and no longer simply announces the annihilation of all meaning. As a result of the history of the dead and risen Savior, death becomes part of the whole, an element within the creational process. Traditionally death has belonged exclusively to the sphere of redemption. As the cruel consequence of man's fall it has been put to redemptive use by the cross of Jesus. For Teilhard, it belongs to the passivities of life, which together with the activities of life constitute the framework within which creation takes place.[14] We are made not only by what we do but also by what we undergo, including even death. Death belongs to the unitive creative process.

## III

The spiritual journey has often been understood, especially in Western culture, in terms of three stages of progress: the purgative, the illuminative, and the unitive. We have seen that Teilhard's spiritual way strongly emphasizes the illuminative and unitive aspects of the journey while seeming to neglect the purgative. He says himself in his spiritual masterpiece *The Divine Milieu* that he does not intend to address himself specifically to the issue of purification from sin since he is writing primarily for the Christian already somewhat advanced along the spiritual way.[15] Perhaps a creational piety and spirituality such as Teilhard's simply is not prepared temperamentally to give extensive attention to purification from sin any more than it is likely to give careful analytic scrutiny to sin itself or the problem of evil in general. These are, after all, the predominating themes of redemptive visions and their spiritualities. Yet Teilhard does not by any means ignore the purgative aspect of the spiritual journey any more than he ignores the problem of evil. Rather, he incorporates it into the illuminative and unitive aspects. To come to insight and vision involves continuous purification of the capacity to see, continuous transcending of inadequate or distorted ways of seeing. To live the unitive life involves a continuous purification of resistance to communion, continuous transcending of limiting self-interest and egocentricity. Purification is demanded by the ongoing requirement to remove the obstacles standing in the way of a creative participation in the cosmogenetic process through vision and love.

A creative spirituality implies an ascetical discipline all its own; it demands forms of ascetical practice peculiar to itself. The very effort involved in the work of creation possesses an inevitable ascetical component in the very overcoming of spiritual inertia. The need to go beyond every present achievement and attainment toward the future necessitates a detachment from the past and present. It demands an attachment to the future yet to be made that is quite as demanding as the ascetical requirements of traditional redemptive spiritualities. There exists for Teilhard a denial of the self as presently constituted in favor of the self still to be created through illuminative and unitive process, which suggests something of the exigency for self-denial and self-mortification characteristic of more traditional spiritual ways. A creative spirituality is a decidedly costly form of discipleship.[16] The price is death for the sake of new life—"the human epic resembles nothing so much as a way of the Cross."[17] Once again it can be seen that death is no longer merely the enemy to be avoided, but it has become an indispensable part of the way toward the creative end. Death still belongs to the darkness of life, but Teilhard invites us to love the darkness, even this darkness. While giving himself over totally to the service of new consciousness, to the service of the light, Teilhard never loses contact with mystery and darkness, for they also belong to the history of the ascent of consciousness. If death has not yet become exactly a friend, it has ceased to be entirely a foe. Throughout his life Teilhard remained deeply in touch with the goodness of the creational process to which he had dedicated himself. Not even death was able to shake that fundamental trust in the victory of the forces of life. Finally even death itself is understood as serving these very same forces of life. Somehow, mysteriously, it too belongs to the goodness of that creative movement, which will one day issue in Omega.

Teilhard de Chardin is one of the great storytellers of the modern age. He has invented a new creation story out of the storytelling traditions of both the Christian and the scientific communities. He has remythologized[18] the old myth of the biblical tradition and resacralized the new myth of the scientific tradition. This new Teilhardian myth of creation has become also a new context of meaning enabling action and commitment. It is after all the moral (or morality) of the story that most interests Teilhard. It is the story that suggests what is to be done. The story envisions the world as creative process; the moral to be drawn invites to cooperative participation in this process through illumination and communion. The spiritual guide can do little more than tell his story: "This is not a thesis, but a presentation—or, if you like, a summons. The summons of the traveller who has left the road and so by chance has arrived at a viewpoint from which everything is bathed in light, and calls out to his companions, 'Come and see!'"[19] The moral simply awaits enactment.

# 3

# Teilhard's Unity of Knowledge

## Thomas M. King, S.J.

In 1981, the centennial year of Teilhard's birth, together with James Salmon, S.J., I directed a symposium at Georgetown University titled "Teilhard and the Unity of Knowledge." We chose the title and the theme because they best told of our appreciation of Teilhard. That is, Teilhard had given us the context in which our knowledge of science, our sensitivity to human relationships, and our sense for God could become mutually coherent. Teilhard had provided a unity for the things we knew. We were also aware that a number of scholars in different fields had found in Teilhard a significant context in which they could situate their own work. We invited a number of these scholars to speak.[1] But though I organized the symposium, I have not previously had the occasion to address the issue.

### EVOLUTION AS A CONTEXT FOR ALL KNOWLEDGE

#### *Evolution as Organic*

Any effort to unify knowledge probably requires a unifying theme. For Teilhard this unifying theme was evolution. He writes that the idea of evolution germinated within him when he was about thirty years old. It began haunting his thoughts like a tune. He experienced evolution as "an unsatisfied hunger, like a promise held out to me, like a summons to be answered."[2] Soon he began full-time studies in geology and what is now known as paleo-biology; for such studies evolution easily served as a unifying theme. But eventually Teilhard would extend evolution beyond science to identify it as a "general condition of all knowledge."[3] He would claim, "All the fields of knowledge" have been transformed by evolution. It is not just a theory or a hypothesis:

It is a general condition to which all theories, all hypotheses, all systems must bow and which they must henceforward satisfy if they are to be think-

---

First published in *Teilhard Studies* no. 9 (summer 1983).

able and true. Evolution is a light illuminating all facts, a curve that all lines must follow.[4]

[E]volution has finally invaded everything . . . all nuclear physics, all astral physics, all chemistry are in their manner "evolutionary." And the whole history of civilization and ideas is at least as much so.[5]

It is evolution that has brought the diverse disciplines together, but many people have not realized this fact:

There are still any number of people to whom it comes as a shock if we speak of the physical reality of a mental phenomenon, or of the essentially biological nature of social or moral laws. It is precisely here that the newly opened up vision of a world in a state of evolution intervenes irresistibly, to release us from this sort of flat, hard and fast, dividing of things intellectually into compartments.[6]

Teilhard would define evolution in both a broad and a narrow sense. In a broad sense evolution means that "everything in the world appears and exists in function of the whole."[7] By his broad understanding of evolution Teilhard is introducing a biological model by which to understand the universe. The universe forms a body; it is "corpuscular"; it is made of "organically woven elements and organically linked layers."[8] The reality of anything is to be found in terms of its relation with everything else and its place in a unified totality.

Teilhard tells of trying to descend through levels of knowledge to his own most fundamental intuition. This turns out to be a "live sense of universal relationships of interdependence."[9] The universe is intuited as a totality; it "forms a system endlessly linked in time and space," or, in more biological terms, it is a "complete linked body." Fundamentally, Teilhard does not feel the need to argue this point. The totality "asserts itself with direct evidence"; it "forces itself inexorably on our attention;"[10] to anyone who can see and think the universe shows itself as "an organic unity, a coherence."[11] He would acknowledge that there is a mystical quality about this experience; it is essentially religious. But he would also claim that intuition is at the basis of all profound poetry or music and the dedication of many scientists. The meaning of this experience is that the universe is not an "ensemble" made of "things"; rather it is a "whole" made of "elements."[12] In any case, the unity of knowledge that Teilhard would develop is based on a fundamental intuition of the unity of the universe.

Teilhard does allow that people in earlier centuries saw the world very differently. Space and time were seen as compartments in which objects could be juxtaposed and interchanged at will. It was believed that an object could be abstracted from its context without changing it and without changing everything else in the process. This is a nonorganic model; it sees the universe as an "ensemble of things." In an organism the parts cannot be shifted around at will; in an organism a part does not make sense apart from its place and function in the whole. So, Teilhard would argue, it is with the universe. This is what contemporary science is showing us: biology shows that each living being has its precise place; it is "in series with the whole web of the biosphere." But Teilhard would go further and extend this understanding to the universe, even to the universe through time. Thus, when Teilhard speaks of Paleozoic times he warns the reader that he is not trying to picture it as a human being would have seen it then, for even to imagine a human in that landscape would be a "cosmic contradiction."[13] Through contemporary discoveries scientists came to see that:

> The position of each element was so intimately bound up with the genesis of the whole that it was impossible to alter it at random without rendering it "incoherent," or without having to readjust the distribution and history of the whole around it.[14]

A historian of science once observed that Darwin was primarily a field biologist, but the net result of his work was to send other biologists into the laboratories, from which they did not emerge for several decades. In a laboratory a single organism is cut off from the context that gave rise to the organism and that in some way explains it. Darwin once saw a hummingbird with a notably long beak; from the beak he argued correctly to the existence of a flower whose long trumpet matched the beak. Apart from the place of the bird in nature the beak is a puzzling curio. In a similar way one would misjudge a language if one tried to study it apart from the culture out of which it arose. Teilhard argues that this is what humanists do when they try to understand humanity; they study human beings apart from the context out of which they have arisen. This context is the entire history of the planet. So in writing *The Phenomenon of Man* Teilhard spent the first half of the book telling of the evolution of the Earth before the appearance of humanity.

Teilhard would see it that many scientists err as did the humanists. They try to study matter apart from a striking truth about matter: it has given rise to humanity. Both humanity and matter itself are distorted by a methodology that would abstract one from the other—for the purpose of study—and then not see that the separation encountered has arisen from the methodology they introduced. Neither humanity nor matter make sense apart one from the other. Humanity is the key to understanding the cosmos, and the cosmos is the key to understanding humanity.[15] The two are organically related. Teilhard would even argue that the present moral crisis goes back to this artificial separation. Human beings are not visitors or aliens on the planet that bore them. Their bodies and their blood, their minds and their culture have been formed throughout the millennia of events that have occurred on this planet; and nothing about humans can make sense apart from this context. We continue to speak as though we "came into this world." But we did not come "into" this world; we have come "out" of it—as leaves come out of a tree, we have come out of the universe. As leaves are organically parts of the tree, we are organically parts of the universe.

We are becoming increasingly aware of this organic interrelationship as it applies to all fields. We cannot study a mountain, a language, or a form of religion as a thing-in-itself.[16] Each makes sense only within a whole context of events proceeding through time. That is why Teilhard argues that because of evolution it "has become necessary to transpose our physics, biology and ethics, even our religion."[17]

### Biology Extended

This emphasis on the organic interrelationship of all things gives a particular significance to *life* and biology in the thought of Teilhard. Ordinarily one would think of life as characteristic of only an insignificant portion of the universe. Perhaps this is why scientists think they can omit it from their understanding of matter. But having claimed that the universe should be understood as an organism, Teilhard proceeds to claim that all matter is vitalized.[18] In stronger terms, he would say that the universe is "fundamentally and primarily living."[19] Thus the life we see is not an exception to the general inanimate nature of matter; it is rather the "manifestation of a fundamental tide inherent in all matter." Life has arisen out of a "general fermentation of the universe."[20] The individual living organism is the "visible expression" of a "force which is under pressure everywhere in the universe."[21] Most people regard life as a "peculiar anomaly" of our planet, an "interesting irregularity . . . with no importance for a full understanding of the basic structure of the universe."[22] This is what Teilhard would deny: the whole universe should be seen as living or at least as preliving. While Teilhard does speak of the coming of life or of the advent of life—phrases that would seem to indicate that life was not always present—he explains that here he means the coming of "formal perceived life."[23] Even this "formal perceived life" has arisen in function of the entire planet and ultimately in function of the "total cosmic evolution."[24] By relating life to the total cosmos Teilhard is appealing to the fact that light, gravitation, meteorites, cosmic rays, and so forth coming from the entire universe have continually affected this planet throughout the course of evolution. They have drastically affected the life forms of this planet (consider the recent claim that the dinosaurs were eliminated by meteorites that destroyed the vegetation on which they fed; the elimination of dinosaurs gave rise to the mammals). Teilhard titled his first essay "Cosmic Life" to emphasize his understanding that life has arisen in function of the entire cosmos.

To defend his "biological" understanding of the universe Teilhard considers other ways that the unity of the universe might be understood. It might be seen as having the unity of sand dumped in a heap or of molecules forming a crystal. A heap of sand is composed of parts that can be readily separated; a crystal looked at "biologically" shows that the molecules are linked by "external association . . . without true combination or union."[25] Neither of these nonliving models suggests an intrinsic union of elements (the type of unity that we are increasingly coming to recognize). But when we consider the polymers and even more so when we consider the living cell, Teilhard observes that the elements build up a more complicated interarrangement of parts into an "ever larger and more complex molecule."[26] There is an intrinsic unity of parts. This is how he would have us consider the universe. The parts of a cell have meaning only in terms of the whole. They do not form a simple ensemble (as in a pile of sand), or a simple external linkage (as in a crystal), but the parts of a cell are intrinsically affected by the unity they form. Teilhard would see such an intrinsic involvement extending to all phenomena. All phenomena are joined to form a "complete linked body." Therefore he would regard any particular organism as a manifestation of "the very essence of phenomenon."[27] He would accordingly speak of each organism as a microcosm within the total organism, and the total organism is the macrocosm.[28]

Teilhard has introduced one of his essays as "a sort of appeal addressed by a biologist to his colleagues in the fields of physics and chemistry." He explains that he does not wish to intrude into their areas of competence; he would simply like to offer them a point of view that might reconcile their work "with closely parallel work now being carried out in the domain of life."[29] It is again as a "biologist" that he makes appeals to the social sciences. He introduces *The Phenomenon of Man* by saying that one of his basic assumptions is a "biological" interpretation of society.[30] In the course of the work he tells of "the organic nature of mankind," and sees the future unity of humanity as "biologically necessary."[31] He would argue that if one accepts the biological nature of humanity, then it "becomes legitimate to talk in the sphere of economics of the existence and development of a circulatory or a nutritional system applicable to mankind as a whole."[32] For Teilhard, the laws developed by any society are regarded as the laws of a growing organism, and modern means of communication are spoken of as forming a "general nervous system."[33] This outlook is possible because social phenomena are "closely linked with biology."[34] At the same time he would warn against transposing literally the terms from physiology or anatomy into social structures.[35] Teilhard would write an essay to show how modern technology fits into the general biology of mankind;[36] the development of electromagnetic waves is identified as a "prodigious biological event."[37] To historians he would offer "a plausible biological interpretation of human history."[38] He believed economists could learn from biology how to understand the unemployment of the 1930s: "Economists are horrified by the growing number of idle hands. Why do they not look to biology for guidance and enlightenment?"[39]

Teilhard would also apply this biological understanding to human relationships. He would ask that we see love not just as a joyous or sentimental power, but in "its full biological reality."[40] Love is identified as the inner affinity of one being with another and ultimately the affinity of all the elements of the universe; love is the power that has been binding the elements together since the beginning. It is the power that binds the elements together to form an organism. Since this cosmic dimension of love is being ignored, Teilhard suggests that "biologists" advise society on how to direct its powers of love.[41] Since love is the power that draws the elements together, Teilhard would urge that Christ's command to "love God and our neighbor" is not to be viewed as something extrinsic to the life of the universe and superimposed upon it from without. Rather, "it is Life, Life in the integrity of its aspirations."[42] Teilhard repeatedly objected to the extrinsic understanding of Christianity that has generally been preached. Christianity seems to be an alien "thing-in-itself" added to the universe from without. But for Teilhard it is the culmination of the entire cosmic movement, and Christ emerges from that movement as the Lord of evolution. Christianity itself is identified as a form of "biological progress"[43] that acts with the rigor of "biological laws."[44] Though other teachers have offered visions that compete with Christianity in the scope of their vision—he refers to the worldviews proposed by Plato, Hegel, and Spinoza—these ideologies are less than Christianity for they have not succeeded in "begetting life."[45] The church is identified as a "mystical organism,"[46] a "supernatural organism."[47] And the kingdom of God is said to be a "prodigious biological operation."[48] Even the mysticism of Teilhard is rooted in biology: "I can feel God, touch Him, 'live' Him in the deep biological current that runs through my soul."[49]

### Converging Evolution

Thus, Teilhard would unify knowledge around the theme of evolution. By speaking of evolution in a broad sense Teilhard would offer all fields of knowledge a biological model: the universe itself is an organism. But the word *evolution* would seem to say more. In a strict sense Teilhard's pan-evolutionism means that the biological character of the universe is increasing: that is, the general interrelatedness of all things is intensifying through time. This progressive convergence is identified also as a "general condition of our knowledge.[50] This convergence is indicated by a number of phrases, for example, "matter contrives to organize itself in particles . . . ever more highly organized";[51] "[t]he universe appears to be affected by a convergent curvature into which the substance of all things is gradually being forced,"[52] in a "structurally convergent cosmos."[53] Because of a general "compression," things are undergoing a "forced coalescence."[54] There is a "movement of involution," an "immense coiling movement," a "cosmic coiling," a "monstrous inflorescence" as the universe "folds in on itself."[55] There is a "gigantic and planetary contraction" in which the world become more compressed upon itself.[56]

Teilhard frequently uses the image of a cone to illustrate this general convergence. The original elements of matter are seen to be spread out at the base; in the course of time they rise toward the apex and in the process come more closely together ("Everything that rises must converge")—that is how the cone is formed.[57] Elements rise "by tightening the cone," and thus "move towards the apex."[58] There is a progressive unification "towards a peak."[59] Each individual person is identified as a "peak of spirit," for the person is a partial center of the converging cosmos. Since each person is seen as a peak or a cone, there are many "peaks of spirit."[60] But ultimately these are being drawn to form a single summit. This is the final divine center of the whole process; Christ is found "at the peak of evolution."[61] He is at "the dominating position of all inclusive Centre in which everything is gathered together."[62] He is "shining at the apex of evolution," at "the apex of the world," and is the "God of . . . evolution."[63]

Because of this general convergence, Teilhard would argue, it is becoming *increasingly* inaccurate to think of ourselves as separate individuals. We are increasingly involved in a common fabric, and this is how we must understand ourselves. "The social unification of the earth is the state towards which evolution is drawing us."[64] Social, political, and economic bonds are becoming global. It is becoming ever more inaccurate and unviable to think of nations as things-in-themselves. "The age of nations is past; it remains for us now, if we do not wish to perish, to set aside the ancient prejudices and build the earth."[65]

## UNITY AND A FUNDAMENTAL DUALISM

### *Without and Within*

Every philosopher—and perhaps every scientist—has tried to introduce a unity into his knowledge. Some philosophers have tried this in a very explicit way. For example, Descartes, early in his career, set out to form an all-embracing system of knowledge that he called a "universal wisdom" (see Rule 1 of *Rules for the Direction of the Mind*). His unifying theme was mathematics, more precisely, geometry. But in developing his unity of knowledge, Descartes came up with a radical dualism in his universe: there is both thought and extension, that is, mind and body, or, perhaps, subject and object. Descartes did not invent this dualism, but his forceful presentation has left it deeply embedded in the Western tradition. This dualism has come down to us in many forms; it is generally identified as the mind–body problem. Each of us is a "ghost in the machine." Sartre wrote in the Cartesian tradition and likewise told of reality as radically divided: there is consciousness (the *pour-soi*) and the object (the *en-soi*). They form "two regions of being absolutely separated."[66]

Philosophers are generally uncomfortable with dualisms. Some philosophers have tried to resolve this particular dualism by eliminating one of the opposing elements. They could be termed "reductionists" in that they try to reduce one of the elements to the other. Those who deny the reality of mind have generally taken a unifying theme from mechanics. They would be the materialists, who have tried to explain all reality in terms of physical particles in motion. Teilhard would see this approach as common in the last century, when physicists tried to reduce everything "to calculable movements of invariable masses" with the result that "mind lost its value and even its reality."[67] Teilhard argues that now that science has not been able to find an ultimate particle, the "great fixed lower point" on which the materialists had been basing their understanding has disappeared. Thus, they would no longer have a viable position.

A second group of reductionists would be the idealists, who have to explain all things in terms of Mind. Teilhard would see them as "obstinately determined not to go outside a kind of solitary introspection." Without the physical world, their knowledge soon becomes pure speculation. Thus, for one group there is only a Without—matter in external relationships; for the other there is only the Within. Teilhard would have it that each of these schools sees only half of the problem.[68] He would like to construct "one coherent explanation for both realities; he would like to form a phenomenology" in which the internal aspect of things as well as the external aspect of the world will be taken into account.[69]

Teilhard would argue against this dualism both in terms of common knowledge and in terms of modern science. It is a matter of common knowledge that in order to think we must eat. It is also evident that the thoughts we have can affect our physical health. Thus the two orders are evidently interrelated. At one time science seemed able to overlook this interrelationship. Scientists assumed that we could see things "just as they are," "without being mixed up in them." Scientists studied the universe "without even being aware of belonging intrinsically to the system which they were analysing."[70] They looked at the world "from outside, like gods." They thought "they could look down from a great height upon a world which their consciousness could penetrate without being submitted to it or changing it."[71] But with the coming of relativity, "the objectivity of the physicist" seemed to vanish; they came to see that their theories contain as much of themselves as of the object they study. This involvement of the observer is even more evident in biology. When a biologist first considered evolution he remained "isolated and apart, a spectator, not an actor in evolution."[72] Now we have come to see that the consciousness of the observer is part of the process; and in the very act of observing this consciousness continues to evolve. That is, we have come to see that we are evolution conscious of itself. Scientists now can see that they are "caught body and soul in the network of relationships they thought to cast upon things from outside."[73]

It was his awareness of evolution that enabled Teilhard to see beyond this subject–object dualism. He claims that both his education and his religion had presented him with the "fundamental heterogeneity between Matter and Mind." They were treated as two different substances or two species of being; he was left with a "paralyzing" and "static dualism."[74] He experienced immense relief when he took his

first still hesitant steps into an "evolutive" universe, and saw that the dualism in which I had hitherto been enclosed was disappearing like the mist before the rising sun. Matter and Mind: these were no longer two things, but two states or two aspects of one and the same cosmic stuff.[75]

It was evolution that allowed him see "the disappearance of the alleged barrier that separates the Within of things from the Without."[76] The process of evolution shows that the Without (the material world) has been increasingly developing a Within (a consciousness). We are that consciousness, and now we must see our mind and the matter from which we have arisen as intrinsically related.

When evolution is regarded objectively, it shows that increasingly larger physical syntheses are being formed. But then in the development of our knowledge we find that increasingly larger syntheses are being formed in human consciousness. Teilhard would connect the outer process with the inner one and see Life and Thought as two phases of a common development: "Life is carried forward into Thought."[77] So he would speak of "the biological properties of thought,"[78] or speak of Thought as "evolution internalized."[79] With the first appearance of

Thought on Earth Teilhard would see evolution passing beyond the physical-chemical organization of bodies to develop "a new organizing power vastly concentric to the first—the cognitive organization of the universe."[80] The same synthesizing power that has been active in the physical world is now continuing its activity in the psyche. "If evolution shows itself as a process of Arrangement, by what right does one place an absolute division between an arrangement of atoms or neurons and an arrangement of visions, emotions, or sensations?"[81]

The absolute division to which he objects is the absolute division that we habitually introduce between matter and mind. Teilhard argues that the evolution of matter proceeds into the evolution of mind by a continuous process. Thus, he would compare the evolution of life with the evolution of ideas.[82] The development of ideas proceeds like the evolution of life: by a series of preliminary trials and gropings; it is a creative process.[83] Ideas are also subject to a "survival of the fittest," and some lines of thought have died out. The reality of evolution is so basic to our own inner processes that Teilhard would ask if scientists have really discovered evolution in the external world, or if they have only been expressing themselves in the theory.[84]

Because of the continuity of evolution from the outer world to the inner world, Teilhard would interpret the anxieties and joys of scientific discovery in a more cosmic context. The wave of enthusiasm that we feel in moments of discovery "was not formed in ourselves. It comes to us from far away; it set out at the same time as the light from the first stars. It reaches us after creating everything on the way. The spirit of research and conquest is the permanent soul of evolution."[85] In a dualistic world this enthusiasm would be interpreted as an emotional tone in my individual psyche. For Teilhard this inner enthusiasm is part of a universal process. A single evolutionary drive has been building the universe; now within my psyche it is continuing the process. The deeper emotions that I feel are part of the wider current of things. The love that seems to realign my inner world is the same love that has been realigning matter from the beginning. And instinctively this is how it is felt: it seems to be a cosmic upheaval. It is only when I turn back to a habitual (and indefensible) body–mind dualism that I lose the true sense of being in love, the sense of participating in a cosmic process.

We are not alien consciousnesses facing a world that is "other." We are rather that world itself come to consciousness. We are the "stuff of the universe . . . becoming thinking."[86] In each one of us it is "evolution perceiving itself and reflecting on itself."[87] Our human reflection is not simply an act of our individual psyches; rather it is the general process wherein "Matter thinks itself."[88] Perhaps in Cartesian terms it could be said that the world is both the object and the subject of my cogito. Teilhard tells of standing on a large heap of rock and having the sensation that it was no longer himself thinking, rather it was "the Earth acting."[89] It is "the universe, in one of its fundamental movements, that would emerge in our consciousness, and the universe battling deep down in our wills."[90] Many individuals come together in love, and humans come together to form a society. It is not so much themselves acting as the universe "animating itself"; it is "the universe fulfilling itself in a synthesis."[91]

Collections of Teilhard's essays have been titled *The Hymn of the Universe* and *The Prayer of the Universe*.[92] Our prayer is more than a turning of our own individual psyches to God; it is the universe itself as found in our knowledge turning to God through us. In the same way, when we love God, the act is not restricted to our individual psyches; rather we love God "with every fibre of the unifying universe."[93] The consciousness of each one of us is where evolution is occurring today, so it is "from universal evolution God emerges in our consciousness."[94] But there is still an ambiguity about the location: "whether above me or in the depths of my being I cannot say."[95] Ultimately, the difficulty is in trying to locate God simply as Within or Without; the one Lord can be equally identified as being above the universe or in the depths of one's heart.[96]

### Dualists and Biology

It is interesting to note that the biological theme around which Teilhard built his unity of knowledge is a particular blind spot for such body–mind dualists as Descartes and Sartre. Descartes reduced animals to being machines, much like wind-up toys, which really have no life. The parts of a machine have purely external relations with one another; the machine can be completely understood "from Without." At the same time Descartes would leave the observer or thinker confined completely within himself (enclosed in his cogito). The Without and the Within are radically separated. But this is precisely what Teilhard's biological image would deny. It affirms that matter cannot be understood simply as a without, and it affirms that the human observer cannot be understood simply as a within.

Sartre tells of his own dislike for vegetation. In *Nausea* he tells of having seen "enough of living things, of dogs and men, of all flabby masses that move spontaneously."[97] So he goes to where there are "treeless sidewalks." He tells of being "frightened in the presence of nature," of feeling alarmed at being in "a heap of living things." He feels "trapped in an immense, amorphous and gratuitous existence."[98] He speaks of wanting to wash himself clean with abstract thought as a "Cartesian," but it will not work.

When Sartre speaks of a "heap of living things" he shows an inability to see the interrelationships of an evolutionary world. But he also has difficulty in accepting any living organism, that is, a body animated by a soul (human, animal, or vegetable). For any body–soul unity is opposed to the habitual Cartesian dualism. These passages from Sartre are taken from his early writings. I have argued elsewhere that Sartre later rejected this dualism and came to develop a very different philosophy.[99] I also have argued that relinquishing this dualism became the fundamental theme of Sartre's plays and novels. It involves an "awakening," an "enlightenment"—followed by a decision. It recalls Teilhard's account of taking hesitant steps out of a "paralyzing" dualism into an "evolutive universe," while seeing the enclosing dualism disappear like the mist before the rising sun.

## KNOWLEDGE AND DARKNESS

This paper has developed Teilhard's understanding of the unity of knowledge around the theme of evolving Life. But I am also aware that one of the best and the most respected of Teilhard scholars, Henri de Lubac, has said that all of the writings of Teilhard are "one long meditation on death."[100] The phrase is surprising for those who have not spent time with the texts of Teilhard, yet it points to an awesome and even an unsettling quality that underlies the optimism that is so evident.

At the end of *The Phenomenon of Man* Teilhard added an epilogue that tells of his being reproached for having presented a "naive or exaggerated optimism," as if "evil and its problem have tided away and no longer count in the structure of the world."[101] Teilhard was surprised by the criticism. He tells of finding evil, death, disorder, and anxiety creeping through every sinew of his system. He allows that he has presented only the positive essence without telling of "the depths of the abysses between the peaks." But he adds that in showing a photograph one need not present the negative that made the picture possible. Teilhard would write other essays that also seem to omit mention of evil—until it is named in a striking final passage.[102] For any system wherein the unity of life is the great good, the disintegration of death is the great evil, the great absurdity. That is, it cannot be understood; it cannot become knowledge.

For Teilhard, knowledge always involves a unity; so that which escapes unity, what Teilhard calls "the pure multiple," cannot be known. Or, as Teilhard would say, it escapes "the direct grasp of thought";[103] "our intelligence is baffled by the multiple."[104] But the multiple is a matter of experience. So it is with death. Death is the absurdity that cannot be understood. But wherever there is a feel for life, a sense of death is vaguely present.

Teilhard has identified himself as an explorer. He traveled much to distant places that are little known. But he was also an explorer of the height and depth of human experience. His vision shows that he has been to the mountain, but it also lets us know that he explored "the depths of the abysses between the peaks." If the light he saw was brighter than that which most people see, his darkness was darker.

The writings of Teilhard have spoken directly to many people. Yet many of those affected are not able to explain his systematic thought. They have been touched by something that is beyond the theology, the geology, the biology, and the unity of ideas he has left us. For the writings of Teilhard give us a sense of the man himself. A man is not contained in his knowledge—but he is contained in his faith (that is what makes the act of faith so frightening). Teilhard has shared his faith with his readers. Faith must include all of one's knowledge and also the strange darkness that extends beyond one's ability to know. Teilhard has presented a stunning vision of the unity of knowledge, but running beneath his optimistic vision one can sense the fear and trembling that remind us that Teilhard lived by faith.

# 4

# The Letters of Teilhard de Chardin and Lucile Swan

## A *Personal Interpretation*

### Ursula King

The long-awaited correspondence between Teilhard de Chardin and Lucile Swan has now appeared in print. The letters have been superbly edited and annotated by Thomas M. King, S.J., and Lucile's cousin, Mary Wood Gilbert. They are accompanied by photographs, explanatory essays, and a helpful chronology of the lives of the two correspondents.[1] It has long been known that a deep friendship existed between Teilhard and Lucile, yet few details were available before. We had to await the full text of this correspondence to discover the strong, loving bonds that existed between these two great souls.

Many volumes of Teilhard de Chardin's letters have appeared in print, made available by those who were their recipients, since Teilhard never kept any copies himself. Previously published letters give us many insights into Teilhard's personal life and manner of working, his travels around the world, and his friendships with people from different backgrounds. Teilhard was a beloved and precious friend to many. Several of his close friends were women, among them his cousin Marguerite Teilhard Chambon, the philosopher Léontine Zanta, Solange Lemaitre, Ida Treat, Rhoda de Terra, and the American sculptor Malvina Hoffman. Some, but not all, of Teilhard's letters to these women have been published much earlier, whereas his letters to Lucile Swan have only now become available. They represent not simply another correspondence with one of his women friends, but they are a unique collection of very special letters which throw new light on Teilhard as a person and put his ideas, especially those about the nature and power of love, into a hitherto unknown perspective.

It is an unusual correspondence between two unusual people, the French scientist, priest, and mystic, Pierre Teilhard de Chardin, and the American sculptor Lucile Swan. They spent many happy hours together during the years when both

First published in *Teilhard Studies* no. 32 (fall 1995).

were working in Peking; they wrote to each other during their absences and travels, a correspondence that continued when both lived later in the United States and lasted until Teilhard's death in 1955. Until recently, only a few people knew of these letters, in which Teilhard speaks at his most personal and intimate, with a depth of feeling and intensity of commitment matched perhaps only in his prayers, retreat notes, and diary entries. Here we catch a glimpse of his mind and soul, of the vibrance of his feelings and the strength of his emotions, which only rarely surface elsewhere. These letters express a great and unusual love, a love that nourished and strengthened much of Teilhard's thought, but also a love that was not without difficulties and turbulences.

Most of the letters are Teilhard's, but the correspondence is unusual in that it includes replies from the person to whom Teilhard wrote. Lucile's letters are much fewer in number, but they have been preserved because Lucile had a habit of keeping carbon copies of her typed letters, whereas Teilhard used to number his. Some letters are missing, however; they may have been lost in the mail or may not have been preserved, as it is known that Lucile destroyed and edited letters before her death in 1965.

The correspondence falls into two parts. The first belongs to what Teilhard later called "the Chinese phase" of their lives, which lasted from 1929 to 1941. Teilhard and Lucile both lived in Peking during that time, and a strong bond of love and friendship developed between them. The second part might be called "the American phase," dating from 1948 to 1955, when their relationship was quite altered. This period was preceded by intermittent contacts during the years of 1941-1948 when, because of World War II and Lucile's return to the United States, they did not see each other at all. These seven years of separation led to a distancing of their relationship, producing tensions and misunderstandings that lasted until Teilhard's death.[2] In this correspondence the thoughts and feelings, the dreams and hopes, as well as the difficulties and disappointments of both sides are openly expressed and shared. More than anything else, these letters highlight the relationship between Teilhard and Lucile, but they also give us many details about his life and work. They provide numerous clues for understanding and interpreting the essays that Teilhard wrote between 1929 and 1941 and give glimpses of *The Human Phenomenon* in the making. This correspondence is, therefore, a particularly rich source for the interpreters of Teilhard's *oeuvre* that cannot be exhaustively described in one essay. However, I would like to offer a personal interpretation by sharing some questions and reflections that other readers of the correspondence may find helpful.

The letters of Teilhard and Lucile Swan tell a beautiful and deeply moving story about human love, a love inextricably intertwined with another love, the love and search for God. A subtle, elusive quality, a radiant beauty and light emerge from their pages, but also a sadness about the precariousness and frailty of human emotions. I was immensely thrilled when I first read this correspondence because these letters opened up a completely new perspective on Teilhard's thought and answered many questions about Teilhard's personal life; they also raised many new ones. I have read and reread these letters and pondered over their meaning. Although different readers may understand this correspondence in many different ways, I hope they will be able to savor the fragrance of a beautiful spiritual love and friendship, so movingly expressed in these letters, which speak of laughter, joy and pain, spiritual union and separation, sadness, doubts, and peace in God.

In earlier years of his life, especially during World War I when his literary activity first emerged, Teilhard had been deeply in love with his cousin Marguerite. This is well known, but his letters to her, found in *The Making of a Mind*,[3] do not directly speak of these feelings of love, nor do we possess any letters from his cousin. Marguerite was a devout Roman Catholic who shared the same family background and religious beliefs as Teilhard. Given these circumstances, both would naturally have felt restrained in giving full expression to their emotions, especially as he was an ordained priest. When Teilhard met Lucile in 1929, the situation was quite different. He was more than ten years older now, widely traveled, and belonging to an international scientific and diplomatic elite in Peking. At the height of his creativity and scientific career, he was closely associated with the Chinese Geological Survey, the excavations at Chou-kou-tien and the findings of *Homo sinanthropus*.[4] He was also increasingly critical of the past, of his own as much as of the past-oriented nature of his scientific work. Thus, he was looking for new horizons, for a new energy, and was turning more and more toward the future. Lucile had been brought up an Episcopalian, but she had drifted away from the church and all formal religion. Unlike Marguerite, she did not feel bound by traditional religious beliefs and attitudes, and she was a creative artist who had lived in an avant-garde milieu before coming to Peking. Her vivacious personality reacted with a spontaneity and freshness to Teilhard, which must have made her all the more attractive to him. She did not feel inhibited in finding words to express their mutual attraction and love, words that Teilhard reciprocated over and over again.

Who was Lucile? We know far more about Teilhard than about her. Teilhard's biographers have told us little about his relationship to Lucile Swan, and what they have told is not always supported by these letters. After reading the deep expressions of love and friendship Teilhard addressed to her, one understands why Lucile wanted her side to be known. But by the time she died, she still had kept most of her story to herself except for what she told her cousin, Mary Wood Gilbert, who is one of the editors of the correspondence. Seeing photos of Lucile sculpting in her Peking studio or in front of her little temple house, one gets the impression of a sensitive, thoughtful woman with much warmth and charm. The happy smile on her face expresses a great joy of life, a sense of exuberance and vivaciousness—traits that are supported by remarks in the letters. Perhaps one day someone might attempt a fuller portrait of Lucile, and also a new biography of Teilhard in the light of his relationship to Lucile. I can offer only a few comments on what I have gleaned from the correspondence and also from two unpublished autobiographical sketches that Lucile wrote in 1957 and 1965, where she hints at, but never fully discloses, the intensity of love between Teilhard and her as documented in the published correspondence.

Lucile and Teilhard first met in 1929 at a dinner party in Dr. Grabau's house in Peking. Almost thirty years later, Lucile wrote in her reminiscences that this first meeting was to change her life.[5] Born in 1887, she was only a few years younger than Teilhard. As an artist she had belonged to a bohemian milieu in New York. Her marriage to another artist in 1912 had been dissolved by 1924. In 1929 she came to China with her friend Elizabeth Spencer, called "Betty," who later married John Carter Vincent. At that time Lucile was looking for a sense of direction, for a meaning to her life and creative work. Although she had turned away from traditional religion, she had retained a deep spiritual longing which she felt found a response in Teilhard's words and vision.

She was impressed with Teilhard's special spiritual radiance and was pleasantly surprised when she discovered herself seated next to him. They quickly fell into conversation, and Lucile was not insensitive to Teilhard's physical attractiveness. As he talked about Christ and the Divine Milieu she found herself awakening to a new interest in the presence of God in her life and in the work of the world.[6]

Their friendship must have grown gradually, but we possess no written evidence about their early years of contact. Teilhard's first letter is dated August 30, 1932, when he was returning to France after the arduous "Yellow Expedition" across the Gobi Desert and Sinkiang. This first extant letter is so brief and casual that one may presume that other letters, now lost, preceded it. In the second letter, written two months later, there is mention of their friendship, a friendship that became much stronger during 1933, when Teilhard was back in Peking. Lucile then sculpted her first bust of him, and during his regular sittings their conversations and friendship must have grown greatly in closeness and intimacy. Lucile's house became a home for Teilhard during the years 1932-1941; he went there every afternoon for tea at five o'clock when he was in Peking. They often went for walks together around Peking, especially in the park.

The first strong declaration of Teilhard's love is found in a letter of March 9, 1934, where he replied to a "glorious letter" from her. Reading it was "one of the most precious minutes" in his life. He wrote: "You have entered more deep than ever, as an active seed, the innermost of myself. You bring me what I need for carrying on the work which is before me; a tide of life. . . . You and I, we are two wild birds on the Mother Earth. May be, for years, our paths are going to run close to each other. May be, also, the wind is going to separate our external ways. . . . And be patient (even with yourself), peaceful and happy.—I *know* that what is born between us is to live forever."[7]

This assurance was often to be repeated between them. But Teilhard's remarks about their paths proved prophetic. They kept close together for many years, but eventually their external ways separated. Lucile provided a sustaining, loving presence throughout Teilhard's long years in Peking. What would he have done without this intimacy and warmth, without the feeling that only Lucile really understood him, shared all his ideas, and even helped to develop them? Teilhard's sense of loss and separation is acutely expressed in the letters after mid-1941, when Lucile had left for the United States: "I miss you in my heart—and in my mind too. I was thinking in you, and through you—you know it. And because you are not here, I have sometimes the feeling that my thoughts do not mature in the same way, as before, when I could search myself in you."[8] They were most dear and precious to each other. Lucile referred to Teilhard's initials "PT" as "precious Teilhard," and frequently used the term "precious" when describing him or addressing him in a warm way. She found it to be a very appropriate term to characterize a very unique quality of this great man.[9]

Lucile longed for a fuller giving in those years, for a complete union, not only a spiritual love and friendship. Yet Teilhard's loyalty and faithfulness belonged to a higher vision, a love of God which Lucile at first did not understand. While she expected some physical confirmation of their affection—they often turned to this subject as their "pet discussion"—Teilhard had clearly stated his position in an early letter: "The fundamental bearing of my life, you know it, is to prove to the others and firstly to myself, that the love of God does not destroy, but exalt and purify any earthly power of understanding and loving. I dream of going to God under the pressure of the strongest and wildest spirits of the world. . . . But because your friend, Lucile, belongs to Something Else, he cannot be yours—(and you would find very few left in him, of what attracts you, if he tried to be yours)—just and merely for being momentarily happy with you."[10]

Lucile found this difficult to understand and felt, perhaps quite rightly, that his friendship was better than his ideas, that he was more interested in the human phenomenon and love in general than in individual people and personal love. She expressed her difficulties with Teilhard's view, not in a letter but in a note to herself:

> You've become more important in my life every day. Yes. The live, physical, real you, all of you. I want you so terribly and I am trying so hard to understand and incorporate into my being your philosophy, your views on life. I read and reread and I think I understand, but why do they not make me feel them more deeply. I want to so much—I must for my own salvation—I can't have you. Not really, so I must learn your way of having each other.[11]

He frankly admitted, "The problem, I told you, exists for me just as for you—although, for some complex reasons, I believe I have to stick somewhat to an old solution. My line of answer, let me observe, does not exclude the 'physical' element,—since it is not some abstract spirit,—but the 'woman,'—which I discover in you."[12]

Their spiritual intimacy was so great that he let her read his notebook, which perhaps no one else ever saw. The finest expression of the depth of her love comes in a passage written on July 27, 1934, where she declares her intention not to write so passionately. She says:

> I have read your notebook and realize how much of you is unworldly. And I wrote you just before you left in which I spoke of the "physical." Please don't think I mean just sex, although that is very strong. It would make a bond between us that would add a strength that I believe nothing else can

give. However, that is only a part. I want to be with you when you are well
and when you are ill. Go see beautiful things with you and walk through
the country. In other words, I want to stand beside you always, to laugh and
play and pray with you. Don't you realize what a big part of life that is, and
how that is what is right and normal and God-given. But I cannot. *Ne puis
pas.*[13]

Teilhard taught Lucile to share his vision and look deeper into things. He gave
her ever so much in their many talks on God, love, and life. She reciprocated by
giving her best to him, convinced that over the years her efforts had greatly
enriched their friendship. When physically awkward moments would arise during their closeness, they would restrain themselves, trust in God, and go forward
in the belief that such discipline would actually make their relationship
stronger.[14]

During 1933 and early 1934, when they so openly expressed their love for
each other, Teilhard was working on his essay "The Evolution of Chastity."[15]
Here, as elsewhere, the matrix of Teilhard's thought is experience, deep personal
experience. This essay, together with others that speak about the power and transformation of love, must be reinterpreted in the light of what we now know about
the relationship between Teilhard and Lucile. Teilhard admits in "The Evolution
of Chastity" that he had been "through some difficult passages" with regard to
human love, but that he did not lose his way. For him love is going through a
"change of state," and he concludes this important essay with the often quoted
words: "The day will come when, after harnessing the ether, the winds, the tides,
gravitation, we shall harness for God the energies of love. And, on that day, for
the second time in the history of the world, man will have discovered fire."[16]
There is much talk of the fire of love in this correspondence. Lucile realized that
a passionate love and fire consumed Teilhard's life and that to the end she associated this fire with the sense of his presence.[17]

Teilhard always remained faithful to his vocation as a priest, to his vow of
chastity and his vision of God and the world. Although firm in his decision, he
was not without doubts. He once said that he was not a preacher but a desperate
searcher. He affirmed again and again that Lucile had become part of his deepest
life, but when she questioned his position, he replied, "You object once more that
I am denying, by chastity, one of the fundamental laws of the Universe. I told you
already how *hesitating* I am in the position which I still keep because I have the
dim impression that it preserves and saves a deep tendency (and a hope) of the
World."[18] He apologized for the extraordinary path along which he had taken her,
the apparently "unnatural situation" of their relationship and assured Lucile "that
there is nothing which I do not do for compensating, on the possible grounds, the
things which for higher reasons, I cannot give you (and it is hard for me not to
give you). Sometimes I think that this very privation I must impose on you makes
me ten times more devoted to you. Anyhow, something seems *sure* to me; even
admitted that I am materially wrong, and that, some day, 'chastity' will definitely
prove not to be connected with a higher spirituality, it remains that love needs

presently a deep transformation in order to become the great human energy and that we are working and praying for this transformation."[19]

During the 1930s Teilhard had difficulties with his church and order, and some of these are mentioned in the letters. Lucile gave him continuing support, but she also questioned his unswerving loyalty. In her view his order had nothing to do with this age, whereas Teilhard had so much to give. She noted in her *Journal*, "I know I had hoped there might be some definite break with his order— but it did not come—in fact I had subconsciously counted on it more than I realized and it was almost hard to realize and accept things as they were—that we were more and closer to each other I am sure—but how to live and express this love is still a problem that sometimes brought up difficulties. . . ."[20] Teilhard maintained that he could not give himself entirely and exclusively to anybody. His method was to yield to his superiors as far as necessary so as not break relations in a premature way. This he would have considered a disaster for what he wanted to develop and spread.

In a letter of August 1938, to which Lucile referred later with great joy, Teilhard expressed in a beautiful way what had grown between them: "You can and you must help me to go on straight ahead, by giving me light and warmth. Keep me alive on Earth, whilst I try to bring you closer to God. This seems to me to be the meaning and the definition of our mutual union. Make me more myself, as I dream to make you reaching the best of yourself. . . . And thank you, *so much,* for forgetting as you do, for me, what you might naturally expect, but what, for higher reasons, I cannot give you. I love you so much the more for this 'renouncement.' And there is nothing I will not do for you, in order to repay you."[21]

Because of the Japanese occupation, Teilhard and Lucile were confined to the city of Peking during the years 1939-1941. They had two years almost completely to themselves, "two precious years of constant presence and uninterrupted mutual confidence," which sealed their friendship, as Teilhard wrote in his farewell letter to Lucile when she departed for the United States. She had come to accept his view of the world transparent with divine glory, of the evolution of all life toward God, and of his deep love for the universal Christ. When she left in 1941, he sent her the only "pious" object left on his working table, a small picture of Christ which he described as "a vague representation of the universal 'foyer' of attraction which we are aiming for. In this atmosphere we can always love each other more and better."[22]

There are no letters to tell us about Lucile's feelings. Teilhard missed her deeply and wrote "that makes such a difference for me not to have you, dearest, to tell and divide *everything.* So many things I have to keep for myself, now; and so many things probably, which do not get born in my mind because you are not there to give me . . . the 'internal impetus.'"[23] Although he felt that their friendship was now strong enough to face everything, seven years of separation so profoundly affected their relationship that it became deeply altered after the war. When Teilhard eventually returned to France in 1946, he did not meet Lucile again until 1948. He was much older then and also more infirm as he had suffered from illness. Another woman friend, Mrs. Rhoda de Terra, whom he had first encountered in late 1937 on his visit to Burma, became a frequent visitor and companion, first in Paris and later in New York. This led to tensions with Lucile, who now felt she was no longer part of his work as in Peking. She was jealous of Rhoda's friendship with Teilhard and her accompanying him on his visit to South Africa in 1951. She wrote: "It seems to me that now she has EVERY-THING that used to be mine, the daily visits, the sharing of all the intimate things and friends—well, all that makes life sweet and worthwhile."[24]

It is difficult to assess Teilhard's relationship to Rhoda in the last years of his life. He had long and openly corresponded with her and refers to her in many letters to Lucile. Teilhard's letters to Rhoda, written between 1938 and 1950, have been published,[25] but they do not reveal anything about their personal feelings for each other, especially as there are no letters of the years 1951-1955, when both Teilhard and Rhoda lived in New York. Lucile, during that time, was settled in Washington but traveled a great deal. Teilhard and Lucile paid each other mutual visits or wrote fairly regularly, and the published correspondence includes almost twice as many letters by Lucile from the period after 1941 as from the period before.

One gets the impression from these letters of the "American period" that sometimes the relationship between Teilhard and Lucile seemed as it was in earlier years, and at other times it was so troubled that Lucile even thought of breaking it off altogether. The letters refer to tense emotions, frustration and ill ease and include several suggestions not to meet too often. On January 24, 1953, Teilhard wrote, "Well, emotions are strange. And the truth is we still disturb each other whereas, both of us, we need absolutely 'peace.'"[26] Lucile objected to being put into a motherly role and expressed her deep disappointment at the way their relationship had developed: "We meet and act as if nothing had ever existed between us."[27]

The difficulties seem to have been more on Teilhard's side than on hers. Lucile admitted that she had reoriented her life since meeting him again in 1948 and had acquired a real inner peace; a peace she wished for Teilhard too. Thus she could write to him, "Again many thanks to you for all the wonderfully happy times we had together—and even more for helping me to try to realize God and stimulating my desire to find a more spiritual way of life. That is always most precious."[28]

Teilhard always used to say mass for Lucile on the feast day of St. Lucia in December and for her birthday in May. On her last birthday before his death he wrote, "My mass of May 9 will be for you,—as every year;—for you and somewhat at the same time for me, so that we should at last! find 'each other' in the best and the highest possible way."[29] Here, as elsewhere, Teilhard's remarks convey calm and serenity, but several letters give the impression that nonetheless he remained emotionally troubled till the end, especially as he was suffering from a nervous condition. In his last letter, written shortly before his death, he expressed the hope that, emotionally speaking, things might gradually settle, but that they should perhaps not see each other more than two or three times during the winter. Lucile felt that she was partly the cause of his malaise. But she strongly affirmed that she had found inner peace and that, more than anything else, she was longing for "the real Peace of God's presence."[30] At her death in 1965, a prayer signed "PT" was found among her papers. It read: "Oh my God, since Thou art with me, and I must now, in obedience to Thy commands, apply my mind to these outward things, I beseech Thee to grant me the grace to continue in Thy presence; and to this end do Thou prosper me with Thy assistance, receive all my works, and possess all my affections."

One wonders how far her integration and peace may have been helped by her contact with Indian thought, to which she refers in some of her letters. During her extensive travels Lucile had visited India in 1949 and, on her return, she had joined Swami Nikhilananda's Vedanta group in New York. But there is already a passing reference to Indian thought in one of her earlier letters, in 1934. On January 13, 1952, Teilhard wrote to his friend, Père Leroy: "Lucile finds her peace in a group . . . directed by a Swami. . . . The spirituality there seems terribly vague to me. But is this not the only solution for so many men and women who are unable from the outside to pierce through the formidable, hardened envelope which theologians characterize by the name of orthodoxy?"[31]

In 1951, Lucile had sent Teilhard one of Swami Nikhilananda's essays for reading and comment. Teilhard said he read it carefully. While criticizing it on several important points, he nonetheless admitted that he might be prejudiced and wrong, in which case he was ready to apologize. Lucile considered his criticisms unfair and expressed the view that the Swami's beliefs were more like Teilhard's than anything she had come across before. Teilhard was probably unwilling to admit such affinity of thought and may even have resented it. Lucile stated clearly what she had learned from the Vedanta group and not found elsewhere: "And the closer we are to God, the better will be the results of our efforts. And they help to show you how to feel God and to be closer to Him. I mean in the way of meditation and reading and thinking and self-discipline—things that I have not found in Christian teaching. Or do you know any books that give one that kind of help? And as for LOVE! I wish I could understand what you mean by it. It seems to me that both Christian nations and individuals TAKE what they want and to hell with the other fellow."[32] The same letter also says that "the USUAL Christian God is NOT big enough. . . . We must find a greater face for HIM." This is not unlike a remark made years earlier when she wrote, "But Pierre, your God seems so cold, so far away. Am I all wrong in thinking that I could help you to feel Him more warmly by giving you a deep and constant human love?"[33]

Was the letter sent in April 1951 Lucile's strong reaction against Teilhard's attitude toward her? Is this the deep cry of a heart that felt rejected? Was Teilhard, after taking so much from her, not giving enough of himself? Lucile's emotions did break through again and again. She felt discouraged and depressed by this, but even if her emotions were misdirected at times, she felt that at least they were not dead. She learned from her mistakes and eventually gained serenity. If one remembers Teilhard's and Lucile's intimacy during their Peking years and his repeated assurances of love, friendship, and spiritual union, one feels that Lucile, in spite of her occasional emotional outbursts, showed a great deal of equanimity and selflessness in the American period of their lives. The letters confirm that Lucile shared closely in the production of essays that Teilhard wrote between 1932 and 1941 and that even later he kept her informed of his work. During that decade Teilhard wrote such well-known essays as "Christology and Evolution," "The Evolution of Chastity," "How I Believe," "A Personalistic Universe," "The Phenomenon of Spirituality," "Human Energy," and "The Mysticism of Science," to name only a few. Most important of all, he wrote his famous book *The Human Phenomenon* during that time. So far, Lucile has only been given credit for having translated "How I Believe," but it is evident from this correspondence that she translated several other essays, typed them (she learned to type in 1935) and helped to get them printed for private circulation. Teilhard shared his ideas and discussed all of his work with Lucile, who was a patient listener and a challenging critic. After she had translated his essays into English, they would go over the translation together in order to ensure that everything was expressed as he wanted it. When traveling on a boat between China and America, as she did several times, she always took some of Teilhard's papers with her. She found that the translation work gave a direction and meaning to her day.[34]

Readers familiar with Teilhard's thought will find illuminating passages about several essays in these letters, especially about "How I Believe" and "A Personalistic Universe." *The Human Phenomenon* is mentioned several times and Lucile wrote about it in her autobiography.[35]

Lucile questioned and challenged Teilhard. Although Teilhard still believed that the church was healthy at its root, he did have his moments of impatience. At such times he would respond by delving even more deeply into the wisdom and life of Christ.[36]

The letters of the American period repeatedly refer to Teilhard's difficulties in not getting his books published. He still shared some of his ideas with Lucile and sent her his spiritual autobiography, the essay "The Heart of Matter,"[37] which he described as "a sort of history of my spiritual adventure, 'the Quest of Spirit through Matter' . . . , these pages are an effort to express an internal evolution deeply impressed by you. . . . It is utterly impossible for me not to see (and to say) what I see. And I am so sure that God cannot be smaller than our biggest and wildest conceptions! Of course, I cannot print. But printing is not essential."[38]

"The Heart of Matter" had been written in his native Auvergne. Years earlier he had sent a letter from the same place to Lucile in which he had briefly sketched his inner development, which he was later so beautifully to describe in this essay. He wrote from his brother's country house: "Never before, perhaps, did I perceive so clearly the possible meaning of the deep evolution of my internal life: the dark purple of the universal Matter, first passing for me into the gold of Spirit, then into the white incandescence of Personality—then finally (and this is the present stage) into the immaterial (or rather super-material) ardour of Love—And never before, too, did I realize in such a tangible way how much people, around one, are starving for the same light, which perhaps I can transmit to them."[39]

Lucile was delighted with what Teilhard wrote to her about "The Heart of Matter." It reminded her of their earlier years of collaboration: "how proud and happy I was when you said how much I helped to clarify your ideas, to talk them over with me and so it was OUR work—and you say so kindly in this last letter, the internal evolution so deeply impressed by you. Perhaps it was something like this that you meant when you wrote over and over again 'what is born between us is for ever.'" In the same letter she also mentions his earlier *Milieu Divine,* which she had read once again: "Oh Pierre, . . . I understand why it has been loved by so many people, and it is of special delight to me because it somehow so vividly recalls to mind the YOU as you were when I first knew you, the eager searcher, the mystic who was so full of the love of the world and to whom God was so close, so much a part of you that everyone who came in contact with you was aware of His Presence. I like to hold to this picture for it broadens my own feeling and vision."[40]

Lucile must have known all Teilhard's essays most intimately. After his death, during the spring and summer of 1955, she collected notes in her "Blue Book," which include passages from Teilhard's essays written during World War I, especially an almost complete word-for-word translation of "Christ in Matter—Three Stories in the style of Benson" and later reflections on Christian love, on God and the world, on Christ Omega, and on death. The excerpts conclude with the following words: "Grace to finish well, in the most efficient manner for the prestige of the Christ Omega! The Grace of Graces. An existence dominated by the unique passion of promoting the synthesis of Christ and the Universe. Therefore love of the two (especially of the Christ church, supreme axis). Communion through death (the death-communion). That which arrives finally: the Adorable One. I go to meet Him who comes."[41] Were these words of prayer and praise the words Lucile lived and was sustained by during the last ten years of her life?

Immediately after Teilhard's death controversies broke out concerning several of his friendships. Jealousies were expressed, especially by some of the women friends he had known. Few of those who knew either Teilhard or Lucile are alive today, and with these letters coming to light, the time has come to reassess the significance of important friendships in Teilhard's life and thought. While most of his previously published letters are concerned with his ideas or travels, the correspondence between Teilhard and Lucile Swan reveals more than any other Teilhard's great capacity for love and intimate friendship as well as his own need for the intimacy and warmth of human love. Thus, these letters provide us with many insights not easily gained elsewhere. They throw light on the relationship between human love and the love of God. They raise questions about love as the greatest source of human energy, but also about the role of chastity and its relationship to spirituality, and about Teilhard's teaching that "union differentiates."

Yet there are many aspects of the relationship between Teilhard and Lucile one must criticize and question, especially from a woman's point of view. However unusual their friendship was, it somehow still seems to conform to a traditional male–female pattern. For Teilhard, his vision and work came above everything, so that in the end Lucile had to fit in with his interpretation of the world. He wanted her "womanliness," as he once said, but she from the depth of her heart wanted above all his presence, forever—to give him her love, more and more. Although she had her own creative work, her social life and her travels, all these appear subordinate to her experience of love and tenderness for Teilhard. She wanted all of him, and he wanted the world—the world for God.

Were Lucile's demands unreasonable, given that Teilhard had vowed his life to God? Her relentless questioning of his position must have been a great temptation, especially as he loved her so deeply. It was truly a trial by fire in which he remained faithful to the end. How much more might we learn and understand if we had access to Teilhard's diaries of the Peking years which seem to be lost. Thus it is difficult to gain further insight into their relationship apart from what we read in these letters themselves.

Lucile gave Teilhard light, energy, warmth, and love. She was his "star," his "sounding board," his "spark," a "tide of life" and "rejuvenation," the "very expression of his life." Did Teilhard not use Lucile for his own ends? She did so much for him—read and translated his essays; discussed them; got them typed, printed, and sent out to friends; walked and traveled with him; made him tea every afternoon and was available whenever he needed and wanted her. Is that not a traditional role which countless other women perform for their loved ones? To be fair, Teilhard was a helpful and welcome critic of her own work, constantly encouraging her to achieve the best. He gave her life direction and led her back to God. As he expressed in one of his early letters, while she enlightened his life, he wanted to give her a new energy for becoming more herself, but he did not want to be the center of her entire life. "To be an energy, and yet not a center. Is that mere utopia?" And yet his dream was to make her "gloriously happy."[42]

The letters also raise important questions about the nature of celibacy as distinct from marriage. Is it legitimate for a celibate priest to enter such a deep emotional bond and have a spiritual union deeper than many a marriage might ever attain? Although chastity was formally maintained, what is its value and meaning in a union otherwise so close and creative as if their work "were in a single and common activity?"[43]

Teilhard was fully aware of the unusualness of his position and the unusual nature of their relationship. Did he want to prove to himself and others the power of love transformed, of human and divine love combined in one single movement? He maintained that what paralyzes love is a lack of faith and audacity. Does not the attraction of his own life consist above all in having combined faith with adventure, an exploration of frontiers with utter faithfulness to his roots and religious commitment? In many ways he broke through the barriers of a traditional celibate life, but one can still ask, did he really free himself? Is there not also a sense of repression, a tension that remains unresolved to the end, when not only the strength of his love but also the transitoriness of emotions can be felt? Or was it simply his complete unworldliness, his living on a higher plane and the transparent purity of his mind and soul that made him behave as he did? As he considered it one of his tasks to work for "the birth of a new consciousness in the world,"[44] do our questions perhaps remain too constrained by an old way of thinking?

Toward the end of his life Teilhard related to Lucile perhaps more as counselor, guide, and teacher than as the intimate companion he had been in earlier years. But she loved and esteemed him until the end. She knew of the utter loneliness of his last few years, the disappointment about his main works remaining unpublished, the lack of understanding and recognition. Toward the end of her life she recalled his lack of self-pity and his continuous dedication to his next work even if it had to be written secretly and in private. In 1954 Teilhard was still writing about his profound attachment to Christ while declaring how clearly and strongly he also saw His identity as a "Super-Christ."[45]

In her personal reflections she stressed above all Teilhard's spiritual qualities, his radiant love, the strength of his vision and its importance for the world, and the help Teilhard had given to so many people, including herself: "How many who would not have approached an ordinary man of the Church, went to him for help and always found it, for he talked to them in language that they understood and could act upon. . . . How often have I heard someone say, 'I could not have gone on without his spiritual help and strength'? He believed so definitely in Man and in his ability to evolve and love."[46]

Is this fire of spiritual love, fueled by the joy of creation and adoration, not the highest love humans can attain to, capable of transforming the world and transcending death? What a great and precious gift for Teilhard and Lucile to have known and lived such a love.[47]

# 5

# Teilhard in the Ecological Age

## THOMAS BERRY

This is a complex and turbulent century, with amazing scientific discoveries, technological inventions, industrial and commercial expansion, population increase, social transformations, new systems of transportation and communication, vast educational and research establishments, ventures into space: a brilliant century no doubt, the human achievement of which radiates over the past making it among the most exalted periods in human history.

But there is another aspect of this century, its destructive aspect: mountains are ripped apart for the underlying coal and ore deposits; rivers are polluted with human and industrial waste; the air is saturated with toxic substances; the rain is turned to acid; the soil is sterile with chemicals; the higher forms of life are endangered; the great sea mammals have been killed off almost to the point of extinction; the tropical forests are being ruined; and many coral reefs are damaged beyond repair.

The structure of the planet and its living forms have been altered on a geological and a biological scale. Change on such an order of magnitude makes of this century something more than another historical period or another cultural change. This is destruction, beyond recovery, of forms that took hundreds of millions, even billions of years to bring about. The entire structure of the biosphere is affected; some hundreds of thousands of present living species could be extinguished by the very near future. There will likely be a third more carbon dioxide in the atmosphere than in the preindustrial period. Here in the United States we are losing perhaps four billion tons of topsoil every year.

The glory of the human has become the desolation of the Earth. This I would consider an appropriate way to summarize the twentieth century. A further statement that might be made is that the desolation of the Earth is becoming the destiny of the human. Indeed the total fabric of living beings is so closely woven that none of its components can be damaged without harming the others.

An even further statement might suggest that one way of evaluating persons, programs, professions, institutions, and activities would be the extent to which

First published in *Teilhard Studies* no. 7 (fall 1982).

they foster or obstruct the creative functioning of the Earth community, the community of all the living and nonliving components of the Earth.

This subject of human–Earth relations is not a new subject of discussion. One of the oldest questions ever dealt with in the long course of human reflection, this discussion has been a prominent issue in the various cultures of the world and in differing historical periods. But at no time in the prior history of the Earth was there such urgency in developing a human role that would be beneficent in its effects; for never before have humans had such power over the air, the soil, and the seas. Indeed the human species that was formerly controlled mainly by the Earth process is now for the first time extensively in control of the Earth process.

It seems appropriate then to discuss Teilhard in this context, to inquire concerning his way of dealing with the issues that caused the glory of the human to become the desolation of the Earth, to inquire also concerning the assistance he offers for healing the Earth and fostering an integral and creative communion of all the living and nonliving components of the Earth.

Teilhard was profoundly aware of the glory of the human achieved in this remarkable century of human development. Finally, he thought, human culture has broken loose from the neolithic constraints into a truly worthy mode of existence, an accomplishment that originated in the Western world but that henceforth must be accepted as establishing the new norms for the human quality and conduct of life throughout the human community. This glory was manifest especially in the increasing human controls over the natural world, designated as "progress."

Teilhard was absolutely dedicated to the idea of progress, the governing idea of Western society since the seventeenth century, the idea that originated in the work of René Descartes and Francis Bacon but was first clearly stated in the writings of Bernard Fontenelle (1657-1757). From that time until the present a sense of progress has dominated first Western society, and now the greater part of the human community. While norms of judgment concerning progress have differed extensively, the general acceptance of the progressive unfolding of reality has become pervasive.

To Teilhard, progress was evident throughout the cosmic historical process. In this human order progress could be observed in expanded modes of consciousness, in the convergence of human societies, in the profound unification beyond all political or institutional divisions, and in an upward spiritual transformation that found its fulfillment in the human–divine presence to each other. All of this was, to his mind, identified with and supported by the emergent evolutionary process. This process, which originated some billions of years ago, was only now reaching its fullest expressions.

Even while such progress was taking place, social discontent was leading to skepticism, to a conscious rejection of this entire cosmic Earth–human venture. Having observed the beginnings of existentialist *Angst* in the decade of the 1930s and its full expression in the late 1940s, Teilhard dedicated himself to reassuring the human community of its basic values and of the need to push on even more urgently in the scientific and social tasks that devolved upon this generation. It all had profoundly religious and mystical as well as cosmological significance.

Indeed his teaching concerned the ultimate identity of these different aspects of the total Earth process.

So entranced with the glory of the human, Teilhard, however, had no awareness of the increasing desolation of the Earth. His few references to the limitation of physical resources are given only in passing and with reassuring phrases that human genius will discover ways to supply any deficiencies. Fewer still are references to the damage being done to the natural world. This was outside his concern. He took no notice of the conservation movements that had already begun in his time. Nor did Teilhard perceive that the pressures he invoked to achieve the ultrahuman were themselves supporting a general economic and social development leading to ecological disaster and to a diminishment of the human quality of life.

From the letters of Teilhard we can see that he had an exceptional aesthetic-emotional response to the natural world as well as a scientific and mystical sense of Earth's grandeur. What was missing was the feeling for an interdependent biological community of the human with the natural world as the functional context for earthly existence. That the bioregions of Earth were ultimately fragile did not impress Teilhard. Possibly this was due to the resilient ecosystem of the European region that constituted the environment of his early life experience. There an abiding balance seemed to be struck between the natural world and an urban-industrial world that as yet did not impinge too heavily on the natural biotic communities, although over the centuries the rich variety of natural life systems was considerably impoverished throughout Europe.

Yet since Teilhard traveled widely and was so deeply concerned with the larger questions of the Earth–human process, we might have expected a certain feeling of concern for a planet that was obviously being damaged by the industrial process.

Here we might step back a little to look at the work of Teilhard in some of its main concerns to understand more fully just where he fits into the history of this century. Indeed he is the first person to outline, in some full detail and with some meaningful insight, the four phases of the evolutionary process: galactic evolution, Earth evolution, life evolution, human evolution. He sees all this in its encompassing unity, and with such descriptive detail of the outer process and the inner forces that sustained the unfolding sequence. Probably no one at the humanistic, spiritual, or moral level ever attended so powerfully to this evolutionary process as did Teilhard. Completely fascinated with this transformation sequence, he was absorbed into his vision as much as Isaiah was caught up in his vision of the historical process or as John in his apocalyptic vision or as Dante in the vision of the *Commedia*. It was an entrancement that inspired research, imagination, teaching, lyrical writing, and philosophical and religious essays.

*The first concern of Teilhard* is the evolutionary origin and development. "Is evolution a theory, a system or a hypothesis? It is much more; it is a general condition to which all theories, all hypotheses, all systems must bow and which they must satisfy henceforth if they are to be thinkable and true. Evolution is a lamp illuminating all facts, a curve that all lines must follow."[1]

The major work in which he expressed this vision, *The Phenomenon of Man*, is a unique synthesis of the vast intellectual, social, and spiritual attainments of the twentieth century. If there is or can be a comprehensive *Summa* of the modern mode of consciousness that reaches from the particular details of the various sciences to the mystical modes of insight available to us, then this work of Teilhard can be seen as the nearest approximation that we have. Here Teilhard has suggested a possible governing myth of the future.

*The second concern of Teilhard* was with the human as the consciousness mode of the universe and as fulfillment of the evolutionary process. The human is neither an intrusion or an addendum to the universe but the central reality of the universe. In his view the full dynamism of the evolutionary process is now contained within the human. The dominant transition now is a convergence of the differing human groups. The ultrahuman is being activated through this convergence. Because of this special role, the human is necessarily the key to understanding the entire evolutionary process. The human must be considered in every science and in every explanation of the various parts of the universe.

By identifying the psychic, consciousness aspect of the evolutionary process from the beginning Teilhard overcomes the materialist view of the universe as this was associated with the Newtonian tradition. In a special manner Teilhard insisted on the human aspect of cosmology. A place for the human must be found in the physics of the universe and in the science of the Earth. Alienation of the human by the scientist is unacceptable. The human mind and its thinking are as much Earth as are the rocks and the rivers and the other living beings who belong to the Earth.

*The third concern of Teilhard* is with the sacred dimension of the universe. He shifted the central focus of Western religious tradition from redemption to creation. This new orientation might be considered the single most powerful aspect of Teilhard's theological thinking. Possibly it can be considered among the most significant theological changes since the sixteenth century. By placing the Christian-religious issue within the context of an emergent creation process Teilhard was asserting a position that had not been asserted before with such convincing evidence. The cosmic Christ of St. John, St. Paul, and the Orthodox churches of the East becomes identified in Teilhard's view with an emergent universe and can be referred to as Christ the Evolver. While this emphasis on an evolving Christ in the modern evolutionary context has not been extensively taken up by Christian theologians, it remains the statement of a powerful Christian position; it enables Christians to relate their faith experience with the contemporary sense of the real in a significant way. The Christian story identifies with the cosmic story told by modern science, although it sees in this story a sacred significance far beyond what is seen by the secular scientist. This can be the beginning of a new era in both the religious and the secular history of our times.

*A fourth concern of Teilhard* is with the activation of energy. The energy issue as he saw it was of utmost concern. For there has been a tendency throughout this century to avoid the effort needed to sustain the evolutionary process. a most critical issue in the existentialist period. While the writings of Jean-Paul Sartre and Albert Camus were extensively known by Teilhard only on his return from Peking in 1946, after the war, his concern for the interior dynamism of the human is expressed earlier. As the movement of human affairs enters the supreme transformation experience toward its final convergence a new intensity of psychic effort is required.

There is need especially to overcome the sense of an absurd universe, of interhuman violence, the absence of affection, and especially the lack of some worthy objective to justify the endurance of so much pain and to evoke the sustained effort needed to resolve the enduring social and cultural tensions. Beyond all these a sense of boredom is afflicting an age feeling that the entire range of human affairs had been dealt with, that there is no longer any vast creative venture to be undertaken. That the evolutionary process is presently in the midst of one of its most significant transitions seemed to Teilhard the only valid way to interpret the present and to evoke the energies needed for the transition.

> Mark my word: though man stands on great stacks of wheat, on mountains of uranium and coal, on oceans of oil, he will cease to develop his unity, and he will perish, if he does not watch over and foster in the first place the source of psychic energy which maintains in him the passion for action and knowledge—which means for growing greater and evolving—from which comes unity of mind.[2]

*A fifth concern of Teilhard* is with the role of science. Advance in knowledge is absolutely essential to the total Earth process. This process Teilhard saw as a vast psychic enterprise into which the human entered by research, thought, and reflection. Thus the fundamental nobility of the scientific endeavor.

His great contribution to the scientific endeavor was to lead the scientific profession into the macrophase of its concerns. This is presently the greatest need of all the sciences, of all branches of knowledge, as well as all phases of human endeavor. For this aspect of his work he remains unforgiven in scientific as well as in religious circles, although it is precisely this largeness of horizon that makes his work so attractive to New Age people—that is, to those who perceive the present impasse created by trying to solve macrophase issues in a microphase perspective. That the various sciences are becoming less rigid in this regard can be seen in the wide acceptance of the biological writings of Lewis Thomas and also in the physics of persons such as David Bohm. In discussions of evolution the most serious difficulty is still the attempt by the biologists to deal with macrophase evolution in terms of microphase processes.

In asserting the role of science as a basic mystical discipline of the West, Teilhard revealed the true dignity of research and intellectual inquiry. This much-needed discipline could again be established on a profoundly religious basis for the first time since the Newtonian period. Some of the greatest passages ever written concerning science are contained in his essays. Taken as a whole, these passages constitute a unique appreciation of the inner nature of the scientific endeavor, its ultimate mystical qualities, its revelatory aspect, and its central role in the planetary process.

In all five of these issues Teilhard's dominant concern is to evoke the mystique needed to fulfill the destinies of the universe, the destinies that had been prepared over some billions of years in the galactic systems, had advanced through the geological and biological formations of Earth, and now were being activated in their highest expression in human consciousness.

For any one of these five achievements Teilhard might well be remembered among the significant thinkers of this century. But to have carried through the entire series of correctives in the thought life of the twentieth century is an accomplishment of admirable dimensions.

[*Editor's Note: At this point in the original publication, Thomas Berry surveys Western philosophical and cultural traditions in their mechanistic, natural history, mystical and arcadian phases to serve as background for understanding Teilhard's position. The present article resumes with the material that followed this background discussion.*]

## TEILHARD AND THE NEW ECOLOGY

The problem that we now face is how the basic achievements that Teilhard turned toward the imperialist attitude to nature can be turned toward sustaining an integral Earth community in which the human becomes a functional component and not an oppressive destroyer. This is needed, since, as we have suggested in the beginning of this paper, any person, program, profession, institution, or activity can at this time be judged by the extent to which the person, program, profession, institution, or activity fosters or obstructs the integral functioning of the Earth community.

The future of Teilhard's thought will progressively depend on this issue, since this is the most urgent of all issues confronting the human community: the quality of human life on a depleted planet, or even survival at an acceptable level of human satisfaction. It is to be expected that a work of the magnitude of Teilhard's should be confronted with the need for readjustment on an equivalent order of magnitude. Probably the adjustment of thinkers from a preevolutionary context to an evolutionary context of interpretation is the best parallel, in the order of magnitude of its adjustment, to the adjustment from an anthropocentric to a biocentric orientation of consciousness. This latter is the adjustment that we are suggesting for the vision of Teilhard.

My own suggestion is that we take the major themes of Teilhard as outlined in the earlier sections of this paper and press them further than Teilhard pressed them. In this manner we can move forward within his overall perspectives and possibly bring his vision to more comprehensive conclusions than those he himself proposed. What must be observed, however, is that the mode of consciousness that is needed in the emerging ecological age is something that has never before existed. There have been over the centuries different approaches to an understanding of the relationship of the human with the natural world. Yet because this relationship is constantly changing no abiding ideal can be invoked. A functioning relationship is needed. This has in the past been supplied by the great religions of the world. But now something new must appear since the religions of the past functioned in a cyclical cosmological context quite different from the emergent evolutionary context of our times. This remains a primary issue of the human itself, the manner in which the human functions in relation to the larger planetary process.

At present the human is struggling with its self-identity more than ever, even with the experience of so many centuries and the experience of so many cultures of the world. From none of these historical ages nor from these cultural formations do we find the model that we need. The Inca, in pre-Columbian America, accomplished much in their dealings with the land. In China the Confucians had a great cosmological insight. The Taoists had a unique naturalist tradition that advocated living lightly upon the Earth. Although the Chinese were never able to function in any completely satisfactory relationship with the land, they did succeed to an admirable degree in sustaining the fertility of their soil over these many centuries.

In the modern Western world the strange thing is the relative silence of Christian traditions in dealing with this basic issue of human relationships with the Earth, a situation that is undoubtedly due to the strong emphasis on the redemption experience with relatively little concern for the functional processes of the created world. Although this is essentially a religious, a spiritual, and an ethical issue, our religious traditions, our spiritualities, and our moral codes do not generally function in this order of magnitude. We can identify the moral evil of suicide, homicide and genocide, yet we have so far elucidated no sufficient principles on which to deal with biocide and geocide, evils that are infinitely greater in their consequences and in their absolute range as moral acts. It is clear that neither the spiritual nor the humanist traditions of the Western world can deal adequately with these issues out of their own resources.

Nor can any of the professions as they presently exist—whether the legal profession, the medical profession, the business profession, or the banking profession. None of these begin to envisage the changes that are needed. Nor can education yet shape a program adequate to the needs of this planetary situation. We are then functionally caught up in a context that is resulting in devastating consequences, and we have no adequate language, religion, professions, models, or conceptual context in which to reflect on the situation.

What we do have is a complex of traditions that must all be turned toward a creative interaction with the functioning of the Earth. The one thing necessary is to appreciate that the Earth itself and all its living and nonliving components is a community, that the human is a member of this integral community and finds its proper role in advancing the well-being of this community. There can be no sustained well-being of any part of the community that does not relate effectively to the well-being of the total community. We might note particularly that we cannot have a healthy human community on a sickened, disintegrated, toxic planet. This is the norm enunciated earlier in this paper, where we noted that one way of evaluating persons, programs, professions, institutions, and activities is the extent to which they foster or obstruct the creative functioning of the larger Earth community, the community of all those components that constitute the planet.

This principle of a total Earth community, along with the imaginative and emotional qualities associated with the functioning of this principle, can be dimly perceived, perhaps, as a suppressed aspect of Western cultural traditions, possibly a carryover of pagan attitudes that were never assimilated into the tradition but were kept in the realm of the unconscious and permitted only vague and inadequate expression. A certain fear of these natural forces seems to exist in both religious and humanist traditions, fear lest established beliefs be weakened or some dark power from a realm of evil pervade the human order. Those most sensitive to this larger Earth community feel a certain alienation from the biblical traditions; persons such as Henry Thoreau and John Muir. Others too in the romantic Western tradition associated these attitudes with a kind of pagan exuberance in this communion with the Earth.

We have then as resources the depth of unconscious feeling for the Earth and the enunciation of this experience in the unassimilated aspects of paganism, especially as these come to us through the natural history essayists and nature-oriented scholars of the nineteenth and early twentieth centuries. This was given further expression in the conservation movements of this same period, until they became associated with what might presently be considered the more mystical-emotional elements of the ecological movement. This attitude presently exists in a rising tension and conflict with the exploitive and destructive industrial, commercial, and military establishments.

While national governments have progressively been forced to consider ecological issues by the volume of toxic poisoning of the air, water, and soil, only inadequate measures have so far been taken to establish truly functional relationships with the various regions of the Earth. This is now an imperative throughout the planet. The outstanding achievement in the political order is the *World Charter for Nature,* adopted by the United Nations General Assembly in 1982. This charter can be considered the most significant public document of the twentieth century in articulating the context for the integral survival of planet Earth. That this document should emerge in a political rather than a religious context is perhaps best understood when we consider the widespread suspicion of religion that exists in these times, yet it is another indication of the inadequacies of traditional religions as they presently exist that none of these could make a statement of any comparable order of significance.

That the most advanced Christian thinker of the century with a scientific background could not himself perceive what was happening in human–Earth relations is a further indication of the inadequacies of the spiritual traditions of the Western world. Yet the context that Teilhard provides is so comprehensive in its overarching perspectives and such an improvement over prior expressions of a Christian vision that we must press on in the basic context of his thought even while adapting his vision to a planetary crisis that he did not anticipate.

This adaptation of Teilhard is a critical necessity also because of the danger lest the power of Teilhard's thought be turned toward further aggravation of human–Earth relations. For although Teilhard had no adequate concern for the biological well-being of the planet, he does provide a way of interpreting our present situation that is of utmost importance. The context provided by Teilhard is urgently needed to save the ecological movement from trivialization, while the ecological orientation is needed to save Teilhard from irrelevance in relation to the biological future of the Earth community. To achieve these mutually beneficial results we must simply extend the principal concerns of Teilhard further than he himself extended them.

*The first concern of Teilhard* that needs extension is his interpretation of the evolutionary process. On his own principles of totality we might say that the evolutionary process finds its highest expression in the Earth community seen in its comprehensive dimensions not simply in a human community reigning in triumphal dominion over the other components of the Earth community. The same evolutionary process has produced all the living and nonliving components of the planet. The human is not intelligible except in this larger community context. Thus Teilhard's principle of convergent evolution should include not only the human community but also the functional convergence of all the planetary components. The great variety of components that constitute the Earth is precisely what enables the planet to function as "a single cell." That there are distinctive aspects of the human convergence can be easily understood; but there is also a bond of convergence that is strengthened throughout the world of the living and indeed throughout the entire realm of all those articulated modes of being out of which the living world itself emerges into existence. Convergence is not simply a human process. Human convergence at the expense of planetary convergence is inherently destructive for both the human community and the planetary community. There can be only one final destiny for the entire community.

In the variety of intimate relations within this convergent community the ancient principle of "plenitude" finds its fulfillment. This principle, in its classical and medieval expression, states that diversity in the creative process takes place because the divine reality wishes to express itself and to communicate its being and its joy in the fullest manner possible. Since this expression of itself could not be realized in any single being or species of being, a great variety of beings was brought into existence with such intimate presence to each other that in this vast unity of different beings the divine image would be realized most perfectly and the joy of creatures would be most complete.

While analytical scientists have little patience with such modes of thinking about the universe, most comprehensive scientists begin to perceive, from the data available to them, that the galaxies, the solar system, and planet Earth all function in a complex of relationships that enables the whole to be seen as a single process, a universe. In a corresponding manner the Earth can be seen as an ecosystem that has been in the making since the universe first came into being, an ecosystem that provides in its ever-increasing variety and unity a sense of the direction of its development throughout this long period of evolutionary time. Although he was not primarily concerned with the evolutionary process, Alfred North Whitehead has presented the functional unity of the universe in his doctrine of Organicism. The unity of the evolutionary process is seen quite clearly by Erich Jantsch in his exposition of *The Self-Organizing Universe.*[3]

In its modern orientations the human mind seems to be caught between a downward reductionism of the mechanists and the upward reductionism of the spiritualists. Matter and spirit are abundantly served, while the living community is devastated by industrial-technological exploitation and withered by spiritual neglect. The difficulty with all these, as with Teilhard, is inadequate attention to the integral functioning of the natural world in the encompassing variety of its manifold activities. This neglect of the living world can be seen also in recent preoccupations with the dual aspects of the brain. One side of the brain seems to control the rational and the analytical, while the other side of the brain seems to function in the intuitive, mystical order. The living world of nature does not appear as a primary concern with either of these functions of the brain.

There are sufficient references in Teilhard to the "living Earth" to justify a shift in emphasis toward the more inclusive evolutionary process that we are indicating. In doing this we can preserve the unique aspects of the human with which Teilhard was so vitally concerned. That he could not himself take this further step is apparently due to his preoccupation with articulating the unique qualities of the human as this was demanded by the religious commitments of his times.

*The second concern of Teilhard* that needs to be extended is his concern for the consciousness dimension of the universe from the beginning. This interiority finds expression especially in its Earth manifestations. We are born out of this larger community context; we live totally within this context and find our fulfillment in union with this context. As the emergence of life revealed the latent powers of the planet, so the emergence of human consciousness revealed an even deeper and more extensive power of the planet, its power of reflecting on itself and even of controlling itself extensively in and through human intelligence. Indeed the human might better think of itself as a mode of being of the Earth rather than simply as a separate being on the Earth.

Because the universe is integral with itself, any point in the universe or any moment in the emergent process is integral with the total universe in its spatial extension and in its sequential manifestation. The whole and the part are dimensions of each other both spatially and temporally. So the human moment, the human mode of consciousness, expresses a quality that belongs to the universe as such and especially to planet Earth; otherwise the human would be an addendum or an intrusion. It would not properly belong to the universe or to the Earth as these are known to us.

Seen in this way we can consider that the human and its activities, its thought, emotion, and imagination, are as much Earth as are water and rocks and trees and birds and their activities. Just as we cannot understand the elements of nitrogen, carbon, and oxygen until we observe how these elements express themselves in cellular life, so we cannot understand these elements until we observe their function in producing thought, emotion, and imagination at the human level. Thus the integral functioning of the human coincides with the integral functioning of the various elements and the integral functioning of the planet.

While the vision of Teilhard indicates a clear awareness of this Earth quality of the human and this human quality of the Earth, this integral vision is not carried out in its implications in his work. Teilhard establishes the human as his exclusive norm of values, a norm that requires the human to invade and to control rationally the spontaneities of nature out of which the human emerged and by which the human is sustained in all its activities. Thus an extension is required in Teilhard's work, an extension that would clearly articulate the comprehensive context of the Earth community. Within this larger context the limitations of human artifice in relation to the spontaneities of nature would be better appreciated. We must question the reductionist statement that in a deeper understanding "there ceases to be any distinction between the artificial and the natural, between technology and life, since all organisms are the result of invention; if there is any difference, the advantage is on the side of the artificial."[4] That human intelligence should establish an intimate relation with the natural world and with many of its most vital functions can be accepted so long as the deep mysteries of nature are respected. The evidence at present is that human cunning has far overreached itself in substituting human artifice for natural functioning. Already we are in a catastrophic situation in establishing a technosphere with deadly consequences on the integral functioning of the biosphere. The brilliance of our scientists and the grand managerial skills of our technocrats are producing a historical period that seems to justify the proposed designation of the next decades as the coming "Age of Slaughter." Perhaps it would be beneficial for everyone to reflect on the statement of biologist Lewis Thomas that "[t]he greatest single achievement of science in this most scientifically productive of centuries is the discovery that we are profoundly ignorant; we know very little about nature and we understand even less."[5] If we consider another statement in the same article—"There is no limit to the ingenuity of nature of this planet"—then we might hesitate and think profoundly before we impose human artifice as improvement upon the basic functioning of the natural world. Above all we might appreciate the necessity of integrating human technologies with the technologies of the natural world.

The proper role of human intelligence would be not to exploit but to enhance the natural world and its functioning. The basic norm would be not the human but the well-being and integral functioning of the Earth community. The anti-natural aspects of Western thought seem to have lingered even in the mind of Teilhard and to have inspired in him a sense of conquering and controlling the natural world rather than a sense of intimacy with living beings as component members of the single community of the living. While he has supplanted the rationalism of the French Enlightenment with a vital mysticism, he still retains an overwhelming need to supplant the spontaneities of nature with the controls of human intelligence.

By removing this aggressiveness from Teilhard's approach we can move toward activating, through human thought, emotion, and imagination, a further diversity and expansion of living species rather than extinguishing species by exploiting the planet for human advantage. In this manner Teilhard's own principles of human solidarity with the Earth would be fulfilled and a limitation in his thought would be removed. His powerful vision of the entire evolutionary process and its higher meaning would provide a context for the ecological movement. This could assist in saving the ecological movement from becoming merely a branch of thermodynamics. The ecological movement in turn could save Teilhard from fostering further disruption of human–Earth relations.

*The third concern of Teilhard* that needs extension is his concern that Western religious thought turn from its dominant redemption orientation to a dominant creation orientation. Teilhard saw quite early in his life that Western religious thought was increasingly alienated from the modern commitment to human values and to the role of human intelligence. This critique he expressed with rare incisiveness in his essay written in 1929 entitled "The Sense of Man."

> Fundamentally, the Church has never understood, as we understand it, the fine pride of man, nor the sacred passion for enquiry, which are the two basic elements of modern thought. However specious the explanations that may be appended to it, Pius IX's Syllabus was an attempt to condemn all that is most solid in our present hopes. . . . What must mark the Christian in the future is *an unparalleled zeal for creation.*[6]

Teilhard saw that a remarkable opportunity existed for extending the Christian vision of the universe and for reinterpreting Christian thought within this context. Yet while he carried out this task with unique efficacy he never succeeded in working out a proper functional relationship between the human community and the natural world. By turning the attention of Christians to the created world, Teilhard was in reality turning their attention to the human sciences and to the technological controls over the natural world. He was not really turning Christian thought to the created world in its full natural splendor. The human and religious mission to nurture the biosphere was lost in this excessive drive toward higher states of scientific and spiritual consciousness.

Although present to some extent from its very origins, the dedication of Western religious thought to redemption processes was fostered by a certain fear of the Earth and its seductive aspects, which seems to have developed in the fourteenth century after the traumatic experience of the Black Death. This alienation was further strengthened by the perfect integration achieved in the medieval period of Christian belief with Aristotelian cosmology. An additional cause for the emphasis on salvation processes to the neglect of creation processes was in the mechanistic mode of scientific thought about the universe that obtained after the period of Descartes and Galileo and Newton. A final cause for the difficulty can be found in the utilitarian values of science and technology that were fostered by Francis Bacon and his followers in England and France.

While these alienating influences posed serious problems for religious thought, there did exist throughout this period from Descartes to the present a remarkable expansion in human understanding of the physical and biological worlds, an expansion that reached climactic heights in the work of Darwin, Einstein, and in the later twentieth-century physicists, astronomers, and biologists.

The need now is to reaffirm within Teilhard's own principles the values of the vast complex of interacting life systems that constitutes the biosphere. To assert these values in themselves is now an imperative lest all that Teilhard derived from the natural world be swept away forever in the rising tide of human aggression against the living world about us. The human mission to nurture the biosphere tends to be lost in an excessive drive toward higher states of scientific or religious consciousness. When these modes of consciousness, instead of reacting creatively with the biosphere, abandon the living world to technologies that destroy the experience out of which religions, poetry, science, and technology themselves emerge and by which they are nourished, then the human subject itself is victimized; it is setting afire the context in which it lives and thinks and acts.

The absence in Teilhard of any reconciliation between his general affirmations of the sublimity of the natural world and his support for activities destructive of the natural world can be remedied by developing within the context of his thought a religious concern for the natural world. Without such concern the religious experience itself becomes impoverished. If possibly a million living species are lost by the end of this century we will have lost some of our most splendid modes of divine presence. We will have lost many of the finest resources of our emotional sensitivity and our imaginative powers. Our thinking powers, too, would be diminished until our inner world would reflect a deteriorated rather than a flourishing planet.

*The fourth concern of Teilhard* that needs extension is his concern for the activation of human energies at a new level of intensity. In this concern Teilhard has shown extraordinary sensitivity to one of the basic needs of these times. The decline of psychic energy that can be observed in this century, especially in the existentialist period of the middle decades, has been extreme. This enervation, which has continued on into the later decades of the century, originates in the attitude that the universe is fundamentally absurd, that acceptance of this fact and adjustment to its consequences are the only realistic attitude to adopt toward life.

Teilhard, recognizing the critical nature of this attitude, wrote almost unceasingly of this subject during the last ten years of his life. His proposal was that a change of a unique order of magnitude was taking place, not simply in human affairs, but in a larger unfolding of the emergent evolutionary process itself, a change comparable only with the great transitions from nonlife to life, from life to consciousness. He also compared the present with the rise of the neolithic stage of human development. Naturally a transformation of such magnitude required the dissolution of a prior life form with all the inherent agonies associated with such a death–rebirth experience. That such disorganization, such alienation, such a loss of direction should become manifest was only to be expected. Anything less would not be proportionate to the process taking place. He dealt with this subject in a short essay written in 1949, "The Phenomenon of Counter-Evolution in Human Biology: Or the Existential Fear." Here the darkness of the existentialist life vision is dealt with in its ultimate significance as a counterevolutionary process. He describes existentialist fear as rising to a certain paroxysm when confronted with the immensity of the universe, its opacity, and its apparent impersonality. In reality we should experience the universe as a vast supportive process with the basic lines of its evolutionary process evident to the simplest effort at reflection. The universe can be seen as converging to an ultimate intimacy in mutual indwelling of personalities in the supreme personal destiny that awaits us. Because of this convergence toward unity, "The universe was dark, icy and blind; now it lights up, becomes warm, and is animated. . . . We have escaped from our agony. We are made free. And all this because the world has a heart."[7]

Once this brightness of the new vision breaks in upon the modern world, then the necessary energies will emerge as in flood tide. But here, too, we find that Teilhard does not find the solace and inspiration that are available in the natural world, in the marvelous manifestations of life that surround us, in the remarkable intercommunion of life energies that is taking place throughout the planet. These manifestations of the natural world that have over the ages awakened in the human soul an awareness of divine presence and its unlimited powers—these need to be brought into the picture. The reading public addressed by Teilhard could not, of course, enter into such expressions of nature romanticism or such religious lyricism, yet the entire corpus of Teilhard's essays reveals that he had little sense of the importance of living forms in the development of the human qualities of life. His excitement for life was in a conquest over these natural forms rather than for deepened intimacy with them. He had none of the concerns of Alexander von Humboldt, or Henry Thoreau, John Muir, Aldo Leopold, Rachel Carson, or Wendell Berry. Indeed, within Teilhard's perspective these would all belong to the retarding forces in the evolutionary process.

It did not occur to Teilhard that the desolation of these times, the paralysis manifested, might be a consequence of the profound disengagement of industrial-technological society from the natural world. Within the context of modern industrial society the loss of spiritual sense might be beyond effective remedy. Enclosing the human within a world of manipulative technologies might be depriving the human emotions and the human soul of experiences that are integral to any desirable form of human development. To insist that the mechanization of life, the exploitation of the natural world, the rise of massive bureaucracies are all part of a sublime evolutionary process might not be fully adequate to the situation.

Thus the proposal here that Teilhard's thought concerning the activation of energy be extended into a greater appreciation of the dynamism that flows into the human soul in and through contact with the spontaneities of the natural world. It might also help considerably to feel that the natural world that brought the human into being is also the continuing source of support for the human not only in its physical needs but also in its psychic structure, its emotional sensitivities, its intellectual comprehension, its social relations, and finally in its communion with those numinous mysteries manifested throughout the entire universe, but especially in the living phenomena of the Earth.

*A fifth concern of Teilhard* that needs extension is his concern for the scientific endeavor. His appreciation for the mystical quality of the scientific endeavor is entirely valid. Yet he understood the scientific endeavor not only as mystical communion with the deep mysteries of the universe but also as conquest and domination over the spontaneities of the natural world. The metaphors of conflict, confrontation, attack and conquest appear much too often in Teilhard's understanding of science and technology in relation to the natural world. He is too ready to accept exploitive technologies as manifestations of high spiritual powers.

The true mystique of science is not simply in the advance of human intelligence into the mysterious functioning of the universe by analytical inquiry; science also has a nurturing role to fulfill in the world of life, a role that it has hardly begun to play at the present time. Only when science and its associated technologies take on this activating role in following and fostering the spontaneities of nature will science have discovered its true identity.

The nurturing role of science in the biosphere has become a critical issue with recent discoveries in the realm of genetics and the development of manipulative processes known as genetic engineering. Such a mechanistic metaphor becomes frightening when we observe what the engineering profession has done to the North American continent. Yet genetic engineering is presently about to follow in the sequence from construction engineering, to electrical engineering, to chemical engineering. Whatever the benefits from these earlier engineering projects, they have led to a planetary devastation beyond measuring. If greater wisdom is not used in the realm of biological engineering, the possible consequences may be even greater than the devastation experienced on the North American continent through these earlier forms of engineering. Such knowledge, power, and technological skill have given to Western society a cunning whereby the integral functioning of the natural world has been subverted for human advantage. The consequence has been to lay waste large areas of the planet and to make toxic the soil, air, and water.

A true extension of Teilhard's view of science and its associated technologies would lead us to create a healing context for the living world. The norm of judgment would be the well-being of the Earth community in the full extent and variety of its manifestations. To understand this and to modify our industrial engineering in all its phases in accord with this norm would be the fulfillment of an undeveloped aspect of Teilhard's vision. Once this positive role of enhancing our understanding and participation in the spontaneities of the natural world becomes a dominant aspect of the scientific endeavor, then the attractiveness of science itself will be increased. New areas of achievement could be expected. Activities such as those already begun in saving species, purifying the environment, increasing our mental, emotional, and imaginative communion with the larger realms of life would be carried out more fully. The human quality of life, which has been shriveled by exclusive concern for the mechanistic on the one hand and the spiritual on the other would be renewed by intimacy with the brilliance and variety of natural forms and activities. This can all be done in the context of Teilhard's sense of the scientific endeavor.

In conclusion: Teilhard is carrying out a unique role in guiding human affairs to their fulfillment in the twentieth century. He provides a comprehensive vision of the universe in its evolutionary sequence with a powerful sense of the emergent consciousness manifested by this sequence. His overview of the way into the future is strengthened by the scientific research on which he bases his thought and by the entire religious and humanistic heritage of Western tradition which is present throughout his work. These scientific, humanistic, and religious influences find lyrical expression with a refinement of feeling and with a depth of understanding that is reminiscent at times of Dante Alighieri in his *Commedia.* These qualities of his writing are undoubtedly what make Teilhard a dominant influence with the New Age movements that have arisen in recent times in America.

But while Teilhard is indispensable for understanding the larger patterns of life orientation that are needed, his thought must not become fixated. Issues that were secondary or dimly perceived during his lifetime are now imposing themselves with increasing urgency. Foremost among these issues is the problem of human–Earth relations that we have been considering in this paper. This issue began to be evident as early as the late eighteenth century in the writings of Michel Jean de Crevecoeur in a series of writings entitled *Letters from an American Farmer,* published in London in 1782. Already it was evident that the people of America were abusing their land. This became a more conscious issue in the nineteenth-century naturalists: Henry Thoreau and John Muir. A more precise articulation appears in the work of Aldo Leopold, whose remarkable essay entitled "A Land Ethic" was written in 1948, at the time when Teilhard was doing some of his most effective writing. Then in the last years of Teilhard's life, Edward Hyams published *Soil and Civilization* with his description of the destruction of both earthly and human affairs brought about by mistreatment of the soil upon which the living beings of Earth depend for their existence.[8]

That the situation had become even more virulent in the Western world through the petrochemical industry was seen by Rachel Carson and described in extensive detail in *Silent Spring.*[9] While Edward Hyams identifies the human as parasitical in its draining of life in a nonrenewing way from the living planet, Rachel Carson identifies the human as a poisoning agent in reference to those life-giving sources on which the human itself depends.

Finally we have *The Global 2000 Report to the President* (1980) with its extensive data on the influences presently exhausting natural resources and devastating the living forms of the Earth and even making the planet inhospitable toward life itself.

Thus, while Teilhard was presenting the activation of higher life expression, the destruction of existing life expression has been taking place. To the critique of Teilhard's work from the scientific community and the critique from the theological community must now be added the critique from the ecological community. In the first two instances the critique has brought out the deeper qualities of Teilhard's work and the fundamental correctness of his basic insights. Now the challenge of the ecological disturbance of the planetary functioning that is consequent on modern scientific technologies is forcing Teilhard's thought to a more profound level of self-criticism and this in confrontation with problems never fully envisaged by Teilhard. The other objections to his work from the scientific community and from the theological community were generally presented during his own lifetime. He had the opportunity to deal with them in extensive detail. Neither Teilhard nor his opponents seems to have realized that the greatest challenge to his work would derive from the planetary disturbance consequent on the ideas of "progress" that were then being proposed throughout Western society. They could not see that the glory of the human was becoming the desolation of the Earth or that the desolation of the Earth was becoming the destiny of the human.

Now that this is being seen with some clarity, the great need is not to cancel out the grand visions of the past but to bring them to a new and more fruitful efficacy in the present; for the ecological movement itself is threatened by trivialization, by reduction to a branch of thermodynamics. The deeper meaning of the Earth process that is carried in the great thinkers of the past must be brought to a more integral expression. A vision is needed with such depth that the solutions offered to the present situation will not be trivial or temporary solutions, but solutions that can provide the fullness of meaning and the energy required to activate a new human age in which peace with the Earth will be established and the emergent creative process will move on toward its next stage of fulfillment in the great age of the Earth community that is before us.

# PART TWO

# AN ECOLOGY
## FOR THE 21ST CENTURY

Teilhard's holistic compass locates the human within an enveloping natural biosphere and its developing noosphere of the mind. The "planetization" he foresaw is now in full force, but appears, if present trends continue, more destructive than sustainable. A product of the technological optimism of the mid-twentieth century, Teilhard extolled the noosphere's positive potential, while noting, as early as 1948, the dangers that could occur. The three studies of part 2 demonstrate how a Teilhardian perspective can inform and enhance environmental concerns even as it is enlarged to embrace our contemporary challenges.

Thomas Berry's pathbreaking chapter, "The New Story: Comments on the Origin, Identification, and Transmission of Values," launched the *Teilhard Studies* series twenty-five years ago. This seminal work became the basis of Berry's later books *The Dream of the Earth* and *The Universe Story*. Here Berry sets forth for the first time his distinctive vision of the limits of a religious emphasis on redemption at the expense of creation. This has left us without a functional cosmology integral with the scientific story of evolution. Berry's "New Story" draws on a Teilhardian perspective to identify human values within the dynamics of evolutionary processes of differentiation, subjectivity, and communion.

Teilhard experienced directly the numinous quality of matter in the rocks and geology of his native Auvergne. He went on in his studies to speak of realms of matter (geosphere), life (biosphere), and mind (noosphere). Our current obsession with mega-technology and industrialization ignores the limitations of the biosphere. In her article "Education and Ecology: Earth Literacy and the Technological Trance," Mary Evelyn Tucker pairs Teilhard and Thomas Berry to call for an "Earth literacy" curriculum that situates the human within the framework of Earth history and cosmic evolution.

In recent years the phrase "sustainable development" has come to signify an ecologically stable economy and lifestyle. The next author argues, however, that this has not been properly grounded in the fluid processes and carrying capacities of the biosphere and can be used as cover for continuous growth. In his updated and retitled study, "Sustainable Development and the Ecosphere: Concepts and Principles," the senior University of British Columbia ecologist William E. Rees specifies the thermodynamic and ecosystem budgets that must be respected.

# 6

# The New Story

## *Comments on the Origin, Identification, and Transmission of Values*

### Thomas Berry

It's all a question of story. We are in trouble just now because we do not have a good story. We are in between stories. The Old Story—the account of how the world came to be and how we fit into it—is not functioning properly, and we have not learned the New Story. The Old Story sustained us for a long time. It shaped our emotional attitudes, provided us with life purpose, energized action. It consecrated suffering, integrated knowledge, guided education. We awoke in the morning and knew where we were. We could identify crime and punish criminals. Everything was taken care of because the story was there. It did not make men good; it did not take away the pains and stupidities of life, or make for unfailing warmth in human association. But it did provide a context in which life could function in a meaningful manner.

Today, however, our traditional story is nonfunctional in its larger social dimensions even though some persons believe it firmly and act according to its dictates. It works in its limited orbit. It is an encouragement to us as individuals. Yet the dissolution of our institutions and our life programs continues. We see this in every phase of our present society. Aware of the nonfunctional aspects of the traditional program, some persons have moved on into different modern programs. But these programs, for the most part, have quickly become tangential. Most are revealed as ephemeral, as incapable of sustaining the life situation of this late twentieth century. Other persons are returning to the earlier religious fundamentalism. But this too is quickly seen as a sterile gesture. Security is not there. The basic elements in the religious community of the modern world have become trivialized. What we offer our society serves only a temporary function. It simply enables us to keep a semblance of meaning in our institutions and in our public life.

First published in *Teilhard Studies* no. 1 (winter 1978).

When we look outside the traditional believing community we see a society that is also dysfunctional. Even with advanced science and technology, with superb techniques in manufacturing and commerce, in communications and computation, our secular society remains without satisfactory meaning or capacity to restrain the violence of its own members. Our miracle machines serve ephemeral purposes.

So we begin to talk about values. Where can we begin? My suggestion is that we begin where everything begins in human affairs, with the basic story, the account of how things came to be at all, how they came to be as they are, and how the future life of humanity can be given some satisfying direction. We need a story that will educate human beings, heal them, guide them.

## THE BELIEVING REDEMPTION COMMUNITY

Western society did have a functional story up until somewhere around the fourteenth century. The Black Death can be taken as the traumatic moment of our civilization. It is estimated that this plague, which began in Constantinople in 1334, within twenty years killed off between one-third and one-half of the population. Throughout the fourteenth and fifteenth centuries there was a decline in the whole of Europe. In London the last of the great plagues was in 1665. There were two basic responses to this terrifying experience of the plague. From these two responses were formed the two communities of the present: the believing religious community and the secular scientific community.

The believing community had recourse to supernatural forces, to the spirit-world, to the renewal of esoteric traditions, sometimes to pre-Christian beliefs and rituals that had been neglected in their deeper dynamics since the coming of Christianity. Even within traditional Christianity there was an intensification of the faith experience, an effort to activate supernatural forces with special powers of intervention in the phenomenal world now viewed as threatening to human life. The sense of human depravity increased. The need for an outpouring of influences from the higher numinous world was intensified. Faith dominated the mental faculty. Redemption mystique became the dominant form of Christian experience. This excessive emphasis on redemption, to the neglect of creation doctrines, had from the beginning been one of the possibilities in Christian development. The creed itself is overbalanced in favor of redemption. Thus, the integrity of the story was affected. The primary doctrine of the Christian creed, belief in a personal creative principle, became increasingly less important in its functional role. Cosmology was not of any particular significance. This response, with its emphasis on redemptive spirituality, continued through the religious upheavals of the sixteenth century, on through the Puritanism and Jansenism of the seventeenth century. This attitude was further strengthened by the shock of the Enlightenment and revolution periods of the eighteenth and nineteenth centuries.

We in America who remain members of the believing redemptive community represent the most modern phase of this tradition. We have kept this Christian story and shaped our world accordingly. We have our parallel society, our own schools, our own hospitals, our own social groups, our own worship, our own moral teaching, our own aesthetic, our own professional societies, our own associations at every level, our own publications, our own financial resources.

This American version of the ancient Christian Story has functioned well in its institutional efficiency and in its moral efficacy. But it is no longer the Story of the Earth, nor is it the integral Story of Humankind. It is a sectarian story. At its center there is an intensive preoccupation with the personality of the Savior, with the interior spiritual process of the faithful, and with the salvific community. It is little wonder that we now discover that our story is dysfunctional in the larger cultural, historical, and cosmic perspectives. The tragedy is that for a while we came to accept this situation as the normal, even the desirable thing. As with every isolated life system, however, this system is inevitably experiencing a deactivation. The believing community is in an entropy phase of its existence.

## THE SCIENTIFIC CREATION COMMUNITY

The other response to the Black Death was the reaction that led eventually to the scientific, secular community of our times. This reaction sought to remedy earthly terror not by supernatural or religious powers but by an understanding of the Earth process. Although those working in this trend were at first involved to a certain degree with the esoteric and Platonic traditions, they did emphasize the necessity for empirical examination of the phenomenal world and its expression in quantitative terms. Scientific inquiry became the controlling human preoccupation, pushed by obscure forces in the unconscious depths of the Western psyche. The telescope and microscope were invented. New forms of mathematical expression were created. A scientific priesthood came to govern the thought life of our society. Men looked at the Earth in its physical reality and projected new theories of how it functioned. The celestial bodies were scrutinized more intently, the phenomenon of light was examined, new ways of understanding energy evolved. New sciences emerged: the *Novum Organum* of Francis Bacon appeared in 1620, the *Principia* of Isaac Newton in 1687, the *Nuova Scienza* of Giambattista Vico in 1725.

All of this led to an awareness that the human mind was advancing. This in turn led to the Enlightenment period of the eighteenth century and to the sense of absolute progress of human inquiry. This found expression in Marie Jean de Condorcet's *Historical Survey of the Progress of the Human Mind.* Here he outlined the ten stages of transformation that human cognition had gone through in its various periods of development until his own time. In the early nineteenth century G. W. F. Hegel was concerned with the inner dialectic of reality within both an ontological and a historical context. At this time also came the doctrines of social development with Jean Baptiste Fourier, Comte de Saint-Simon, and Auguste Comte. Karl Marx brought this movement to its most realistic expression in his *Manifesto.*

All of this was only preparatory to a new discovery whose magnitude and effects on human life are still not measured. While these changes in the mode of human perception and of social structure were taking place, evidences were appearing in the realms of geology and paleontology indicating that there was a time sequence in the very formation of the Earth and of all life forms upon the Earth. Finally it dawned upon Western consciousness that earlier life forms were of a simpler nature than later life forms, that the later forms were derived from the earlier forms. The complex of life manifestations had not existed from the beginning by some external divine creative act setting all things in their place. The Earth in all its parts, especially in its life forms, was in a state of continuing transformation. Discovery of this life sequence was brought to its first full expression by Charles Darwin in his *Origin of Species* in 1859. After Darwin the physicists in their study of light and radiation came almost simultaneously to an understanding of the infra-atomic world and the entire galactic system. Insight into both the microphase and macrophase of the phenomenal world was obtained, and the great unity of this universe became apparent in its spatial expansion and its time sequence. A new story of the universe was available in its basic outline.

Just at this moment, however, a sudden shift in the mode of consciousness took place. The scientist-priest-mystic suddenly became aware that the opaqueness of matter had dissolved. His science was ultimately not the objective grasping of some reality extrinsic to himself; it was rather a moment of subjective communion in which the human saw itself less an isolated, Olympian, knowing principle than a being in whom the universe in its evolutionary dimension became conscious of itself.

Thus the sequence from an awareness of spiritual development of the biblical world to the mental development of the Enlightenment, to the social and historical development of the sociologists, to the ontological development of Hegel, to the biological development of Alfred Russel Wallace and Darwin, to the later cosmic development of the twentieth-century physicists. The final stage has been to see that the human person is not a detached observer of this development but one that is integral to the entire process. Indeed the human may now be defined as the latest expression of the cosmic-Earth process, as that being in whom the cosmic-Earth-human process becomes conscious of itself.

Thus, a new creation story has evolved in the secular scientific community, the equivalent in modern times of the creation stories of antiquity. This creation story differs from the traditional Eurasian creation stories much more than these differ from each other. It seems destined to become the universal story taught to every child who receives formal education in the modern form anywhere in the world.

## THE EARLIER CHRISTIAN COSMOLOGY

The redemptive believing community, first dazzled by this new vision of developmental time, then frustrated by an inability to cope with the new data, lapsed unenthusiastically into its traditional attitudes. In recent centuries the believing community has not been concerned with any cosmology, ancient or modern, for the believing community has its real values concentrated in the Savior, the human person, and the believing church.

There is, indeed, a surviving cosmology in which even the redemption story takes place and which to some extent still plays a role in the Christian story. According to this story the cosmos and every being in the cosmos reflect the divine exemplar considered by Plato as the *Agathon* ("the Good"), by Plotinus as the One, by Christians as God. All things are beautiful by this beauty. The supremely beautiful is the integrity and harmony of the total cosmic order as St. Thomas Aquinas insists so constantly. This requires the perfection of each part, the proper relating of the parts to each other, and the final integrating of the parts in the whole. Thus, there is the love of oneself, of others, then of the total cosmic complex, and finally the love of God, who is the primordial eternal reality in whom every reality finds its primordial eternal image.

The human mind ascends to the contemplation of the divine by rising through the various grades of being from the lowliest forms of existence in the Earth with its mountains and seas to the various forms of living things, and so to the human and consciousness, to the soul and from the inner life of the soul to God. This sequence is portrayed most beautifully in the *Symposium* of Plato and in the *Soliloquy* of Augustine as he meditated with his mother by the window. So Bonaventure could write on the reduction of all the arts and sciences to theology, for all eventually depended upon the divine reference. So too the journey of Dante through the various spheres of reality up to the divine vision in itself. Initiation into the basic human and Christian values was initiation into this cosmology. Christian spirituality was built up in this manner. The mysteries of Christianity were integral with this cosmology. The difficulty with this cosmology is that it presents the world as an ordered complex of beings that are ontologically related as an image of the divine; it does not present the world as a continuing process of emergence in which there is an inner organic bond of descent of each reality from an earlier reality.

## THE IMPASSE

In their functional roles neither this traditional cosmology nor the new scientific cosmology is of serious concern because of the shift in the Western religious tradition from a dominant creation mystique to a dominant redemption mystique. This Christian redemptive mystique is little concerned with any cosmological order or process, since the essential thing is redemption out of the world through a relationship with a personal Savior that transcends all such concerns. Even the earlier mystical experiences of ascending to the divine through the realms of created perfections are diminished. There eventuates an acosmic, ahistorical religious mood as a dominant response to the awesome experience of the Earth and its demonic powers. But now this excessive redemptive emphasis is played out. It cannot effectively dynamize activity in time because it is an inadequate story of time. The redemption story has grown apart not only from the historical story but also from the Earth story. Consequently an isolated power has eventuated that is being victimized by entropy.

If this is the impasse from the side of the believing redemption community of America, the impasse from the side of the secular scientific community, committed to a developmental universe, is its commitment to the realm of the physical to the exclusion of the spiritual in the creation story. This has been the tough, the realistic position, the rule of no-nonsense action. Thus the Darwinian principle of natural selection involves no psychic or conscious process but a fierce struggle for earthly survival which gives to the world its variety of form and function. Because this story became too exclusive in its physical biological version of the cosmic-Earth process, the society supported by this vision is also victimized by entropy, expressed in its lack of meaning. It is not an integral story.

We must not think that these two communities, both now in a state of entropy, have no regard for each other. Extensive courtesies are extended, extensive cooperation is offered. Persons in the secular scientific professions as well as in modern manufacturing and commercial pursuits have high regard for the religious dimension of life. But this is either an extrinsic dedication of their profession or their business to religious goals or a simple form of reverence. Many are themselves religious personalities of intense dedication to the saving mysteries of religious faith. They spend time and energy in seeking to make the faith prosper. They wish to serve, to give themselves a spiritual discipline.

Those in the religious community have their own esteem for the integrity of those engaged in scientific technological commercial activities. These phases of life have their consecration. Training in the professions takes place in the religious schools. It even dominates the curriculum. So what's the fuss about? The answer is that surface agreement is not depth communion or the basis of sound cosmic-Earth-human values. The antagonisms are deeper than they appear to be. An integral story has not emerged, and no community can exist without a community story. This is precisely why communication between these two is so unsatisfying. No sustaining values have emerged. The problems of the human are not resolved. The human adventure is not dynamized.

Both traditions are trivialized. The human venture remains stuck in its impasse. There is no Divine Comedy. The Platonic vision no longer has the excitement it had for Augustine or for Bonaventure or for Dante. Even when we read Plato or Augustine or Bonaventure or Dante we no longer have the experience they had. Their suppositions are not ours. The child who enters school and begins his or her Earth studies or life studies does not experience any numinous presence. This teaching, which enables children to discover their place in the world of time and space, is one of the most important of all events in their life. Students need a story that will encompass this, and the school at present cannot provide the mystique that should be associated with this story. Even the religious-oriented school that has only extrinsically adopted the modern sense of the Earth cannot evoke this experience in the child.

The story is not complete; it has no human or spiritual aspect. This is especially significant because the child's schooling now fulfills a role in our society similar to the role of the initiation ceremonies in earlier societies. The secular society does not see the significance of its own story, while the religious society rejects the story because it is presented only in its physical aspect. The creation process has been sublimated by the redemption process. The totality of the numinous is subsumed in the redemption experience. All real values are redemptive values. Yet, as we have seen, these values have become nonfunctional in the larger dimensions of the human community. Because they are dysfunctional in the larger community they have become dysfunctional for the individual. Therefore the need exists to establish a deeper understanding of the spiritual dynamics of the cosmic-Earth process within which the redemption process functions. From the empirical inquiry into the real it has become increasingly clear that from its beginning in the galactic system to its earthly expression in human consciousness the universe carries within itself a psychic as well as a physical dimension. Otherwise human consciousness emerges out of nowhere and finds no real place in the cosmic story. The human is an addendum or an intrusion.

So far, however, spiritually oriented personalities have been pleased because this cleavage provides the human with superior, unearthly quality. The scientist also is pleased, since this leaves him or her free to structure the world of quantitative measurements with the problem of human consciousness. Thus both scientist and believer conspire to keep their positions disengaged from the profound understanding of the Earth process itself. Neither seems to be looking at the reality before oneself; else it would be evident that the cosmic-Earth-human process requires both a physical and a psychic phase from the beginning. As soon as this is recognized, and the story of the universe is presented in its integral form, a new world appears for both the scientific and the believing community. Once again a universal cosmological myth attains its primacy in human understanding of the universe and in the direction of human affairs. The work of Teilhard de Chardin has been to give the integral Story the most complete expression that it has so far attained.

## THE STORY

The Story of the Universe is the story of the emergence of a galactic system in which each new level of being emerges through the urgency of self-transcendence. Hydrogen in the presence of some millions of degrees of heat emerges into helium. After the stars take shape as oceans of fire in the heavens, they go through a sequence of transformations. Some eventually explode into the stardust out of which the solar system and the Earth take shape. Earth gives unique expression of itself in its rock and crystalline structures and in the variety and splendor of living forms until the human appears as the moment in which the unfolding universe becomes conscious of itself. The human being emerges not only as an earthling but also as a worldling. Human persons bear the universe in their being as the universe bears them in its being. The two have a total presence to each other.

If this integral vision is something new both to the scientist and to the believer, both are gradually becoming aware of this view of reality and its meaning for the human. It might be considered a new revelatory experience. Because we are moving into a new mythic age, it is little wonder if a kind of mutation is taking place in the entire Earth-human order. A new paradigm of what it is to be human emerges. This is what is so exciting, yet so painful and so disrupting. One aspect of this change involves the shift in Earth–human relations, for the human now in large measure determines the Earth process that once determined men and women. In a more integral way we could say that the Earth that controlled itself directly in the former period now to an extensive degree controls itself through human beings.

## CREATION OF VALUES

In this new context the question appears as to where the values are, how they are determined, how transmitted. First it can be said that, whereas formerly values consisted in the perfection of the earthly image reflecting an eternal Logos in a world of fixed natures, values are now determined by the sensitivity of the human responding to the creative urgencies of a developing world. The transforming sequence is in the direction of an increasing differentiation, a deepening subjectivity, and a more comprehensive communion within the total order of the real. The scientists themselves—often unknowingly—are drawn by the mystical attraction of communion with the emerging creative process. This would not be possible unless it was a call of subject to subject, if it were not an effort at total self-realization on the part of the scientists. Their taste for the real is what gives to their work its admirable quality. They wish to experience the real in its tangible, opaque, material aspect and to respond to this by establishing an interaction with the world that will advance the total Earth-human process. If the demand for objectivity and the quantitative aspect of the real have led scientists to neglect subjectivity and the qualitative aspect of the real, this has been until now a condition for their fulfilling this historical task. The most notable single development within science in recent years, however, has been a growing awareness of the integral physical-psychic dimension of reality. The scientific community is possibly more advanced than the religious community in accepting the total dimensions of the New Story. An abundant interpretative literature has appeared that gives an entrancing, humanly understandable description of the universe, the emergence of life, and the appearance of the human.

The believing redemption community is awakening only slowly to this new contest of understanding. There is a fear, a distrust, even a profound aversion to the Earth and all its processes. Probably no Catholic theological seminary in the country has an adequate course on creation as it is experienced in these times, whereas there is a long list of courses on redemption: Soteriology, Christology,

Ecclesiology, the Sacraments, Grace, Pastoral Ministry, and others concerned with redemption and how it functions in aiding human beings to transcend the world. Some years ago it was noted in a survey published in the journal *Science* that Catholics ranked lowest of religious traditions in the country in their production of scientists. Although this has been challenged in its particulars, it probably can stand in its general implications. Such a situation cannot long endure, however, since a new sense of the Earth is arising in the believing community. The Earth will not be ignored, nor will it long endure being despised, neglected, or mistreated. The dynamics of creation are demanding attention once more in a form unknown to the orthodox Christian for centuries.

## IDENTIFYING VALUES

In identifying values in this new situation a new type of difficulty emerges. Even when there is a responsiveness to the inner dynamics of the Earth process there is a certain dislocation from the clearly established directives of a prior paradigm of the human. Even though this paradigm is no longer effective in dealing with the most basic issues of the present, there is a tendency to continue problem solving within the paradigm rather than an effort to change the paradigm as the only way of dealing with the problems. The basic norms of the new paradigm are continued differentiation, subjectivity, and communion. As regards differentiation, it seems that one of the primordial intentions of the Earth process is to produce variety in all things from the atomic structures of the living world of plant and animal forms to the appearance of the human, where individuals differ from each other more extensively than in any other kingdom. This applies not only to individuals but also to social structures and historical periods of humankind's development. Thus, the law of differentiation is of primary importance in the appreciation of the entire Earth process. There can be no doubt that this is the primary aspect of the New Story that is being written, how this differentiation took place in time and space to produce such a variety of manifestations. Here is a first fundamental value, the inherent indestructible value of the individual. But here also is the difficulty in the human order, for there is no absolute model for the individual. Such personal realization involves a unique creative effort in response to all those interior and exterior forces that enter into individual life. So too with each historical age and each cultural form there is need to create a reality for which, again, there is no adequate model. This is precisely the American difficulty, a difficulty for which there is no complete answer but only a striving toward. At each moment we must simply be what we are and be open to a larger life.

After differentiation, by far the most important value is subjectivity, interiority. Every being has its own interior, its self, its mystery, its numinous aspect. To deprive any being of this sacred quality is to disrupt the total order of the universe. Reverence will be total, or it will not be at all. The universe does not come to us in pieces any more than a human individual stands before us with some part of one's being. Preservation of this feeling for reality in its depths has been considerably upset in these past two centuries of scientific analysis and technological manipulation of the Earth and its energies. During this period the human mind lived in the narrowest bonds that it has ever experienced. The vast mythic, visionary, symbolic world with its all-pervasive numinous qualities was lost. Because of this loss human beings made their terrifying assault upon the Earth with an irrationality that is stunning in its enormity, while we were being assured that this was the way to a better, more humane, more reasonable world.

Such treatment of the external physical world deprived of subjectivity could not long avoid encompassing the human also. Thus, we have the most vast paradox of all, human persons as free, intelligent, numinous beings while negating these very interior qualities by their own objective reasoning mind and subserving their own rationalization. Finally a reversal has begun, and the reality and value of the interior, subjective, numinous aspect of the entire cosmic order are being appreciated as the basic condition in which the story makes any sense at all. If the first theme of the story is differentiation, the second theme is the ever-increasing awakening of interior consciousness.

The third determining theme of the New Story is the intercommunion of the universe within itself and of each part with the whole. Each atomic particle is in communion with every other atom in the vast web of the universe. This web of relationships throughout the universe is what first impinges on the waking consciousness of the human from the beginning. If the larger story of the world process is the account of differentiation and subjectivity it is also the account of deepening communion at every level of reality. It is a more intense communion within the material world that enables life to emerge into being. The living form is more differentiated, with greater subjectivity and more intensive communion within itself and within its environment. All these factors are multiplied on a new scale of magnitude in the realm of consciousness. There a supreme mode of communion exists within the individual, within the human community, within the Earth-human complex. Increased capacity for differentiation is inseparable from this capacity for communion. Together this distance and this intimacy establish the basic norms of being, of life, of value. It is the destiny of our present and all future generations to develop this capacity for communion on new and more comprehensive levels.

## TRANSMITTING VALUES

As we move now from the creation and identification of value to transmission of values, we must first note that we no longer have the functional initiation techniques whereby the vision and values of earlier generations were transmitted to succeeding generations. Yet there is an abiding need to assist a succeeding generation to fulfill its proper role in the ongoing adventure of the Earth process. In the human realm education must supply what instinct supplies in the prehuman realm. There is need for a program to aid the young to identify themselves in the comprehensive dimensions of space and time. This task was easier in the world of the *Timaeus,* where the Earth was seen as an image of the eternal Logos. In such a world St. Thomas could compose his *Summa Theologica,* which could then be summarized in catechetical form and taught to succeeding generations.

Now a new way of understanding values is required. The *Summa* that is presently being written is the story of the universe in its cosmic-Earth-human phases as this is now emerging into consciousness. In this story human development has gone through a primal phase dominated by its tribal character, a civilizational phase of the more massive societies, a technological phase wherein the new discoveries were made. Now a numinous integration phase of the Earth process is taking place.

It is of utmost importance that the next generation become aware of this larger story here outlined and the numinous, the sacred values that have been present in an expanding sequence over this entire time scale of the world's existence. Within this context all human affairs, all professions, occupations, and creations of the human have their meaning precisely insofar as they enhance this emerging world of subjective intercommunion within the total range of reality. Within this context the scientific community and the religious community have a common basis. The limitations of redemption rhetoric and scientific rhetoric can both be seen, and a new more integral language of being and value can emerge.

## CONCLUSION

I would offer a few observations in conclusion. Within this story a structure of knowledge can be established with its human significance from the physics of the universe and chemistry, through geology and biology to anthropology, and so on to an understanding of the entire range of human endeavor from language, literature, art, history, and religion to medicine and law, to psychology and sociology, to economics and commerce, and so to all those studies whereby human beings fulfill their role in the Earth process. In all these studies and in all these functions, the basic values depend on conformity with the Earth process. To harm the Earth is to harm the human; to ruin the Earth is to destroy humankind.

Second, there is no possibility of discovering a functional story for American society or the human community except by discovering the functional story of the cosmic-Earth process. If the way of Western culture and Western religion was once the way of election and differentiation from others and from the Earth, the way now is the way of intimate communion with the larger human community and with the cosmic-Earth process.

Third, the basic mood of the future might well be one of confidence in the continuing revelation that takes place in and through the Earth. If the dynamics of the universe from the beginning shaped the course of the heavens, lighted the sun, and formed the Earth—if this same dynamism brought forth the continents and seas and atmosphere, if it awakened life in the primordial cell and then brought into being the unnumbered variety of living beings and finally brought human persons into being and guided them safely through the turbulent centuries—there is reason to believe that this same guiding process is precisely what has awakened in the human the present understanding of ourselves and our relation to this stupendous process. Sensitized to this guidance we can have confidence in the future that awaits the human venture.

Fourth, by means of this story the new paradigm of the human is established. With its support we can awaken in the morning and know where we are. We can answer the questions of our children. We can interpret suffering, integrate knowledge, guide education. We can have a context in which life can function in a meaningful way.

# 7

# Education and Ecology

## Earth Literacy and the Technological Trance

### MARY EVELYN TUCKER

> To understand the world knowledge is not enough,
> you must see it, touch it, live in its presence
> and drink the vital heat of existence
> in the very heart of reality.
> —Pierre Teilhard de Chardin,
> *The Heart of Matter,* p. 70

The reality of a growing environmental crisis of immense proportions was the focus of the United Nations World Summit on Sustainable Development in Johannesburg in September 2002. This crisis, global in scope but local in impact, has created an urgent agenda in this new millennium that must be met with innovative political, economic, social, and educational programs. There are calls now for new forms of global governance, ecological economics, social equity, and alleviation of poverty. All of this requires creative approaches to educating for a sustainable future.

Those of us interested in education and in the work of Pierre Teilhard de Chardin and Thomas Berry are especially challenged to create the conditions for healing the biosphere in the twenty-first century. Teilhard's call to "build the future" and to inspire the energies for that future is an essential part of the educational vision needed in our time. As Thomas Berry has noted, we will be unable to make the necessary changes without a clear analysis of the global challenges faced by the human community and without a sufficiently comprehensive historical and geological context, namely, a planetary perspective.[1] As educators, we are challenged to motivate the next generation of students to go beyond the technological trance of a consumer society toward creating mutually beneficial human–Earth relations. This requires an understanding of Earth's evolution within the context of the universe story. It calls us to see our role at a critical

First published in *Teilhard Studies* no. 28 (spring 1993).

moment in history as a determining factor in the future course of evolution itself. We are a planetary species that can move toward the enhancement of life or its radical diminishment for future generations.

Accordingly, this study begins with a survey of some of the problems we face as we attempt to move beyond military-based economic systems toward economies engaged in sustainable interactions with nature and appropriate uses of natural resources. Next, a reassessment is made of the myth of progress and the lure of quick technological fixes for environmental problems. After a review of some of the present inadequacies of education, we will outline a broadened perspective of time and space through an appreciation of the emerging story of the universe. Here the evolutionary cosmology of Teilhard de Chardin, Thomas Berry, and Brian Swimme is essential.[2] In conclusion, the study will propose that we develop an Earth literacy sensitive to the voices of the whole Earth community. Several innovative individuals and programs attempting this kind of education are noted.

## THE SHIFT FROM MILITARY INDUSTRIAL SOCIETIES TO SUSTAINABLE ECONOMIC DEVELOPMENT

The litany of military excesses is familiar. During 1986, designated as the International Year of Peace, global military expenditures reached $900 billion.[3] This was more than twenty-five times the amount spent on development assistance to countries in need.[4] Until the collapse of the former Soviet Union the United States and the Soviet Union together were spending about $1.5 billion a day on military defense. The U.S. national defense budget is now more than $1 billion a day. With a $396 billion dollar defense budget, the United States spends more on the military than the rest of the G8 countries combined and six times more than Russia, the second-largest spender.[5] Present nuclear arsenals still represent over 26,000 times the explosive force of all armaments used in World War II. This continues at a time when at least one person in five in developing countries is undernourished.[6] The juxtaposition of such impoverishment and such overkill, one might suggest, has never been matched in human history. The pressing question is how to convert modern economies from following a rapacious military industrial model to one that promises some equitable distribution of resources for both first and third world peoples. A further requirement is to respond to ecological devastation in various parts of the world including Africa, Asia, and Latin America, as well as Eastern Europe and Russia. The legacy of pollution from the production and deployment of nuclear and chemical weapons worldwide is just one example of this problem.[7]

### The State of the Environment and the Use of Natural Resources

The injuries to the Earth are manifold from military waste and from extractive industrial processes. One-third of the world's cropland is losing soil to erosion. Acid rain from industrial pollution causes the death of forests and lakes in the

United States, Canada, the former Soviet Union, and Europe. Tropical rain forests are being destroyed at the rate of hundreds of acres a day in South and Central America and in Southeast Asia. Current estimates are that at least one hundred species a day are being eliminated. No comparable rate of extinction has occurred since the Cretaceous period sixty-five million years ago. The effect of the depletion of the ozone layer is already being felt in the widespread increase in skin cancer. The warming of the planet due to the greenhouse effect has contributed to severe droughts as well as devastating storms and flooding.

Water is now becoming a precious commodity across the United States and around the world. In many areas intestinal diseases occur because of polluted drinking water. In the United States the easy technical fix to concerns about water quality is to buy bottled water or put a filter on the faucet. Deeper causes of contamination are not addressed. The danger is that we adjust so readily if a simple technological solution is at hand. As the World Summit on Sustainable Development noted, the availability and use of water are increasingly a key issue worldwide as all life forms are so clearly dependent on it.

Still another impact on the environment comes from technological and chemical "advancements." Ecologist Barry Commoner puts it this way:

New production technologies have replaced old ones. Soap powder has been displaced by synthetic detergents; natural fibers (cotton and wool) have been displaced by synthetic ones; steel and lumber have been displaced by aluminum, plastics, and concrete; . . . returnable bottles have been displaced by nonreturnable ones. On the farm . . . the amount of harvest acreage has decreased; fertilizer (much of it synthetic) has displaced land. Older methods of insect control have been displaced by synthetic insecticides . . . and for controlling weeds the cultivator has been displaced by the herbicide spray. Range-feeding of livestock has been displaced by feedlots.[8]

Our synthetic, plastic, throwaway world is taken for granted and hailed as progress, but we are beginning to realize that it is *progress with a price.* With the increased capacity of inappropriate technologies to alter or destroy ecosystems, the rethinking of economic development and growth becomes more urgent. Even simple technologies like the chainsaw are implicated in the rapid depletion of the tropical and temperate forests. Technology has clearly been a mixed blessing, bringing both advances and destruction in its wake.

## THE MYTH OF PROGRESS

As the participants in the United Nations World Summit on Sustainable Development noted, the challenges faced by the entire human community are of grave proportions. Affluent societies live within a nonsustainable industrial bubble that will inevitably burst, third world societies understandably want its material benefits, and yet few question the myth of progress that supports it.

Unlimited progress and economic development through the consumption of non-renewable resources are seen as inevitable and desirable. To question such progress or continuous growth is considered to be romantic or impractical, or, even worse, unpatriotic and anticapitalist.

The rush to consume is so blind and unrestrained that we pollute our rivers, foul the atmosphere, destroy forests, poison the soil, and eliminate species all in the name of progress. The ultimate danger today is the precipitous and irrevocable destruction of the life-sustaining biosphere. It is not only terrorism against one another that we need to fear, but also terrorism against the planet itself.

In the United States the rhetoric and allure of unbridled consumption are mirrored from Madison Avenue to Hollywood. Our educational system has largely become an instrument to provide labor and consumers to perpetuate this cycle. Worthwhile employment in service industries or nonprofit groups is not lucrative and therefore is less attractive to young people. Religious organizations valiantly concentrate on issues of personal salvation and charitable acts while individuals are unable to find a sense of larger meaning and values in the modern world. Our crisis is thus educational and religious as well as economic and environmental.

Is this too dramatic a scenario? Not according to the Worldwatch Institute's annual *State of the World* reports or the *Global 2000 Report to the President of the U.S.* by Gerald Barney or *Agenda 21* published by the United Nations Environment Programme after the Rio Earth Summit.[9] The Worldwatch Institute has observed that the radical changes brought about by humans in altering atmospheric chemistry, global temperatures, and the abundance of living species "reflect the crossings that may impair the Earth's capacity to sustain an ever-growing human population. A frustrating paradox is emerging. Efforts to improve living standards are themselves beginning to threaten the health of the global economy. The very notion of progress begs for redefinition in light of the intolerable consequences unfolding as a result of its pursuit." In calling for a transition to a sustainable society the Worldwatch study goes on to say that:

> A sustainable society satisfies its needs without diminishing the prospects of the next generation. By many measures, contemporary society fails to meet this criterion. Questions of ecological sustainability are arising on every continent. The scale of human activities has begun to threaten the habitability of the Earth itself. Nothing short of fundamental adjustments in population and energy policies will stave off the host of costly changes now unfolding, changes that could overwhelm our long-standing efforts to improve the human condition.[10]

Lester Brown notes that we need to awake to the illusion of progress, and he suggests using a new method of cost accounting that would consider the consequences to the environment of various economic activities.[11] He observes that a schizophrenic perspective is emerging between a conventional economic position that is optimistic about "growth," "development," and "progress" and an environmental one that is far less optimistic when pollution and depletion of resources are factored in.[12] He states bluntly, "The ecological view holds that continuing the simple-minded pursuit of growth will lead eventually to economic collapse."[13]

In a similar vein the *Global 2000 Report* cites critical deficits that will worsen in the present decade:

> The environment will have lost important life-sustaining capabilities. By 2000, 40 percent of the forests still remaining in the LDC's [less developed countries] in 1978 will have been razed. The atmospheric concentration of carbon dioxide will be nearly one-third higher than pre-industrial levels. Soil erosion will have removed, on the average, several inches of soil from croplands all over the world. Desertification (including salinization) may have claimed a significant fraction of the world's rangeland and cropland. Over little more than two decades, 15-20 percent of the Earth's total species of plants and animals will have become extinct—a loss of at least 500,000 species.[14]

The report goes on to note that "once such global environmental problems are in motion they are very difficult to reverse. In fact, few if any of the problems addressed in the Global 2000 Study are amenable to quick technological or policy 'fixes'; rather, they are inextricably mixed with the world's most perplexing social and economic problems."[15]

The environmentalist Bill McKibben, in his book *The End of Nature,* observes that our relationship with nature is now forever changed because much of our technological imprint on nature is irreversible.[16] The director of the Missouri Botanical Garden, Peter Raven, put it starkly in his keynote address to the American Association for the Advancement of Science, entitled "We're Killing Our World." He states at the outset: ". . . the world that provides our evolutionary and ecological context is in serious trouble, trouble of a kind that demands our urgent attention. By formulating adequate plans for dealing with these large-scale problems, we will be laying the foundation for peace and prosperity in the future; by ignoring them, drifting passively while attending to what may seem more urgent, personal priorities, we are courting disaster."

## A Response through Education for Earth Literacy

The environmental crisis we face, then, is occurring on the scale of a major geological epoch in terms of alterations of ecosystems and impact on humans and other species on the planet. While previous geological ages or extinctions happened naturally, this one is being driven largely by human blindness, intransigence, and greed. The fact that we are in the midst of a sixth extinction period of loss of species is being acknowledged by the scientific community. Like species loss, global warming is seen by the Intergovernmental Panel on Climate Change (IPCC) as caused in large part by humans.

For some people, the sheer enormity of our difficulties results in a paralyzing inability and an unwillingness to make changes that are necessary. It is easier to continue with a consumptive lifestyle with no regard for future generations. Many are caught in the patterns of addiction that pervade American society. Drugs and alcohol are only surface manifestations of the larger addictions to wealth and excess. These obsessions produce an altered state, a kind of trance, like the fascination with technology that we assume will solve our problems. Thomas Berry has called this addiction and the concomitant belief in the myth of progress a "technological trance."[17]

How to break this trance becomes a crucial question for educators. Our specific concern is how to imbue the next generation with radically new values that can recognize the need for sustainable development, appropriate technologies, alternative energy sources, and changes in lifestyles. This will require a deeper understanding of the concepts not only of "sustainable development" but also of *sustainable life* for future generations. A vital goal should be teaching courses in Earth literacy to foster both a scientific comprehension of the natural world and a comprehensive environmental ethics based on principles of ecojustice. Issues of poverty and environment need to be solved in tandem. A change of values, perspectives, and priorities is central to this effort. As Lester Brown cogently puts it: "The goal of the cold war was to get others to change their values and behavior, but winning the battle to save the planet depends on changing our own values and behavior."[18]

A major obstacle to achieving an effective and comprehensive global environmental ethics is the inadequacy of an educational system in which the sciences and the humanities are two separate and often unrelated entities. The lack of communication between scientists and humanists in the universities with regard to issues of planetary survival is endemic. An atmosphere of mistrust and misunderstanding exists on many campuses between these disciplines. Thus the complementary perspectives of scientific research and moral questioning are rarely found in dialogue, much less in fruitful collaboration. Knowledge has consequently become compartmentalized, highly specialized, and ineffectual in relation to the multiple global crises faced by the Earth community. Similarly, both within and outside of academia, religion and science are seen as largely incompatible. Each tends to claim an exclusive hold on truth that allows little room for substantive dialogue. It is ironic that while our educational system pushes toward the frontiers of knowledge many religious institutions claim an ever more exclusive salvific wisdom.

Students are thus caught unwittingly in two traps. One is the labyrinth of compartmentalized disciplines; the other is an often-desperate obsession with marketability and job skills. There is little opportunity to synthesize the knowledge they receive in high school or college. Their reasoning powers are being challenged through a current focus on "critical thinking" in the curriculum. Yet an intellectual integration or personalization of what they have learned is rarely accomplished. Quantitative analysis and assessment are frequently emphasized over qualitative, creative, or holistic learning processes. We need to foster appreciative learning, not simply critical thinking. We need multidisciplinary synthesis, not only disciplinary specialization.

The popularity of courses in business, computer science, and engineering reflects the pragmatic attitude of students and the materialistic preoccupation of our society. Studying these areas instills ways of thinking that promote short-range "progress" and bottom-line profits. One learns to manipulate natural processes with little attention to long-range effects. Our universities thus contribute to the technological trance and the industrial bubble with little concern for the consequences of unlimited growth or for encouraging alternative means of employment. It is a formidable dilemma that educational establishments prefer not to address because their own futures often rest on support from industry and government.

Clearly these are not black-and-white issues. Technology has contributed substantially to the betterment of human life; but it has also demanded a price, especially with respect to the environment. Asbestos, for example, was first used successfully for thermal insulation and was only later found to have harmful health consequences; drugs that cure one ailment may have unforeseen side effects; pesticides can kill certain insects but upset a whole ecosystem. Our fascination with technology makes us unwilling to employ a precautionary approach before using various kinds of technologies or chemicals.

This does not mean we are advocating a nontechnological, pristine utopia. More realistically, we need new perspectives on a natural context for the education of future generations. This implies a more comprehensive and integrated understanding of our evolutionary relationship to the whole Earth. We now have the capacity either to destroy or to assist in the unfolding of basic life processes. We need to foster an appreciation of how to work with nature, not against it, and to understand ecological interconnectedness *before* interfering with nature, not afterward. As Barry Commoner has suggested, the best way to control pollution is to prevent it before it happens, not to try and clean it up later.[19] This is the basis of the precautionary principle.

Such an agenda requires the articulation of an Earth literacy. Many teachers and students are virtually illiterate in understanding the intricacy of ecosystems and thus are deficient in knowing effective ways to protect the environment such as intermediate technologies, alternative energy sources, organic agriculture, and recycling processes. An understanding of Earth literacy and an application of these alternative and organic approaches will surely foster sustainable life of the planet. The work in alternative technologies of John and Nancy Todd is significant here, as is the research on conservation and alternative energy by Amory and Hunter Lovins.[20] In the area of sustainable agriculture the work of Wes Jackson, Wendell Berry, Miriam MacGillis, and countless others has been invaluable.[21]

## A NEW RELATEDNESS TO THE EARTH

Having identified some of the issues we are facing regarding military spending versus sustainable development, the protection of the environment in relation to economic growth, natural resources and appropriate technology, and the challenges these issues pose to education, it can be said that a primary premise of effective education in the future must be the appreciation of our intimate relationship to the Earth. This is the basis for Earth literacy, for this is the ultimate matrix for both survival and sustainability of life. The assault on the planet has been under way for several centuries, especially since the beginning of the industrial revolution. Of late it has been escalated by technological excesses and growth without limits. But the Earth can no longer serve passively as our dumping ground or our place of endless extraction of resources. It can no longer be viewed, as Thomas Berry suggests, as something only to be used for us. It is a community of life, not a commodity of resources. Our role as educators is crucial to this new realization. Indeed, it is essential to the process of creating the possibility of peace among peoples through peace with the planet. It will require *imagination* and *evocation* as well as *programs* and *practicality*. We will briefly discuss these four points.

We need first to cultivate both a scientific understanding and an imaginative appreciation of nature in ourselves as educators as well as in our students. A difficulty is that the scientific method has seemingly outpaced the imaginative and creative arts. The next phase of an education for an Earth literacy will require a creative synthesis of science, social sciences, and humanities. As teachers we must become students again to learn interdisciplinary approaches to our understanding of nature and its complex self-organizing dynamics.

New ways of imagining and thinking, of reasoning and relating, of valuing and judging need to arise not as separate, testable processes but as holistic ways of seeing. Teilhard opens *The Human Phenomenon* with the following statement:

> Seeing. One could say that the whole of life lies in seeing. . . . That is probably why the history of the living world can be reduced to the elaboration of ever more perfect eyes of the heart of a cosmos where it is always possible to discern more. . . . See or perish. This is the situation imposed on every element of the universe by the mysterious gift of existence.[22]

Two perspectives that can facilitate such a vision in students are a new understanding of evolution and the view of the Earth from the moon. Both of these involve an evocation of our place in nature and our role as humans in the larger universe. It will be important to encourage students to move from an *anthropocentric* view of human dominion and management of nature to an *anthropocosmic* one of reciprocity and respect between humans and all life forms on the Earth.[23] An anthropocosmic perspective implies one where humans acknowledge their embeddedness in nature and their evolution from the larger cosmos.

It is useful to recall that Darwin's theory of evolution is little more than one hundred years old, a short time in relation to Earth history, and it is still not fully assimilated into human consciousness. An evolutionary view requires a radical rethinking of time, which many religious fundamentalists vigorously resist. Nonetheless, a new cosmological paradigm is emerging in our midst. The thought of Pierre Teilhard de Chardin, Thomas Berry, Brian Swimme, and others has been critical to its development. Indeed, Teilhard sees how radically the idea of evolution changes our perspective: "This is something we must fully understand once and for all: henceforth, for us and for our descendants, there is a complete change of psychological time-relationships and dimensions."[24] This is true, he observes, because: "For our age, to have become conscious of evolution means something very different from and much more than having discovered one further fact. . . . It means (as happens with a child when he acquires the sense of perspective) that we have become alive to a new dimension."[25]

### Cosmology: New Views of Time and Space

Central to a change of consciousness necessary for Earth literacy education is an enlarged understanding of cosmology, namely, of the cosmic evolutionary processes. As Thomas Berry has said, we must become familiar with the comprehensive "new story" of the universe as it has emerged over some 13.7 billion years.[26] A vital message Teilhard sought to convey is that we live not in a static cosmos but within a creative cosmogenesis. He writes: "Phenomenally speaking we see the world not merely as a system that is simply in movement but as one that is in a state of genesis."[27]

The several millennia of Judeo-Christian history need to be brought into relationship with the scope and complexity of the environmental crisis we are facing. As Teilhard noted, to see ourselves as a human phenomenon integral with this dynamic evolutionary story is essential. Only then can we begin to appreciate our role in fostering a mutual balance between human needs and those of the myriad other forms of life on a common Earthly home. Teilhard clearly saw how powerful this sense of interconnection is from an evolutionary perspective:

> We have in the first place realized that every constituent element of the world has of necessity emerged from that which preceded it—so much so that it is physically impossible for us to conceive of a thing in Time without "something before it" as it would be to imagine the same thing in Space without "something beside it." In this sense every particle of reality, instead of constituting an approximate point in itself, extends from the previous fragment to the next in an indivisible thread running back into infinity.[28]

Here are the ancient lineaments of the natural history of the Earth after the emergence of the universe some 13.7 billion years ago. Our solar system itself was formed some 5 billion years ago while the Earth began to take shape 4.6 billion years ago, and the sun was born 4.5 billion years ago. Life flourished through four major extinctions before the dinosaurs. The oceans took shape shortly thereafter. Fossil cells of self-replicating molecules date from 3.6 billion years ago. Free oxygen began to accumulate 2 billion years ago and complex cells with nuclei about 1.5 billion years ago. Then the protective ozone layer formed and life on land began to emerge. The dinosaurs ruled for 160 million years before their extinction 65 million years ago. During the last 135 million years flowering vegetation spread. Homo sapiens appeared some 200,000 years ago and the great traditional civilizations about 4,500 years ago. In the last half-century we have harnessed the atom, cracked the genetic code, launched into space, and changed the face of the planet. This is the cosmological story of the emerging universe that can provide an appropriate context for Earth literacy.[29]

The expansive view of time just outlined is complemented by the integral image of the Earth from the moon. As James Lovelock articulates in his Gaia hypothesis, Earth is a self-regulating living organism protected by the thin covering of our atmosphere. He writes:

> The new understanding has come from going forth and looking back to see the Earth from space. The vision of that splendid white flecked blue sphere stirred us all, no matter that by now it is almost a visual cliché. It even opens the mind's eye, just as a voyage away from home enlarges the perspective of our love for those who remain there.
>
> The first impact of those voyages was the sense of wonder given to the astronauts and to us as we shared their experience vicariously. . . .
>
> We now see that the air, the ocean and the soil are much more than a mere environment for life; they are a part of life itself. Thus the air is to life just as is the fur to a cat or the nest for a bird. Not living but something made by living things to protect against an otherwise hostile world. For life on Earth the air is our protection against the cold depths and fierce radiations of space.
>
> There is nothing unusual in the idea of life on Earth interacting with the air, sea and rocks, but it took a view from outside to glimpse the possibility that this combination might constitute a single giant living system and one with the capacity to keep the Earth always at a state most favorable for the life upon it.[30]

Such an expansion of the parameters of space and time marks a new era in the human imagination. How to visualize ourselves as arising from an intricate system of evolving life forms that is some 4.6 billion years old and as part of a blue-green planet floating in space is a challenge that humankind has just begun to encounter. Meeting the challenge will require imaginative stories, meditations, poems, paintings, dances, and dramas that reorient us to a universe that is much larger, more complex, and more mysterious than we had previously thought. This will guide us in our journey to becoming a planetary species that is enhancing rather than inhibiting the flourishing of the larger Earth community.

Poised as we are between an old and a new story, the place of the human in relation to other species is the subject of a debate among the social ecologists and the deep ecologists.[31] The social ecologists emphasize the significance of humans, while deep ecologists point out that we are one of thousands of species and that an anthropocentric arrogance has contributed to our global environmental crisis. It will be important to resolve this argument in order to rethink priorities with regard to species extinction and human survival on a damaged biosphere. An *anthropocosmic perspective supported by Earth literacy* may be the most comprehensive grounding to educate for the long-term viability of life on the planet.

### *Proposals for Innovative Programs*

A core feature of an educational curriculum for the twenty-first century is rec-ognizing that in some fundamental way *the Earth is the basic curriculum.* Here is a conceptual expansion far beyond most undergraduate or graduate programs for training teachers. Yet Thomas Berry observed some years ago that the Earth is the primary educator; it is as simple and as complex as that. The Earth is the primary healer, lawgiver, and producer of life.[32]

A reliable guide to its implementation may be found in the phrase "Think globally; act locally" or "Think cosmically; act bioregionally." With such an inte-gration of macro and micro scales we gain a way to help both ourselves and our students assimilate these vast temporal and spatial dimensions of universe emer-gence. The narrative story of evolution provides the most comprehensive context for any curriculum, especially for an understanding of world history, literature, and religion. It is a practical matrix for teaching the natural sciences and envi-ronmental studies, and for investigating specific bioregions. A complementarity of the universal and the particular is vital if we are to be effective teachers and indeed midwives for the emergence of a holistic cosmological paradigm for this new millennium.

One of the most helpful works on Earth literacy is David Orr's *Ecological Lit-eracy: Education and the Transition to a Postmodern World.* Also of major sig-nificance for potential curricular changes is Mary Clark's *Ariadne's Thread: The Search for New Modes of Thinking.* In addition, there is an edited volume by Robert Costanza on *Ecological Economics: The Science and Management of Sustainability.*[33] Chet Bowers has also made significant contributions to ecolog-ical education in his many publications. Mitchell Thomashaw's book *Bring the Biosphere Home* is also an important contribution to ecological education. Vari-ous Earth literacy centers have emerged to meet this growing need of learning to live in harmony with nature in a postindustrial society.[34] At the Center for the Respect of Life and Environment in Washington, D.C., there is a network of Uni-versity Leaders for a Sustainable Future (USLF; www.ulsf.org). Moreover, the Earth Charter has also become a central vehicle for education for a sustainable future (www.earthcharter.org). Universities such as Harvard and Columbia have developed comprehensive multidisciplinary environmental programs, while oth-ers such as Florida Gulf Coast University have organized curricula for environ-mental sustainability. The University of Buffalo, University of Colorado at Boulder, Penn State, and the Associated Colleges of the South have become lead-ing institutions in environmental education. Colleges such as Middlebury, Brown, Colorado College, Williams, Prescott, Warren Wilson, Oberlin, Antioch, Berea in Kentucky, St. Thomas in Miami, and St. John's in Minnesota have developed curriculum, centers, and buildings that are models in the field of envi-ronmental education.

There are, of course, numerous activities that can be undertaken by children in schools to enhance their sense of Earth literacy, and many Montessori schools do just that within the context of the universe story. A goal would be to instill care for the Earth not only for the present but for future generations as well. If Earth literacy activities are undertaken so as to encourage in children a respect for the Earth itself as the sustainer of life, a new context for ethics can emerge. Aldo Leopold first wrote of such a "Land Ethic" more than forty years ago, and it is further developed in Roderick Nash's book *The Rights of Nature*.[35] Environmental philosophers such as Baird Callicott, Holmes Rolston, Byran Norton, Laura Westra, and others have made great progress in articulating an effective environmental ethics. A sense of morality toward the land and animal and plant species would inspire us to nurture life rather than to exploit it. Violence against the Earth and all its life forms would be as unacceptable as violence against human beings. An Earth literacy would give students a vision of their oneness with nature while making them aware of the consequences of damage to the encompassing biosphere.

## A REFLECTION UPON LISTENING TO THE EARTH'S VOICES

We conclude with examples of both the global mode of *reflecting* on evolutionary processes and the local mode of *relating* to particular forms of life as complementary aspects of a viable Earth literacy. In each selection the telling of a "story" is crucial. The first two passages are from Loren Eiseley's book *The Immense Journey*.[36] One describes the evolution of flowers; the other is a meditation on the innate patterns in nature as revealed in a snowflake. The universal and the particular, developmental time and immediate time, interact in Eiseley's experience and imagination. He summons for us the wonder of the prolific diversity and interconnected complexity of life. In the chapter titled "How Flowers Changed the World" Eiseley writes:

> Once upon a time there were no flowers at all. A little while ago—about one hundred million years, as the geologist estimates time in the history of our four-billion-year old planet—flowers were not to be found anywhere on the five continents. Wherever one might have looked, from the poles to the equator, one would have seen only the cold dark monotonous green of a world whose plant life possessed no other color.
>
> Somewhere, just a short time before the close of the Age of Reptiles, there occurred a soundless, violent explosion. It lasted millions of years, but it was an explosion, nevertheless. It marked the emergence of the angiosperms—the flowering plants. Even the great evolutionist, Charles Darwin, called them "an abominable mystery," because they appeared so suddenly and spread so fast.
>
> Flowers changed the face of the planet. Without them, the world we know—even man himself—would never have existed. Francis Thompson, the English poet, once wrote that one could not pluck a flower without troubling a star. Intuitively he had sensed, like a naturalist, the enormous interlinked complexity of life. Today we know that the appearance of the flowers contained also the equally mystifying emergence of man.[37]

Eiseley further describes his own affinity with the dynamics of nature in a chapter titled "The Flow of the River." He concludes the chapter with a reflection on the intrinsic self-organizing principles that have molded and shaped life. The unique quality of water and the intricate mystery of a snowflake recall this special intuition of being part of the evolution of life forms:

> It is then, when the wind comes straitly across the barren marshes and the snow rises and beats in endless waves against the traveler, that I remember best, by some trick of the imagination, my summer voyage on the river. I remember my green extensions, my catfish nuzzlings and minnow wrigglings, my gelatinous materializations out of the mother ooze. And as I walk on through the white smother, it is the magic of water that leaves me a final sign.
>
> Men talk much of matter and energy, of the struggle for existence that molds the shape of life. These things exist, it is true; but more delicate, elusive, quicker than the fins in water, is that mysterious principle known as "organization," which leaves all other mysteries concerned with life stale and insignificant by comparison. For that without organization life does not persist is obvious. Yet this organization itself is not strictly the product of life, nor of selection. Like some dark and passing shadow within matter, it cups out the eyes' small windows or spaces the notes of a meadow lark's song in the interior of a mottled egg. That principle—I am beginning to suspect—was there before the living in the deeps of water.
>
> The temperature has risen. The little stinging needles have given way to huge flakes floating in like white leaves blown from some great tree in open space. In the car, switching on the lights, I examine one intricate crystal on my sleeve before it melts. No utilitarian philosophy explains a snow crystal, no doctrine of use or disuse. Water has merely leapt out of vapor and thin nothingness in the night sky to array itself in form. There is no logical reason for the existence of a snowflake any more than there is for evolution. It is an apparition from that mysterious shadow world beyond nature, that final world which contains—if anything contains—the explanation of men and catfish and green leaves.[38]

Finally, we turn to the writing of Wendell Berry, the Kentucky farmer and poet, who evokes a sense of place and an identity with a native bioregion that is his distinctive gift. In doing so he reflects on the mixture of violence, peace, and joy in the lives of animals and birds—thus commenting on the integrity and celebration of nature in itself.

> In spite of all the talk about the law of tooth and fang and the struggle for survival, there is in the lives of the animals and birds a great peacefulness. It is not all fear and flight, pursuit and killing. That is part of it, certainly; and there is cold and hunger; there is the likelihood that death, when it comes, will be violent. But there is peace, too, and I think that the intervals of peace are frequent and prolonged. These are the times when the creature

rests, communes with himself or with his kind, takes pleasure in being alive. . . .

But there is not only peacefulness, there is joy. And the joy, less deniable in its evidence than the peacefulness, is the confirmation of it. I sat one summer evening and watched a great blue heron make his descent from the top of the hill into the valley. He came down at a measured deliberate pace, stately as always, like a dignitary going down a stair. And then, at a point I judged to be midway over the river, without at all varying his wingbeat he did a backward turn in the air, a loop-the-loop. It could only have been a gesture of pure exuberance, of joy—a speaking of his sense of the evening, the day's fulfillment, his descent homeward. He made just the one slow turn, and then flew on out of sight in the direction of a slew farther down in the bottom. The movement was incredibly beautiful, at once exultant and stately, a benediction on the evening and on the river and on me. It seemed so perfectly to confirm the presence of a free nonhuman joy in the world—a joy I feel a great need to believe in—that I had the skeptic's impulse to doubt that I had seen it. If I had, I thought, it would be a sign of the presence of something heavenly in Earth. And then, one evening a year later I saw it again.[39]

Such an exquisite resonance with the life forces of the natural world challenges us to nurture these same sensitivities. Such extraordinary meditations as these on the ordinary rhythms and mysteries of nature reawaken our sense of intimate connection to life in all its varied forms. To see deeply into the myriad patterns of life on the Earth will give us, our children, and our students a revitalized communion with our bioregion and with the larger unfolding processes of the universe story. The voices of the Earth are calling to us. It is urgent that we begin to listen once again.

# 8

# Sustainable Development
# and the Ecosphere

## Concepts and Principles

### WILLIAM E. REES

### INTRODUCTION, PURPOSE, AND SCOPE

Since being popularized by *Our Common Future*, the Report of the World
Commission on Environment and Development,[1] the venerable concept of "sustainable development" has inspired the enthusiasm of people on all sides of the
economy–environment debate. In light of worsening global ecological trends,
any concept that implies that we can eat our developmental cake and have the
environment too is bound to have a certain attraction. But there is little agreement
as to the nature of future development. To some, sustainable development is a
long-awaited call for political recognition of environmental decay, for economic
justice, and for limits to material growth. It therefore represents an opportunity
for humanity to correct a historical error and begin a more benign, balanced, and
stable relationship with the natural world.[2] This view of sustainable development
also raises moral considerations such as the need in a finite world for an equitable sharing and conservation of its natural bounty.[3]

Other people read a different message in *Our Common Future*. The World
Commission itself equated sustainable development with "more rapid economic
growth in both industrial and developing countries" on grounds that "economic
growth and diversification . . . will help developing countries mitigate the strains
on the rural environment, raise productivity and consumption standards, and
allow nations to move beyond dependence on one or two primary products for
their export earnings."[4] Accordingly, the commission indicates that "a five- to
ten-fold increase in world industrial output can be anticipated by the time world
population stabilizes some time in the next century."[5]

To those who see present levels of industrial activity as the cause of wide-

First published in *Teilhard Studies* no. 23 (spring/summer 1990).

spread damage to the biosphere, the commission's appeal for a "revitalization" of economic expansion on this scale seems paradoxical at best. Nevertheless, the power of the growth paradigm is not to be underestimated. As sustainable development is gradually embraced by the political mainstream, its meaning drifts ever further from the ideal of a viable environment toward the seductive temptation of sustained material growth.

In this essay I consider some ecological and thermodynamic principles and their ramifications to reach an environment-economy integration appropriate for sustainable development. My premise is that our current environmental dilemma is due, in part, to a much distorted perception of reality. Modern economic society operates from an outdated mechanistic perception of the natural dynamics of the Earth. If this premise is correct, our understanding of the environmental crisis is dangerously superficial, and the possibility of sustainable development based on the growth-oriented assumptions of neoclassical economics is illusory. No amount of ethical axiology or legal, policy, and technological engineering is going to solve problems that are misunderstood.[6] It follows that significant changes in sociocultural beliefs, attitudes, and behavior will be required before sustainable development can acquire any substantive meaning.

## THE CULTURAL ROOTS OF REALITY

How a society relates to the world is profoundly affected by an elaborate set of evident facts, unquestioned assumptions, and entrenched beliefs. These are derived from the shared experience of a people in the course of their social development and are transmitted culturally to each new individual as she or he matures in that particular milieu. Such a common philosophy or worldview shapes every culture's social relationships, its political institutions, and the nature of its economic enterprise.

### Worldview as Social Myth

It is important to realize that there can be as many worldviews as there are cultures and that each worldview only more or less coincides with reality. Our most sacred beliefs, however well based on the evidence to date, may simply be wrong. While we think we act from factual knowledge, much individual action and government policy is based on unsubstantiated belief. As the systems scientist Stafford Beer writes in the *Teilhard Review*, much of our worldview may be little more than social myth, a collection of "shared illusions."[7]

In past centuries it has been of no great consequence when cultural beliefs such as that of an unbounded Earth depart from external reality. However, certain activities, long consistent with a prevailing worldview, may produce a crisis if the cumulative effect comes in conflict with previously unknown constraints. In these circumstances, a society must be prepared to modify its worldview to conform to the new knowledge and realities. Like a disadvantageous genetic mutation, a maladaptive worldview can be "selected" out by the environment. I argue that industrial civilization has reached such a critical juncture in its relationship with the global environment and that radical new assumptions are needed to inform the concept of sustainable development.

### Nature Estranged: The Clockwork Universe

The scientific worldview that presently dominates Western society is characterized by a mechanical model of the universe as "a vast machine, wound up by God to tick forever, and consisting of two basic entities: matter and motion."[8] Although it has deeper roots, this view flowered in the seventeenth century and is most closely associated with René Descartes, Francis Bacon, and Isaac Newton.

Descartes set the stage by splitting reality into the independent realms of mind and matter and by proposing a universal mathematics to measure and order the external world.[9] The ultimate rationalist, Descartes saw even a person's activity as a thinking being as purely mechanical. The mind has a certain method and confronts the world as a separate object: "It applies this method to the object, again and again and again, and eventually it will know all there is to know."[10] Through the separation of the observer from the observed, Descartes helped formalize the notion of objective knowledge. His reductionist approach provided the methodological framework for subsequent scientific inquiry.

Bacon represents the empiricist pole. He reasoned that to know nature one had to "vex" her, "torture nature's secrets from her," thus forcing unambiguous answers.[11] In addition to this essence of experimental method, Bacon gave the new science its *raison d'être*. He argued that knowledge should be put to work allowing mankind to take command over the natural world, its objects, and its mechanical powers. "From this perspective, knowledge is regarded not as an end but as a means, expressed and applied in technology, by which humans assume power over the material world."[12]

However, it was Newton who most succeeded in validating the Cartesian view of the universe. His *Principia* (1686) revealed the laws of mass and motion, which seemed to describe the universe as a mechanical machine of unlimited dimensions behaving according to strict mathematical rules. By the end of the seventeenth century the founders of the scientific worldview had abolished the ancient perception of the Earth as an organic living entity, a nurturing mother. "By separating and then eliminating all the qualities of life from the quantities of which they are a part, the architects of the machine paradigm [left us] with a cold, inert universe made up entirely of dead matter."[13]

### The Material Human

Two additional thinkers went on to apply the mechanical scheme directly to human institutions and affairs. John Locke sought to determine the "natural" basis of society. With God alienated from nature, Locke reasoned that religion could no longer provide the rational basis for government. People had to create their own meaning, and the purpose of society was reduced to protecting and facilitating the increase of the property of its members. Locke argued that the ownership of property conveyed not only rights but an obligation to generate wealth: "He who appropriates land to himself by his labour, does not lessen but increases the common stock of mankind,"[14] and "land that is left wholly to nature . . . is called, as indeed it is, waste."[15]

Similar logic underpinned the "invisible hand" of Adam Smith. Just as planets conform to natural laws, so must economic behavior obey subtle forces. Smith, like Locke, believed that the basis of all human activity was material self-interest, "but the study of [a person's] own advantage naturally, or rather necessarily, leads him to prefer that employment which is most advantageous to society."[16] By this reasoning, "any attempt by society to guide 'natural' economic forces [would be] inefficient." Interference with the workings of the "invisible hand" for whatever noble purpose would only stifle economic growth. Significantly, this effectively excluded morality from the realm of political economy. "There are no ethical choices to be made, only utilitarian judgments exercised by each individual pursuing self-interest."[17]

From its roots in the Cartesian paradigm, the utilitarian social mechanics of Locke and Smith thus succeeded in reducing human beings to selfish egoists devoted mainly to economic production and consumption in the pursuit of endless material abundance.

## A MODERN MYTH: THE MECHANICAL ECONOMY

Modern economics is still based on this worldview. The founders of the neoclassical school, impressed with the successes of Newtonian physics, strove to create economics as a sister science, "the mechanics of utility and self-interest."[18] The major consequence of the mechanical model is an entrenched view of economic process as "a self-sustaining circular flow between production and consumption. . . ." By this perception, supply and demand functions continually readjust to each other: "everything turns out to be just a pendulum movement. One business 'cycle' follows another. . . . If events alter the supply and demand propensities, the economic world returns to its previous position as soon as these events fade out." In short, "complete reversibility is the general rule, just as in mechanics."[19]

### The Worship of Growth

An economy chugging away machine-like in an infinite universe assumes potentially unlimited growth. Even today some economic planners believe "not only in the possibility of continuous material growth, but in its axiomatic necessity."[20] Our "largely uncritical worship of . . . economic growth is as central to [capitalism's] nature as the similar veneration of . . . divine kingship or doctrinal orthodoxy has been for other regimes."[21] Accordingly, the annual increase in gross national product (GNP) is still taken as every nation's primary indicator of national health. Rates under 3 percent are considered sluggish, but even 3 percent implies a doubling of economic activity in just twenty-three years!

We should note in the context of sustainable development that capitalist states depend on the increasing size of the economic pie to ensure that the poor receive enough of the national income to survive. Indeed, economic growth is a major instrument of social policy. By holding out hope for improvement, it relieves the pressure for policies aimed at more equitable distribution of wealth. In addition, while GNP—a deeply flawed index—is accepted as a measure of economic welfare, we have no universal metric for the state of environment or perceived quality of life. This is a revealing comment on societal perceptions, priorities, and the staying power of the materialist paradigm.

## ECOLOGICAL REALITY

The emerging ecological crisis reveals several fundamentally erroneous misconceptions of the prevailing worldview. A fatal dissonance exists in economy-environment relationships that must be acknowledged if we are ever to appreciate the policy implications of sustainable development.

### From Environment to Ecosphere

A first step is to recognize that the objectification of the natural world is due to the Cartesian subject–object dualism. In effect, environment-as-separate-entity is a human invention. The psychological consequences of this separation are quite profound. By definition, "environment" is its own pejorative, alluding to whatever surrounds some other thing of greater interest or value—it "diffidently declares itself to be peripheral, unimportant, not to be taken seriously."[22] We may recognize the environment as a source of resources and sink for wastes, but beyond that it is perceived as just a static backdrop to human affairs. By this perception there is no compelling need to love, cherish, or even husband nature, to do anything beyond exploiting its bounty to our own advantage. As a corollary, impacts of economic activity on natural Earth processes are perceived to be of little long-term consequence. Should something go awry, a simple retraction or technological fix will set things right.

That the economy has an independent life is a cultural myth, one of our most cherished illusions. In reality, the economy and the environment have always been fully and inextricably integrated everywhere but in the Cartesian mind. For all its political and institutional sophistication, the human economy is "fundamentally directed toward a problem encountered by all other species—the dependence for life on materials from elsewhere in the biosphere."[23] The fact is there is only a single functional matrix, the biosphere, of which humankind has always been a part. We next explore the implications of this whole Earth system.

### The Economy as Black Hole:
### Growth Is a Thermodynamic Process

The mechanical metaphor has inhibited economic theory from acknowledging the second law of thermodynamics. This omission is at the heart of our ecological crisis. The second law states that in an isolated system—a system that cannot exchange energy or material with its "environment—any change involves the degradation of available energy and matter to an unavailable state and the progressive disordering of the system."[24] Simply put, entropy increases. But the same forces of entropic decay operate on all complex evolving systems whether isolated or not. Since the economy is one such system, why does the economy not simply unravel and run down like an isolated system? The answer is that the economy is an open system that overcomes the entropy law by importing available energy and material (negentropy) from the ecosphere and using it to maintain itself and grow. It also exports the resultant waste (entropy) back into the ecosphere. In effect then, the economy is potentially an entropic parasite on the ecosphere. It is a *growing* subsystem embedded within the *nongrowing* ecosphere; it treats the ecosphere both as a source of sustenance and as a sink for wastes.

This is a sobering perspective. We are accustomed to thinking of the economy as a dynamic, productive system—witness the continuously expanding outpouring of goods and services. However, the fact is that at present *all* economic activity is dependent on declining stocks of nonrenewable energy and material resources and on various renewable resources produced by the ecosphere. Moreover, the economy eventually returns all the resources it uses to the ecosphere as useless waste. This includes the material embodied in consumer products—which are generally discarded when worn out—as well as the immediate waste by-products of the production process.[25] Thus, in light of the second law, the economy is seen as a "dissipative structure," and all material economic production is revealed as consumption. A constantly growing material economy, therefore, *necessarily* ultimately consumes and degrades the very resource base that sustains it. Rather than the circular flow of exchange value, a realistic model of the economy might be based on the unidirectional throughput of useful energy and matter.

There are no exemptions from the second law—all forms of economic activity contribute to global entropy through the dissipation of energy and matter. A finished automobile or computer represents only a fraction of the energy and material that have been permanently degraded and dissipated in the production process; modern energy-subsidized agriculture consumes many calories of fossil energy for every calorie of food energy produced (high-input agriculture has been called the use of land to convert petroleum into food); even the service and knowledge-based sectors use large quantities of material and electrical energy. It follows from thermodynamic law that, contrary to the assumptions of neoclassical theory:

- There can be no equilibrium in energy and material relationships between an open, growing industrial economy and a materially closed nongrowing ecosphere.

- Sustainable development based on prevailing growth-based development assumptions and existing patterns of resource use is not even theoretically conceivable.

- There is a fundamental contradiction between the goal of continuous material growth—the anticipated fivefold expansion of the world economy during the first five decades of the twenty-first century—and the necessity of maintaining global ecological integrity.

These corollaries to the second law suggest that the latter may well be the ultimate regulator of economic activity and that the most important limits to growth are thermodynamic limits. They also suggest a novel criterion for sustainable global development. Sustainable development is development in which the rate of resource consumption by the economy is compatible with rates of production by the ecosphere. That is, sustainable development is thermodynamically balanced, limited development that over the long term does not contribute in net terms to the dissipation and disordering of the ecosphere.

### The Special Case of Ecosystems

Ecosystems, like economic systems, depend on fixed stocks of material resources. However, the stuff of ecosystems is constantly being transformed and recycled throughout the system via food-webs at the local level and biogeochemical cycles on a global scale. In addition, evolution and succession in natural communities tend toward greater net order and resilience. Thus, also like economies, ecosystems appear at first glance to defy the entropy law. Ecosystems are inherently self-organizing and self-sustaining and work continuously to reduce their internal entropy. Indeed, the ecosphere as a whole exhibits an important property of ecosystem dynamics: through numerous positive and negative feedback mechanisms "[the system] is in many respects self-generating—its productivity and stability determined largely through its internal interactions."[26]

The organizational property that enables ecosystems and other living systems to produce and sustain themselves is known as autopoiesis.[27] Autopoiesis is a product of the complex, interdependent relationships (energy, material, and information flows) linking the system's major components. The important point is that the structural integrity of these relationships is essential not only to the functioning of the system, but also for the production and maintenance of the participating components themselves.

Autopoiesis is reflected in the homeostatic or self-regulating behavior of the ecosphere. Over geological time life processes have maintained the physical environment of Earth within limits narrow enough that life has been able to persist.[28] Thus, even such physical conditions for life as mean global temperature and the relative composition of gases in the atmosphere are dependent on autopoiesis and the homeostatic properties of the biosphere.[29]

Self-production by the ecosphere differs in one critically important respect from self-production by the economy. As described above, the economy grows and develops by dissipating and polluting the ecosphere. By contrast, the ecosphere evolves and maintains itself by dissipating an extraplanetary source of free energy, solar radiation, and the entropic waste (low-grade heat) is reradiated back into space. A steady stream of solar energy sustains essentially all biological activity and makes possible the diversity of life on Earth. Through photosynthesis, living systems concentrate simple dispersed chemicals such as water and carbon dioxide and use them to synthesize the most complex substances known (fats, carbohydrates, proteins, nucleic acids). Thus, in contrast to economic systems, ecosystems steadily contribute to the accumulation of concentrated energy, matter, and order within the ecosphere. In thermodynamic terms, photosynthesis is the most important productive process on the planet and the source of most renewable resources used by the human economy. Moreover, since the flow of solar radiation is constant, steady, and reliable, resource production in the ecosphere is potentially sustainable over any time scale relevant to humankind.

But only potentially. Ecological productivity is limited by the availability of nutrients, photosynthetic efficiency, and ultimately the rate of energy input (the "solar flux") itself. Ecosystems therefore do not grow indefinitely. Unlike the economy, which expands through resource conversion and positive feedback, ecosystems are held in "steady-state" or dynamic equilibrium by limiting factors and negative feedback.[30]

### The Pathology of Current
### Economy and Environment Integrations

This difference is significant because human beings and their economies are now a dominant component of all the world's major ecosystems. Since our economies are growing and the ecosystems within which they are embedded are not, the consumption of ecological resources everywhere has begun to exceed sustainable rates of biological production. By the late 1980s, nearly 40 percent of net terrestrial primary productivity (photosynthesis) was already being used or co-opted by humans, one species among millions, and the fraction is steadily increasing.[31]

Should this trend continue, overharvesting, including species extinction and the outright destruction of whole ecosystems, may eventually undermine the autopoietic organization of the ecosphere and its ability to produce the type of "environment" necessary to sustain human beings. Moreover, the destabilizing effect of overexploitation is exacerbated by pollution, which impairs the remaining productivity of ecosystems. The death of lakes and forest dieback due to acid precipitation in Europe and eastern North America are familiar examples.

Unfortunately, neoliberal economics is uninformed by autopoiesis and related ecological concepts (ironically so, because the economy is itself an autopoietic system!). Historically, we have all but ignored the major "downstream" consequences of pollution,[32] and most economists argue that concern for resource scarcity (the "Malthusian spectre") has been permanently put to rest.[33] According to these economists, technology and the magic of the marketplace will facilitate both conservation and the substitution of technology for natural resources as the latter become scarce.

This is dangerous reasoning. While market signals may be adequate to stimulate technical solutions for the depletion of certain nonrenewable resources such as copper or petroleum, they are an unreliable solution to the depletion of biophysical resources and processes on at least the following grounds:

1. Because of the lag and threshold effects characteristic of complex dynamic systems, price- or scarcity-induced conservation or substitution may occur too late to avoid the extinction of priced biophysical resources that have been overexploited.

2. Efficient markets assume that all participants have perfect knowledge of all present and future markets. This condition cannot even be met theoretically in the case of natural capital because biophysical systems are characterized by chaotic behavior that is inherently unpredictable.

3. Resources extracted from nature and their prices in the marketplace do not reflect key qualities and values of the systems that produced them. For example, the price of a log for market does not reflect the flood- and climate-control values, the carbon sink value, the wildlife fisheries and other recreational values, the aesthetic and existence values, and so on, of a functional forest. The log is therefore undervalued by its market price.

4. Certain resources for which there are markets and price signals (e.g., agricultural and forest products) may depend on other unpriced material or process resources (e.g., soils and soil-building processes).

5. The economy and the marketplace do not even recognize certain well-known biophysical entities (e.g., the ozone layer) and processes (e.g., climate modification) as resources, so their scarcity value may go unnoticed until it is too late.

6. Key biophysical functions of species and whole ecosystems may not be readily apparent and may remain unknown until the entity in question has been destroyed. Again, in the absence of a market there can be no price signal of impending scarcity.

These factors emphasize that while markets may be able to price the direct material inputs to manufacturing, they remain silent on the positive economic value of critical resources and life-support functions supplied by ecosystems. Consequently, society receives no signal from the marketplace that the biophysical basis of our wealth (and life itself) is being permanently eroded. Various unpriced—and often unpriceable—components of our natural capital are disappearing and may be unsubstitutable. In many cases, there is no evident solution to this problem short of limiting human impacts.

We should acknowledge that economics is concerned primarily with the efficient allocation of relatively scarce resources and that many ecological resources have heretofore been ignored (considered as "free goods") only because of their seemingly unlimited abundance. It might be argued, therefore, that establishing property rights in these resources as they become scarce will mitigate our problems. This explains the recent flurry of interest among economists in privatizing the natural environment and allowing the free market to determine the "proper" price for such things as pollution rights.[34]

However, in addition to the limitations listed above, proposals to extend the market raise several new objections. Most immediate is the difficulty in establishing property rights to many "open access" resources and processes.[35] How do we (and should we) privatize the ozone layer? There is also a strong case that far from protecting ecological resources, profit maximization and similar economically rational behavior by private owners may actually lead to resource extinction.[36] Perhaps most important in the long run are the philosophical arguments against market approaches.[37] "Commoditizing" the ecosphere is a technical solution that merely extends the materialist worldview without questioning society's fundamental values and assumptions.

### Consuming the Capital

The surplus . . . whether great or small is usually torn from the producers, either by [government or individuals] who by superior force . . . have established themselves as lords of the soil.[38]

Clearly, any human activity dependent on the consumptive use of biophysical resources (forestry, fisheries, agriculture, waste disposal, urban sprawl onto agricultural land) cannot be sustained indefinitely if it consumes not only the annual production of the ecosphere (the "natural interest") but also cuts into the standing stock (the "natural capital"). Herein lies the essence of our environmental crisis. Persistent trends in key ecological variables indicate that we have not only been living off the interest but also consuming our biophysical capital. This is the inevitable consequence of exponential material growth in a finite environment.

Among the most familiar trends are encroaching deserts (growing by 6 million hectares/year); rising sea-levels (1.2-2.2 meters by 2100); deforestation (11 million hectares/year); acid precipitation; resultant forest dieback (31 million hectares damaged); toxic contamination of food supplies; soil oxidation and erosion (26 billion tons/year in excess of formation); marine pollution; extinction of species (1,000 species/year); collapse of fisheries; drawdown and pollution of water tables everywhere; ozone depletion; greenhouse gas buildup; and climate change.

Viewing the decline of the ecosphere alongside our rising per capita consumption provides a novel perspective on at least one source of our unprecedented wealth. The intersecting curves reveal that throughout the industrial revolution we have been busily converting biophysical capital into economic capital. In short, the growing global economy is cannibalizing the finite biosphere! Much of our wealth is illusion—we have simply drawn down one account (the biosphere) to add to another (material wealth). It might even be argued that we have been collectively impoverished in the process. Much potentially renewable ecological capital has been permanently converted into machinery, plant, and possessions that will eventually wear out and have to be replaced at the cost of additional natural capital.[39]

The economist Robert Heilbroner notes that the origin of surplus in the era of industrial capitalism "has gradually moved from trade through direct wage labour exploitation toward technological rents, and that modern-day profits consist of combinations of all three."[40] We can now add a fourth profit source to Heilbroner's list—capitalist society gains much of its surplus from the irreversible conversion of biological resources. (We should note that the form of state capitalism practiced in socialist countries differs little in its ecological effect from the industrial capitalism of Western market economies.)

To put it another way, we've long been enjoying a free ride for which payment has now come due. Forest products, food, and manufactured goods are undervalued in the marketplace to the extent that the prices we pay do not include the costs of natural capital maintenance. Corporate profits are excessive at least to the extent that the resource base which produced them has been run down. A family's second car may represent capital that was not ploughed back into forest regeneration, soils management, and waste control. In short, the "good life" for some humans has been subsidized at the expense of other life on the planet, including future generations.

## HUMAN CARRYING CAPACITY

For most species, carrying capacity is the maximum population that can be supported indefinitely in a given habitat without permanently damaging the ecosystem. For human society, carrying capacity can be defined as the maximum rate of resource consumption and waste discharge that could be sustained indefinitely in a distinct planning region—or the entire planet—without progressively impairing ecological productivity and integrity.[41] The corresponding maximum human population is therefore a function of per capita rates of resource consumption and waste production (system capacity divided by per capita demand).

### *How Close to Global Limits?*

The deteriorating biosphere suggests that human populations and the present scale of economic activity may already exceed global carrying capacity. Many ecological processes have been overloaded, and the long-term dependability of certain critical life-support functions is in jeopardy. Indeed, we may not be far from their absolute limits.

Reid Bryson approached this issue in 1986 through a thermodynamic analysis of food production. He showed that we would need about 900 square meters of cropland to produce the average per capita food energy requirements assuming year-round cropping. With an average growing season of only 180 days, each hectare of agricultural land will theoretically support about five and a half people. World population density was then about three persons per arable hectare and within less than one population doubling of the "sunshine limit" to growth. Bryson felt that limit would be reached within thirty-five years.[42]

These calculations make no allowances for either resource degradation or technological advances. While such uncertainties make prediction about food limits hazardous, Lester Brown observed in 1988 that per capita grain production had declined since 1984, "falling 14 percent over the last four years"; that available data on erosion and falling water tables suggest "sustainable world food output is now running well below consumption"; and that "the backlog of unused agricultural technologies that farmers can draw on in some countries is dwindling."[43] These data give reason enough to ponder absolute limits in a world where even in 2000 the human population was still increasing by 78 million people per year.

Another factor related to global stability is that the closer we push the ecosphere to its limits, the more likely we are to reach critical thresholds of unpredictable and possibly irreversible systems behavior.[44] At certain points in the cumulative process, additional incremental changes and individual actions may acquire great significance. The probability of resultant homeostatic breakdown increases the more human beings overexploit and simplify the ecosphere. Humankind cannot risk the destabilization of major biophysical systems from which there would be no short-term recovery (e.g., large shifts in historic patterns of climate). From the perspective of carrying capacity, persistent negative ecological trends are clear signals that the human population and its economic activities already threaten to disrupt the very processes and relationships that sustain us.

It should be understood that while human society depends on many ecological resources and functions for survival, carrying capacity is ultimately determined by the single vital resource or function in least supply. On the global scale, loss of the protective ozone layer or a substantial increase in the greenhouse effect from accumulating carbon dioxide and other greenhouse gases alone could be catastrophic.[45]

Such considerations call seriously into question the Brundtland Commission's route to sustainable development through a five- to tenfold increase in industrial activity. Indeed, it forces a reevaluation of the entire growth ethic, the central pillar of industrial capitalism.

## CUMULATIVE EFFECTS AND REGIONAL LIMITS[46]

A major force behind the call for sustainable development is concern about the cumulative environmental and social effects of human activity at all spatial scales. Cumulative impacts result from the additive or synergistic effects of numerous actions usually ignored as individually too small to be regulated through such instruments as environmental assessment. Sometimes concern is over cumulative changes in single variables from a variety of similar sources, sometimes over the impacts on numerous variables from unrelated activities. Most of the known global ecological problems facing us today are the end result of myriad individual actions and economic processes.

Society rarely notices gradual changes in environmental parameters until it is too late for effective mitigative action. Often the homeostasis (negative feedback) of ecosystems "absorbs" incremental impacts for long periods without obvious ill effect. This produces a false sense of security when, in fact, we are being led into an ecological trap. The consequent inaction means that we may add a final economic straw that breaks the environmental camel's back. A valuable fishery, a whole ecosystem, or even historic climatic patterns, may suddenly collapse, leaving any dependent population in the lurch.

Any planning for truly sustainable development will require systematic identification and monitoring of progressive negative trends in significant environmental variables. Whether these trends are driven wholly by local activity or are the result of more global factors, the necessary corrective action will often be implemented locally. This suggests that the management of cumulative effects might best be carried out within ecological planning regions identified for this purpose.

### Regional Carrying Capacity—The Idealized Concept

Monitoring these additive effects has no practical utility unless it is in relation to recognized limits of ecological and social impact within the planning or management region. Working within regional carrying capacity does not preclude some environmental damage in the course of development (buildings and roads must occupy some space); nor does it preclude using nature's services (e.g., organic waste processing and recycling) to capacity. The key is to ensure that sufficient stable ecological capital remains in place to support the anticipated dependent population indefinitely at an acceptable standard of living. Trade confuses matters—for example, some of the "dependent population" may live outside the region.

I wish to stress that maintaining sustainable levels of economic activity would require more environmentally rigorous approaches to regional planning than at present. Long-term ecological factors rather than short-term market forces would be the primary determinants of land use and resource management decisions as limits are approached.

Persistent deterioration in key ecological variables could not be tolerated. Each planning region would, therefore, have to develop a comprehensive inventory of lands, water, and associated resources and implement a resource systems monitoring program to ensure the maintenance of essential natural capital stocks. Such comprehensive regional monitoring would become an operational form of cumulative environmental assessment and would provide the means to prevent the region from eroding its biophysical resource base.

The regional approach also provides what has long been recognized as the missing context for project-specific environmental assessments. Knowing regional carrying capacity enables new development proposals to be evaluated, as they should be, in light of preceding development, opportunity costs, and the remaining capacity of biophysical and social systems to cope with stress. Project-specific assessments would in turn provide data for the ongoing cumulative assessment program and an opportunity to test specific hypotheses on environment-development relationships.

### The Problem of Interregional Trade

While the notion of regional carrying capacity is conceptually simple, various factors make it difficult to put into practice. For example, interregional flows and commercial trade in biophysical goods and services presently obscure the immediate people–land relationship. These flows include the movement of air and water in natural cycles throughout the ecosphere and trade in fisheries, forestry, and agricultural products. Because natural products can be imported, the populations of many regions today unknowingly exceed their local carrying capacity with impunity. In the absence of feedback from the land on their lifestyles or economy, there is no direct incentive for such populations to practice sustainable management of local resources. The psychological effect is that people forget their obligatory dependence on the natural environment. Why should the citizens of Region A be concerned about the urbanization of their limited agricultural land when they can always import food from Region B?

The problem is that as one region's population undermines its own environment, it becomes dependent on apparent excess carrying capacity "imported" from other regions over which it has no direct management control. In these circumstances, the populations of exporting regions could not then rise to the level of their own regional carrying capacity without potentially compromising people in dependent importing regions. We should also acknowledge the ecological inequity that arises from inequity in the distribution of the world's wealth. The perceived need for development and foreign exchange drives many impoverished developing countries into borrowing and accepting structural adjustment programs imposed by the World Bank that require them to export nonsurplus carrying capacity in the form of cash crops to wealthy industrialized nations. This jeopardizes production of staples for domestic consumption, thus harming their own people. Such situations are unsustainable.[47]

These points are crucial for policy development when we realize that (a) there is generally no permanent commitment by export regions to dependent regions, and that (b) "management" practices in the export regions (which are under pressure to pay back their loans) may be undermining critical ecosystems. Under a carrying-capacity approach to sustainable development, inhabitants of significant trading regions would enter formal contractual relationships to ensure fair exchange and compliance with required management principles. In effect, trade requires that carrying capacity be based on aggregate biocapacity and total demand.

The necessary negotiations would be oriented to creating a morally and politically acceptable basis of exchange and would serve a valuable educational function. Documenting the nature of interregional dependencies would both increase public awareness of ecological limits and contribute to interregional equity. For example, importers would have to pay a surcharge for reserving and maintaining extraterritorial carrying capacity. At present, the residents of developed countries are not even aware of the impacts their imports of luxury crops have on such factors in the exporting developing countries as local food production, land use and ownership patterns, and ecological conditions.

Although interregional trade reduces the incentive to husband local ecosystems, making it politically more difficult to implement a carrying-capacity approach, trade *per se* is not at fault. If by adopting an ecological-development paradigm, the population of each planning region were to achieve intraregional ecostability (i.e., no progressive environmental degradation) regardless of its trade balance, the aggregate effect would be a sustainable level of development within global carrying capacity. (To achieve this ideal would require a reasonable degree of interregional equity and assumes that global carrying capacity has not already been breached.)

## SUSTAINABILITY IN THE REAL WORLD: LIVING ON THE INTEREST

This analysis of the pathological relationship between environment and economy and the implications of carrying capacity for future development represents a serious challenge to the central assumptions of our economy and our way of life. In essence, compatible economy-environment integration requires that we recognize ecological limits to material growth and the need to live on the interest of our remaining ecological capital. Consistent with the overall argument, I propose the following principles as a practical guide to sustainable global development:

- The economy is an integral dependent subsystem of the ecosphere. The future of society, therefore, rests on our ability to restore and maintain the self-producing structure and functional relationships of the ecosphere (autopoiesis).

- The maximum sustainable level of global economic activity is limited by the health and productivity of the ecosphere. Exceeding current limits will reduce future productive potential in proportion to the depreciation of natural capital (i.e., the loss of species diversity and total biomass).

- We must move from a society oriented to satisfying the artificial wants of a few to one committed to satisfying the basic needs of all. Our present economic system encourages continuous material growth (consumption). By contrast, sustainable development requires that we limit resource exploitation and minimize entropic decay.

- Harvest rates in the renewable resource sectors must be held to average rates of production and not be responsive to ever-increasing market demand. Bottom-line economics often encourages the liquidation of ecological capital stock (fish, forests, soil, etc.).[48] By contrast, sustainable development requires that society live on the "interest" of our ecological endowment. This is not an option but an absolute necessity for a sustainable future.

- Rates of waste discharge (including pesticide use) must be limited to the rate at which ecosystems can absorb and denature the wastes. Significant processing capacity generally exists only for ecologically benign organic waste and nutrients.

- In the case of radioactive substances, carcinogens, and similar dangerous compounds, zero tolerance is warranted.

- Society at large will have to pay the true costs of goods "production." In general, market prices should reflect producers' costs for maintenance of ecosystems (e.g., forest restocking, soils management). In some cases, an entropy tax should be imposed to provide public funds for common property systems maintenance. (An entropy tax on fossil fuels could be used to plant carbon sink forests to help stabilize atmospheric CO levels.)[49] Where serious damage has already been done, society may have to devote substantial resources to rehabilitation of ecosystems. All this implies significant increases in operating costs and market prices.

- As society makes the above adjustments, special measures must be put in place to ensure that the burden does not fall unfairly on working people and the poor. The basic necessities for a decent life must be affordable to all.

- We must recognize that historic levels of profits may not be compatible with sustainable development. For example, resources corporations should be required to demonstrate adequate maintenance of the resource base (including investment in alternative forms of productive capital in the case of depletable resources) before declaring a dividend.

- Global population control must become an international priority. The maximum sustainable human population (global carrying capacity) is a function of the nature of economic activity, technological sophistication, and mean per capita consumption (material standard of living). All these factors are subject to public policy adjustment. Any population growth beyond current carrying capacity can be justified only by improving technology or must be accompanied by a proportional decline in standard of living.

- New systems of national economic-ecological accounts must be adopted to monitor the ecosphere. Remarkably, macroeconomic indicators such as GNP only monitor consumption and income flows, not the state of productive capital. Thus, "glowing economic reports . . . are possible when the policies that generate them are destroying the resource base."[50]

- The new indicators might include Adjusted National Product (ANP), consisting of GNP with natural capital depreciation and defensive "social and environmental costs deducted from it, rather than added to it."[51] Other accounts should monitor the state of key autopoietic processes such as pollution absorption, nutrient cycling, soils maintenance, radiation balance, atmospheric regulation, and primary production (photosynthesis).

- In the absence of such accounts, interregional trade obscures people's sense of a region's dependence on the ecosphere. Importing biophysical goods and services means importing carrying capacity from elsewhere and encourages people to destroy their own local ecosystems through "development" at no apparent cost to themselves. Many regions and nations with excellent economic accounts (e.g., the Netherlands) would be unviable as isolated ecological units.

- Trade also has important implications for equity in achieving global sustainable development. For example, when wealthy nations import carrying capacity from poor regions it may be at great unaccounted cost to the latter. This is the case when the global financial system compels developing nations to grow cash crops for export on their best lands at the expense of local staples production. This leads, in turn, to overexploitation of marginal agricultural and forest lands as impoverished local people struggle to survive. Revised interregional economic-ecological accounting would help to internalize these real cost factors into the terms of trade.

- Sustainable development requires defining development regions for ecological accounting purposes and monitoring cumulative impacts against carrying capacity. In current practice "taking environmental factors into account" usually means that long-term ecological productivity is "traded off" for short-term economic gain. Thus, while individual developments are approved on economic grounds the cumulative ecological impacts will eventually exceed regional and global carrying capacity.

- Seemingly underdeveloped ecological assets in one region may actually be performing vital functions that are already being fully utilized by people elsewhere. This is most evident when there are markets for specific products but is less obvious in the case of unaccounted vital services. Tropical rain forests are of concern to people everywhere for their role in maintaining a viable atmosphere, the global energy budget and a stable climate.

- When the carrying capacity of a given management region has been reached, ecological factors must necessarily override economic considerations. The next project cannot be built. If each nation or management region achieves regional ecological stability, the net effect would be global stability. Conversely, if most regions exceed their domestic carrying capacities, global destruction is assured.

- Well-documented ecological trends such as atmospheric change, ozone depletion, deforestation, and falling per capita food production indicate that we have already breached global carrying capacity. Thus, even current levels of economic activity are not sustainable with present technology. People in the industrialized countries may well have to lower their material expectations and even accept a decline in present material standards to achieve global sustainability.

- Economic growth should no longer be considered a basic element of social policy. Considerations of social justice and equity may, therefore, require creative new policies for income redistribution. We may even have to move beyond paid employment as the means of access to the basic requirements of life to some other system of entitlement.

- Sustainable development may force significant restructuring of national economies in the developed nations (for example, in the petroleum, auto-motive, and forestry sectors). This may require new forms of social safety nets to catch and retrain workers displaced from ecologically unsustainable employment. At the same time, new jobs will be created in developing and producing the energy and materially efficient products and technologies of the future.

- Sustainable development reintroduces equity and moral considerations into global economic development. The wealthiest 26 percent of the world's population consumes 80 to 86 percent of nonrenewable resources and 34 to 50 percent of food supplies.[52] In a finite world, reducing the gap in living standards between the rich and the poor requires that any capacity for future material economic growth be redirected to the third world. Forgiving inter-national debt, aid to rehabilitate tropical ecosystems, the programs to develop ecologically appropriate technology for the developing countries are examples of strategies the developed nations might implement to help redistribute global wealth.

- Sustainable development represents an opportunity to shift the emphasis from quantitative to qualitative considerations. We might rediscover that development has more to do with community relationship, self-reliance, and personal growth (qualitative improvements) than it does with increased eco-nomic capacity (quantitative growth).

- Socially sensitive interpretations of sustainable development emphasize the opportunity for a return to community values, local control over resources, community-based development, and other forms of decentralized gover-nance. This, too, confronts the current trends toward concentrated economic power and centralized political decision making.

- Global sustainable development demands new forms of international coop-eration and regulation to ensure acceptable standards for ecological stabil-ity. This is contrary to the current emphasis on competition, exploitation of comparative advantage, and deregulation as means to stimulate world eco-nomic growth.

- Sustainable development presents an opportunity to eliminate the arms race and free up the resources required for planetary rehabilitation. By the mid-1980s, armaments already consumed a trillion dollars annually or "more than the total income of the poorest half of humanity."[53] Increasing numbers of nations will come to realize that national security lies more in rehabili-tating ecological capital than in retaining military might.[54]

## CONCLUSION:
## A DIFFICULT PATH TO AN IMPROVED ECOSPHERE

Most social and political discussion of sustainable development today emphasizes the need to foster economic growth. It assumes that we can take care of the environment just through proper pricing, greater efficiency of resource use, improved technology, better pollution control, and wider use of environmental assessment. Such an incremental approach would hardly affect the growth-bound status quo and would require a minimum of adjustment by either industry or individuals.

This study offers a dramatically different picture illuminated by thermodynamic principles and the concept of ecological carrying capacity. In light of this evidence, we may be fast approaching absolute limits to material economic growth. We no longer have the luxury of "trading off" ecological damage for economic benefits if we are to achieve a sustainable ecosphere. The maintenance of global ecological integrity must become our highest priority and must be factored into every local and regional development decision.

While our conceptual framework merely stresses the obvious—a dependent part cannot grow indefinitely within a limited whole—the acceptance of this fact demands a profound shift in societal values and attitudes and a major restructuring of national and global economies. However, the requisite changes in worldview and policies have the potential of creating a more politically secure, ecologically stable, and economically just global society.

## REFLECTIONS ON THE ORIGINAL ARTICLE

My views on sustainability and the human prospect have changed little since "Sustainable Development and the Biosphere" first appeared. Certainly the world seems little reformed—if anything, the growth model of sustainable development seems more firmly entrenched in mainstream thinking than ever, despite the persistence and increasingly sophisticated counteranalyses of environmentally and socially motivated nongovernment organizations (NGOs). Meanwhile, the degradation of ecosystems and the loss of biodiversity keep dismal pace with every increase of the human "ecological footprint" on the known world. Meanwhile, governments are busily staking their claims to the ocean floor in the continuing scramble for more energy and mineral riches to exploit.

Why do people seem so immune to data and analyses showing that they are literally consuming and dissipating the only planetary home they are ever likely to know? This is the question that guides my current research. I have recently argued, on evolutionary and historic grounds, that *H. sapiens* may well be inherently unsustainable. As Joseph Tainter pointed out, "What is perhaps most intriguing in the evolution of human societies is the regularity with which the pattern of increasing complexity is interrupted by collapse. . . ."[55] Consistent with this pattern, I argue the case that unsustainability is an inevitable "emergent property" of the interaction of techno-industrial society and the ecosphere.[56]

Ironically, the root cause of the problem is the unique combination of physiological, genetic, and cultural properties that have made humans so formidably successful in the Darwinian struggle for existence. In essence, *H. sapiens* is a large, demanding, competitive, and highly adaptable mammal with a natural genetic predisposition to expand into all available ecological space. Moreover, because we possess language and cultural memory (cumulative technology), we get progressively better at exploiting our expanding habitat. Humans are also endowed with a universal penchant for cultural myth making, a tendency that has served us well in the course of our evolution. Cultural myths explain the mysteries of the universe, even to "primitive" people, thus reducing fear and bolstering personal security; they also provide shared stories that reinforce social cohesion and confer a sense of tribal identity. At various times or for certain peoples, spiritual or religious myths may even have served to inhibit ecologically destructive individual or social activities.

Today's dominant cultural myth—the "shared story" that is giving shape and direction to societies all over the world—is the myth of infinite wealth acquired through economic globalization fueled by open markets and expanding trade. This grand illusion obviously reflects and reinforces the tendency of human societies to grow to the limits of local/regional carrying capacity. As has happened repeatedly in the past, human society is presently breaching the biophysical limits to growth, but this time on a *global* scale. As a result, the very qualities that once assured humanity's remarkable evolutionary success are now threatening to do us in.

All is not dark. Humans are uniquely self-conscious and self-aware. In theory, therefore, we should be able to override any biocultural predispositions that have become dysfunctional and threaten the species at large. The first step, of course, is to raise these predispositions to consciousness and to acknowledge that they are at least partially "at cause" of our sustainability conundrum. More difficult still is the need to reach agreement on what is to be done. It seems that humanity must rise to the challenge of creating an international legal and institutional framework that will inhibit the self-interested behavior of our multiple tribes and enforce sustainable economic behavior in the interests of the common good. (Garrett Hardin was right: to control the rogue in us humans will require what he succinctly called "mutual coercion mutually agreed upon.")

Needless to say, this agenda would require an unprecedented degree of international agreement, political will, and spiritual unity—and for these very reasons it may be impossible to achieve in the real world. History does not seem to be on our side, and the human species is obviously slipping badly back into militant tribalism as war clouds gather in the post–9/11 world. As I write these words, the fate of the United Nations, our flawed but last best hope for united action, is at stake as an increasingly fractious world community debates the (de)merits of war on Iraq.

Whatever happens in the Middle East, sustainability demands that humanity ultimately succeed in overriding primitive behavioral tendencies that can lead only to geopolitical chaos and ecological collapse. We must develop a new global cultural myth that celebrates both the diversity of humanity and the diversity of other life, one that is based on a fairer sharing of the world's limited ecological and economic abundance.

Ironically, compassion for "the other" may now be prerequisite for the continuance of civilized society on our finite planet. Cynics may prefer to think of this simply as enlightened self-interest, but whatever we call it, we need a new kind of social glue to bind the world's peoples together in the common purpose of protecting the Earth from ourselves. Success in this endeavor would mark the ascendance of cultural evolution over mere biology and would herald the most significant advance in human evolution since the invention of language.

On the other hand . . . Well, the other hand is simply too depressing to contemplate.

# PART THREE

# COSMOGENESIS

Teilhard's vision of evolution stands in contrast to the dominant secular, materialist paradigm. In the latter view, humans are seen as an unintended addendum to the universe. For Teilhard, human beings are the central, forward-edge phenomenon of a cosmogenesis and the bearers of creative consciousness. The three studies in this part consider how his thought can reveal the unity of evolution and especially its convergence with and confirmation by the new sciences of complex systems.

In the early 1980s Brian Swimme joined the insights of Thomas Berry and Teilhard into an evolutionary narrative of great import for both persons and the planet. A mathematical cosmologist and noted author, Swimme employs his capacity for a vivid turn of phrase in a chapter entitled "The New Natural Selection" to describe and evoke an unfolding universe in transition to a viable Earth community.

Decades after Teilhard's death, in a major scientific revolution, his intuition of a spontaneous, sequential rise of complexity and consciousness is being verified by new discoveries of an inherently self-organizing universe. These new sciences and their affinity with Teilhard are the subject of the study by Kathleen Duffy, professor of physics at Chestnut Hill College. Her essay, "The Texture of the Evolutionary Cosmos: Matter and Spirit in Teilhard de Chardin," provides a comprehensive introduction to these new sciences within the metaphorical context of an organically woven cosmic tapestry.

This theme continues in Arthur Fabel's millennium retrospective "Teilhard 2000: The Vision of a Cosmic Genesis at the Millennium." An engineer, writer, and editor of *Teilhard Studies* for ten years, Fabel describes a dynamically creative system present everywhere, which is becoming understood through the new complexity sciences. As a result, a new emergent cosmos with a central axis of life's intricacy, sentience, selfhood, and community shows how the latest findings are validating Teilhard's prescient vision.

# 9

# The New Natural Selection

## Brian Swimme

We are living out a myth that has many similarities with that of Oedipus. We can see that we live in a sickened state of life. The realm deepens in its pathology each day, and yet we do not quite know what to do. We thrash about, but it seems only to make matters worse. Needless suffering is on the increase; worse scenarios threaten beyond the horizon; and we ourselves agonize in the central role of the drama. It is not one thing that is wrong; it is everything. It is not a single situation that depresses us; it is the wide choice of disasters, cruelties, and toxins. We stagger into the future tragically aware of our responsibility in all this as Americans, as Westerners, even as humans, but we remain callous and arrogant concerning what we might do to bring health to the whole Earth community.

Our central shortcoming is precisely our failure to evolve into our larger role as earthlings. We have performed so mightily in our role as Americans; we have succeeded in our role as scientific Westerners. Even as humans in the role of subduing, conquering, and controlling the environment we have accomplished wonders. But we have failed as yet to evolve further into our role as human earthlings, and this lies behind our present pathological impasse. Our deep-seated arrogance toward the nonhuman components of the Earth community has crippled evolutionary advance. The nuclear impasse stems from our delusion that territorial and ideological disputes qualify as issues for which the four-billion-year process of life can be sacrificed. The commercial-industrial impasse results from our delusion that consumer demands are reason enough to ruin any habitat, any community of life, even the very conditions from which life emerges and evolves on this planet. The sickness of the present situation will continue to escalate with ever more cruelty and suffering until we learn the fuller dimensions of our role within evolution's unfoldment. Oedipus could not move toward health until he discovered that he had unknowingly been violating his mother. We are only now realizing that we have been violating Mother Earth for some time. The task of furthering evolution is the task of becoming full earthlings. It is, as Thomas Berry has suggested, the challenge of living within a new story, a story of cosmic and planetary dimensions.[1]

---

First published in *Teilhard Studies* no. 10 (fall 1983).

We must concern ourselves, then, with discovering this macrophase role of the human. We must learn to conceive of ourselves and our genetic powers within the total life process of this planet. Previous conceptions of the human have failed to reach this larger planetary dimension. Former conceptions might well have been adequate for certain earlier historical periods, each with its own specific needs, but those situations have now disappeared. Even the ancient threat of survival in the midst of a violent natural world no longer obtains. We must ask the basic questions all over again. What is the nature of the human and its powers of mind? What is the purpose and place of this creature in the larger dynamics of evolutionary unfolding within the integral Earth process?

I am proposing that the present evolutionary impasse will be broken only when humans go beyond their arrogance toward the nonhuman components of the Earth and further activate their own deeper planetary dimensions of being. When we learn to live as evolutionary unfoldment brought into the conscious mode, the genuine ripening of the Earth will occur. In particular, I would like to discuss what it might mean to bring the dynamics of natural selection into a conscious mode of being. What it might mean for the dynamics that have been operative in the Earth process for billions of years to advance suddenly into the modality of consciousness through the human component of the planet.

## NATURAL SELECTION

Natural selection principles are dynamics that whole systems of life exhibit, whether we are considering a forest, a seashore community, or a major bioregion. Natural selection is a holistic concept pointing to the dynamics of interaction among the beings of the community. An organism that finds itself in the midst of an ecological community must learn to mesh with the existing order of relationships so that it may live and continue its genetic line within this context of life. If the new organism cannot fit into the existing order it either leaves or dies. As Gregory Bateson has emphasized, it is a question of fitness.[2] The survival of the fittest refers to those organisms that can fit into the existing coherence of the interacting systems of life within the community. Fitness cannot be reduced to strength alone. Strength is but one aspect of the many involved when an organism confronts a community. Natural selection is the holistic phenomenon that amounts to a test for each new organism or species, and determines if it is able to fit into the existing patterns of life within the community.

It is when we move beyond the biological realm and attempt to include cultural activities in our discussion of natural selection principles that our difficulties begin. What can the principles of natural selection say concerning art, politics, mathematics, music, technology, law? Our cultural disposition is to regard each of these activities as largely disconnected from the dynamics of the natural world. And of all our cultural activities, mathematics resists inclusion in the natural world more so than any other. Our 2,500 years of Western intellectual philosophical development has assumed in large part that the human mind is ontologically distinct from the natural world. This claim has been championed especially on the basis of our abstract system of mathematics. We have assumed for millennia that mathematical truths have a certainty that places them outside time, in a transcendent and eternal realm.

To see the place of mathematical activity within evolutionary dynamics, we begin by identifying the principles of natural selection with the proof procedures of logic. Just as natural selection tests a new organism before allowing it to enter the community of life, so do the proof procedures test new mathematical propositions before allowing them to enter the body of mathematical knowledge. If through logic the proposition can be shown to be true, the proposition is allowed into mathematical knowledge. If the logical procedures can show that the proposition is false, it is rejected from the body of mathematical knowledge. Logic decides which novel mathematical ideas shall be accepted and which shall be rejected in a manner similar to the way natural selection principles decide which novel organisms shall be accepted into the community of life and which shall be rejected. The logical procedures represent a form of natural selection brought into the conscious phase.

Throughout the centuries of Western intellectual development, at least as far back as Plato, the proof procedures of mathematics have been regarded as transcendent. They were altogether separate from the conditions characterizing the natural world. Mathematical knowledge then was certain, eternal, transcendent. The proof procedure provided a method of making absolutely sure that mathematical knowledge was of this eternal and certain quality. We saw ourselves as arriving at ideas and knowledge that were separated by a chasm from the activities and generation and transience of the natural world and this primary assumption about the human mind deepened our Western alienation from the natural world.

But twentieth-century mathematics has discovered that the proof procedures of mathematics are developmental. The most abstract creations of the human mind can now be understood as sharing in fundamental dynamics of the evolutionary unfoldment. An ancient tradition in the West has been called into question in our century, for now an understanding of mathematics has come to mean an understanding of its development. This interpretation is possible only through the work done in the foundations of mathematics that culminated in the stirring results of Kurt Goedel. The notion of a transcendent logic that can be employed for arriving at eternal, certain truths outside of time has been shown to be false. Our ancient assumption that human knowledge is ontologically distinct from the developing universe has been undermined, and in this development within our most theoretical enterprise, we can find hope that the alienation that has split the human from the nonhuman for so many centuries is finally ending.

An evolutionary understanding of mathematical logic begins with the observation that the bodies of mathematical knowledge exist first. Arithmetic and geometry and their truths emerge in human experience before any attempts are made to articulate a logic. Logic is understood simply as a later explication of a fundamental coherence tying any body of mathematical knowledge into a fundamental unity. Humans examining the knowledge extract those forms of interconnectivity that hold the body together. That coherence does characterize any established body of knowledge can be recognized by inspection. The articulation of the patterns of coherence and interconnectivity is logic. And since each age develops and extends the knowledge it has received from its ancestors, the logic develops as well. Logic, understood in this manner, is a characteristic of the body of knowledge in a particular historical period; it is the pattern of coherency of the whole. To say that we have proven a mathematical result through logic is to say that the new mathematical proposition can be shown to fit into the patterns of coherency of the existing body of knowledge. To say that a mathematical proposition has been shown through logic to be false is to say that it violates the coherence of the knowledge. Thus logic is a holistic phenomenon of a system that tests for fitness novel mathematical ideas, just as natural selection is a holistic phenomenon that tests for the fitness of novel organisms or species. And further, logic develops as the body of mathematics develops, just as the selection principles with the natural world develop as the ecosystem evolves.

For our purposes, the most important analogy between mathematical logic and natural selection is the concern of each for the vitality of the whole. Established mathematical knowledge is a precious and highly complex reality. Proof procedures through logic are created to protect this vitality from the crippling that would ensue should fundamental contradictions be allowed into the body of mathematics and entangle themselves so deeply in the organism that their final extirpation would be nearly impossible. Just so, the principles of selection in the natural world ensure that the most vital, most interesting, most capable organisms, those that are able to fill out all the various niches available in an ecosystem, will be the ones contributing to the future of the species of the whole community. An ecosystem is as fragile as foam on a seawave; and should genetic mediocrity be allowed to dominate the future generations of the community, the whole system risks collapse with a much greater probability. Both logic and natural selection work to promote the vigor and vitality of the whole systems in which they operate.

By analogy, we can see how the selection dynamics of evolution operate within all the cultural activities. The literary critic serves as an agent of selection dynamics in literature and the arts generally. The body of classical works is protected from the enervation that would follow should simply all cultural novelties whatsoever be included. Through a test with the works of excellence, both the diversity of achievement and the intensity of activity are evoked, and through this the vitality of the enterprise is protected and enhanced. But perhaps it is in law that the clearest example of the conscious phase of selection dynamics can be seen. The work of lawyers and courts is fundamentally the work of testing particular patterns of behavior against the established patterns of the acceptable norm. Those patterns that do not fit the accepted coherence of the norm are known to be debilitating and are to be extirpated for the sake of the vitality of the whole society. In all this we see how humans have been operating within patterns that are extensions of the dynamics of evolution's unfolding.

## QUALITATIVE ADVANCE

Within any stable biological or cultural regime, the dynamic interaction between novel creations and selection principles proceeds with a smooth overall growth in complexity and vitality. But moments occur when the regime breaks down. The stability of the system is ruined. It is, as Erich Jantsch calls it, an introduction of a disequilibrium that throws the previously functioning stable regime toward chaos.[3] In such a situation the principles of natural selection cannot maintain the previous system's stability, for the novel organism or the novel conception is so powerful or alien that it overrides all the tests for fitness that are put to it. The system enters a time of breakdown and chaos as this new organism unfolds its novel powers and enters the community.

In the biological perspective, the most important example presently of a disequilibrium that disrupted a previous harmonious community is the arrival of *Homo sapiens* into the Earth community. Considered from the four billion years of life's development, the scientific-technological human has been on the Earth one instant, and yet in that instant everything has changed on the planet. From a negligible creature that had to make its way into the existing patterns of feeding, mating, eating, preying, hiding, and nurturing that were established within the community of beings, the human has erupted during the last two centuries into the dominant organism of the planet. Rather than having to adjust and fit into the patterns of interaction of the rest of the Earth community, the human has come to dominate the Earth process involving every other life system. Indeed, changes now wrought by the scientific-technological phase of *Homo sapiens* accomplish —or destroy— in a week what required millions of years of fashioning with the prehuman Earth community.

Thus we lay down hundreds of thousands of miles of asphalt; we let loose millions upon millions of steel machines that crisscross the land and crowd the skies; we infiltrate the atmosphere with chemical creations never experienced before in the Earth community; and we spew millions of tons of materials noxious to all forms of life through our waterways and our soil communities. Suddenly, this negligible creature is creating the total environment into which all other life systems must either fit or perish. Once we were frightened creatures attempting to learn the patterns of the Earth community so that we might fit in and survive. Now we are the dominant fact in this world. Every other species must approach us with even more fright and terror than that with which we first approached them. Our cultural novelties overwhelm the entire system of natural selection devised to protect the health of evolution's development.

Fundamental to any qualitative emergence within a biological or cultural system is the total breakdown of the existing principles of natural selection. Even in the 1700s the principles of the Earth community that had been developing over the previous millions of years functioned throughout the major portions of the Earth. The 700 million humans who had lived up until that time had certainly created some deleterious situations, for example, in the forest destructions of Europe and China; in the disastrous agricultural regimes in the Middle East and elsewhere; in the aggregation of stone and dead wood in the urban centers. But the presence of the human was the presence of one rather strange organism among others. And the interactions between the human and the natural world were not substantially different from what they had been for the previous eight thousand years, and not enormously different from what they had been for the previous two million years.

But with the emergence of the power of scientific-technological knowledge and development, the fundamental principles of natural selection failed to assure the vitality and health of the whole Earth community. The Earth's organism could not effectively interact with bulldozers. The Earth's community cannot select against agricultural machines and chemicals that, for instance, destroy four billion tons of topsoil on the North American continent each year. It took thousands of years to fashion the topsoil, and it disappears forever in a season. The principles of selection are impotent in the face of the noxious chemicals rained upon the land. A glut of oil invades a seashore community and a billion interactions and selections and novel emergences vanish. Ancient achievements are nothing when confronted with our machines designed to gut a forest. We have broken the very principles of natural selection constructed to safeguard the vitality of the planet's life.

I would like to compare this biological scenario with a situation from the history of mathematics. The introduction of calculus in the seventeenth century was a disequilibrium event that has no rival in the history of mathematics. Through the creations of Isaac Newton, Gottfried Leibniz, and Pierre Fermat, mathematics as a whole was profoundly transformed over the course of two centuries. Indeed, all of science was transformed. And yet, from the beginning, these novel mathematical ideas could not *be proven.* This strange fact did not go unnoticed at the time. Bishop Berkeley, for one, made a career of ridiculing the attempts of both Newton and Leibniz to prove their calculus. A strange situation—tremendous new mathematical ideas and yet no one could prove they were actually mathematical knowledge. We see here a novelty that overwhelmed the principle of selection that was supposed to test these novelties. No one could prove these mathematical assertions and no one could answer Berkeley's criticisms.

As these new ideas of calculus entered Europe, a creative blossoming of science and mathematics followed. No branch of the sciences remained the same. Humans had gotten hold of something new, strange, powerful, and fertile, and for the rest of the century and throughout the eighteenth as well they extended and deepened these new ideas. It is doubtful if there has ever been a more significant period of mathematical activity in the history of scientific thought. European science was buzzing with these transformed modes of thought, which soon permeated areas of culture much removed from the strictly scientific. And though many mathematicians continued to try to prove these results within the logic then available, they repeatedly failed. The principles of natural selection that had served for so long were suddenly unable to test effectively against these novel conceptions following on the calculus.

This rapid creative outburst of mathematical development did not come without a price. From the beginning, discrepancies had appeared within the great new body of work. Contradictions and ambiguities could be found in many areas of development. Most disheartening were the situations when the greatest minds of the eighteenth century produced proofs for opposite results. Were these indications of deep structural contradictions in the calculus and its development? Sensitive minds began demanding a process that would enable mathematicians to decide what was to be accepted and what was to be rejected. It was a demand that the vitality of the whole enterprise of modern mathematics be protected. It was, in essence, a demand for a new set of selection principles that could be used to test the many extravagant creations, the many bizarre novelties.

Beginning in the early nineteenth century with the work of Augustin-Louis Cauchy and proceeding throughout the century in the work of people such as Karl Weierstrauss, the principles of selection to be used in the great body of mathematical analysis were constructed. These logical principles were extracted from the existing body of mathematical knowledge and represented the fundamental patterns of intelligibility of the whole achievement. After all, calculus and its developments had already been in existence for over a century. That was adequate time for humans to observe the form and structure of these new conceptions. It had grown organically into its own special interconnected shapes, and the fundamental and essential structure could be extracted and codified in the processes of the limit of uniform convergence, in the definitions of the integral and the derivative and the continuous function. The health and vitality of the mathematical enterprise as a whole were the aims of this endeavor, and the mathematicians proceeded with vigor to construct these principles of natural selection. They wanted to be able to recognize and pluck out the powerful and vital ideas while rejecting the sickly and unimportant. Their success in establishing these principles endowed nineteenth-century mathematics with unparalleled depth, nuance, confidence, and imaginative freedom. The mathematical sciences had never been so vibrant; their overall health never so apparent.

## THE TASK OF THE EARTH COMMUNITY

If we return now to the consideration of the planet and the violent disequilibrium caused by industrialization, we can see that the basic task before the Earth community today is the creation of a new set of natural selection principles out of the ruined conditions we find ourselves in. The emergence of this powerful and talented species has overwhelmed the Earth and has destroyed those very principles the Earth community created for its vitality through millions of previous years of evolution. But just as the emergence of calculus led to a wild proliferation of mathematical ideas and then to the recognition that the mathematicians must create a new set of selection principles, so too do we awaken to our fundamental task within the impasse of our situation. The Earth community has been watching the human being over these last two centuries and has been able to determine the kinds of powers and extravagances and constructions that are possible for this new member of the family of life. It is now time to create norms to promote life's flourishing for the whole Earth community so that the vitality and the continuing evolutionary unfolding of the entire planet will be protected.

The creation of these selection principles depends on one central act. The human must activate its cosmic and planetary dimensions of life. Previous to our era, humans considered themselves to be beings within the small context of the tribe, or within time boundaries of a religious or cultural group, or as members of a scientific-technological nation-state. A few even regarded themselves as members of what was considered the ultimate universal context, members of the human species. All of these self-definitions are true, but a further dimension has emerged during these last two centuries. The full context of the human must include the cosmic and planetary dimension of life and being. Humans are, as Teilhard celebrated, the conscious mode of co-evolution.

In the past we created principles of natural selection—in our law codes, for instance—that reflected the boundaries of our limited self-conceptions. We understood justice in terms of those principles that protected human from human. We protected the state and the religious institution. We protected our businesses with our selection principles. In all of these contexts we have established codes and norms that test patterns of behavior as well as conceptions that might weaken the whole person, the whole state, the whole corporation. But our task at the present time is much vaster. We are called to create selection principles that will enable the evolutionary processes of unfoldment to deepen throughout the Earth process. Presently we are called upon to evoke those macrophase dimensions of the human person that will allow the dynamics of evolutionary process to blossom into its conscious mode within the Earth community. That is the task of the human community today: we are called upon to represent the whole planet as its conscious mode of life and being.

Oedipus too needed to bring a larger awareness into his realm. So long as he continued to live within his limited framework, he only worsened the sickness of his world. Our situation over the whole planet is the same today. So long as the evolutionary process exists in its present crippled state, the pathology and the fundamentally rancid nature of the whole planet will continue. Only when the deeper dynamics of evolution break through and assume their destined role in a conscious mode will we move through this impasse and into the more harmonious beauty possible within our planetary system of living and nonliving beings.

## GUIDELINES FOR ARTICULATION
## OF A MACROPHASE FLOURISHING OF LIFE

Principles of natural selection exist in any ecologically interconnected community of beings. These principles are profoundly embedded in the functioning systems of this planet. We speak only from an examination of the history of this Earth when we speak of the natural and spontaneous emergence of ordered and harmonious wholes throughout life's development. The coherence of the living world is taken as a fact, just as the coherence of established bodies of knowledge is taken as a fact. It is not something that is proved. But it is most definitely something that can be observed throughout billions of developments in the history of the planet.

To attempt to discover those principles of natural selection against which we must test all future technological, commercial, industrial, political, and economic decisions and inventions we turn not to a priori assumptions about the nature of life, but rather to the whole display of life's dynamic development. It is through its history that we encounter the actuality of life's emergence into our world. In the last two centuries of scientific-technological development we have come to understand the nature of life and the development of life in ways that are stupendous to contemplate. From this great body of knowledge we extract those central dynamics. The process of evolution teaches us how we must proceed to bring the inner dynamics of unfoldment into a greater conscious expression for the vitality, vigor, and splendor of this planet and all its systems of life and being.

I have indicated that our selection principles of the past are inadequate for the task before us at this time. Thus, though some principles were used to test commercial and technological processes, these were microphase concerns focusing on the individual person, or the individual business, or the state. Beyond those tests, there was the simple and dominant test of profits. In the main, if a device or a process or a program or policy would eventuate in greater profits, it would find its way into the planetary system. Our failure to develop the planetary dimensions of the human person is clearly indicated in our insensitive complacency before such obviously inadequate selection principles for the vitality of the Earth. The evolutionary development of our integral community demands more comprehensive criteria for its living and nonliving components than that of profits.

I present, then, three principles that characterize the dynamics of the life process on this planet. It is upon these that we will create our macrophase principles of natural selection.

### Depth of Being

Scientific investigation has revealed that every individual organism, every mineral, every ecological community possesses within itself a significant story in relation to the whole emergence of life on Earth. Each existent being or community of beings can be considered a voice that speaks from thirteen billion years of cosmic development. We are only just now understanding how to listen to the voice that speaks in these systems of life and being. Only in the last few decades have we been able to listen to the story of the universe's origin that is contained in the radiant energy that bathes the Earth. Each wave of these photons brings even more information from the earliest moments of the universe. Then, too, it is only in the last few years that we have been able to listen to the story contained in the continents of their journey through the transformations of the Earth. And only now are we able to hear the story of the prokaryotes and their symbiotic fashioning to create the eukaryotic cells some one and a half billion years ago. Only in the last few years have we realized that all the nuclei even of our own skin must be considered fossils from the ancient origins of the symmetry breaks in the heart of the primordial fireball. In these and many other examples we are beginning to appreciate the way in which every existent being is the whole universe's story told from a particular viewpoint and history. We must, therefore, hope that future humans recognize and respect this great truth, this great mystery of history's presence within each being. A voice that is lost means knowledge and information lost for all time, a story that will never be recaptured. We must move into the future with a deep reverence for all beings and the story that each is able to tell.

Now that we have come to understand that the remaining primal peoples of the Earth must be cherished as a precious source for the story and wisdom they have to speak into the world, we must extend this stance to include all the living and nonliving systems of being. We must insist on this reverential stance toward every species of plants and animals, every major geological formation. The Himalayas and the Philippines and Southern California are permeated with the history of this planet's journey; should they be demolished or blacktopped a billionfold voice of our past and its meaning and wonder are silenced forever. We must understand that every living being, every community, every underwater formation rests quietly with a great realm of intelligent history folded into its being. If we are yet unable to read these stories, we must not deny the possibility that a future generation might learn to listen and learn from them.

### Creative Power

The one stubborn fact of our cosmic creative unfolding is the dependence of each being's emergence on the totality of evolution's previous achievement. Only because the stars created the chemicals that form our bodies and the bodies of every form of life could the Earth emerge with all its splendor. Only because prokaryotes created the oxygen of the early Earth system could the higher animals emerge. Only because the microorganism created the basic set of genes could their later complex combinations allow the higher animals and eventually consciousness to emerge into the planetary system. We are certain of one thing surely: the future unfolding of evolutionary development depends on precisely those beings—and their inherent creative powers—that presently inhabit the Earth system.

If we remove any species from the Earth system, we are in that act forever limiting the possibilities of the future. Remove all the species and there is no future. Remove a significant portion of them and the future possibilities are profoundly diminished. Our ignorance of the dynamics of this mystery is overwhelming. We do not know in either a general or a specific sense anything about the interactions and processes that will enable the future to unfold. All we know for certain is that all future possibilities, all unrevealed beauty, are presently contained in just those beings that exist in Earth's system. No species and no individual can be considered redundant or unnecessary for the ongoing unfolding. We live in a vast multiform event that has required all thirteen billion years of the universe's creativity. We must begin now with a profound reverence for the inherent power of self-emergence that each being possesses. It is precisely out of, because of, and through these powers of creativity that all future destinies of the Earth will be fashioned. We are evolutionary dynamics brought into its conscious phase when we act with an awareness that these creative powers need to be evoked, defended, and nurtured with the fear and trembling that reflect our awareness of the future on our present actions.

### Intimacy of Community

Though untold millions of species have vanished from the Earth system, the present community is more complex and diversified and intimately involved as a single community than any previous Earth. The overall effect of this stupendous story of life's emergence in this Earth system is a story of a continued growth in the great complexity and diversity and community of being. The vitality of this complex whole must take precedence over all else. Though our human processes might involve destruction, it must be a destruction that promises to nurture those conditions enabling an even more diversified emergence of life. All aims and all policies and all values must begin with this affirmation of the total community of beings on this planet. The integral community—complex, splendid, vastly differentiated—is the principal accomplishment of the long history of the Earth process. Our principles of natural selection must work to enhance this fundamental achievement, to aid in the development of an even richer and more intimately interrelated Earth community.

We, like Oedipus, must admit that we are blind, even though we think we have eyes. We have attempted to see this planet through the eyes of the industrial exploitation of both capitalism and socialism, but that was not seeing at all. The eyes we must use to see the Earth are provided by centuries of work in mathematics, physics, chemistry, biology, astronomy, paleontology, and anthropology. From that perspective our present economics are seen to be ignorant of the context of life on our planet. The medieval doctors in their ignorance thought they could bleed their patients to health. The industrial nation-states in their ignorance thought they could bleed the planet and arrive at wealth. Both must be regarded in light of present scientific understanding of the Earth process as profoundly confused.

The continued evolutionary unfolding into the unknown, unimaginable, and unspoken splendor begins when we leave the dead end of human arrogance and disregard for the integral dynamics enfolding this planet into a single process. We must activate the deeper dimensions of the human person so that our legitimate demands for a vibrant Earth community will enter their macrophase role as planetary selection principles. Only then will we restore health and vitality and vigor to our planet, for only in that way will we be entering upon our destined role as the planetary process brought into a conscious phase of unfolding.

# 10

# The Texture of the Evolutionary Cosmos

## Matter and Spirit
## in Teilhard de Chardin

### Kathleen Duffy, S.S.J.

### Introduction

Pierre Teilhard de Chardin was born in 1881 in central France. After becoming a Jesuit, he practiced geology and paleontology in Europe, Asia, and Africa and wrote a series of essays in which he attempted to integrate his scientific understanding of the evolutionary world with his religious beliefs. But due to the controversial nature of his work at the time, he died without having received permission from his Jesuit superiors to publish these essays. Since his death in 1955, however, they have all appeared in print and have been studied extensively.

Teilhard's imagery is vivid, even sensuous, attractive even when, at times, his precise meaning is difficult to grasp. Stored within his imagery are a depth and a richness that will take many more decades to plumb. Although Teilhard relied heavily on images from physics, he often referred to the texture of things. In an early lecture, for instance, he muses about "the ultimate texture of the world"[1] and writes later about analyzing the "texture" of the stuff of the universe.[2] He also ventures into the realm of spirit, stating that the "pattern . . . in which our experience unfolds [things] may very well disclose to us the fundamental texture of Spirit."[3] Moreover, a careful reading of his works reveals a pervasion of textural images such as weaving and spinning, looms and tapestries, fibers and threads.[4] Teilhard extends the concept of texture to the realms of biology, physics, and mathematics, referring to evolutionary landscapes, topological surfaces, and space-time diagrams.

In this essay, I weave together some of Teilhard's many textural references, especially those dealing with fibers and threads, and show how this particular strand of imagery elucidates his view of the relationship between matter and spirit. I begin by investigating how he conceptualizes the texture of matter and

First published in *Teilhard Studies* no. 43 (fall 2001).

explore what he means by the texture of spirit. Then, after a short introduction to chaos and complexity theories, I point out the concepts, vocabulary, and purpose that Teilhard holds in common with the complexity scientists and show how his synthesis would be enhanced by including these modern scientific theories.

## TEXTURE IN TEILHARD'S EARLY LIFE

In *The Heart of Matter,* Teilhard describes his spiritual journey as a tapestry and recounts how his view of the cosmic texture developed over the years. In this biographical essay, he tells his "complicated story in which the various threads were formed and began to be woven together into what was one day to become for [him] the fabric of the Stuff of the Universe."[5] These reflections on his own story give insight into the forces at work in his life.

Still, it is difficult to pinpoint the source of Teilhard's fascination with texture. An early childhood experience might have catalyzed his interest. He tells how one day, while sitting by the fire, he watched a lock of his hair that his mother had just clipped fall into the fire and burn to ash. This traumatic experience of texture change affected him deeply.[6] He was disheartened to realize that part of his body could so easily be destroyed. From that moment, he began a lifelong search for the "Durable." At first he looked for it "in its most closely-defined and concentrated, and heaviest forms." To the young Teilhard, these were first metal and then rock. In the hard and dense, he sensed something more durable than the threads of his perishable hair, something deeper than its external texture. As a young adult, volcanic rock and continental shelves allured him into the study of geology, a study that deepened his desire to be fused with the Earth that he loved and one that allowed him to deepen his relationship with what he describes as "a sort of universal root or matrix of beings." Even at the peak of his spiritual trajectory, he continued to feel most at home when "immersed in an Ocean of Matter."[7]

As a young Jesuit, Teilhard was greatly puzzled by what seemed competing loves: his love for God and his love for the "Science of Rocks." He shared his dilemma with his novice master, expecting to be told to relinquish his interest in geology. Luckily, good advice prevented him from abandoning either love, and although he continued to experience and wonder at what seemed opposing tugs,[8] he continued his work in geology and pursued the study of paleontology. Perhaps his sensitivity as geologist and paleontologist to the shape of the arrowhead and the print of the fossil[9] also heightened his sensitivity to the texture of matter and led him to conjecture about the texture of spirit.

While studying theology at Hastings, Teilhard was exposed to two strands of thought that influenced him profoundly. The first was the theory of evolution, which he encountered in Henri Bergson's *Creative Evolution.* The second strand was a scripture passage from Colossians referring to Christ: "All things hold together in him" (1:17b). Presented at the time as a summation statement for all of Christian theology,[10] this passage, along with several others from Paul's letters, suggested a way to integrate the theory of evolution with his religious tradition; it helped him to visualize the unity of matter and spirit, and eventually it reversed his focus from the texture of rocks to the texture of Spirit. The theory of evolution helped him to visualize the threads that make up the cosmic tapestry; the passage from Colossians, the loom on which these threads are woven. A new understanding of the consistence of matter, for which he had been searching from his boyhood,[11] gradually began to develop in him. However, Teilhard would not be satisfied until he experienced a true synthesis of matter and spirit and was able to articulate it clearly. This would become his lifelong task.

Teilhard began writing essays to describe his amazing vision while he worked as a stretcher-bearer in the trenches during World War I. It was during the lulls between battles that he had the leisure to explore his ideas and to try to articulate, in a set of essays, the profound insights that resulted from his personal struggle.

Teilhard traveled widely during his lifetime. Many of the letters sent to his friends during these voyages are rich with sensuous details describing Earth's texture. He tells of an "atmosphere heavy with the smell of orange trees in bloom," the "hot desert regions of Arabia, all perfumed with incense and coffee," "large black butterflies with metallic-green reflections and long tails," "metamorphosed schist and granite running from north to south following the great fold axes." He notes that "the sea often becomes sleek and oily . . . its surface looks white and opaque, like milk" and that "the storms that break over the mountain of Africa form thick clouds which the setting sun paints glorious colors."[12] In one of these wartime essays, he confesses, "I have contemplated nature for so long and have so loved her countenance, recognized unmistakably as her."[13] His senses seem to be attuned to the slightest nuance within what he calls "the crimson gleams of Matter."[14]

On his way to China in 1926, however, he wrote to a friend that "nature is almost dead for me. I used to be passionately fond of the outward apparel of the Earth. Now it seems to me that I love only the Life which is at the bottom of its heart." Yet, despite this reversal, his letters continue to be full of the rich detail that bespeaks his love and reverence for Earth's texture and his need for prolonged contact with nature. While contemplating Earth's beauty during a passage through the Red Sea, he says, "All this is magnificent, because it provides a kind of new and constantly renewed expression of the aspirations and expectations of the spirit and the heart, so that it is something that you pass through and that passes through you."[15] It is the profound interplay of matter and spirit as they weave an intricate texture that moves Teilhard so deeply.

## THE TEXTURE OF MATTER IN TEILHARD'S WORK

Early in his major work, *The Human Phenomenon*, Teilhard notes that "each element of the cosmos is woven . . . from all the others."[16] We might wonder how elements that are generally thought to be particle-like can be woven together. To illustrate the meaning of his claim, Teilhard introduces a space-time view of the cosmos that allows him to look at the evolutionary process as a whole.

Ever since Einstein proposed the theory of relativity, it has become increasingly clear that time is inextricably connected to space. Because our senses have been fashioned to perceive only what is happening in the present, and because our experience of the cosmos is so short compared to its history of approximately fifteen billion years, we experience only a relatively miniscule cross-section of its complex texture at each moment and perceive matter as ultimately made of particles—hence, our predilection for reductionism. Taking both time and space into account, however, enhances our ability to see the cosmos as a whole.

To set up such a cosmic view, Teilhard suggests plotting the activity of evolution in space-time, coupling the idea of a dynamic topological surface with an image of an emerging tapestry. Consistent with the Aristotelian view of matter still prevalent in his day, Teilhard envisioned an early universe filled with proto-matter waiting to be called into being. Then, as this proto-matter begins to react, proto-particles begin to form new unities, giving birth to elementary particles, atoms, and molecules, and then, with the coming of life, more and more complex structures. When the positions of the original particles of the evolving cosmos are plotted as a function of time, a surprising texture is generated. The curve for the position of a single particle forms a thread that intertwines and unravels with other curves as forces attract and repel, form new entities, and fall apart. Duration thus provides texture to a world that only appears particulate.

In the early universe, the weaving fibers that are the extensions of the proto-matter of the early universe are not at all correlated.[17] At first the particles (and thus the threads) repel one another. Then the weaving begins. The space-time fibers become much more interrelated, more interconnected as they learn, despite their natural tendencies, to form complex wholes. Each new complexity prepares the way for still richer forms. The cosmic fibers experience what Teilhard calls *creative union*. As they interweave, they preserve their identities while yet becoming something more.[18]

As the cosmic drama unfolds and the threads intertwine and unravel and intertwine again, organic connections within the dynamic four-dimensional fabric are enhanced. Even though the number of species and individuals within each species multiplies with time, more of the once disparate elementary matter is now interrelated and weaving more complex patterns. Individual patterns come undone, but as time progresses, the texture of the fabric as a whole becomes more complex, more beautiful. Rather than as a sea of particles, then, matter can be viewed as a network of threads weaving in and out, responding to forces that encourage complexity, originality, and beauty. In fact, if the evolutionary project could be viewed from outside rather than from the center, it would look like a giant tapestry in process, "woven in a single piece," presenting a holistic and integrated approach to the cosmogonic process. However, this is ordinarily so difficult to envision because we are so firmly immersed within it.[19]

To provide further insight into the structure and texture of space-time, Teilhard singles out one of the many threads to guide his encounter with the cosmos. Centrally placed in *The Human Phenomenon*, "Ariadne's Thread," as he calls it, acts as a pivot on which he reenacts for us his own experience of reversal. This thread not only is a guide but also becomes for him an arrow pointing in the direction of increasing complexity-consciousness in the cosmos.[20] It is this thread that convinces him that evolution has a direction.

Ariadne was the daughter of King Minos of Crete, who attacked Athens after his son was murdered there. The Athenians submitted and, as a consequence, each year had to sacrifice fourteen youths to the Minotaur, a monster half bull and half human, who stayed in the king's labyrinth. The princess Ariadne fell in love with Theseus, a young man who had volunteered to be sacrificed to the Minotaur. To rescue him from disaster, Ariadne gave Theseus a ball of thread directing him to fasten one end close to the entrance of the maze and to unwind it as he went. Theseus confronted the Minotaur asleep in the depth of the labyrinth and, after destroying the monster, led the youths to safety by rewinding the thread.[21]

Teilhard grasps Ariadne's thread and begins his descent into his own cosmic labyrinth. There he confronts his minotaurs: pantheism, luring him to merge with matter,[22] and materialism,[23] suggesting that he objectify it. As he gapes at the maze of fibers, "the innumerable strands which form the web of chance, the very stuff of which the universe and [his] own small individuality are woven" give him pause. He feels "the distress characteristic to a particle adrift in the universe."[24] At each step of the descent, once-familiar patterns seem to come and go at random and finally unravel. As he reaches the disparate multiple and watches the dissolution of all that is familiar, he concludes that although we are all made from the same stuff, its principle of unity is not to be found within matter itself.[25]

Still clutching his prized thread, Teilhard reverses his direction still in search of cosmic consistence. Following the arrow of time, he notes that the cross-sectional patterns, made by slicing the four-dimensional tapestry at particular points in time, display more complex structures. He wonders at the "slender . . . threads from which [his] existence is woven, extending from the initial starting-point of the cosmic processes . . . to the meeting of [his] parents. . . . Had but a single one of those threads snapped [his] spirit would never have emerged into existence."[26] Like Theseus, he sees clearly the importance of Ariadne's thread, which begins "to disclose a complex and delicate fabric in what had been thought our most spiritual substance." Although he had considered himself extremely simple and very much his own master, in the ascent, he finds himself "made up of all sorts of fibres . . . fibres that come from every quarter and from very far afield, each with its own history and life."[27] Now he sees himself as part of humanity, as part of the cosmos, as part of a synthetic process.

As Teilhard approaches the present, it becomes clear that today "evolution is now busy elsewhere, in a richer, more complex domain, constructing spirit, with all our minds and hearts put together."[28] This reassures him that not only is the cosmos complexifying but it also has a "psychically convergent structure." Teilhard concludes that "Matter is the matrix of Spirit."[29]

He continues to follow Ariadne's thread to the end to see where it is leading,[30] to extrapolate into the billions of years that lie ahead. He discovers that the texture of the ever-complexifying tapestry does in fact "disclose to us the fundamental texture of Spirit."[31] As the weaving proceeds, the cosmic fibers will continue to become more tightly knit, and more complex patterns will continue to emerge.

This holistic view of the cosmic tapestry changes Teilhard's perplexity to ecstasy. He says that "as the scales fall from our eyes, we discover that we are not an element lost in the cosmic solitudes, but that within us a universal will to live converges and is hominized."[32] Teilhard returns from his labyrinthine journey full of insight. The universe has become for him a dynamic, organic whole with humanity at the front riding the crest of a wave as evolution moves into the future.

For Teilhard, spirit and matter are not separate entities, since they are so intricately woven together. Rather, like the threads of the cosmic tapestry and the spaces between them, matter and spirit form complementary textures, textures carved and shaped by complementary processes. They form "two *states* or two aspects of one and the same cosmic Stuff."[33] The quanta of matter and spirit that once permeated the early universe become fibers of matter influenced by gravity and threads of spirit drawn by love. Together, they form what Teilhard calls a mystical *milieu*, a "support common to all substances . . . a universal substratum, extremely refined and tenuous, through which the totality of beings subsists," a matrix on which *"spirit* is made *through the medium of matter."*[34] *It is the interplay of spirit with matter on the cosmic loom that encourages the creativity needed for quanta of spirit to weave a common soul.*

Extrapolating from his own experience of confronting the tensions within his spirit, Teilhard realizes that there must be something or someone at the center of the evolution drawing all creation together. He speculates on the nature of the force that allures the threads. He finds that "a transcendent form of action begins to emerge, which embraces and fuses together . . . the whole medley of things which . . . appear to us to conflict with and neutralize one another."[35] He suggests that as we explore the texture of the space-time tapestry, "we are gradually introduced . . . to the concept of a first, supreme centre, an omega, in which all the fibres, the threads, the generating lines, of the universe are knit together."[36] For Teilhard, the irresistible and universal center of convergence to which we are attracted[37] is a Person whom he calls Omega and eventually identifies with the cosmic Christ.

To Teilhard's surprise, the elusive "Durable" for which he was searching is found not in rocks and metal but in a tapestry of organic complexity. On the cosmic loom, the dissonance he experienced between the God of evolution and the Christian God resolves into a single, unified Force.[38] What began for him as grief over perishable strands of hair, culminates in ecstasy over durable threads of spirit. He summarizes the weaving process.

Crimson gleams of Matter, gliding imperceptibly into the gold of Spirit, ultimately to become transformed into the incandescence of a Universe that is Person—and through all this there blows, animating it and spreading over it a fragrant balm, a zephyr of Union.[39]

Viewed in space-time, gleams of Matter become crimson threads that swirl into the golden fibers of Spirit. Supported by an alluring and ensuring presence, the threads of the cosmic tapestry experiment with novel patterns as they grope their way toward the incandescence of the Cosmic Christ[40] who is, for Teilhard, truly and "organically clothed in the very majesty of his creation."[41]

It is its holistic character that makes Teilhard's synthesis so compelling. Over and over, he insists "order and design appear only in the whole,"[42] in the tapestry that is "endless and untearable, so closely woven in one piece that there is not one single knot in it that does not depend upon the whole fabric."[43]

## Chaos and Complexity—What Are They?

Given Teilhard's propensity for texture and for the holistic, and given the holistic nature of the complexity theories, it would be interesting to try to imagine how Teilhard might have incorporated them into his synthesis. Although his work preceded the onset of chaos and complexity theory by several decades, there are hints that he would have applauded many of the features of these theories.

Defining precisely what is meant by complexity is still difficult. There are presently at least three ways to approach it. The first two define ways to measure the complexity of a system. The mathematical approach counts the number of steps in the shortest program that will accomplish a particular task, while the connective approach counts the number of significant connections among the subunits of a complex system. Instead of an operational definition, the inductive approach enumerates the main properties of a system that can be considered complex: it is nonlinear, open, dynamic, emergent, poised between order and disorder.[44]

Because of their nonlinearity and openness to the environment, complex systems tend to be spontaneous, disorderly, and alive. They are made up of a great number of elements that interact with one another in complex ways. The richness of their interaction allows them to undergo spontaneous self-organization. Every living organism is a complex system. So too are a flock of birds and a group of individuals in economic interaction with one another. The elements that make up a complex system somehow manage to transcend themselves, constantly adapt to one another, organize themselves into exquisitely tuned patterns and together acquire collective properties such as life, thought, and purpose that they would never have possessed individually.[45]

On the forefront of research into the nature of complex systems, the Santa Fe Institute in New Mexico is an interdisciplinary group of scientists headed by Nobel Laureate in physics Murray Gell-Mann. These scientists want to determine the fundamental mechanisms that systems use to construct complex wholes. They are trying to provide a mathematical language to describe the stable yet flexible creativity found in the cosmos, phenomena as diverse as spiral galaxies, the colorful and intricate patterns on butterfly wings and the complex social organizations of cultures.

To plumb the nature of such phenomena, complexity scientists are asking new questions, devising new theories, discovering new relationships. Their questions address topics such as morphogenesis, emergence, and self-organization. They are interested in how organisms evolve and why certain structures exist. Theirs are questions that treat the dynamic, emergent processes at work in the cosmos. They are finding that when a few simple rules are applied to a variety of simple systems, intricate patterns begin to emerge. Because the fate of a complex system is so profoundly intertwined with its environment, its study requires a more holistic treatment than has generally been practiced in the sciences.

Classical biologists, for instance, have been interested in how organisms work. They ask questions about their makeup and the mechanisms that affect their behavior. Once they understand how organisms function, they try to predict their behavior and sometimes find ways to interact with them to their own advantage. Many advances have been made in biology in recent years by focusing on the gene as primary in determining the properties of organisms. According to neo-Darwinian evolutionary theory, new types of organisms arise from the interplay of random mutations of genes and natural selection. Complexity theorists, on the other hand, point to the inadequacies of natural selection as the sole explanation for emergent phenomena[46] and try to go a step further. They want to understand how the cell organizes itself into stable patterns of activity. Obviously, the pattern depends on genetic activity, but the new question is, in what particular ways?

One of the properties characterizing the complex response of a dissipative system made up of huge numbers of particles is its coherent behavior. An example of this kind of behavior occurs in a Benard convection cell, in which fluid is trapped between two plates, one heated at the bottom to sustain a constant temperature difference. To set up a convection pattern, the fluid is driven far from equilibrium by increasing the difference in temperature to a critical value. At this value, millions of molecules begin to move coherently, forming hexagonal convection cells of a characteristic size.[47] These patterns are obviously absent when there is no temperature gradient and the fluid becomes turbulent for larger temperature gradients. In the convective fluid, molecules seem to be independent and usually interact only through short-ranged intermolecular forces. However, when they are in the chaotic regime, correlations between particles become long-ranged.[48] That means, for instance, that even though a molecule is situated at a relatively large distance from its partner, it acts as though it knows what its partner is doing and responds accordingly. Through the interplay of two opposing forces, convection and gravitation, molecules seem almost to be communicating with one another.

Unlike complex systems, chaotic systems are usually simple. However, because they are nonlinear and influenced by positive feedback and information from their environments, they respond to stimuli in very complex ways. The order found in chaotic systems is radically different from previous notions of order. Although chaotic systems are deterministic, that is, governed by universal physical laws and not by chance, they are extremely sensitive to the environment. A small change in energy input, in the initial values of their variables, produces an entirely new response. Before the dawn of the computer, it was literally impossible to determine and describe chaotic behavior. Now the availability of high-speed computers has made it possible to explore their response. A flurry of research into all sorts of nonlinear phenomena in a variety of disciplines has resulted.

Graphs help scientists to see and understand a system's dynamics. A particularly helpful kind of graph often used to explore chaotic behavior is the phase plot. On a phase plot, the state of a system is plotted in a space with as many dimensions as there are variables needed to describe the state of the system. For instance, a mass oscillating on a spring in one dimension can be described by two variables, its position and its velocity. When the velocity of the mass is plotted against its position, a picture of its orbit results. The orbit provides insight into the behavior of the mass. For regular oscillatory or circular motion, the phase plot is called a limit cycle. Its elliptical shape represents the orderly behavior of a dependable, periodic process that continually repeats, preserving a fixed pattern. If the motion of the spring-mass is overdamped as it would be if the oscillating mass were immersed in molasses, the orbit will spiral in to a stable point. This kind of attractor is called a fixed point, since all initial conditions within the attractor will eventually lead to the same final state of rest.

When the spring-mass system is operating in the chaotic region, on the other hand, a collection of profoundly intricate and beautiful orbits arise. Patterns, such as the well-known Lorenz attractor, often called the "butterfly attractor" because of its shape, have captured the public imagination. Called "strange attractors," these orbits embody an unpredictable and intricate order. A strange attractor is often compared to a lake that exerts an attractive, gravitational force on the water from the rivers and streams that flow into it.[49] Water from these streams always moves toward the lake to which it is attracted and never escapes in the reverse direction. However, since the lake has no drain, any stream of water that flows into the lake remains there and, as if driven by an invisible force, continues to flow in complex spirals throughout the lake. The orbit of a truly chaotic system executes fairly complex dynamics within the limits of its center of attraction. Although the motion of a particular orbit never repeats itself and is hard to predict, order is maintained because, despite its tendency to wander, it is always being pulled back in toward its center of attraction.

Chaotic dynamics produce fractal structures whose irregular yet beautiful shapes are so unlike Euclidean geometrical forms. Fractals are intricate images that can be produced by the iteration of a few simple coupled nonlinear equations. The turbulent flow of air in the atmosphere forms fractal cloud patterns from condensing water vapor; over millennia, buffeting winds and rain produce jagged mountains; turbulent oceans form jagged coastlines; the violent pumping of blood by the heart fashions a fractal blood stream. The surf-pounded coastline, the blood vessels of the heart (a very violent pump), and the wind- and rain-buffeted mountain exhibit fractal shapes. The resultant fractal shapes are due to the interplay of powerful and turbulent driving forces and the strong damping forces that act to subdue them. Because of the aggressive nature of both types of force, the resulting fractal forms often turn out to be more robust than other forms.[50] Fractal boundaries also tend to be more fluid, and their patterns are more graceful and artistically appealing.

The study of these intricate structures reveals several interesting features. First of all, fractals are self-similar; that is, as the fractal image is enlarged, the pattern of the whole is found embedded in each smaller scale. Because a characteristic pattern appears on many scales, no scale predominates. Second, fractals have no characteristic length; each level is as important as any other. Fractal boundaries are also curious. As the fractal boundary is magnified, more and more detail can be seen and the length of the boundary becomes infinite. Finally, every fractal structure has a characteristic dimension that is non-integer. Unlike our familiar one-, two-, and three-dimensional spaces, a fractal fits into a non-integer dimensional space that seems strange to our Euclidean way of thinking.

Complex arrangement requires that two opposing forces such as convection and gravitation simultaneously act on the system. This is what the complexity scientists call conflicting design criteria. While one force dissipates energy, the other force supplies energy to the system to keep it far from equilibrium. One force seeks to bring it into homeostasis; the other, to destabilize it. The overall result is that, because the system is not in equilibrium, it is able to avoid thermal disorder and create new forms. The process of evolution also relies simultaneously on two opposing forces: self-organization and natural selection. Self-organization is the energy-enhancing process, and natural selection the limiting process.[51] Together they maintain a complex order.

The transition region that exists between ordered stability and chaotic instability is called "the edge of chaos." Although it is a place of homeostasis, "the edge of chaos" is a particularly creative region, a regime of complex order. In this regime, the complex system is slightly unstable, and thus is able to interact with its environment. In the process, stable structures are formed. Complex systems are not rigid. In fact, they cannot evolve unless they become somewhat unstable, unless they begin to fall apart. In nature, a process of radical change necessitates the movement of a stable structure from its stable environment into a far-from-equilibrium situation, into a more turbulent environment, into "the edge of chaos."

## TEILHARD AND COMPLEXITY THEORY—THE RESONANCE

Clearly, Teilhard senses and is attracted by the same deep laws of organization that complexity theorists are searching for. Just as Teilhard finds the evolutionary paradigm an overarching theme, so he would probably consider the emergence paradigm central to his synthesis. In fact, even though he knew nothing of complexity theory as it is practiced today, his words resonate with the amazement of scientists like L. V. Beloussov and Anatol M. Zhabotinsky, who first noticed that a far-from-equilibrium structure such as a chemical clock exhibits complex order[52] or Swinney and Golub, as they watched the patterned flow of fluid between two cylinders rotating with respect to each other that formerly would have been thought to produce turbulence.[53]

It is interesting to compare Teilhard's references to order, chaos, and complexity with concepts from complexity science. Santa Fe Institute's Stuart Kauffman, for instance, is struck by "the extraordinary surge toward order"[54] and expects his research to uncover "a deep theory of order in biology."[55] Teilhard, too, has an innate sense of complex order. And like the complexity scientists, he realizes that order often masquerades in apparent chaos. In the essay entitled "My Universe," he alludes to this. "My only concern will be to show how it is possible, by approaching the vast disorder of things from a certain angle, suddenly to see their obscurity and discord become transformed in a vibration that passes all description, inexhaustible in the richness of its tones and its notes, interminable in the perfection of its unity." Just as the chaotic-looking data that describe Lorenz's butterfly attractor turn out to be quite orderly when plotted in a certain way, so too, for Teilhard, the data that support evolution make sense of the world—but only if viewed from a certain angle. Otherwise, Teilhard tells us, what is "fundamentally directed by a power that is eminently in control of the elements that make up the universe" will seem like "an unimaginable tangle of chances and mishaps."[56]

Teilhard names complexity as a third infinite along with the infinitesimal and the immense and laments the fact that physics has ignored it. For him, "the gap between the extreme simplicity and the extreme complexity is as astronomically great as that between stellar and atomic magnitudes."[57] He tries to quantify complexity and defines it in a way similar to the connective approach[58] used by complexity theorists. He says that complexity can be expressed "numerically . . . simply by the number of elements in combination." He wants to include complexity as a state variable, envisioning a complexities-axis "to connect the phenomena of life—consciousness, freedom, inventive power—to the phenomena of matter: in other words, to find a natural place for biology as part of physics."[59]

Like the complexity scientists who are looking for deep fundamental laws of arrangement, Teilhard notices that "deep down, there is in the substance of the cosmos a primordial disposition . . . for self-arrangement and self-involution."[60] Arrangement, for him, consists not simply in the homogeneous interlocking of similar units as in crystal formation,[61] but the coherence brought about by the complex interaction that occurs in the formation of living things. He finds that "the multiple is bound together into the coherence of one solid whole or one single impulse";[62] thus the cosmos cannot be reduced to its constituent parts. If it is, if the inherent interconnection among all the seeming fragments is ignored, then the borders of the cosmic network fray and come undone.[63]

Unlike most complexity scientists, Teilhard extrapolates into the realm of spirit. He would remind us, for instance, that complex wholes are not purely spatial; they can also be psychic. The longer he considered the evidence, the more he found himself "inevitably, and paradoxically, obliged to identify the extreme Solidity of things with *an extreme organic complexity*."[64] (He was convinced that "the progressive spiritualization of conscious being is the only parameter that enables us to follow . . . the essential curve of Becoming through the labyrinth of individual evolution."[65])

In some of his later works and in his journals, Teilhard draws a simple curve, "the arrangement-curve," plotting a variable he calls arrangement as a function of time. He uses this plot to illustrate how matter and spirit complexify. He explains: "Thus, in the process of becoming, organic complexity and psychic simplicity are not in opposition: the one, in fact, is the condition for the appearance of the other."[66] Thus, both matter and spirit increase proportionately in complexity up to a certain peak value, at which point they bifurcate. At death, matter follows the law of entropy and decays back to its most probable form, while spirit continues to rise.[67] The tapestry threads of matter unravel in order to be recycled, but those of spirit survive and continue to complexify.

Though unaware of the existence of the term "the edge of chaos," Teilhard realized that the creativity of the cosmos depends on two opposing processes. The "process of 'arrangement' . . . produces the infinite variety (ever more complex and ever more 'psychized') of atoms, molecules, living cells, etc. . . . and the process of 'disarrangement' (Entropy), which is constantly bringing arranged Energy back to its most probable . . . forms." Sometimes he calls them two tides of consciousness. They are, for him, the two spiritual ingredients that, when brought together, react "endlessly upon one another in a flash of extraordinary brilliance, releasing by their implosion a light so intense that it transfigured . . . for [him] the very depths of the World."[68]

Teilhard describes a personal encounter with the "edge-of-chaos" in one of his early essays, "Nostalgia for the Front." As he reflects on his experience in the trenches while serving as a stretcher-bearer during World War I, he notices the feelings of freedom, unanimity, and exhilaration that only those experience who know the danger of the battle front. Writing to his cousin, Marguerite, he describes the front as "the final boundary between what has already been achieved and what is striving to emerge the *extreme boundary* between what one is already aware of, and what is still in process of formation."[69] The front becomes a metaphor for the far-from-equilibrium region, "essentially relative and shifting,"[70] like "the edge of chaos" that separates the chaotic zone from the stable zone. It is a place of creativity where there is enough stability to maintain a structure but also enough dynamism to keep the system alive and seeking for new ways to stabilize.

The focus throughout the history of science on linear systems that produce only orderly limit cycles has distorted our perception of the dynamics of the cosmos. By avoiding the difficult case of turbulence as if it were an exception we expect too narrow a spectrum of physical outcomes. This approach has affected our perception of social and spiritual phenomena as well. Teilhard alludes to this in the following passage, "The visible world formed a completely unvarying framework, within which, until the end of time, man was to repeat himself, ever identical; and with no function other than to restore to God, by *intellectual obedience and temperance in their use,* the manifold objects which were harmoniously ordered once and for all by the Creation." Referring to powerful thinkers such as Aristotle, Plato, Thomas Aquinas, Bossuet, and Ignatius of Loyola, Teilhard notes how for these sages all change was cyclical. Much like the limit cycles of classical physics, cyclical change "never amounted to more than accidental diversification or repetition of uniform cycles."[71] As his own synthesis becomes more fully formed, Teilhard becomes disappointed with his church's fear of evolution and its lack of interest in integrating evolutionary insights into its doctrine. Likewise, he grows weary of the science of the past. Instead, he becomes more and more interested in how the creative, dynamic processes that have influenced the past and have led the cosmos to the present are moving humanity into the future. In his later years, he expands his interest more and more beyond science toward the social implications of cosmic tapestry weaving.

Teilhard alludes to the fractal texture of the cosmic tapestry noting that at each scale of the cosmic hierarchy, self-similar structures reappear. He points, for example, to patterns on diatoms that resolve "almost indefinitely under stronger magnifications into new patterns."[72] He also notes that humanity, if it could be viewed by a distant observer, appears "if not the same as, at any rate akin to, all the other magnitudes of which the cosmos is the assembly."[73] He argues that we can see similarities between levels only if we treat the cosmos as a whole. The cosmos, he says, "taken as a whole, discloses with increasing clarity strange analogies which oblige us to treat it as a single organic object."[74]

Chaotic maps form by stretching and folding in on themselves. With the emergence of the human, Teilhard sees a similar development in the universe as it folds in upon itself through the process of reflection.[75] According to Teilhard, thought, that specifically human phenomenon, has been developing in the cosmos since the beginning within even the simplest of elements. He sees it emerging in proportion to the complexity of the material matrix, the interconnectedness of the threads. Little by little, this latent power within the cosmos becomes consciousness, and as it does it, more responsibility for the future of the cosmos rests with the human species.

Using self-similar arguments, Teilhard extrapolates his knowledge of the cosmos into the social and spiritual realms. He notes that "there is not . . . a single phenomenon extracted by biology . . . for which we cannot find an equivalent in the human social complex."[76] He also alludes to the power of self-similarity in directing his spiritual life and encouraging his continued participation in what he calls the great work, the continual knitting together of the cosmic tapestry. Embedded within this tapestry, we never see what is happening to the tapestry as a whole. We can only imagine the patterns that emerge as the threads intertwine. Drawing on the wisdom he acquired in his labyrinthian journey, Teilhard recognizes that "all the roads that life tries in order to effect the synthesis of the Multiple are not equally profitable."[77] However, since threads of matter and threads of spirit interweave in self-similar ways, he suggests that the self-similarity of nature can act as a guide as we try to construct a more coherent tapestry design. Because what is learned from nature can help in discernment, Teilhard places a high value on the study of science, on learning more about cosmic processes. He concludes that *"to explain the shape of the world means to explain the genesis of Spirit."*[78] Perhaps today he would say that the fractal texture of matter reveals the fractal texture of spirit.[79]

The strange attractors of chaos theory, with their fractal basin boundaries, would enhance Teilhard's image of the cosmic tapestry. Teilhard realizes, for instance, that evolution is not a matter of a "gentle drift toward equilibrium" but an "irresistible 'Vortex' . . . spinning it into ever more . . . complicated nuclei."[80] Teilhard's cosmic tapestry threads swirl like currents of water moving in whirlpools, behaving like streams of water draining from a basin under the influence of gravity.[81] From the chaos perspective, the cosmic tapestry threads form orbits or local patterns within the attractor. The mystical *milieu* corresponds to the basin of attraction in which the orbits unfold. Limit cycles, fixed points, and strange attractors intertwine to form tangles at each level of the cosmic hierarchy. Each thread weaves a fractal attractor in phase space. If the states of all of these threads as they whirl in space-time are projected onto phase-space diagrams, the result would be a tangle of intertwined orbits, weaving the rich texture of a supporting matrix for spirit.[82]

Yet these orbits are not forming simply local patterns. Each local pattern, responding to the Center of Centers, is being attracted to an absolute, common center[83] and participating in a single cosmic orbit. In the language of chaos theory, Omega would be the Super-Attractor who guides the cosmic becoming, the unification of matter and spirit. Yet just as a chaotic orbit is extremely sensitive to its environment, so each local orbit responds to influences that make its dynamics unpredictable. This allows naturally for both the freedom and the novelty that characterize the universal becoming. Responding to Omega, the Center of Centers, each local pattern would participate in patterns of varying magnitudes. These would eventually "meet together at a deeper level"[84] in a single cosmic orbit. They would not necessarily be packed tightly in space but would behave like coherent macroscopic systems communicating with and responding to one another at great physical distances. As it becomes more intercorrelated, matter provides a better milieu for spirit formation, since, according to Teilhard, spirit can complexify only in proportion to the complexity of the matter with which it interacts.

Teilhard would extrapolate this centering process to the end. Eventually, in a final act of union, all will become one with Omega, the attractor who draws all to the Center. Thus, the multiple is made one under the influence of the Super-Attractor. Teilhard says, "If things hold, and are held together, it is only by reason of complexity, from above." In fact, "the world would have no internal coherence were Christ not at hand to give it a centre and to consummate it. Christ, on the other hand, would not be divine if his spirit could not be recognized as underlying the processes which are even now recreating the soul of the earth."[85]

As a boy at play, as a paleontologist at work, and as a traveler on the way, Teilhard noticed, delighted in, and was extremely sensitive to texture in whatever form it appeared. This interest encouraged him to create a holistic, synthetic image of cosmogenesis that not only models the science and theology of his day but is also flexible and farsighted enough to include some present developments. In science, there is a resonance with pioneering work in complexity theory, fractal forms and chaotic dynamics and, in theology, with the notion of the Cosmic Christ. Because Teilhard's cosmic tapestry can be viewed alternatively as a topological space-time surface with convergent properties by the scientist and as a tapestry of finely woven threads by the artist, it finds itself somewhere between a mathematical model and a poetic image. Scientific layers of meaning add depth to an already powerful image capable not only of conveying scientific information but also of stimulating an aesthetic response. Thus, the tapestry image acts as a bridge between two disciplines that are rarely able to communicate so well.

## COMMENTS ADDED FOR THIS BOOK

In spite of the ongoing risk to reputation, career, and health, the Jesuit paleontologist Pierre Teilhard de Chardin attempted to lay out a daring synthesis of the theory of evolution with the doctrine of the incarnation. Such a synthesis is difficult, especially in a world in which both fields have become so technical and have, over the years, grown so far apart in their methods of viewing reality. Science tends to ignore the religious implications of its findings, while mainstream theology is not much closer to discovering a God for evolution than it was in Teilhard's day. Today, it is still quite rare to find a serious scholar of either science or theology willing to spend a lifetime on this task.

However, as the fact of evolution continues to permeate our popular culture and a keener understanding of its implications becomes apparent, it is consoling to have the words of a man, at once scientifically astute and deeply spiritual, reflecting on its deeper meaning. In a unique way, Teilhard allows the language of science to provide insight into the nature of God and God's action in our world and to help him to articulate his insight. He takes seriously the dynamics of the evolutionary process as major input for his theology, his spirituality, his understanding of himself, and his interaction with God and the world. At the same time, he takes seriously his own religious experience and tradition, drawing great inspiration from both the *Exercises* of St. Ignatius and the letters of St. Paul. It is Teilhard's profound reinterpretation of many scripture passages in the light of his understanding of evolution that returns to them their vigor.

Teilhard does more than simply refashion scriptural understanding. Evolution, at work everywhere in the cosmos, had profound implications for the way he lived and worked. In the context of the evolutionary paradigm, Teilhard's writings proclaim truths and values essential for our day: the profound presence of God at the heart of matter, the deep interconnectedness of all creation, the need to recognize each creature as subject, and the essential unity to which we are called. If we follow his line of thought, we find ourselves at the heart of the cosmos and at the forefront of the evolutionary endeavor, challenged to be co-creators, co-dreamers with the Cosmic Christ, who allures creation toward a future full of hope.

Yet Teilhard never presumed his work to be complete. His synthesis is not a once-and-for-all task. Just as the landscape of our knowledge is evolving, it seems logical that our understanding of the God whom we find at its center will deepen and evolve. As science continues to learn more about the composition and intricate dynamics of the cosmos, as psychology continues to fathom the growth and development of the psyche, our understanding of God should also become heightened. It is in this arena that Teilhard continues to model for us an urgently needed approach to the science/religion dialogue. Although he was not a theologian and although some of his science needs updating, Teilhard's work deserves to be studied carefully, and the witness of a life dedicated to this task must continue to inspire and to challenge our religious and scientific institutions.

## 11

## Teilhard 2000

### *The Vision of a Cosmic Genesis at the Millennium*

#### ARTHUR FABEL

Pierre Teilhard de Chardin achieved his prescient vision of a spiritually oriented evolution, a cosmic synthesis of science and religion, in the first half of this century. As the century draws to a close marking the turn of a millennium, it is an appropriate time to revisit the state of this project.

To set the scene, one might speak in terms of paradigms, a reigning worldview that subsumes everything in its premise. In the twentieth century, the vested assumption has been of a sterile cosmos, a material mechanism fundamentally indifferent to life. It is evolutionary but without direction or soul. This gloom is touted in a recent book, *The End of Science* by John Horgan, which claims that science is in its twilight since all the particles, genes, and galaxies, all the origins and fates, are found without any signs of a design.[1] We are left with a postmodern "ironic science" of untestable Borgesian speculation. An initial observation is that, since everyone Horgan interviews or cites, except Lynn Margulis, is a man, it seems a narrow "left-brain" surmise unable to imagine connections between the reductionist fragments.

Teilhard's legacy has been to represent the holistic alternative: "I shall try to show how it is possible if we look at things from a sufficiently elevated position, to see the confusions of detail in which we think we are lost, merge into one vast organic, guided, operation, in which each of us has a place."[2] From this vantage, Teilhard could perceive a progressive genesis developing by nested spheres of organic complexity. A companion axis of consciousness brings forth the personalization of the Earth in its noospheric human phase. Humankind is to be known as an exemplary phenomenon of a greater creation, however vicarious, thus gaining a sense of hope and purpose.

In an earlier Teilhard Study, circa 1980, I tried to show how scientists and authors were beginning to glimpse and verify this scenario.[3] Now, almost two

First published in *Teilhard Studies* no. 36 (spring 1998).

decades later, the evidence appears sufficiently strong, if gathered altogether, to presage a new paradigm, a Copernican revolution on a cosmic scale, that could fulfill Teilhard's mission. To address Horgan's establishment realistically, these reasons must be clearly stated and supported, which is our aim here. A website is noted at the end with a much expanded bibliography in this regard.

The issue is as much one of inclination as of detail. An erudite scientist such as biologist Harold Morowitz can reach a quite opposite reading: "The record from stromatolites to human societies seems by any measure to show a progressive increase of complexity."[4] We appear poised between two cosmologies, the physical machine of the past three centuries and a nascent embryonic organism.

The attraction of Teilhard's achievement may lie in three areas: its expansiveness to take in the vista of a developing cosmos, an attentiveness to a comprehensible design, and the realization that this can be made intelligible by an episodically emergent principle whereby complexity and consciousness rise in tandem. And it is all centered on and moving toward a New Being: "With cosmogenesis being transformed into Christogenesis, it is the stuff, the main stream, the very being of the world which is now *being personalized. Someone,* and no longer something, is in gestation in the universe."[5] As we will suggest, the concept of evolution as a planetary and cosmic individuation is central to appreciating what Teilhard was onto. At the cusp of 2000, such a "grand option" may at last be coming into sight.

Our path will take us to the noosphere as a new locus of discovery, the cosmos seen as a genesis, its fractal intricacy and axial sentience, how these result in an emergent self, now manifest in humankind, so as to arrive at an incarnate rationale for social justice and environmental responsibility.

## THE NOOSPHERE

At the outset it is worthwhile to state the context, the perceptual basis, for the content to follow. The aspect of Teilhard's vision that has gained most popular appeal is the *noosphere,* a planetary "thinking layer" composed of the collective sum of human cognition. It is lately reaching actualization in the worldwide computer network of the Internet, an exponential increase in interconnected minds expected to produce a new phase of global intelligence. As Jennifer Cobb writes in *Wired,* Teilhard gave us "the philosophical framework for planetary, Net-based consciousness."[6]

If such a cerebral faculty is forming over the Earth it might provide a way to resolve the conceptual standoff. This spherical envelope is noticed to develop in the same analogous fashion as a human brain whose self-organizing neural networks bring it to a point of thought and awareness.[7] Belgian system scientists Francis Heylighen and Johan Bollen perceive the Internet as a "giant associative network," "the collective wisdom of all people," and capable of learning and "knowledge discovery" on its own.[8]

To pursue this, if the noosphere is truly seen as an inchoate brain, might it conceivably come to its own understanding? By definition it would be all-inclusive and would take in every individual contribution at once. In the older scheme, the world still looks for one person, a new Darwin or Einstein, to state a final theory. But this has not happened. Might it be that a novel perspective is needed to see humankind itself reaching its own witness and knowledge?

The situation comes into focus by considering the trajectory of intellectual history. For millennia people lived in the thrall of a magical, animate, but undifferentiated matrix. Experimental science began to study and catalogue ponderable nature, but by its method lost an innate vitality. This analytical phase explored infinitesimal atomic matter and infinite celestial space, but the third infinity of the fecund complexity of life remained inexplicable in a cosmos bent on a fire or ice fate. As a planetary science now converges in computer graphic visualization, it may reach a new unity, a noospheric "right brain." In such a dimension we might find the integrative scope to reveal a natural genesis not visible otherwise. Incidentally, this historical round is similar to the way a brain develops from a rudimentary right mode to discrete neurons, which then form axons and synapses leading to a higher synthetic capacity. Computers likewise evolved from mainframes to PCs to networks.

Along with the purview of humankind, a requisite state of mind is essential to seek a generative cosmic order rather than summarily dismissing it. In the motion picture *Contact,* about the search for extraterrestrial intelligence, it is necessary both to expect a message and, if found, to be able to interpret its illustrative code. Nature was once understood as a book to be read, a second scripture, made comprehensible by an analogic frame from the microcosmic human to the numinous macrocosm.[9] But this has been forgotten in our secular modernity. As a brain learns by matching new experience with memory, humankind might recall to its benefit this perennial key most exemplified in the masculine and feminine archetypes. As the human phenomenon possesses an incredible propensity to learn, moving from falling apples to quantum cosmologies in a few hundred years, might humankind altogether be closing on its own discovery, if we are mindful to look for it?

## A COSMIC GENESIS

The imminent advent of a life-affirming worldview is evoked by systems theorist Sally Goerner.[10] "This book describes a broad cultural shift and a parallel scientific shift. Western civilization is moving away from a Newtonian, clockwork-machine universe toward a vision of a living, evolving, ecological universe." Three aspects are cited: a holistic perspective, the "nonlinear revolution" of the sciences of self-organizing complexity, and their societal implications.

The theoretical basis of an embryonic cosmos is the reunification of physics and biology, whereby life can be understood as springing from its intrinsic development. The French biologist and Nobel Laureate Christian de Duve contrasts Jacques Monod, also a Nobel Laureate biologist, with Teilhard as representatives of the two options.[11] Monod, in his 1970 *Chance and Necessity,* bleakly set out an existential view of life and the human as a random accident. De Duve, writing in 1993, claims that this is fallacious; the universe can now be scientifically known as organic in kind and made to evolve intricate, sentient, and "meaningful" life.

The convergence of the sciences is clear if they are seen in the compass of a singular historical endeavor. They logically began as isolated efforts to identify and measure the substantial world and its linear laws. At mid-century, the origins of life, the DNA genetic code, and the cosmic background radiation were still unknown. Before computers able to process and display the nonlinear mathematics of evolutionary complexity, life remained a thermodynamic fluke. The present task would seem to be to merge and join all the domains and theories, the pieces of the puzzle, so a coherent image can be discerned.

A most sophisticated synthesis has been proposed by theoretical physicist Lee Smolin in his *Life of the Cosmos*.[12] Smolin acknowledges the gulf between physical science and an evolving universe that spawns life but advises that the gulf can be bridged if the cosmos is recognized as a nonequilibrium, self-organizing system. As such, it takes on organic qualities as it generates the sequential hierarchy of life from biomolecules to the biosphere. The entire universe can be known as a product of natural selection from an ensemble of possible universes whereby its laws and parameters are optimized for the formation of stars, planets, and life. This view takes us beyond the anthropic principle which notes how finely tuned for life these constants are but which is not amenable to experiment, to an empirical regimen able to explain a cosmic genesis.

Smolin's exposition goes on to suggest a spiritual vector: "But if life, order and structure are the natural state of the cosmos itself, then our existence, indeed our spirit, might finally be comprehended as created naturally, by the world, rather than unnaturally and in opposition to it." A collaboration with the Santa Fe Institute biologist Stuart Kauffman suggests a congruence between self-organization in quantum gravity and evolutionary networks.[13] Their argument is that to unify general relativity and quantum theory requires a universe made to organize itself into living systems.

An emphatic break with the dominant paradigm is likewise proposed by George Smoot, the astrophysicist director of the COBE (Cosmic Background Explorer) satellite team that detected the origin of galaxies, which shows how much one's predilection governs what is seen.[14] He takes issue with his former professor, Steven Weinberg, who made the oft-quoted remark that the more the universe is comprehended, the more hostile and pointless it seems. Smoot finds just the opposite. Life is written in from the beginning and unfolds as if from a "cosmic DNA." If the "macrocosm" and "microcosm" are unified as the same subject—a universe inherently developing into complexity—intelligence and its human observer are obvious.

Accordingly there seems "in the air," through a noospheric lens, an incipient recognition of a fertile cosmos wherein life and the human are again at home. Physicist and author Paul Davies: "I have arrived at the belief that the emergence of life and consciousness is inevitable from a study of the processes of self-organizing complexity in the non-biological realm."[15] Davies then offers a lucid insight. A person can gain "phenomenological" knowledge of the world by direct observation. But there is another, invisible domain of the systemic, creative principles that only humankind can perceive. To Davies, as earlier to Galileo, here is nature seen as a testament we might learn to read together.

## FRACTAL COMPLEXITY

In 1980 a glimpse of an evolutionary dynamics antecedent to selection was just dawning, mainly through the nonequilibrium thermodynamics of Ilya Prigogine. Today a robust science of complexity can describe ubiquitous patterns and processes that evolve stages of animate intricacy from atoms to galaxies. The many versions such as autopoietic systems, neural networks, hypercycles, cellular automata, hierarchy theory, synergetics and chaotic dynamics now serve to articulate a natural order and aim.

A prime contributor is biologist Stuart Kauffman.[16] Bacterial colonies, genetic networks, evolving populations and democratic societies are to be seen as open systems, composed of diverse agents and their interactions, which arrange themselves into an oriented emergence opposed to entropic disorder. A salient feature of such self-organization is its tendency to develop into a nested, modular series of wholes within wholes, where common principles apply at each tier. This works the same way whether for a prairie ecosystem, a human brain, or the ramifying universe.

In addition, life and its evolution appear to be poised at the edge between order and chaos. What is described is a scale-free process of "self-organized criticality" that characterizes a spontaneous, stepwise genesis as the cosmos evolves in time. This impetus applies in the same way to genomic webs, species diversification and succession, personality formation, ecological biota and commercial enterprises as they take on an unsuspected affinity.

A further achievement of the nonlinear sciences is to identify a complementary system that applies everywhere. A constant cycle of autonomous entities and their relational connections, an interplay of independence and unity, generates and sustains the living realm. Neurons and axons in a brain, precursor biomolecules at the origin of life, and participants in a market economy are typical examples. What is found is a general "complex adaptive system" composed of archetypal complements that occurs at each phase and occasion.

A common sequence in the passage to a further level of organization is also evident. Peter Schuster, a theoretical biologist at the University of Vienna, notes several steps.[17] A cycle begins with many replicators or agents in competition. A mutual dependence arises as cooperation becomes more advantageous. This leads to a coupling of agents into beneficial assembly. Finally these emerge as a new class of evolving "individuals." The microbiological stage of such an evolution by symbiosis has been described by Lynn Margulis of the University of Massachusetts: nucleated, eukaryotic cells arose by the synergistic merger of diverse prokaryotic bacteria. The importance of these contributions is to specify an episodic ascent by means of a "creative union" of diverse autonomy and salutary community.

To enter some growing signs of an evolution revolution, an innate propagative structure is apparent to British biologist Brian Goodwin in consideration of the sources of morphological form.[18] Complex organisms, although unlimited in variety, are attracted to just a few basic "Bauplans." The shape of a leaf or a wing is not arbitrary or stochastic but reflects independent generative laws. Goodwin contends: "There is an inherent rationality to life that makes it intelligible at a much deeper level than functional utility and historical accident." In a comparison of a wide range of mammalian brains, Cornell neuroscientists Barbara Finlay and Richard Darlington find a predictable regularity with regard to component size such as the neocortex.[19] They believe such results imply that life evolves along specific guidelines as opposed to pure happenstance.

The realization of a heretofore undetected order and advance in nature and evolution thus seems under way by the composite sciences of humankind. We find quantification of Teilhard's strata of complexity along with his insight that greater unity actually fosters personal liberty. This updated "law of recurrence" can illuminate an ingrained motif and axis in evolutionary proliferation and point to its future florescence.[20]

A significant attribute in this regard is that such a periodic evolution possesses a fractal-like geometry. The French mathematician Benoit Mandelbrot has recognized that living nature does not conform to a linear Euclidean geometry but is infinitely variegated according to fractional dimensions.[21] Consider a fern or a coastline. What is of interest is that the same shapes occur over and over at every viewpoint. An extensive study, for example, finds body size and physiology to be defined by the same fractal rule across twenty-one orders of magnitude from microbes to whales.[22] But the novel application is to evolution itself. The late Harvard paleontologist Stephen Jay Gould saw beyond a strict Darwinism to observe a hierarchical, punctuated scale that forms "a kind of fractal pattern in self-similarity."[23]

How nature may become intelligible by means of a universal viable system is eloquently conveyed by Lynn Margulis and Dorion Sagan in their volume *What Is Life?* "Life on earth is a complex, photosynthetically based, chemical system fractally arranged into individuals at different levels of organization. We cannot rise above nature, for nature itself transcends."[24] With reference to Russian geochemist Vladimir Vernadsky, Teilhard's contemporary, humankind is seen in the midst of a transition to a "new level of organic being" of a fractally developing planetary mind. And this is the consciousness that has risen with the frame of complexity from the outset: "Mind and Body, perceiving and living, are equally self-referring, self-reflexive processes already present in the earliest bacteria."

From a deep mythic sensitivity, psychologist Jean Houston arrives at the same epiphany of a nested resonance. The correspondence of broccoli florets, a firefly's eye, courtship rituals, and dreamscapes with galactic nebula reveal a natural, folded up self-similarity. "These examples point to the universality of the fractal as a central organizing principle of our universe; wherever we look, the complex systems of nature and time in nature seem to preserve the look of details at finer and finer scales. Fractals show a hidden holistic order behind things, a harmony in which everything affects everything else."[25]

In this study, to restate our aims at midcourse, we are attempting to survey and sample, within the arc of the noosphere, the frontiers of the sciences and humanities to suggest how they are coming to perceive a true cosmic genesis. A prime feature is the directional emergence of better brains, intelligence, and mindfulness, which is considered next.

## THE AXIS OF CONSCIOUSNESS

What distinguishes Teilhard's hypothesis is not only a somatic complexification but how this facilitates the attendant rise of consciousness. "The more complex a being is, so our Scale of Complexity tells us, the more is it centered upon itself and therefore the more conscious does it become. In other words, the higher the degree of complexity in a living creature, the higher its consciousness."[26]

Although an issue under discussion, a consensus is forming that sentient awareness is not a spurious epiphenomenon but is real and primal. Interdisciplinary conferences entitled "Toward a Science of Consciousness" are now held biannually at the University of Arizona to explore the multifaceted qualities of consciousness.[27] From roots in the quantum domain, consciousness is seen to ascend by scalar degrees to break through into human self-awareness. Once outside the confines of a corporeal Darwinism, a wider view of evolution is gaining acceptance as due to nonlinear dynamics, which trace a central path of increasing cerebral capacity and behavioral repertoire.

This ascent of mind is explicable when evolution is not defined by genetic drift alone but is seen primarily as a cognitive process. At the forefront of this effort, such neural architecture and activity are seen as fractal in kind as "many spatial scales are recursively embedded."[28] An evolutionary epistemology perceives most of all a knowledge gaining experience. To Austrian philosopher Franz Wuketits "evolution is a universal cognition and learning process and there is a nested hierarchy of such processes from unicellular animals to humans."[29] Swedish neuroscientists Peter Arhem and Hans Liljenstrom report a co-evolution of consciousness and intelligence as nervous systems complexify.[30] As a result, a phylogenetic enlightenment seems to characterize the entirety of life as it develops in a broadly comparable manner to the ontogenetic path of an individual organism.

Another axial component is the informational, semiotic character of the quickening cosmos. In addition to matter and energy, information and its communication are seen as fundamental to evolutionary self-organization. A formative program appears to emerge with autocatalytic molecules, chromosomal networks, epigenetic inheritance, and human language as they encode and transmit knowledge. This new universe is pervaded by signs; it is a "semiogenesis," a "cosmic code" and testament waiting to be read.

By these accounts we may find the Teilhardian feature, missed by a fossil-based paradigm, of an "Adriadne's Thread," a developmental direction. We can now move on to consider its personalizing interiority.

## An Emergent Self

An aspect of Teilhard's thought that is often misunderstood is that the unification of a new stage or sphere does not limit the freedom of its members; rather it heightens their creativity in a symbiotic reciprocity of individual and community. And this holds from the atomic state to organisms and the noosphere. The scale of complexity-consciousness in fact describes an intensifying selfhood: union differentiates and personalizes in a cosmic process of personalization.

An interpretation of the complex adaptive system attributed to Chilean biologist Francisco Varela is relevant.[31] Varela's model is known as an autopoietic system to designate its capacity to produce and maintain its own identity and vitality. These dynamic networks continuously regenerate their viability so as to create distinct "selves." Varela finds this general system at each evolutionary plane from life's origin to social groups whereby local entities exist in a "reciprocal causality" with the communal whole. Here is another insight into how the universe becomes more organized when simpler, distributed entities interact to form a stratified assembly, "like a fractal," of complication and sentience. In so doing autopoiesis brings forth a cognitive self; it is inherently a "self-making" activity.

In the last two decades evolutionary theory has expanded from an emphasis on just genes or organisms to admit distinct levels of selection. These "units of evolution" form by means of a novel way to transmit information at each stage such as template replication or language. What is significant is how each autopoietic locus is seen as a new individual. Israeli philosopher of science Eva Jablonka finds an "emergence of new levels of individuality" from protocells to cultural groups.[32] She also observes that a new phase occurs when communication between agents makes cooperation and interdependence more beneficial than conflict. Systems biologist Stanley Salthe concurs that such developmental self-organization is engaged in the "individuation" of life.[33]

An example of a visionary synthesis from a feminine perspective is *The Ecological Self* by the Australian philosopher and environmentalist Freya Mathews.[34] After citing an atomistic worldview as the cause of ecological devastation, she argues that new versions of quantum theory are rightly organic in essence. The core drive of cosmic and biological development is an impetus toward self-realization effected by the individuating selves of each being. The Gaian biosphere epitomizes this for the whole Earth. Mathews advocates an accord of substance and system, autonomy and connectedness, by which human selves, in harmony with the "ecocosm," can participate in "the Self-realization of the universe."

In another version conceived by the Norwegian ecophilosopher Arne Naess and imbued in deep ecology, human beings ought to appreciate the expanded role of their interconnection with and embeddedness in a living nature; one is the rain forest.[35] But two aspects are involved. At the same time that communion with a greater Self is warranted, a person needs to proceed on the path toward one's own, integral self. Teilhard, while stressing the embrace of a sacred cosmos, would see evolution primarily as the gestation of a new, personal being, now reaching planetary proportions.

## THE PHENOMENON OF HUMANKIND

The convergent civilization on a finite globe that Teilhard foresaw is apparent today in the intense commercial, political, intellectual, and media planetization, especially since the demise of the totalitarian states. Yet it threatens to slide into cultural, economic, and environmental anarchy without a cohesive bond and purpose. To this end, how might a transition to an equitable humankind and a viable Earth be realized as a phenomenon of a cosmic genesis?

In the first place, it requires a change of mind and paradigm whence life is not alien nor the world a collection of objects but understood as reflective of a deeper dynamic. We noted earlier how global computer networks seem to be taking on the rudiments of a brain. Biologist David Sloan Wilson and philosopher Elliott Sober have extended the evolutionary scale to the social realm whereby human groups form a new organic level.[36] The acceptance of multilevel selection extending to societies follows the same course from a holistic origin a century ago with Emile Durkheim's group consciousness, to its denial in a genetic fixation to a new sense that social groups are "adaptive cognitive units" with a modicum of a collective thought.

In another revision against the competitive Western grain, cooperation and altruism are being recognized as a major agency in evolution. Systems scientist Peter Corning proposes a "Holistic Darwinism" that can admit the complementary synergies at work from DNA to ecosystems.[37] The occurrence of unsuspected patterns on a social plane is further revealed by applying fractal geometry to the growth of cities. British architect Michael Batty has found their structure and function to be self-similar across many ranges from neighborhoods to a metropolis.[38]

As the principles of nonlinear dynamics are applied to the human sciences, they bring a previously elusive theoretical basis. A "dynamical social psychology" finds the same forms and forces that impel and shape evolution to be present in interpersonal relations, that thought and action proceed in a fractal manner.[39] This societal realm is achieved by the free association of people from which an overall cohesion arises. Human behavior was initially seen as separate from nature, then as a product of Darwinian selection, and newly as reflecting the universal self-creation.

To ground this in a practical illustration, a novel form of community in Amherst, Massachusetts, offers an example. Known as Cohousing, a movement begun in Scandinavia, it was organized and designed by its members, who represent a diverse mix of economic, vocational, and familial situations. Composed of some thirty-five affordable homes clustered around a common house, it has minimum impact on the landscape. A member gains the benefits of shared living, which then allows time and resources for personal pursuits. If such intentional communities could be seen as a fledgling manifestation of a greater genesis, they might provide a model by which to reinhabit a peaceful, sustainable world. To move beyond the current globalization debate, by reading a constantly recurring natural system, the next phase could be appreciated as a network of diverse eco-villages in a beneficial global unity.

## "Someone in Gestation"

In our review of the state of Teilhard's project, two recent criticisms ought to be addressed. According to philosopher Daniel Dennett, "evolution is a mindless, purposeless, algorithmic process" and we will just have to accept it.[40] Teilhard is a "loser" whose apologetic would be fatal to this Darwinian doom if true. But Dennett, in his one man's opinion, seems to bend everything, including Kauffman, to his case while missing the sequential arrow of life and mind. Theologian Karl Schmitz-Moormann advises that Teilhard's universe is to be understood by referring not to some formula, an arcane theory of everything but to its teleological result, "not its starting point, but in the fully realized being,"[41]

The second contention is by historian Theodore Roszak.[42] In an otherwise commendable work on ecopsychology, he cites Teilhard as the worst example of an anthropomorphic "authoritarian centralism." Yet Roszak rightly observes that it is the very "non-anthropomorphic cosmology" wherein human life has no meaning that is at the root of rapacious environmental degradation. Roszak simply misreads Teilhard to appropriate him to his argument.

If humankind is indeed meant to fathom what the cosmos and its phenomenal self might be, a built-in guide ought to be provided, and, as we have seen, it is. In the medieval scholastic age, an analogical ladder held sway. Lost to scientific reduction, it is being revived in the image of a self-similar universe developing by a ubiquitous creative system.[43] In her celebration of the evolutionary epic, science writer Connie Barlow catches this by noting the "great metaphysical binaries." The venerable Yin and Yang can return a meaningful depth in the form of the interplay of differentiation and integration, strife and synergy, individual and community.[44] As Teilhard and tradition intimated, once again we may glimpse a complementary structure and process that occurs everywhere in spontaneous exuberance.

A work that expresses well the pivotal moment is *The Passion of the Western Mind* by Richard Tarnas.[45] The intellectual history of the West is a cosmological and philosophic estrangement, which at its nadir may be saved by a participatory, ecological, feminine vision. For it has been an "overwhelmingly masculine" endeavor. A persistent dialectic in terms of the feminine and masculine occurs in the perinatal event, the path of self-integration, the Judeo-Christian fall and salvation and, as we saw earlier, the span of history from a maternal milieu through patriarchal alienation to a redemptive synthesis. For Tarnas, the millennial reprieve is a reunification with the feminine matrix of being. A universe so conceived is engaged in the conception of a new self, a "resacralization of the cosmos," the "Incarnation" of a personified, planetary humankind.[46]

A similar fusion is reached by Sr. Catherine O'Connor in her study of Teilhard and Carl Jung. The feminine is the ground and goal of being, Beatrice inspiring Dante, the love that personalizes.[47] Theologian Ursula King likewise believes that Teilhard's sense of the feminine as the unitive element in the cosmos can nourish and inform an immanent ecological spirituality.[48]

A closure between Teilhard's prescience, the nascent genesis vision, an emergent self and traditional teachings may be likewise found in psychologist Sanford Drob's account of the wisdom of the Kabbalah: "The goal of both the cosmos and humanity is a union between self and other, psychologically between man and woman, and cosmically between God and humanity. Such an encounter and union between souls is, according to the Kabbalists, the goal of both cosmic and personal existence. However, the cosmos and the individual must each become fully individuated prior to being reunited with the creator."[49]

By projecting the scale of recurrence, Teilhard went on to imagine a future genesis of "noospheres" joining together in a galactic domain. But a collective resolve may first be necessary. If the levels of self-organization and selection are extended to the entire biosphere, to a sentient Gaia, it may be imperative for a planet to "select itself" as a viable center of cosmic life. Such an incentive and challenge might inspire humankind to a requisite degree of social justice and environmental concern, which it does not at present have.

In the twentieth century, Teilhard has often represented the alternative of a cosmic genesis to a profane science and philosophy. In this regard Steven Weinberg and Stuart Kauffman offer diametrically opposed statements as to whether life is meant to be or not. Weinberg contends life is a stranger while Kauffman believes the universe naturally develops into animate complexity and sentience. Here may be the root issue for the twenty-first century. Yet some sixty years after Teilhard wrote *The Phenomenon of Man* an incipient discovery by humankind may be dawning not of a moribund cosmos but of a numinous, embryonic creation becoming conscious of itself.

## SUGGESTIONS FOR FURTHER READING

As an update to this study, the reader is referred to an annotated bibliography entitled "The Emerging Discovery of a Self-Organizing Universe," prepared by Arthur Fabel in collaboration with Mary Evelyn Tucker, Brian Swimme, and John Grim. It is posted at the Forum for Religion and Ecology website: www.environment.harvard.edu/religion. Many hundreds of references are cited that further attest to and document the growing explanation of a cosmic genesis. At the accelerating rate of scientific advance nowadays, in the five years since the present study was written, the evidence for a life and people-friendly universe in a process of organic, personal, and spiritual development, which Teilhard sought to express, seems to be reaching its threshold of acceptance.

# PART FOUR

# THEOLOGICAL
# AND SOCIAL DIMENSIONS

The final four studies in this volume explore Teilhard's unique synthesis of religion and science through its aspects of liberation, an incarnate creativity, feminine wisdom, and human solidarity. In the first of them, "Liberation Theology and Teilhard de Chardin," the Filipino-American theologian Eulalio Baltazar provides an overview of liberation theology that then gains import through Teilhard's rich evolutionary perspective.

As noted earlier, "Cosmogenesis," the vision of a self-organizing universe, is today being discussed at the frontiers of science. In "Chaos, Complexity, and Theology," Georgetown University theologian John Haught, S.J., surveys seemingly "chaotic" systems that in fact are marked by deep order. He then shows the integral accord of these systems with key ideas in the process philosophy of Alfred North Whitehead and with Teilhard's dynamic cosmogenesis. These understandings, he indicates, can anchor a vision of how divine action in the world can be seen as an ongoing creation.

In "Divine Wisdom: Her Significance for Today," theologian Eleanor Rae describes Wisdom as the feminine divine in Judaism and Christianity. She explores the idea of biblical wisdom literature as a source of creation theology, suggesting that the person of Wisdom as a religious figure related to the Earth needs to be studied in all the world's religions.

The book concludes with a vision for the possibility of a more encompassing justice and enduring peace based on human solidarity with evolutionary processes. The late Sacred Heart University theologian Joseph Grau writes in "The Creative Union of Person and Community: A Geo-Humanist Ethic" that "personalizing a Christic Universe through Love Energy" can be realized in an organically viable human–Earth community.

# 12

# Liberation Theology
# and Teilhard de Chardin

## Eulalio Baltazar

In this study we will attempt to show how the evolutionary framework of Teilhard de Chardin might throw light on two vexing problems that critics of the Marxist-influenced Latin American theology of liberation find to be inadequately answered. The first is the criticism that in the effort to make the transcendence of the faith, of God, and of the salvation in Jesus Christ immanent in the world, these doctrines are not sufficiently safeguarded. Liberation theologians are accused of immanentism, of humanism and secularism, of politicization of the faith and of reductionism.[1] In short, the relation between earthly progress and the kingdom of God, or, to put it in more speculative language, the relation between immanence and transcendence, is not sufficiently clarified. As one sympathetic commentator of liberation theology notes:

> The role and significance of the transcendent remains a troubling issue for liberation theologians. . . . Where is God in all this? What has happened to the Lord of history? Is eschatology a strictly human enterprise? For example . . . Rubem Alves accentuates the human and immanent so strongly in his later writings that he sounds like a secular humanist.
>
> It is important for liberation theologians that the immanent and transcendent be understood as part of the same process. The crucial problem here is to find the kind of language that will not suggest a "two realm" theory of reality yet will still allow for a sense of divine sovereignty and mystery in the larger scheme of things. Liberation theologians refuse to interpret the eschatological dimension as primarily transhistorical, for the only history we humans know is the history of our present existence. One cannot be saved apart from this historical condition.[2]

The second problem we will consider is the relation between Marxism and Christianity within liberation theology. Some critics believe that such an alliance could be a danger to the faith.[3]

---

First published in *Teilhard Studies* no. 20 (fall/winter 1988).

## SUMMARY OF LIBERATION THEOLOGY

Let us at this point give a selective treatment of liberation theology so that we can better see how these two problems arise. As we all know, the historical stimulus for a theology of liberation was and is the massive poverty, exploitation, and oppression of the marginalized and disenfranchised population of Latin America. The European theology that the liberation theologians learned was claimed to be inapplicable to the Latin American situation. As Gustavo Gutiérrez has noted, European theology was addressed to prosperous and enlightened Westerners who have lost their faith in God.[4] The problem in Latin America was not how to preach the Christian God to nonbelievers but how to show that such a God is a God of love to the poor, the hungry, and the oppressed.[5] So the Conference of Latin American Bishops in Medellín (1968) went back to Vatican II, especially to the Pastoral Constitution on The Church in the Modern World (*Gaudium et Spes*), and undertook to translate its teaching in terms of the Latin American situation. The theological and pastoral teachings of Medellín, especially its theme of integral liberation, were crystallized and systematized in the now famous and perhaps most significant theological work in recent times, *A Theology of Liberation*, by Gustavo Gutiérrez.[6]

What Gutiérrez and the other liberation theologians accepted from Vatican II was the shift in the orientation of the church from the otherworldly to the this-worldly. To do this, the classical "two-realm" theology of a supernatural and a natural order was abandoned and a single history of salvation was adopted.[7] Because liberation theologians adopted this single-history-of-salvation framework, they inherited the problem of relating the transcendence of the faith, of salvation, God, the kingdom, grace, and so on to history and historical progress. In the two-realm theology, the transcendent had its own proper sphere, the metaphysical and supernatural, which was separate from the physical and natural order, the realm of temporal and historical realities and structures. In this two-realm view, there was no danger of collapsing the transcendent into the immanent. But if the metaphysical order is done away with, one faces the problem of relocating the transcendent within history. Because of the more urgent pastoral problem of combating oppression and poverty, liberation theologians have not had the time to devote to this speculative problem in an *ex professo* manner.

The second problem, that of the relation of Marxism to liberation theology arises from the nature of the methodology. According to Gutiérrez, liberation theology is a critical reflection on historical action in the light of the word of God.[8] This reflection is done by the people, in this case the basic Christian groups or communities. They analyze their historical situation, which is one of oppression and poverty. The developmental mode of analysis imported from the rich nations of Europe and North America hides the causes of oppression. "Only a class analysis," says Gutiérrez, "will enable us to see what is really involved in the oppression between oppressed countries and dominant peoples." He adds, "the theory of dependence will take the wrong path and lead to deception if the analysis is not put within the framework of the worldwide class struggle."[9] Thus, only the Marxist mode of class analysis will reveal the true features of the historical situation, which can then serve as the true basis for critical reflection in the light of the Word of God.

This brief introduction to liberation theology has identified the origin of the two problems we propose to consider. Before we proceed, it might be appropriate to recall the comment of Pope John Paul II to the bishops of Brazil concerning the merits of liberation theology: "When purified of elements which can adulterate it, with grave consequences for the faith, this theology is not only orthodox but necessary."[10] We would like to think of our effort here as a process toward the purification of liberation theology by the use of Teilhard de Chardin's evolutionary frame of reference.

## MARXIST ANALYSIS
## AND TEILHARD'S EVOLUTIONARY FRAMEWORK

Let us invert the order of discussion and consider first the problem of the alliance between Marxism and liberation theology. The fear of some Christians is that the atheistic materialism of Marxism could adulterate the purity of the Christian faith. Even if it is asserted that only the Marxist mode of analysis is appropriated, the conflictual scheme of Marxism, which accentuates class struggle, still seems to be at variance with the Christian principle of love and brotherhood of all.

In this regard, our strategy to allay the fear of some Christians of the Marxist element in liberation theology is to see whether we can integrate this mode of analysis within the evolutionary vision of Teilhard de Chardin, a framework that provided the context within which the famous Vatican II document *Gaudium et Spes* was formulated. In this document, the Teilhardian view of a single reality in process whose maturation point is Christ-Omega facilitated a rereading of the scriptures, in which creation and redemption constitute two stages of a single process of salvation.

Liberation theologians, taking their cue from *Gaudium et Spes,* base their theology on a single-history matrix. This would seem to provide the possibility of a rapprochement between Teilhard's theology and their own. But while Gutiérrez acknowledges the influence of Teilhard on the affirmation of Christ as the Lord of history and of the cosmos in *Gaudium et Spes,*[11] he sees a difference between Teilhard's theology, which he classifies as developmentalist,[12] and the liberation view, which he claims is dialectical and revolutionary. By developmentalist, Gutiérrez means gradual and incremental change within one and the same framework. What is needed for Latin America, he claims, is a change in the framework itself, hence revolutionary change. Hugo Assmann also admits the influence of Teilhard on the understanding of historical reality, but, like Gutiérrez, he labels Teilhard's theology progressivist, relevant for the developed world but irrelevant to Latin American needs.[13] Liberation discourse, according to these theologians, must go beyond the language of development.

I believe that liberation theologians, without a detailed examination of

Teilhard's evolutionary progress, simply classified it according to the popular scientific view of evolution as gradual change. But development defined as gradual change does not properly and adequately describe the dynamics of evolution as understood by Teilhard. The evolutionary process as seen by Teilhard has various stages: geogenesis as the evolution of matter, biogenesis as the rise of life, noogenesis as the evolution of consciousness. The passage from one stage to the other is not developmental in the sense of gradual, incremental, or quantitative increase but a radical qualitative change, hence revolutionary. But it is not proper to describe the radical qualitative change from matter to life, let us say, as dialectical, if by this change is meant the annihilation or absorption of one of the terms of the dialectic into the other. For Teilhard, the proper term for the radical change that marks evolutionary advance is creative union.[14] This is the underlying dynamism of a universe tending toward convergence in the superpersonal center, Christ-Omega. In creative union, the terms are not lost or absorbed into each other as in dialectical change but are differentiated. As Teilhard notes:

> In any domain . . . whether it be the cells of a body, the members of a society or the elements of a spiritual synthesis—union differentiates. Through a neglect of this universal rule many a system of pantheism has led us astray to the cult of a great All in which individuals were supposed to be merged like a drop in the ocean or like a dissolving grain of salt.[15]

At the social level, creative union takes the form of love. Union through love is closer than purely economic and political association.[16] While Marxist class analysis in terms of a dialectical struggle between the oppressed and the oppressor might be a useful method of understanding the phenomenon of oppression, we need to see the deeper meaning of the cultural and social change of noogenesis as that of creative union. Instead of looking at class struggle as the primary category for social analysis, we need to relativize it and see instead the convergence of classes through creative union as the primary category. By so doing, liberation theology can allay the fear expressed by *Octogesima Adveniens*, that Marxist analysis because of its intimate link to Marxist ideology could lead to a totalitarian and violent society. Further reflection, of course, is needed to adequately integrate Marxist analysis within Teilhard's theistic vision. We have simply tried to show how theology might find in Teilhard rather than in Marx the philosophic frame of reference needed for the articulation of the concept of liberation.

## THE PROBLEM OF IMMANENCE AND TRANSCENDENCE

### *Official Church Teaching*

We begin with the central issue of immanence and transcendence. Recall what we said earlier: a problem arises because of the adoption of a worldview of a single history of salvation. Our first step in the investigation is to survey the teaching of the church on the relation between salvation and liberation, which is also between transcendence and immanence.

*Gaudium et Spes* gives the definitive guideline on the relation between transcendence and immanence when it says that "earthly progress must be carefully distinguished from the growth of Christ's Kingdom" and that "on this earth that kingdom is already present in mystery."[17] The Conference of Latin American Bishops held in Medellín in 1968 following *Gaudium et Spes* adds that "all liberation is already in anticipation of full redemption in Christ."[18] In this statement, some link between salvation and liberation is mentioned, but no explanation is given as to whether liberation is the occasion for salvation or is a causal factor in salvation. In 1975, Pope Paul VI declared, in *Evangelii Nuntiandi,* that "the church . . . has the duty to proclaim the liberation of millions of human beings, many of whom are not her own children. . . . This is not foreign to evangelization."[19] This statement clearly links human liberation and salvation in Jesus Christ without, however, identifying them.[20] The pope names three possible linkages, namely, the anthropological, the theological, and the evangelical. Anthropologically, salvation is related to the socioeconomic order; theologically, redemption is related to creation; and evangelically, charity is related to justice and peace in the temporal order.[21] The pope concludes that "salvation is offered to all . . . a transcendent and eschatological salvation, which indeed has its beginning in this life but which is fulfilled in eternity."[22]

From our cursory examination of the church's teaching, we note that the question has not really advanced beyond the guidelines laid down by *Gaudium et Spes.*[23] We next consider the views of liberation theologians who have come to associate earthly progress with the growth of Christ's kingdom.

### A Survey of Liberation Theologians

Gustavo Gutiérrez, after reviewing the directives of *Gaudium et Spes,* takes the position that human liberation and the growth of the kingdom "have the same goal, but they do not follow parallel roads, not even convergent ones. The growth of the kingdom is a process that occurs historically *in* liberation."[24] He adds: "Without liberating historical events, there would be no growth of the Kingdom."[25]

Another theologian, the Uruguayan Jesuit Juan Luis Segundo, agrees with Gutiérrez by affirming the causal relation between historical liberation and the kingdom.[26] But neither Segundo nor Gutiérrez provides an explanation of how the historical can promote the growth of the eschatological. They merely leave us with the assertion that "salvation is present at the heart of man's history."[27]

Among these theologians, Leonardo Boff, in my view, has given the most thought to this question,[28] one which the International Theological Commission in October 1976 considered to constitute "one of the principal tasks of theology."[29] Boff starts by simply assuming God's presence in history, penetrating and permeating all aspects of reality. This presence of God allows Boff to see a theological element in socioeconomic liberation, thus legitimizing theological discourse which interprets sociological material in the light of faith, an interpretation he terms hermeneutic mediation.[30] The relation between the theological and sociological dimensions is described by Boff thus:

> In Christian faith, "salvation" is a technical term, expressing the eschato-logical condition of the human being, risen and divinized, in the plenitude of the kingdom of God in eternity. But this definitive situation does not spring up full-blown only at the term of history. This situation is antici-pated, prepared for, within the historical process.[31]

Boff offers four noetic models to help us see the convergence of salvation and liberation. These are the Chalcedonian, the sacramental, the agapic, and the anthropological. These models, he explains, "involve both oneness and distinc-tion—*identification* without total *identity*." In the first model, Jesus Christ is of two natures but "these two natures are so unified that they constitute *one and the same* Jesus *Christ*."[32] Our objection to this noetic model is the difficulty if not impossibility of introducing metaphysical discourse in a historical context. How is one to talk of the two natures of Christ within a single historical framework, which liberation theology has adopted? Do the two natures of Christ correspond to two distinct histories? But if the divine nature is historicized, how is its tran-scendence safeguarded? On the other hand, if the divine nature remains meta-physical, how is it immanent in the historical?

The sacramental model sees Christ as the sacrament in which the human and the divine are unified. But here also a dilemma remains. The agapic model sees the presence of God wherever there is love of neighbor, for God is love. Again, the fun-damental problem of how God is present in human historical acts of love is not explained, for if God is metaphysical, that is, otherworldly, nontemporal, and tran-scendent, how can the divine be immanent in the historical and temporal?

Finally, Boff's anthropological model argues that just as the soul is immanent in the body, as body and soul are two principles that compose one being, salva-tion is immanent in historical liberation so that they constitute a single process. A difficulty with Boff's model has to do with the origin of the human soul. In classical theology, which has adopted a two-realm conceptual framework of the metaphysical and the historical realms, the soul is metaphysical, having been directly created by God and then infused into a body prepared for it. But Boff cannot use this metaphysical and anthropological model, since liberation theol-ogy has adopted a single-history matrix. He needs an anthropology valid for a single-history frame of reference, yet he has not provided us with one, nor has any other liberation theologian, for that matter, so that we can judge the validity of the claim that the soul is immanent in the body.

We would note that before theology can even talk about historical liberation, which causes and hastens the growth and coming of the kingdom, it needs to develop a language about God and man that is nonmetaphysical and derived from a single-history view of reality. Marxist sociological discourse, which liberation theologians have chosen as the dialogue partner of theology in place of philoso-phy, does not have the vocabulary to express the transcendence of God and the

Christian Faith. Existential discourse as an alternative is better suited to private salvation than to the social dimension that liberation theology wants to emphasize.

Historical liberation as the means toward salvation as opposed to the classic view of an escape from history is meaningful only if, first, God is shown to be immanent in the world so that his action does indeed endow history with salvific power; and, second, if it is shown that the human composite is wholly historical, for how can the whole person be saved through historical liberation if part of him or her is otherworldly and nonhistorical?

Schubert Ogden faults liberation theologians for being unconcerned with the metaphysical question about the being and action of God. He finds the reason for this unconcern in liberation theology's view of faith as *orthopraxis* as opposed to *orthodoxy*.[33] But even the view of faith as orthopraxis does not exempt its proponents from providing us with a doctrine of God and of man that justifies orthopraxis as historical liberation. If liberation theology rejects the metaphysical views of God and of humans as bourgeois, then it must provide us with an alternative. Such a view must explain how divine transcendence is protected if the metaphysical dimension which in the past served as the basis for God's transcendence is rejected. Similarly, if the metaphysical nature of the human soul is denied, it must be shown how human transcendence can be achieved.

It is not enough to simply say as liberation theologians do that God is immanent in history.[34] It must be shown *how* God is immanent in a single-history framework while at the same time preserving his transcendence.

### God's Immanence in History

Let us therefore review the question of God's immanence in history before we consider the second question of man's total historicity. The liberation theologian Juan Luis Segundo says that God does not so much invade our history as that "our history invades the divine realm."[35] He does not tell us, however, whether for him the divine realm is historical or not. If it is not historical, then we are back in the two-realm framework of metaphysical theology. If the divine is historical, he has to advise us how transcendence is safeguarded.

Our first step to show God's immanence in an evolving world is to go to the scriptures and reread them in the light of a modern evolutionary consciousness that the human phase is evolution becoming conscious of itself.[36] In the scriptures, we are shown that God's life is conceived as unending time rather than as the absence of time, as classical theology influenced by Platonic metaphysics mistakenly thought.[37] God, says the Bible, is both Alpha and Omega, the beginning and the end (Rev. 21:6). God is he who was, who is, and who is to come (Rev. 1:4; 4:8). Thus, God's "divine time overflows, holds together and envelops all other times."[38]

But further critical reflection is necessary. To say that God's life is to be seen in terms of the category of time rather than timelessness does not mean that God's life is historicized, that is, subject to finitude, contingency, and evolution. Rather, God is the Lord of history and of time. God gives everything time to evolve to its maturation point. To use a noetic model, God is like a mother's womb that gives time for the gestation of the fetus. And so, we might metaphorically speak of the womb of God containing the evolving universe, of divine time enveloping history.

For another noetic metaphor, let us use Teilhard's model for the evolving world, which is that of a tree.[39] If we think of the evolving world as a tree, then theologically we must think of God as its ground. To see God's immanence in the evolving world, let us consider how the ground is immanent in a tree. If we reflect on the essential meaning of a tree, we see that the ground is included in its very definition, for when we say that a tree is a living thing with roots, trunk, branches, leaves and so on, we see that the tree in its totality is structured for the ground. The ground is immanent in a tree, not physically but in a much deeper way, by being present in its very essence. And since the essence of a thing is what is deepest in it, it follows that the ground is most immanent in a tree.

Similarly, God is immanent in history as its ground. God is structured in the very meaning of history, or rather, history is structured for God. And since the essence of history is what is deepest in it, therefore, God is more immanent to it than history is to itself. But while God is most immanent in history, God's transcendence is not jeopardized, for as its ground, God is dialectically other than history.

Without a model like Teilhard's, liberation theology will find it difficult to make assertions about God's immanence in history that at the same time safeguard his transcendence. We could end up historicizing God as some Whiteheadian process theologians have done.[40]

Summarizing this section, we can say that God can be known as the immanent ground of history, which unites history to himself in a creative union of love resulting in the growth, maturation, and transformation of history into the kingdom of God. Instead of an escape from time, salvation is now by way of involvement in history. But for humanity to be integrally and totally liberated, it must be wholly historical. God's salvific action through historical liberation cannot save the whole person if a part, namely, one's soul, is, as classical theology holds, unevolved, hence, unhistorical and otherworldly. Therefore it is incumbent on liberation theology to resolve this issue if it is to justify salvation through historical liberation to provide an anthropology in which the whole person is historical but at the same time allows for Christian transcendence. As we noted earlier, Marxist anthropology, while totally historical, fails to provide for Christian transcendence. Having given up the evolutionary framework, the possibility for a solution is closed to liberation theology.

### Human Existence as Wholly Historical

We will now attempt to show the total historicity of the human person within Teilhard's evolutionary framework. For those with a metaphysical mind-set, there is an understandable fear in the proposal that the whole person evolves. The main cause of fear, it seems to me, comes from a faulty understanding of evolution. From a scientific point of view, evolution is a purely natural process in which matter evolves. Given this view, it would not have been God who created the human person but evolution. Furthermore, if it is the case that only matter evolves, then the possibility of a spiritual soul emerging from matter would be negated. From matter can come only matter, a more evolved form, perhaps, but still material. And if the soul is reduced to materiality, the Christian truth of our spiritual transcendence would be endangered.

In contrast to the scientific mode is the philosophic and theological view of evolution, which postulates God as its ground. It follows that God ultimately is the creator of the human person, not instantaneously and nontemporally, as in the metaphysical view, but temporally, by way of evolution. Furthermore, contrary to the popular notion that evolution is a purely material process, we affirm with Teilhard that, in fact, it is spiritual in nature, being the evolution of mind or consciousness. As Teilhard notes, "it is not in their germinal state that beings manifest themselves but in their florescence."[41] Therefore, if evolution gives rise to mind, then this quality must have already have existed in the beginning in an obscure and primordial way.[42] Thus matter is actually inchoate spirit or preconscious reality.[43] Teilhard concludes: "Man was born entirely from the world—not only his flesh and bones but his incredible power of thought."[44] The human is a single reality in which the body is tangential energy and the soul is radial energy; these two energies are but aspects of one and the same reality.

The evolutionary view of human origins described here is not foreign to the scriptures. The Bible teaches us that man is conceived monistically rather than dualistically as in Hellenism.[45] For the Hebrews, "the body is the soul in its outward form."[46] Again, a biblical scholar observes that "in Old Testament Semitic thought, man is an indivisible unity, and this unity is given him by the creator. Unlike hellenistic dualism, they did not see themselves as body and soul but simply as God-given life (nepeš). The same unity characterizes New Testament anthropology."[47]

Having shown the immanence of God in history and the total historicity of the human person within a single historical context, we now have the theological basis for the rightful claim of liberation theology that integral liberation is by way of total immersion and involvement in history. It remains for us to show the relation between historical liberation and salvation—the growth of Christ's kingdom.

## HISTORICAL LIBERATION AND THE COMING OF SALVATION

### *The Kingdom Here and the Kingdom to Come*

We begin our reflection by recalling the parameters set by the church's teaching. *Gaudium et Spes* tells us that earthly progress must be distinguished from Christ's kingdom. *Evangelii Nuntiandi* adds that eschatological salvation is already here in this life but will find its fulfillment in eternity. And the Medellín statement says that "all liberation is already an anticipation of full redemption in Christ."

Let us first consider the relation between the kingdom that is already here and the kingdom that is to come. The use of static categories cannot properly bring out their true relationship. If the kingdom is already here and abides with us, there is no point to speak of its return. One has to think in terms of processive categories and say that the kingdom that is already here is evolving or growing. The kingdom that is yet to come, by contrast, is the kingdom as fully evolved. They are not two distinct entities but phases of growth of one and the same reality. The noetic model that may be helpful is that of birth. The kingdom already here but hidden from view is the kingdom in the womb of God, as it were. The kingdom to come is the one that will be manifested at birth. Or, to use the scriptural metaphor, the kingdom here below is like a seed that is buried in the ground, hence, hidden. God is the ground for the eventual germination and fruition of the kingdom to come. It is incorrect to interpret the hiddenness of the kingdom here below statically, that is, as already finished and evolved but behind a temporal or historical veil. If it were so, the growth of the kingdom of which the church speaks cannot be explained and historical liberation to promote the growth of the kingdom cannot be justified. Time on Earth would then be simply one of patient waiting and passive suffering.

### History and the Kingdom Yet To Come

Having distinguished between the kingdom present and the kingdom to appear, let us next distinguish history from the kingdom to come. How is the kingdom yet to come related to human history? We shall call this variously the eschatological kingdom or the parousia.

The eschatological kingdom is the new Jerusalem peopled by a new humanity in Jesus Christ. History, on the other hand, is the place for the old Adam, the old city. The kingdom as future is not a metaphysical dimension, that is, a region of timelessness. If it were, then we would have a problem showing how the non-historical nature of the coming kingdom could be immanent in history. The eschatological kingdom has to be conceived of processively, that is, as the fullness of time of the kingdom here below. As Pierre Benoit notes, "that world whose centre is the risen Christ, still lives in a certain time, just as it is situated in a certain place." He adds that this certain time and place are in relation to our present time and place, a "new" and "higher" time and place.[48] It is precisely because the eschatological kingdom is in the category of time that it can be immanent in history.

But eschatological time is not the same as historical time. They represent different dimensions of one and the same salvation history and are as different as are the time dimensions of the biosphere and the noosphere. Historical time is the time proper to the noosphere; biological time pertains to the biosphere. Plants and animals are ruled by biological time, while the human being as self-conscious is ruled by historical time. To attain historical time, an animal must evolve toward self-consciousness. So, too, in order for human life to attain the eschatological dimension, it must be transformed into the new life in Christ. History, of course, has its own future in which present structures are transformed, cultures and civilizations evolve, and science and technology develop. This historical future is also the region of the Communist utopia. But the future in which the eschatological kingdom is situated is beyond all these. It cannot be identified with any historical structure, even if such a structure is a liberating one, for all history and its myriad forms will pass away.

To speak of the otherness and transcendence of the kingdom yet to come in relation to history, we use prefixes such as trans-, supra-, post- or ultra-. But we must be careful that we do not translate these terms into metaphysical discourse in which the transhistorical is outside time altogether. The transhistorical must be understood within the category of process as the fullness of time of the historical, the fruition and maturation of history. It is history fully transformed and consummated, the omega of the historical process. As such, it has a qualitatively different form, order, and unity from that of history.

### The Kingdom Here Below and History

Liberation theologians speak of the kingdom here below as being at the heart of history. The *Instruction* from the Congregation for the Doctrine of the Faith (1984), however, warns some liberation theologians that they tend to "identify the kingdom of God and its growth with the human liberation movement, and to make history itself the subject of its own development, as a process of the self-redemption of man by means of the class struggle" (IX, no. 3). They are also accused by the same *Instruction* of politicizing the faith (XI, no. 6) and of sacralizing politics (XI, no. 7).

The problem is how to distinguish the kingdom on Earth and history without separating them into two separate realms, the metaphysical and the physical respectively, as in classical theology, but instead distinguishing them within one and the same single processive view of reality.

The relation between the kingdom here below and history might best be articulated using a processive noetic model, that of a seed that must die in order that it may have new life and form. In this model, there are two distinguishable phases in one and the same process of germination and growth. The first is the dying phase or the dissolution stage, when the seed form breaks down. The second is the germination phase, in which a new form emerges. This noetic model was used by St. Paul to illustrate the mystery of baptism and resurrection (e.g., 1 Cor. 15:36-44). Thus, history represents the dying phase of the salvific process, while the kingdom here represents the resurrection or germination phase.

Political, economic, and social structures of history belong to the dying phase, while the salvation in Christ belongs to the resurrection phase. Thus, historical structures and the kingdom on Earth belong to one and the same process but are not identical. They are as distinct as dying is from rising, and one cannot hope for a greater difference than this. It is impossible to reduce one to the other, yet, paradoxically, they cannot be more closely connected. As history advances toward the eschatological future, death possesses more and more of history. But this passing away of history is not in vain, for Christ incarnated himself in history and is the first fruit of the salvific process. If we die with Christ we will rise with him (Eph. 2:6; Col. 2:12; 2 Tim. 2:17; 1 Cor. 15:36).

Dying with Christ is not merely a private, individualistic process of renouncing one's personal sins but is a social process of struggle against sinful social structures, "burying" these oppressive structures, as it were. As these oppressive structures are changed for less oppressive ones, we gain a measure of sociopolitical and economic liberation. But as long as we are in the sphere of history, we are never completely liberated. Paradoxically, it is by the demise of each succeeding historical structure that the kingdom advances.

To use scriptural imagery, we can look at the kingdom as the people of God advancing toward the land flowing with milk and honey. While on the way, the people of God erect or build "tents," which are provisional structures. Historical structures are precisely "tents" that must sooner or later be pulled down. Historical structures that are preserved beyond their time oppress the people of God. The task of liberation is precisely the relativization of these structures. For we do not have here a lasting city. The kingdom is the final form of history. In order for this to emerge, initial and intermediate forms must give way. To be involved in liberation, then, is to be an undertaker of all these intermediate forms. The task of liberation theology is to assist in the removal of oppressive historical structures and to erect new, less oppressive ones. As Teilhard notes, "in the case of the definitive union with God in omega, we can see that if the world is to be divinized it must, in each one of us and in its totality, lose its visible form." And he adds: "From the Christian point of view, that, in virtue of the death of Christ, is the life-giving function of human death."[49]

Summarizing this section, we note that history and the kingdom here below do not have identical forms. The form of the kingdom, which is eschatological, cannot be identified with any historical form that is relative and provisional. Thus, the danger of destroying the transcendence of the kingdom is avoided. Yet a problem arises. How can the kingdom be immanent in history if it cannot be identified with a historical form, say, a liberating one? Does not logic itself require that to be immanent in history is to be historical? Yet we claim that the kingdom is not historical. How then can it be immanent in history? Are we not in fact separating the kingdom from history and really returning to the two-realm framework? Accordingly, we need to consider as the final part of our study the nature of the immanence of the kingdom in history. It would seem that if the kingdom is transcendent it cannot also be immanent, and if it is made immanent we destroy its transcendence. Classical theology opted for transcendence at the expense of immanence, while liberation theology, it would seem, has opted for immanence at the expense of transcendence.

### The Immanence of the Kingdom in History

The problem facing liberation theologians is to show that the eschatological kingdom, which is transcendent, is also immanent in history without destroying its transcendence. Recall Leonardo Boff's noetic models, namely, the Chalcedonian, the sacramental, the agapic, and the anthropological. These models, however, do not show how the nonhistorical divine nature of Christ can be inside history, how the soul that is unevolved but directly created can be immanent in the evolved animal body. We have already indicated that because the eschatological kingdom is in the category of time rather than timelessness, the possibility of its immanence in historical time is greater than the possibility of a timeless reality being in a temporal one.

This requires that we show how it is possible for one time dimension to be in another. Recall as we said earlier that the kingdom in history is part of a single process that has two phases, death and resurrection. The kingdom, we noted, is the resurrection or emergent phase of the salvific process. It represents the new life in Christ, the new Jerusalem, the new Earth, the new Adam, which are of a higher order of reality than the historical phase, hence, the transcendent phase of history. We now want to show that this transcendent phase is also immanent in the historical phase. But we want to add that it is more immanent to history than history is to itself, and that it is precisely because it is transcendent that it is also immanent. This paradoxical statement becomes a contradiction and an impossibility in a metaphysical frame of reference where what is outside or beyond another cannot also be within it.

To aid us in seeing that what is most transcendent is also most immanent, let us use again the process model of the germinating seed.[50] For the seed, the transcendent phase is its maturation point, when it reaches the fullness of its reality, which in this case is the fruit. The fruit is the omega point, the fullness of being and truth of the seed. It is the fullness of being of the seed because without it, the seed will not germinate. The fruit liberates the seed, as it were, from germinal life. The fruit is also the fullness of truth of the seed because it manifests what the seed is; it reveals or unfolds the meaning hidden in the seed. The process of germination and other transformations of the seed into the seedling, the tree, the flower, and finally the fruit is a process of transcendence, that is, a process tending toward fullness of being and truth. Each stage in the process represents a higher level of transcendence until the fullness of transcendence is reached in the fruit.

Let us return to the stage of the seed and see the fruit in relation to it. In the unfolding of the seed, the fruit is the last to emerge; it is what is most hidden in the seed. The fruit is at the very heart of the seed, so to speak; it is what is deepest in it. It follows that it is most immanent. Thus, the fruit, which is the most transcendent, is also the most immanent in any given reality in process. The omega, which is most transcendent, is also the most immanent.

Taking now historical liberation as a process whose omega is the eschatological kingdom, it follows that the kingdom, which is most transcendent, is also the most immanent to history. The kingdom, we can now rightly say, is at the very heart and center of history. Since Christ is the Omega of history, Christ is what is most immanent to history, more immanent to history than history is to itself.

To identify the kingdom with history is not really to make the kingdom immanent. The *Instruction* on the theology of liberation (1984) from the Congregation for the Doctrine of the Faith holds that to do so is to fall into historicist immanentism (IX, no. 3). But this cannot be so, for history is not really immanent to itself. Historicist immanentism is meaningful only within a two-realm frame of reference in which history is identified with the immanent and the kingdom with the transcendent or metaphysical realm. If the metaphysical realm is abolished and we resituate the kingdom within history, it follows that its transcendence is destroyed and one falls into historicist immanentism.

But within a Teilhardian processive discourse, history is not to be identified with immanence, for history is not immanent to itself. To be immanent to oneself is to be fully revealed to oneself, to be open to one's inmost reality. But history, like a seed, is not fully revealed to itself. For the seed to be immanent to itself, it must be present to itself as fruit. But the fruit is still hidden from view. Therefore the seed is not immanent to itself. Similarly, the inmost meaning of history, which is the kingdom, is still hidden from view. In order for history to be immanent to itself, it must be present to its center. Since the kingdom is at the heart and center of history, it follows that the kingdom is more immanent to history than history is to itself. To identify the kingdom with historical structures and forms is to dislodge it from its proper place, the heart and center of history and to cast it outward toward the periphery, thus destroying both its immanence and its transcendence.

## CONCLUSION

In conclusion, I would again recommend to liberation theology the evolutionary framework of Teilhard de Chardin as the context in which many of its theological issues could be resolved. Among the liberation theologians, Juan Luis Segundo has come closest to Teilhard's evolutionary outlook, using it to articulate the Christian faith. We tried to show here how the major problem of immanence and transcendence, or the relation between liberation and salvation, could be clarified within Teilhard's evolutionary vision. We also briefly indicated the possibility of integrating Marxist class analysis used by liberation theology within Teilhard's framework and by so doing offset the fear of its atheistic orientation and secular stance.

Contrary to the view of many liberation theologians that Teilhard's theology and worldview are Western, my own opinion is that they are transcultural, having evoked sympathetic responses from Marxists, Buddhists, Hindus, and other Eastern philosophies and religions. In a dialogue with liberation theology, a case might be made that Teilhard's thought is in fact a theology of liberation. Indeed, it could be argued that Teilhard's theology of liberation is more comprehensive, for it discusses not only the liberation of the noosphere but also that of the biosphere and the geosphere. Such an overall view corresponds to the scriptural doctrine that integral liberation includes not only humanity but material creation as well, for as Paul says in Romans, all creation is groaning until now to be delivered.

# 13

# Chaos, Complexity, and Theology

## JOHN F. HAUGHT

What are some of the thoughts that occur to a theologian who reads about the new sciences of chaos and complexity? The formal scientific study of chaos and complexity has arrived so recently that very little attention has been devoted so far to their possible theological implications. In this essay, however, I shall propose that the picture of nature now taking shape as a result of reflection on the phenomena of chaos and complexity may be of considerable significance for the theological enterprise.

There is always the question, of course, whether any new scientific developments have lasting theological relevance. A large number of theologians, in fact, find conversations with scientists quite immaterial. The natural world is still not a central theme in most contemporary religious thought, and our departments and schools of theology have not often made knowledge of ecology or cosmology an essential ingredient of their curricula.

In the modern period, after a disastrous flirtation with Newtonian thought, theology all too willingly handed over to science the task of understanding the natural world and left to itself the job of interpreting the more elusive realms of human existence, freedom and history. By compartmentalizing things in this fashion, however, theology made itself largely irrelevant to our understanding of the cosmos—which is, after all, the encompassing context of our existence, our freedom and our history.[1]

At the same time, this divorce impoverished theology. For new developments in science and cosmology can always bring a fresh perspective to our understanding of biblical faith. This has already proven to be the case with evolutionary science, general relativity, and big bang cosmology. Today, however, theology also has much to learn from the so-called sciences of chaos and complexity. Although the studies surrounding these notions are still in the process of formation, there is nevertheless sufficient reason for theology to begin inquiring about their significance for our interpretation of the whole of reality.

---

First published in *Teilhard Studies* no. 30 (summer 1994).

# I

What then do scientists mean when they speak of "chaos" and "complexity"? Chaos is the study of "dynamical systems" in which complex and random behavior arises spontaneously out of simple and ordered physical processes.[2] Stephen Kellert defines chaos as "the qualitative study of unstable aperiodic behavior in deterministic nonlinear dynamical systems."[3] Chaos in common discourse means "disorder," but science is primarily interested in order. In fact, only the assumption that the universe is intelligibly arranged gives scientists the incentive to understand it better. In what sense then can science be interested in chaos? It is interested in chaos because many physical processes that start out with a simple kind of orderliness suddenly move toward turbulence, but end up producing surprisingly richer forms of order out of the chaos, an order often so intricate and complex that it can be mapped only with the help of computers.

Even without computers we can get a glimpse of chaos. For example, a pot of water is sitting cold upon a stove, its molecules in a state of relative equilibrium. If we turn the heat on, the molecules in the liquid start moving excitedly all over the place. Randomness and disorder seem to rule for a moment, but then something remarkable happens. Under appropriate conditions hexagonally shaped convection cells begin to form in the liquid at a state far from the earlier equilibrium. When energy is fed into unstable systems, intriguing varieties of order can "spontaneously" emerge out of the chaos. Today this is cause for much scientific wonder.

Countless happenings in nature exhibit this feature of simple order turning chaotic and then suddenly displaying more intricate states of order far from thermodynamic equilibrium—at the "edge of chaos." Thus, when scientists talk about "chaos" this includes not simply disorder or randomness but also the complex patterns that lie hidden beneath what we had taken to be aimless disarray.

There is much more "chaos" in nature than science ever noticed before. Scientists used to assume that physical reality, based apparently on timeless natural laws, follows rigidly causal pathways. They were convinced that if any deviations from deterministic conceptions of natural processes showed up, these could readily be damped out or explained away. Nature itself could not at bottom waver from linear mathematical ideals. However, today the science of chaos has shown that causally determined processes with *completely* predictable outcomes seldom occur in nature.

The puzzling order that emerges out of chaotic processes can become more visible to us through computer images that sketch the complex phase space transitions and patterns in so-called dynamical systems. Chaotic activity is apparently guided in some largely unknown way by "strange attractors" that hold the chaos within bounds and bestow on it a surprisingly rich pattern. By computer tracking of a system's activity over a period of time we may find that what appeared to be purely random movement has been guided or "attracted" all along by "strange," often intricate and beautiful, forms or "basins" of order.

Of utmost importance in the new scientific developments is the striking fact that the specific character of the complex order that emerges out of chaotic phenomena is extremely sensitive to initial conditions. This means that very slight differences at the start of a sequence can become considerably amplified as the system evolves, a fact that has gone largely unnoticed in previous physics. Two series of events that started out very close to each other will lead to vastly divergent outcomes. A crude but commonly used example is that of placing two paper cups very close to each other at the top of a water rapids. Although their initial conditions are very nearly the same, the very slight difference between them becomes considerably amplified as the cups move through the turbulence of the rapids, and they end up at increasingly greater distances from each other as they move further downstream. Their subsequent positions are thus said to be "extremely sensitive to initial physical conditions."

It is this sensitive dependence on initial conditions that renders most occurrences in nature unpredictable. Since it is utterly impossible to master accurately all the initial conditions, it is also impossible to predict the exact outcome of most natural processes.

The study of chaos overlaps considerably with the broader science of complexity. The term "complexity" refers here to all emergent, adaptive, self-organizing, informationally rich systems in both nonhuman nature and human culture as well.[4] Examples include cells, organisms, brains, immune systems, ecosystems, economic systems—and even religions. Here we shall understand the concept of "complexity" as the broader of the two notions, inclusive of the physics of "chaos."

In both chaos and complexity a striking feature is that self-organizing patterns emerge in a scientifically *unpredictable* way out of processes that we used to consider deterministic. For three centuries we thought the business of science was to make exact forecasts about the future states of systems. Obviously science never succeeded in actually doing this except in the case of trivial physical sequences. But its limited success in these areas gave scientists the confidence that one day predictive kinds of explanation could be carried over into all other areas of experience, including life, consciousness, and human culture. This ideal still guides, or perhaps misguides, much scientific inquiry.[5]

Today, however, science is at least beginning to acknowledge its inability to predict accurately what will happen even in the simplest of natural processes. And in the case of nature's most fascinating phenomena, from turbulence in the atmosphere to the evolution of new species, science is clearly powerless to tell us precisely what is going to occur—even in the near future. We used to hope that we could eventually graph and master everything in a linear way. The expectation was that this would give us scientific control over the future. But now scientists are starting to recognize how exquisitely sensitive natural outcomes are to initial conditions that can never be fully specified. So today they are talking less about predictability and more about the so-called "butterfly effect" (referring here to the way in which the flapping of a butterfly's wings in a remote part of the globe can help initiate an atmospheric disturbance that will end up producing, say, a violent hurricane half a world away). Physical processes are so sensitive to their initial conditions that some scientists have calculated that even to predict the position of a billiard ball accurately after only one minute of motion we would have to take into account the gravitational attraction of an electron at the edge of our galaxy.[6]

Even the possibility that our big bang universe would eventually bring forth living and thinking beings apparently requires that the initial physical conditions at the time of cosmic origins were very precisely and delicately configured. The existence of life and mind is now often said to be "exquisitely dependent" on the most infinitesimal features in the universe's initial conditions and fundamental physical constants. For example, if the rate of cosmic expansion, the force of gravity, or the ratio of electron to proton mass had been just slightly different (say, one part in a million) from what they are, there could have been no life and no mind—at least in our present universe. Something like the butterfly effect seems to apply to the whole cosmic story.

## II

One of the most interesting features of the "scientific" discourse that surrounds chaos and complexity is that the scientists exploring these phenomena are now asking questions about the universe that sound very much like those that formerly echoed only in the chambers of metaphysics and theology. Why, they ask, is the universe so intent upon diversifying into innumerable forms of order? Why does the world have a tendency toward complexity? And why is there not just complexity, but also a cosmic tendency toward increasing, or *emergent,* complexity along the edge of chaos? Why is the universe like this?[7]

Or, as one physicist more pointedly puts it: "How can a purposeless flow of energy wash life and consciousness into the universe?"[8] For more than a century the second law of thermodynamics has dominated both physics and intellectual culture—leading usually to a sort of cosmic pessimism. The universe seemed to be heading down the slopes of entropy to an abyss of absolute disorder. But a growing number of scientists now acknowledge that there is nothing in the notion of entropy itself that helps us understand why the cosmos, from its very beginning, has also moved toward increasingly diverse and more complex forms of order.[9] Granted, there is no violation of the laws of physics in this evolution, but why has the universe taken such a fascinating detour on its journey toward final quiescence (if that is its destiny)—through the production of so much emergent beauty, life, consciousness, and culture?

These are familiar questions, of course, to followers of Teilhard de Chardin or Alfred North Whitehead. In fact they are questions that a few theologians have been dealing with for some time. But now they are creeping back into the conversations and writings of scientists themselves. We need not go so far as to insist that these questions are scientific in the strictest sense (especially since science is supposed to prescind from "why" questions and their implied teleological thrust); but that they are showing up more obviously in the discourse surrounding science is certainly worthy of reflection.

Numerous systems in nature, from cells to organisms, minds, civilizations, and religions, emerge and stabilize for varying periods of time at states far from equilibrium. And it is there—at the edge of chaos—that the most interesting new things happen in cosmic evolution. Scientists are now increasingly asking why nature tends toward this emergent complexity. Of course, they hope to answer this question in a purely naturalistic way, and they quite justifiably push their methodological naturalism as far as it can go. But if any "why" question is pursued all the way, it can scarcely avoid eventual contact with theology.

Theology is being challenged in a fresh way today to think about the biblical God in terms of a universe that is largely "self-organizing." What kind of Maker would create a universe in which novelty and creativity emerge mostly "at the edge of chaos," and in which the order and complexity emergent out of chaos cannot be specified in advance of its arrival? Does the surprising fact that randomness is bounded by strange and intricate forms of order (attractors) tell us anything significant about the relationship of the cosmos to its Creator? Is there any relevance to theology in the new picture of a universe whose features in whole and in part are so sensitive to initial conditions?

## III

These are several of the questions with which science challenges theology today. Obviously I cannot treat them all in detail here. Instead, I shall limit my discussion to six tentative suggestions as to how theology might interact in a general way with the picture of the cosmos as it is now being reconfigured by the sciences of chaos and complexity.

First, and perhaps most obviously, we should note that chaos and complexity have invited scientists to focus in an unprecedented way on the naked fact of patterning in nature. This is not something they are accustomed to doing. Usually their methods have been reductive, breaking things down into constituent parts. But in turning their attention to the fact of complex order, scientists are now getting dangerously close to issues that usually engage metaphysics and theology. In asking about the origin and meaning of pattern the scientists now exploring chaos and complexity are not far from dealing with something as fundamental as being itself.

The philosophers of old taught us that we cannot neatly separate the question of a thing's existence or its "being" from its formal cause. And more recently Alfred North Whitehead reminded us that for anything to exist at all it would have to have at least some internal organization. If there were no arrangement of its component parts it would have no definiteness. A thing simply cannot be actual without being ordered in a specific way. Indefiniteness would be the same as nonactuality.[10] "No order" means "no thing"—that is, "nothing." Thus, when scientists today ask why there is patterned complexity in the universe, this is only a hair's breadth away from the metaphysical and theological question concerning why anything exists at all. Consequently, the new "scientific" inquiry cannot be as cleanly segregated from religious questions as could perhaps the abstract, atomistic, analytical science of the past.

Moreover, it is not inconsequential, theologically speaking, that the new sciences bring out how remarkably generous the universe is in allowing order to arise even where we habitually expect more disorder. It is more evident than ever that something about the cosmos—which science itself has not yet fully specified—holds randomness within bounds. For example, stable systems, which become turbulent when energy is introduced into them, do not always avalanche precipitously toward further chaos, as we might usually expect. Surprisingly, they often take on even richer patterning and stability when they reach a state far from equilibrium. This is not the same universe that we inherited from Newton or even from Einstein. Consequently, our thoughts about its relationship to God, if we have such thoughts at all, cannot just stay the same as in the past. Once again, I believe Teilhard would completely agree.

Why, scientists are now inquiring, does the universe have this wondrous and, we might add, gracious habit of turning confusion into complexity and order? And why is there an overall increase in complexity as evolution moves forward in time? What right do we have to expect the universe to unfold so extravagantly in ever more diverse and often increasingly elaborate array, rather than simply abiding indefinitely at a granular and homogeneous level of existence? The so-called science of complexity has offered us very little so far that is inherently explanatory in this regard. We are of course grateful that it has given new emphasis to the neglected aspects of pattern and emergence, but so far it has been much more descriptive than explanatory. It raises the most fundamental of questions: Why is there order at all rather than sheer indefiniteness? This brings us very close to the Leibniz-Heidegger question: Why are there beings and not nothing?

At all costs we must avoid introducing any "god-of-the-gaps" into the dark regions that science is itself capable of illuminating. However, the question concerning why there is patterning in nature at all is a *fundamental* concern, one that asks about the totality of things and not about any particular problem capable of eventually being solved by science.

This leads us then to a second, and closely related, observation. As much as any recent developments in science, chaos and complexity are pointing us again toward the world's "contingency." And if anything is an opening for theological explanation, it is the alleged contingency of the cosmos.

To say that something is contingent means that its existence is not necessary or that its distinctive character is not required on the basis of what has happened in the past. Much discussion in science and theology comes down in the end to the question of whether the universe is contingent or necessary. Theology obviously cannot accept the idea of a necessary universe, since this would leave no place for divine creation, for gratitude, prayer, hope or worship.

Science, on the other hand, has often been attracted to the idea that the universe is necessary.[11] Scientific method, after all, would be meaningless if the universe were devoid of lawful, regular, orderly, and predictable features. Without such consistency there simply could be no science, and a necessary universe would supply consistency in abundance.[12]

Obviously, then, a universe permeated by necessity would seemingly be more congenial to scientific understanding than one enfeebled by contingency. For if the universe is contingent and not necessary, how can we account for the cosmic consistency that science needs to ground its predictions and laws? For example, unless the coupling force of gravity remains the same always, how could we ever launch satellites or predict eclipses? Unless carbon bonds with hydrogen or oxygen in the same way from age to age, how could we ever explain the emergence of life and the workings of DNA? Could we even formulate scientific theories at all if there were no underlying inevitability in the material realm? It is not hard to see why science wants the universe to be eternal and necessary.

On the other hand, could we meaningfully worship, pray, or hope for the renewal of the world if everything followed from physical necessity and there were no room for the openness of contingency? Can theology tolerate the locked-in sameness of natural schemes of recurrence that science requires in order to formulate coherent theories and invariant laws? In the past—and even today—some scientific thinkers have rejected the biblical idea of a creative, promising God because it does not mesh easily with the necessary, fully determined universe that science prefers. And theologians' distrust of science is at least partially understandable in view of the fact that so much scientific thought has ruled out the idea of a universe open to unpredictable surprise and eventual renewal.

It is well known that Albert Einstein, receptive as he was to a religious sense of mystery, could not accept the biblical God-Creator. He had assumed, at least until his own theories wrecked the notion, that the universe must be eternal. Only a universe without beginning or end would be able to guarantee the lawfulness that science seems to need. Even today, when big bang physics has all but ruled out an eternal universe, a significant number of cosmologists still strive to salvage the idea of cosmic eternity by multiplying "worlds" with such prodigality that the unfathomable totality can thereby avoid ever coming into or passing out of existence.

For over three centuries physicists have tried in this and other ways to exorcise contingency from the cosmos, presenting their timeless mathematical abstractions to us as though they were the concrete actualities of nature. But it is for just this reason that the sciences of chaos and complexity are so interesting theologically. A case can be made that they have brought science face to face with the finitude and contingency of the natural world as forcefully as have general relativity and big bang cosmology.

The most obvious way in which they have done so is in their disclosure that we can no longer deduce the future states of most natural processes from necessary first principles (as both ancient Greek "science" and classical physics had tried to do). Just as the world of Newtonian necessity breaks down when we move into the region of the very small (quantum mechanics), or into the realm of the very fast (relativity), we are now discovering that it also breaks down in the transition to turbulence (chaos). Natural systems get lost in a mathematical fog when they move through irreversible phase transitions and critical bifurcation points. We can learn about their outcomes only by waiting to see how they in fact turn out.

Their resistance to prediction and deduction is best explained by the fact of their contingency. If their outcomes were necessary we would not have to observe them at all. Empirical method would be superfluous. But because the outcomes of chaotic and complex processes can be known only by actually observing them, it is now doubtful that science can ever again find a safe haven from cosmic contingency in the classical ideals of physical inevitability or universality. This, at the very least, makes the new sciences interesting from a theological point of view.

It may be helpful to recall here that in pointing toward a unique cosmic beginning, general relativity and big bang physics had already come upon what most scientists now take to be a temporally finite universe. In demolishing the idea of an everlasting, unoriginated world, science has implicitly challenged the notion that the universe is eternal and necessary. The implication that the universe is a finite totality of interrelated things was quite startling to many scientists. Einstein, for example, originally rejected the suggestion by Willem de Sitter that general relativity requires an expanding cosmos and therefore one that must have begun in a singularity.[13] After all, what would become of science if the universe had so contingent a birth? If it is temporally finite, then on what basis could we defend the universality and necessity of its seemingly inviolable laws?

It is often said that the implied threat by a contingent universe to the eternal security of science may help explain why Einstein doctored his equations in an attempt to damp out the possibility of an expanding, temporal universe. It was not until Edwin Hubble showed him that the galaxies are in fact moving rapidly away from each other that he was compelled to reconsider his original assumptions about the eternity and necessity of the universe.[14]

Today, however, chaos and complexity are serving up just as heavy a portion of contingency on science's platter as did general relativity. Here are some of the reasons for this observation:

• The new emphasis on nature's propensity to branch out into self-organizing patterns places the most interesting features of our world far beyond the pale of what can be subjected to rigid, deterministic, or a priori analysis. The self-organizing nature of complex systems and the sheer spontaneity of complex patterning shatter our expectations of reducing all aspects of physical phenomena to some hidden inevitability.

• The unspecifiability of the literally countless initial conditions affecting any dynamical system shows it to be unpredictable, not only in practice but, as many would argue, even in principle.[15]

• The irreversibility of chaotic processes and complex dynamical systems radically challenges any efforts to retrace the stages of their development in terms of the linear scientific methods that accompany the assumption that nature is totally governed by necessity. In fact, chaos and complexity suggest that it may not be entropy alone that gives irreversibility to cosmic time. Rather, the deepest source of time's arrow could well be the continual breaking of physical symmetries (ever since the time of cosmic origins) and evolution's continually tilting toward disequilibrium and complexity.[16]

• In a similar vein we can say that it is the historical quality of our awareness of chaotic and complex evolving systems that brings home to us the contingency of nature. Science's learning about dynamical and evolutionary systems is in some respects more akin to what we usually call historical reporting than to the abstract analyses of classical physics. The objects of historical study, after all, are actual contingent events or series of events, not abstract principles. Likewise the study of chaos and complexity requires that science look closely at what actually happens in evolution, embryogenesis or atmospheric turbulence. It is not enough to sketch abstract mathematical trajectories of such processes, for in actuality they never completely conform to our idealizations (although chaos theory can have a globally predictive value in some instances). Since chaotic processes are unpredictable, they can be mapped only by following closely behind them—and awaiting their outcomes—not by predicting in advance exactly how they are going to end up.

• Finally, chaos and complexity also accentuate the inherent openness of nature to the future. In keeping with the historicity of nature, they make room once again for novelty and surprise as essential aspects of the universe. Chaos and complexity imply that nature is better understood as an indeterminate striving toward future self-realization than as an inevitable set of results arising out of a dead past. Complexity scientists, for example, have noted the remarkably anticipatory nature of any complex system's process of self-organization.[17] It is almost as though the specific pattern toward which a system is attracted quietly "influences" it out of some misty region of futurity, enticing it away from sheer determination by the past and inviting it to experiment with a wide range of possibilities before it settles into a specific morphological pathway.

It is especially this openness of phenomena toward the future, toward novelty and surprise, that now allows us to situate the natural world, more comfortably perhaps than ever, within the framework of biblical faith. There is the basis in chaos and complexity for a fresh sense of the consonance of science with the idea of a God who comes to meet the world out of the realm of the future.

Wolfhart Pannenberg, like Teilhard, understands God's relationship to the cosmos in such eschatological terms. Reality is fundamentally future, and it is out of this future that God creates the world. Likewise, Pannenberg argues, it is the constant "arrival of the future" into the present (which is also his definition of "revelation") that gives the cosmos all the consistency it needs to make science possible. We do not need to appeal to a timeless, impersonal necessity in order to ground science's ability to formulate laws and theories or to make predictions. Theologically speaking, we can account for nature's coherence by appealing to the fidelity of a promising God who sustains the world and orients it toward eschatological fulfillment.

Viewed in this way, it is not the barren necessity of a deterministic or eternal past that makes nature consistent enough from age to age to allow us to formulate scientific laws. Rather, the reliability of science is grounded in the faithfulness of God who forms a bridge backward from the future, as it were, into the present.[18] At the same time, it is the promising quality of this divine futurity that leaves the present open to the unpredictable surprise and novelty that the sciences of chaos and complexity are now bringing to our attention.

Chaos and complexity are theologically significant, therefore, especially because they require our keeping nature's reliability intimately connected to the aspect of openness to future possibility and novelty. The new sciences rule out both a world at the whim of blind chance and a world ruled by impersonal necessity. What they can teach us is that nature has both an indeterminacy that allows for new creation and a limit to randomness that still permits us to speak meaningfully of divine providence and cosmic purpose. In Teilhard's words, they teach us that "the universe is organically resting on . . . the future as its sole support."[19]

As my third suggestion, chaos and complexity are theologically appealing because they frustrate the horrifying expectation—expressed in the writings of physicists like Steven Weinberg and Stephen Hawking—that some "final theory" in physics lurks just around the corner, threatening to bring with it a conclusive, comprehensive grasp of the fundamental features of nature.[20] Such closure, allegedly, will make science complete, leaving it with nothing of significance left to discover or explain.

Chaos and complexity, however, remind us that spontaneous and unpredictable patterning is no less "fundamental" in nature than the abstracted particle-world of microphysics. Furthermore, if indeterminate quantum effects can be factored into the initial conditions to which dynamical systems are said to be so sensitive, we must despair all the more of ever fully comprehending and demystifying physical reality.[21]

There is no danger at all, in other words, that physical science is getting us any closer to an exhaustive understanding of the world. The phenomena of chaos and complexity convince us that the universe was kind enough, from the earliest moments of its formation, to see to it that we would never run out of fascinating things to explore and explain. If the universe appears simple and determined at one end, it is complex and open at the other. It is now clearer than ever that science cannot expect to arrive at intellectual control over the future of natural processes. This is good news indeed, not only for theology with its need for mystery and hope, but for the future of science as well.

Fourth, chaos and complexity suggest that any theology striving to be consonant with science must represent God as the source not only of cosmic order but also of the novelty that causes chaos to happen in the first place. In such a theological vision novelty constantly enters into the ongoing creation of the universe. But as the cosmos appropriates this novelty, its present order may have to give way to at least transitional periods of chaos. This might be troubling to theology were it not for the dramatic disclosure by chaos theory that turbulence does not always end up in complete disorder; chaos is also the opportunity for the creation of more intricate forms of order. Creativity happens "at the edge of chaos," since it is at this adventurous juncture, rather than in rigid states of stagnant equilibrium, that novelty insinuates itself into the world, concealed as it were in the clothing of turmoil. The good news in chaos theory is that disorder is not the last word.

However, if God is understood as the source of novelty, as the One "who makes all things new" (Rev. 21:5), then divine creativity is much more closely related to disorder than an older natural theology could ever have contemplated. If God were understood exclusively as the source of order (and not of novelty also), then the fact of randomness and chaos might occasion skepticism about God's actuality. However, the God of biblical religion is the author not only of order and life but of *new* order and *new* life. Hence, a biblically based theology is not surprised to find divine creativity hovering very close to turbulence.

Whenever something new is introduced into an already ordered arrangement, the present state of order tends to break down. To be receptive to novelty, rigid orderliness has to give way. It is the habit of nature, as it seeks wider and more intricate patterning, to veer entropically toward the "edge of chaos." The world's atomic, molecular, and organic structures first have to loosen up, as it were, if they are to make way for a more intricate incarnation of information. It is apparently the role of what physics calls "entropy" to provide the conditions for this disassembling. If natural order were absolutely inflexible and resistant to processes like "symmetry breaking," there could be no emergent novelty, no growth, no life, no evolutionary adaptation, no new patterning. From this point of view, entropy is the occasion less for cosmic pessimism than for hope that the universe is always open to new creation.

Chaos, nonlinearity, and chance, then, are not signals that the world exists without the care of God, as scientific skepticism has generally argued.[22] Rather they may be read theologically as consonant with the idea of a God who is concerned that the world will always become something more than what it is. To the theologian they suggest a divine discontent with the status quo, a Creativity that is always fresh and that invites our own complicity in making the world new.

A theology shaped by the religious tradition that traces its ancestry to Abraham understands "faith" as an invitation to look for signs of promise in even the most inauspicious beginnings. The sciences of chaos and complexity show how processes in the natural world (1) begin with an amazing modesty and simplicity, (2) move through a puzzling turbulence or chaos, but then (3) burst out into the richest and most beautiful of patterns. We may take this constellation as a metaphor of the promise that permeates the whole universe. Though either monotony or turbulence seems to reign supreme at times, chaos and complexity point to the possibility of surprising outcomes, for novel forms of order that we must await in patience.

We cannot calculate the character of emergent natural beauty in advance of its actual arrival. This, we have learned at last, is a remarkably different kind of universe from the one given to us by the science of the past. But a world so *pregnant with* surprising new outcomes corresponds remarkably well to the idea of a God whose character is disclosed primarily in the experience of reality's promise.

My fifth point is that chaos theory and the new science of "complexity" put a fresh spin on the origin and evolution of life, and this may also catch the attention of the theologian. For one thing, the picture of nature that arises from the study of so-called "dynamical systems" makes the emergence of complex pat-

terning, such as the origin and evolution of life, exemplify a much more probable occurrence, and less of a cosmic accident, than the older cosmologies could
have anticipated. The sensitive dependence on initial conditions in natural
processes sets these processes on the path toward complexification much earlier
and much more easily than linear science (which took into account only a small
number of initial conditions) could allow.

As long as the cosmological background of evolutionary science is taken to be
the necessity-ridden, inertial, and linear world of classical physical laws, the contingent emergence of life will appear impossibly difficult and improbable. The
cosmology implied in the sciences of chaos and complexity, however, grants to
physical reality an open readiness for dramatic, irreversible, and creative transformations that take less time, and make the emergence and evolution of life
much more likely. And because there is an outer limit to turbulence in natural
systems, complex order can arise spontaneously out of them. It is no longer necessary, in other words, to picture life as a completely anomalous occurrence in
the physical universe.

In addition, chaos and complexity also challenge science to reconsider the
role of natural selection in evolution, and in doing so they affect, at least indirectly, theology's conversations with evolutionary science. In his book *Ever
Since Darwin,* Stephen Jay Gould takes the usual neo-Darwinian line in arguing
that blind natural selection is the sole and sufficient source of creativity in the
biosphere. Like many other evolutionists, he considers the natural selection of
numerous small variations over a long period of time sufficient to account for all
the new things that appear in evolution, including eventually ourselves. If variations arrived already "prepackaged in the right direction," Gould says, then selection would have no creative role to play.[23]

Today, however, complexity science proposes that organisms do indeed arrive
in a "prepackaged" form. Stuart Kauffman, for example, has argued at great
length that living systems (like other complex phenomena) have already organized themselves spontaneously—before selection ever has a chance to choose
some few species for survival and reproduction. Creativity in evolution takes
place *primarily* in the self-organization that occurs at the edge of chaos. Natural
selection, Kauffman thinks, is still a factor, but it is not the only one.[24]

Kauffman's ideas about evolution may have no direct implications for theology. They do nothing, for example, to disturb his own agnosticism. Still, they
indirectly affect theology in its encounter with scientific skepticism. For in order
to bludgeon religious interpretations of evolution skeptics have consistently
fallen back on the assumption that an aimless process of purely "necessary" natural selection is sufficient to account for all of life, including the human species.
Yet, if we are to trust Kauffman's interpretation, nature is more than eager to provide the material for selection in a "prepackaged" form. The process of self-
organization that goes on (in the formation of cells and organisms) before or
alongside of natural selection provides further hints that our universe is not one
that only grudgingly or sparingly allows living and thinking beings to appear as
the cosmic pessimists have always insisted. Rather, nature apparently goes out of
its way to make such momentous emergence possible.[25] Chance and natural

selection still have to play in evolution, but they no longer seem to be as dominant as science has previously supposed.

Sixth, and finally, what are we to make theologically of nature's capacity for
self-organization? That the universe seems to be creatively patterning *itself* is
also of great theological interest. An older natural theology may have been disturbed by all the scientific talk nowadays about nature's self-organizing propensities. After all, a self-organizing universe would seem to leave little room for a
creative and designing deity. Does the world's order, therefore, no longer depend
in any sense on God? Is the universe really so autonomous that it can actively
organize itself?

The science of complexity assumes that nature is actively self-creative at all
levels. Atomic structures, living cells, anthills, immune systems, ecosystems, and
even economic systems seem to come about primarily as the result of an unspeci-
fiable *internal* organizational impulse. Organization seems to "just happen" as
the result of a self-creative impetus built into nature from the start. Even the
emergence of life and mind in all their complexity now appears to science as simply the unfolding of a potential always resident in matter. No special supernatural intervention seems necessary.

How then can we continue to talk meaningfully about God or divine care in
terms of a universe comprised of complex, adaptive, self-organizing patterns?

A very tentative theological response might go something like this: if God is to
create a world truly distinct from the divine being, then such a world would have
to possess an *internal* "self-coherence" or autonomy, simply in order to be distinct from God. Divine creation may perhaps be understood as a "letting be" of
the world. The creation of the world *ex nihilo* does not require a simplistically
direct divine fashioning of things. Even classical theism holds that the world
generally works by way of secondary causation. If the universe were merely
passive putty in a divine pot maker's hands, then it could not be adequately distinct from God, nor could God radically transcend it. If nature is to be clearly
not-God, or if it is to be something other than God—as all forms of theism
require—then it would not be at all surprising that it has a propensity for the kind
of self-organization that the sciences of chaos and complexity are now bringing
to our attention.

This does not contradict the classical understanding of creation, in which the
universe's coming into being and its ongoing existence are grounded in the power
of God. But any notion of creation that attempts to reduce it simply to efficient
causation is both scientifically and theologically problematic, since this would
imply a predestinarian determinism. In order to create a distinct universe, a truly
loving God could also be thought of as paradoxically withholding the exercise of
a too direct kind of power and as withdrawing any intrusive form of presence.
The universe that is then called into being by God would be not only an expression of divine might but just as fundamentally the product of divine humility.

In this interpretation of creation God freely undergoes a self-emptying
(*kenōsis* in Christian thought) so that something "other" than divine reality can
come into existence. At the heart of the divine life, so to speak, there is an eternal self-contracting, a reduction of God's expansiveness, a self-emptying of the

infinite presence and power. In this *kenōsis* God freely gives the divine selfhood completely and unreservedly to the world, and so becomes deeply incarnate in it.[26] This incarnational emptying is paradoxically what allows God's "other," the universe, to emerge in its relative autonomy and self-creativity. It is out of God's humility and loving concern for the full actualization and coherence of this "other" that the universe is endowed, from its inception, with an inherent, though risk-filled, capacity for self-organization.

It is only because we have not thought in sufficient depth about God's loving as a self-emptying and a letting-be that we find ourselves surprised that a divinely created universe is also a self-organizing one. Yet even in adult human relations we are most responsive to others whose love takes the shape of a noninterference that gives us the slack to be ourselves. We feel most liberated and most alive in the presence of those who risk "letting us be," and we are considerably cramped by those who force their presence upon us. We tender our deepest devotion to those who have the strength to restrain their power and presence so as to allow us to be somewhat indeterminate, and we resent those who are too weak to keep their domineering impulses from constantly running our lives. Unfortunately the "power" of God is probably more often understood as the capacity for wielding the intrusive kind of might rather than as bestowing a love that is mighty precisely in its restraint.

In a kenotic theology, however, it is because God is not only infinitely loving, but precisely out of love also infinitely humble, that the self-organizing universe is allowed to appear. Theologians have ignored the aspect of God's humility and have usually presented "Him" (masculine) as "powerful" only in a very coarse sense.[27] The idea of God as "all-mighty" has been understood in a way that often leads to theological contradictions, many of which have been pointed out quite rightly by scientific skeptics. However, God's power (which ultimately means the capacity to influence) is more effectively manifested in a humble inviting into being of a self-organizing universe than in any direct display of divine magicianship. A world capable of self-organization is surely a more integral world, one more intense in being, and paradoxically one more intimately related to God, than a world thought of as merely passive in the hands of its creator.[28]

The ongoing creation of the universe through the self-organizing processes disclosed by the sciences of chaos and complexity, therefore, can be thought of as ultimately made possible by the nonintrusive, persuasive love of God, by a calling-into-being that arrives faithfully out of the realm of an inexhaustible future. It is this promising, yet paradoxically self-restraining and self-outpouring, divine love that invites the world into being and continually challenges it to raise itself every day, as Teilhard would put it, "a little farther above nothingness."[29]

# 14

# Divine Wisdom

## Her Significance for Today

### ELEANOR RAE

The person of Wisdom is the focus of this study. There are certain obvious flaws in the selection of Wisdom, such as the magnification of one aspect of the divinity to be all-encompassing.[1] However, there are also serious problems with images such as Father and Son, which by definition exclude the majority of the human race.[2] At this point in time, Wisdom is my personal choice for imaging the divinity because I know of no other image in my Christian tradition that speaks as powerfully to the three issues to be addressed in this paper. Thus I will present Wisdom as a universal saving figure, as the divine as feminine, and as the presence of the divine in creation as its ground.

## WISDOM AS UNIVERSAL SAVIOR

For the first time in recorded history, all of humankind share a common origin story—the scientific story of how our universe blazed forth into being from an infinitesimal pinpoint.[3] This blazing forth from a common source speaks to us of our unity and our connectedness; all that we know, including ourselves, is basically recycled stardust. This story of the universe gives us pause in regard to the claims made by Christianity. This issue is well stated by Sallie McFague:

"And the Word became flesh and lived among us." (John 1:14a). The scandal of uniqueness is absolutized by Christianity into one of its central doctrines, which claims that God is embodied in one place and one place only: in the man Jesus of Nazareth. He and he alone is "the image of the invisible God" (Col. 1:19). The source, power, and goal of the universe is known through and only through a first-century Mediterranean carpenter. The creator and redeemer of the fifteen-billion-year history of the universe with its

First published in *Teilhard Studies* no. 40 (summer 2000).

hundred billion galaxies (and their billions of stars and planets) is available only in a thirty-year span of one human being's life on planet Earth. The claim, when put in the context of contemporary science, seems skewed, to say the least. When the world consisted of the Roman Empire (with "barbarians" at its frontiers), the limitation of divine presence to Jesus of Nazareth had some plausibility while still being ethnocentric; but for many hundreds of years, well before contemporary cosmology, the claims of other major religious traditions have seriously challenged it. In its traditional form the claim is not only offensive to the integrity and value of other religions but incredible, indeed, absurd, in light of postmodern cosmology. It is not remotely compatible with our current picture of the universe.[4]

It seems to me, as a Christian, that the proper response is to see my Christianity as only one particular part, and a minor one at that, of the universe story. It also motivates me to look for those elements in my faith tradition that speak most powerfully to true universalism. At this time, I find this claim best articulated in the person of Wisdom, who speaks as the creator and sustainer of all of creation.[5]

My own understanding of Wisdom as universal savior originated several years ago as the result of my reading from the Gospel of Luke. I was using Luke as part of my preparation for a retreat presentation and was struck in a new way by 7:35: "Yet wisdom is justified by all her children." At its face value, and coming as it did at the conclusion of the story comparing John and Jesus and the power of the message of each for some members of their society, it seems to indicate that it was Wisdom who was the universal savior. The role of Jesus and John seemed to be that of her messengers.

I shared this insight in my speaking and in my writing. Further, in 1990, I was given the opportunity to test my insight with a prominent scripture scholar. We were working together in an interfaith context and trying to draw up a document that, while honoring our experience of the interfaith community, would speak to the delegates to the upcoming Assembly of the World Council of Churches on the Holy Spirit. I suggested we use Luke 7:35 because of its universalism, but he turned me down, saying there was not enough evidence for my interpretation. Not being a scripture scholar, I acquiesced, perhaps too quickly, to his judgment. Nevertheless, I continued to speak out of my insight and was delighted when, at the 1992 meeting of the Society of Biblical Literature, a scripture scholar did address the meaning of Luke 7:35. His paper included the following: that, for the Q community, John and Jesus are both children of the divine Sophia; that they are the ones of their own generation to whom the divine Sophia has communicated Herself; that, as Her children, they are called upon to justify Her; that the importance of Jesus lies in his role as spokesperson for Sophia—that is to say, in his words and not in his death and resurrection.[6]

It would seem that the research on Q is a worthwhile contemporary means of moving out of an exclusive Christianity and entering into dialogue among the world's religions. In the person of the divine Sophia, it offers us one who may be looked upon as a universal Savior, whose messengers appear in all the major world religions (and in other religions as well) and who may be available at any and all times.

In the tenth chapter of the Wisdom of Solomon, Wisdom is seen as savior in that the key elements of the exodus event are attributed to Her as are key events in the lives of Adam, Noah, Abraham, Lot, Jacob, and Joseph.[7] We read, for example, "She brought them over the Red Sea, and led them through deep waters" (Wis. 10:18). For our purposes, the verse directly preceding chapter ten (9:18) is especially noteworthy, for in this verse we are told that Wisdom's saving agency is extended to all human beings on Earth.[8]

This gift of salvation or offer of life is also the theological vision of the Book of Proverbs. Further, this gift of life is not reserved for the future but is given in the here and now. Life is a gift to be sought, but the giving of that gift rests ultimately on the choice of Lady Wisdom. The images of a fountain and of the tree of life are frequently used to symbolize this gift of life.[9] In Proverbs 10:2 and 11:4, life is equated with virtue, while in Proverbs 12:28, it is seen in relationship to justice.[10] This gift of life is amplified in the Wisdom of Solomon, where wisdom is associated not only with life but with life that is immortal. Here life is presented as undying, incorruptible, and eternal (Wis. 1:15; 2:23; 5:15).[11]

In the Wisdom literature, specifically in Proverbs 8:4, where the call of Wisdom is addressed to the whole of humanity, at least one author finds that biblical universalism has reached its height. Samuel Terrien contrasts the universalism of the wisdom of the sages to the universalism of the prophets and psalmists. He characterizes the latter as eschatological, whereas the former is concerned with the here and now. For example, Wisdom provides a sacramental meal of bread and wine so that her guests may live (Prov. 9:5-6).[12]

The above shows both the particularism and the universalism of Wisdom. Both of these elements are very much a part of who She is. In regard to the particular, it may be said that Wisdom's concern lies in responding to the challenges provided by one's immediate experiences.[13] However, it may also be said that, when the Divine Presence appears absent from history, it may be found in the cosmic order as Wisdom. While Terrien is specifically referring here to the time of the Babylonian capture of Judah, I suggest that it could refer equally as well to our own times.[14]

Given the power of the presence of Lady Wisdom, one cannot but wonder why She was not a more central part of the Western religious heritage. In the Hebrew tradition we find that the universalism of Proverbs 8 is narrowed down in, for example, Sirach 24, and Wisdom is given a dwelling place in Jerusalem. Further, She is identified here with the Torah. This linkage of Wisdom and Torah is continued by Baruch (3:9-4:4).[15] It becomes even more explicit in, for example, *Sayings of the Fathers,* where one finds that several scripture texts about Wisdom, which are found in Proverbs, are taken and applied instead to Torah.[16] Working from within her tradition, Asphodel P. Long has also used the biblical texts, notably Proverbs, but also Psalm 104:24 and Job 28:27, to argue for the universality of Wisdom as well as Her divinity and Her intimate relationship to creation. Long notes that this image of Wisdom raised enormous questions for the monotheistic, patriarchal Hebrews. They dealt with these by equating Wisdom with the Torah (for example, Ben Sirach) or by assigning Her to heaven (for example, Enoch). Through these actions, the feminine Divine was lost, as was "her universality and her relationship with Nature. Rather, wisdom was seen as compliance with commandments and subject to reward and punishment, rather than the origin and sustainer of the natural universe."[17]

In the Christian tradition too, Lady Wisdom was buried and altered. Thus, while the beginnings for a vibrant pneumatology were available in the close identification of Wisdom and the spirit (e.g., Wis. 7:22-23), Wisdom was taken and applied to Christ, both directly, as in Paul (e.g., 1 Cor. 1:24, 30) or indirectly, as in John (for example, the prologue to his Gospel). This was also the path followed by the early church fathers, such as Hermas (*Shepherd*), Justin Martyr, Clement, and Origen. In time, to safeguard the divinity of Christ, the Wisdom tradition was downplayed, only to resurface again in relationship to Mary, who was not officially considered divine. Thus was preserved the monotheism of Christianity.[18] But Wisdom as a universal symbol for the ultimate is resurfacing again in Christianity, as may be seen, for example, in the writing of Elizabeth A. Johnson:

> Wisdom discourse likewise directs belief toward a global, ecumenical perspective respectful of other religious paths. The imagery of wisdom operates today much the way the logos metaphor functioned in the early Christian centuries to signify the play of God's goodness and just order throughout the world, a function now somewhat curtailed for the logos due to its long association with androcentric theology and imperialistic ecclesial history. Sophia, however, is people loving; her light shines everywhere, and those whom she makes to be friends of God and prophets are found throughout the wide world. Jesus-Sophia personally incarnates her gracious care in one particular history, for the benefit of all, while she lays down a multiplicity of paths in diverse cultures by which all people may see, and seeking find her.[19]

Some of the diverse cultures in which Wisdom may be found include the other major world religions—Hinduism, Buddhism, and Islam. Thus, for example, the *Ramayana* tells us: "Wisdom (*saryam*) is God in the world. It is on wisdom that justice always is built. It is in wisdom that everything is rooted. There is no higher level above that."[20]

Likewise in Hinduism is found the goddess Kulakatyayani, or intuitive wisdom.[21] In Buddhism, Wisdom is present in at least two images. One is Prajnaparamita, the perfection of Wisdom. She is seen as the ultimate saving wisdom because she personifies the insight "which perceives the dynamic and interdependent character of reality." She is considered the mother, nourisher and teacher of all the Buddhas.[22]

> The Buddhas in the world-systems in the ten directions
> Bring to mind this perfection of wisdom as their mother.

The Saviours of the world who were in the past, and also are now
   in the ten directions,
Have issued from her, and so will the future ones be.
She is the one who shows this world (for what it is)
   she is the genetrix, the mother of the Buddhas.[23]

A second figure is found in Mahayana Buddhism in the person of Kuan-Yin.
There are more than eighty Sutras (canonical texts) devoted to Kuan-Yin. While
she may originally have been presented as male, by the fifth century she became
identified as female. As such, she expresses concern with liberation in the here
and now. Further, she is regarded by many as the universal principle of salvation
and the giver to all of the light of wisdom. She is sometimes pictured with one
thousand hands and one thousand eyes.[24] Islam, despite its strict monotheism,
has at least one theologian who wrote about divine Wisdom. To Ibn al-Arabi,
who lived in the twelfth and thirteenth centuries, is attributed a poem about
Nizam, a young woman whom he presented as an earthly manifestation of divine
Wisdom. He also wrote about the creative breath of Mercy as a feminine component of the Godhead itself. While he was persecuted for his views in his lifetime, he was too good a theologian to be ignored.[25] As today's Islamic women
receive training in theology, we can look forward with hope to more theologizing on divine Wisdom.

## WISDOM AS THE FEMININE DIVINE[26]

Sometimes the fact that certain key divine symbols are feminine—such as
Ruaḥ and Ḥokmah and Shekhina—is simply acknowledged and then dismissed
as unimportant. At other times, the female gender of these key symbols seems
simply to go unnoticed. For example, in the commentary on the reading from
Proverbs 8:22-31 for Trinity Sunday we are told: "The praise of Wisdom is a kind
of foreshadowing of the doctrine of the Blessed Trinity. Wisdom is personified as
the creative spirit of God speaking in *her* (italics added) own person and later to
be manifested in the person of Jesus Christ."[27] Nor is this ignoring of the femininity of the divine symbols limited to the Christian tradition. For example,
Joanna Macy notes in her writing on Prajnaparamita that her being mother of all
Buddhas is simply overlooked in that tradition.[28] These tactics of belittling and
ignoring the femininity of the divine symbol are specifically confronted by Claudia V. Camp in her study on the book of Proverbs. Camp takes note of the widely
accepted theory that Wisdom is a hypostasis of Yahweh, which theory she views
as problematic because it is "difficult to square with the rather debilitating fact
that wisdom was not a terribly prominent attribute of Yahweh."[29] (This is not
totally surprising, as one should not really expect to find the feminine wisdom to
be prominent in the very masculine Yahweh.) Camp's book as a whole is a study
of Wisdom as feminine and as the unifying element in Proverbs. She uses three
areas of literary analysis—metaphor, personification, and symbol—to illustrate
her hypothesis.[30] For Camp, the use of the feminine noun *ḥokmâ* was not some-

thing that just happened, or something into which writers were forced, but rather was a deliberate choice.[31] The most audacious claim made by female Wisdom is her claim to be mediator of the foremost divine blessing, life itself.[32] This would seem to be a claim reserved for the Divinity alone. But this claim is not altogether surprising in view of the divine origin of Wisdom as presented in Proverbs 8:22-31.[33] For me, this passage speaks to the emptying out of the Divinity into the Spirit (Wisdom), and, while not attested to in this passage, I see this *kenōsis* also taking place with the Word as recipient.

Also commenting on Proverbs 8, Roland Murphy makes the following observations about Wisdom: She speaks publicly and universally on Her own authority; She identifies Herself as being present before creation; She claims that the one who finds Her, finds life; She is both the revelation of the divine and the revelation of creation.[34] In Wisdom of Solomon 7:25-26, Wisdom is the reflection of eternal light—the light that Isaiah 60:19-20 identifies as the Divinity. This passage in the Wisdom of Solomon is a celebration of Her intimacy with the Divinity, moving beyond her "begetting" in Proverbs 8:22-25 or Her coming forth from the mouth of the Most High in Sirach 24:3. In this passage, She is identified with the divine spirit (Wis. 1:7; 9:17; 12:1).[35]

This correlation of Wisdom and the spirit, as found in Wisdom 7:22, is to be found in the New Testament writings of Paul (1 Cor. 2:4-16). It should be noted, however, that while the image of the Holy Spirit as the feminine Divine develops naturally from the Hebrew use of the feminine word *rûaḥ* (spirit or breath), subsequent translations of scripture did not support this development. Thus the Greek of the New Testament rendered Spirit as *pneuma*, which is neuter, while the Latin used the word *spiritus*, which is masculine. Nonetheless, strands of the development of the Holy Spirit as the feminine Divine are to be found in the Christian tradition. But before turning to this development, let us look briefly at the gnostic writings to see what they reveal concerning the feminine imaging of the Divine.

The writers of the gnostic Gospels often viewed the Divine not only as the Divine Father but also as the Divine Mother. According to Elaine Pagels, these writings may be grouped into three different categories. In the first category, the Divine is seen as a dyad of the Divine Mother and the Divine Father. The Divine Mother in this dyad is variously imaged as Grace, Silence, the Womb, the Mother of All and Intelligence (in Greek, the feminine term *epinoia*). She is the source of all that is, including, in some accounts, even the great God Yahweh Himself. A second group of writings describes the Divine Mother as the Holy Spirit. Thus, for example, in the *Apocryphon of John,* she is seen as Mother in a trinitarian vision; in the *Gospel of Thomas,* Jesus contrasts his earthly parents, Mary and Joseph, with his Divine Mother, the Holy Spirit, and with his divine Father; in the *Gospel of Philip,* the Spirit is called the "Mother of many."[36] The *Gospel of the Hebrews,* which is utilized by Clement of Alexandria, Origen, and Jerome, also speaks of the Holy Spirit as Mother. For example, Origen quotes, "Even so did my mother, the Holy Spirit, take me by one of my hairs and carry me away on to the great mountain Tabor," while Jerome sees the Holy Spirit as Mother descending on Jesus at his baptism.[37] Finally, there are some gnostic writers who characterized the Divine Mother as Wisdom. As such she is called the source of all creation, the one who enlightens humanity and makes it wise, the savior of Noah and his family from the wrath of God the Father, the coincidence of opposites, the first and the last.[38]

Pagels, who is interested both in biblical scholarship and in cultural issues, asks the question: Did the gnostic Christian women derive any practical social advantages from this feminine conceptualization of the Divine? Her answer is yes, as evidenced by the fact that women were revered as prophets, teachers, exorcists, and healers; that they presided at the Eucharist and baptism; that they were ordained as priests and bishops; that they were founders of gnostic movements. While she does not always see a universal connection, she does conclude that the weight of evidence indicates a clear correlation between gnostic religious theory and social practice.[39]

Within mainstream Christianity, as in the gnostic writings, the Holy Spirit was experienced in explicitly sexual terms. She is called Mother, Spouse, the New Eve, Sister, Daughter. Traces of these experiences are found in mystical, liturgical, and theological writings. In Ebionism, a tradition that may be characterized as Judeo-Christian in origin, we find the vision of Elkesai. In this vision, he sees two beings of equal and immense dimensions. The masculine he identifies as the Son of God, while the feminine he sees as the Holy Spirit.[40]

Within the Syriac liturgical tradition, a tradition that was also Judeo-Christian, we find the Holy Spirit imaged as the feminine Divine. The signing in the rite of initiation, the laying on of hands in the rite of ordination, and the eucharistic sacrifice were effected by the power of the Holy Spirit, whose action is described as hovering or brooding.[41] She is imaged in the context of the liturgy as a merciful mother.[42] This understanding of the Holy Spirit as feminine Divine was evident in the Syriac liturgy until 400 C.E.[43]

In theological writings, too, the Holy Spirit is represented in sexual images. In *Against Heresies,* Irenaeus states, "Those who do not have a share in the Spirit are not nourished to life by the Mother's breasts" (3.24.1). Likewise, Clement of Alexandria characterizes the Divine in feminine as well as in masculine terms. He refers to the Word as mother, nurse, and teacher, while the Father nourishes us with milk from his breasts. On this basis, in what seems to be a pattern, Clement sees men and women as sharing equally in perfection, and he urges women to participate with men in the community. He backs up his urging for female participation by listing women who have held prominent places in history as rulers, writers, philosophers, poets, and painters.[44] While Clement imaged both the Father and the Word in feminine terms, Methodius of Olympus (d. 311) looked specifically to the Holy Spirit and saw Her as Bride and as the New Eve.[45] For Synesius of Cyrene (d. after 412), the Holy Spirit was mother, sister, and daughter.[46] For the orthodox Syriac theologians, it was commonplace to refer to the Holy Spirit as She. According to Robert Murray, these Syriac theologians are "simply attributing to the Holy Spirit the motherly character which the latter parts of Isaiah (49:14-15; 66:13) find in God."[47]

In addition to the images of the Holy Spirit as mother, spouse, the new Eve, sister, and daughter, She appears to us in the Christian tradition as divine

Wisdom. Some of the early church fathers, for example, Theophilus of Antioch, Irenaeus, and the author of the Clementine Homilies, regarded Wisdom in the Old Testament as prefiguring the Holy Spirit.[48] Justin Martyr also equated the divine intelligence with the Holy Spirit; however, he diverged from biblical pneumatology in that he also equated the divine intelligence with the Logos or Son. For Clement of Alexandria, there was only one principle of enlightenment, the Son. While this imaging of Wisdom as the Son rather than as the Holy Spirit is the basic path followed by Origen, Augustine, and Aquinas, there is an alternate path that does follow the biblical witness. Thus, for Irenaeus, the Father is unknown, transcendent, and mysterious; the Son is the one who executes the Father's will; the Spirit is the divine Wisdom which nourishes, increases, and illumines. This way of theologizing is developed by Gaius Marius Victorinus (baptized c. 354). For Victorinus, the Son is the action of the Father, the one through whom the divine Being is channeled outward and downward into matter; the Spirit is the divine Intelligence, the living thought of the divine that leads us back to the source.[49]

However, this identification of divine Wisdom and the Holy Spirit came to be almost forgotten in time.[50] While there may be few explicit references to an identification of Christ and Wisdom in the New Testament, over time the church fathers did develop a Wisdom Christology, and the identification of Wisdom and the Holy Spirit was virtually forgotten.[51] For example, some of the patristic commentators such as Hippolytus and Cyprian understood Luke 11:49, "God's wisdom has said," as alluding to Jesus. However, Hans Conzelmann sees no identification here between Jesus and Wisdom, as Wisdom is here preexistent while Jesus is not.[52] While this issue of a specific Pneumatology identifying Wisdom and the Holy Spirit is deserving of much further discussion, space restraints necessitate that we move on and turn now to the issue of Wisdom's transcendence and immanence.

The first appearance of a personified figure in the Wisdom literature occurs in Job 28. Commenting on this appearance of Lady Wisdom, Roland Murphy characterizes Her as "the divine secret in the created world."[53] This passage would seem to speak of both Her transcendence (divine secret) and Her immanence (in the created world). Further, Job 28:22 states that Wisdom is inaccessible to the human but that perdition and death claim to "have heard rumor of it." The Divinity attests to having "seen and appraised it" (Job 28:27). This would seem to give wisdom an independent existence apart from Yahweh, who discovers Her. Wisdom's inaccessibility is echoed in Sirach 24:28, where we are told that "the first human never knew wisdom fully, nor will the last succeed in fathoming her." This same message is found also in Baruch 3:15-31. Further, it is alluded to by Gerhard von Rad when he tells us that a message of the Wisdom literature is, no matter what we know, there still remains the element of mystery in the end result. This is so because life is ultimately determined not by rules but by the Divinity.[54] So, in a real sense, Wisdom will never be the possession of the human.

In addition to being transcendent, Wisdom is also immanent. This is noted by many commentators, including Murphy, who sees Wisdom as the divine communication, or extension of self, to human beings.[55] Murphy identifies Wisdom of Solomon 7:24 and 8:1 as passages that present Wisdom as immanent in the world.[56] Terrien also characterizes Wisdom as immanent and, citing Proverbs 8:22-31, describes Her as a divine being who communicates Her unique status, activity, and mediating function; She is the presence of the Divinity to humankind, a presence communicated through play.[57] More on the issue of the divine immanence of Wisdom will be said when we look at Her in the context of creation theology in the next section. But before that I will conclude with a quotation from Elizabeth Johnson that summarizes well the insight into Wisdom as the feminine Divine. After examining the function of Wisdom, Johnson states:

> This lends credence to yet a fifth option, which holds that Sophia is a female personification of God's own being in creative and saving involvement with the world. The chief reason for arriving at this interpretation is the functional equivalence between the deeds of Sophia and those of the biblical God. What she does is already portrayed elsewhere in the scriptures as the field of action of Israel's God under the revered, unpronounceable name YHWH. She fashions all that exists and pervades it with her pure and people-loving spirit. She is all-knowing, all-powerful, and present everywhere, renewing all things. Active in creation, she also works in history to save her chosen people, guiding and protecting them through the vicissitudes of liberating struggle. Her powerful words have the mark of divine address, making the huge claim that listening to them will bring salvation while disobedience will bring destruction. She sends her servants to proclaim her invitation to communion. By her light kings govern justly and the unjust meet their punishment. She is involved in relationships of loving, seeking, and finding with human beings. Whoever loves her receives what in other scriptural texts is given by God alone.[58]

## WISDOM AS THE MATRIX OF CREATION

The idea of the Wisdom literature as creation theology is not a recent development but dates back at least to 1964, when Walther Zimmerli identified Wisdom as being within the framework of a theology of creation.[59] For example, in the book of Ecclesiastes, the Deity presented is preeminently a creator deity. All that is created is beautiful and/or appropriate to its time.[60] "The sages did not analyze nature in the subject/object manner that is ours. Ps. 104 and the saying in Prov. 30 show this. All things, especially all living things, were appreciated for simply existing, for being alive."[61] There seemed to be no dualistic view of creation. Rather, everything had intrinsic worth; things were not objects to be valued because they were useful. There was no sacred versus profane; all was permeated with the Divine Presence. This would lead me to say, in the present environmental crisis, that a wisdom spirituality is to be found in such things as the food I purchase and eat and the way I treat my yard by refraining from the use of poisons. Likewise, the biblical sages, by the use of daily experiences, were able to draw people into the mystery that was the divinity. According to Murphy, they "penetrated into the divine mystery in a manner that even the prophets never equaled."[62]

Von Rad also seems to see a holistic vision in the Wisdom literature. He contends that Israel "did not differentiate between a 'life wisdom' that pertained to the social orders and a 'nature wisdom' because she was unable to objectify these spheres in the form of such abstractions."[63] For von Rad, the continuity of the Wisdom literature is based on seeing Wisdom as self-revelatory. In other words, the Wisdom writers had "unwavering certainty that creation herself will reveal her truth to the man who becomes involved with her and trusts her, because this is what she continually does."[64] Thus it may truly be said that Wisdom is a way of understanding divine revelation.[65] While the more usual way to understand divine revelation has been as salvation history, I would suggest that divine revelation as seen in creation is more appropriate for today. One obvious reason is that it is the story of all of humankind, which story is critically needed today if we are all to act together to save the Earth from ecological disaster.

In the Wisdom literature, there is no separation of the world from the creator. Rather, the two are held in tension—the all-pervasive causality of the divine (for both good and evil) and the autonomy of creation, as seen, for example, in the ants, locusts, lizards, and badgers who teach wisdom (Prov. 30:24-28).[66] Creation is understood as the revelation of the creator (Wis. 13:1).[67] To see the world is to see the creator. However, Wisdom literature displays little interest in the world's origins; rather it is interested in the world as the place of divine activity. This is the world that humans learn from and react to—the surface of the Earth on which Lady Wisdom plays (Prov. 8:31).[68] Thus, for example, in Job, the first biblical book in which personified Wisdom appears, the Divinity reveals itself in creation with the result that Job is transformed (Job 38-39); Job responds to this revelation: "I had heard of you by word of mouth, but now my eye has seen you" (Job 42:5).[69]

It is also in the book of Job that a non-anthropomorphic understanding of creation is presented. God points out to Job that rain falls where human beings do not live (38:26-27); that the Divinity is the one who hunts for the lion (38:39-40); that, as exemplified in the ostrich, the creation includes by design that which the human does not value (39:13-17). Rather than vanquishing the "monsters," as occurs in traditional cosmogonies, God admires them in splendid poetry. Placing Job at the periphery, God celebrates the creation for its own worth, a testament to His power and grace.[70]

The language that creation speaks may be characterized as peculiar (Psalm 19), steady, nonverbal, and heard (Psalm 19:2).[71] In addition to being the language of the sages, the language of Wisdom is also the language of the non-human. The four previously mentioned small creatures—the ants, the badgers, the locusts, the lizards—are referred to as being exceedingly wise; they are so called because of their behavior (Prov. 30: 24-28). Job also cites beasts and birds, reptiles and fish as the teachers of the human (Job 23:7-8). In Sirach 39:12-35, the goodness of all the works of creation is extended to the so-called non-living world. Here the theme is the goodness of all the works of the Divinity; this theme is illustrated through the motif of *kairos,* or right time. Thus even fire and hail, famine and disease are seen as having their proper time. Sirach 43:1-33 is a hymn in praise of creation where all obey including hail, rain, and lightning. The hymn reaches its high point when it cites the Divinity as the source and sustenance of all that is: "He is the all" (43:27). Further, the compassion of the Divinity is extended to all living beings; this is contrasted to the human, who has compassion only for the neighbor (18:13).[72]

The language of the Wisdom literature may also be seen as the language of experience. This may be seen as a pertinent source today for ecofeminists who are developing an experiential ethics. In the Wisdom literature is found, not lofty abstract principles, but the human experience; this includes the human experience of the Divine. The human may be characterized as being always wholly in the world and as having always to deal with the Divinity. The Wisdom literature exhorts us to learn everything we can possibly learn and to use it in our daily living; on the other hand, it warns us that, no matter what we know, there is always the element of mystery in the end result. This is basically an acknowledgment of human limitations. One must always remain open for the completely new experience.[73] Von Rad summarizes this meaning and power of wisdom in the following way:

> There is the fact that the truth about the world and man can never become the object of our theoretical knowledge; that reliable knowledge can be achieved only through a relationship of trust with things; that it is the highest wisdom to abstain from the attempt to control wisdom in abstract terms; that it is much wiser to let things retain their constantly puzzling nature and that means to allow them to become themselves active and, by what they have to say, to set man to rights.[74]

In the Wisdom literature, we find a language that encompasses both good and evil (for example, in Job and Ecclesiastes). Ours is an age in which the reality of evil has appeared in massive proportions—on both the structural and the personal level. Facing this reality, we seem to have even less insight than ages past on how to conceive of a Divinity whom we call good and yet who "allows" such evil to occur. We might begin a contemporary theodicy by looking at the Wisdom literature and acknowledging its insight that all—both things we call good and things we call evil—are somehow the work of the Divinity. If nothing else, this might enable us to rethink the idea of our own deaths. The Earth and all we know is here only because of the death of stars. In the same manner, might not our own deaths be seen, not so much as an evil but as the opportunity for new lives for others? In addition, it seems highly likely that Plato's insight in the *Timaeus,* that the creator was not omnipotent but only doing the best that could be done, may be valid after all. This is in no way meant to play down the human's responsibility for evil actions nor to negate the power of the One who paints purple and pink sunsets that fill half the sky.

Finally, the language of Wisdom is the language found in the public places where the people are gathered: in the streets, the plazas, by the city gates (Prov. 1:20-21). Commenting on this passage, Bernhard Lang observes that "the basic reason is that Wisdom must demonstrate Her usefulness in the arena of public life."[75] Is it not even more necessary today, when the systems such as air, water, and soil, which have made life possible on the Earth and now face destruction, that the voice of Wisdom once again be heard in the public places?

## CONCLUSION

The preceding has been a look at divine Wisdom in the roles of universal Savior, the feminine Divine, and as matrix of creation—roles that have special significance for our world today. It is a preliminary study and will hopefully serve as an opening to the work that needs to be done in each of these three areas. The person of Wisdom as a saving female figure who is related to the Earth needs to be studied in all the world's religions. Only then can we make a determination of Her universality—the universality I found in the Christian scripture in Luke 7:35.

Second, Wisdom as the feminine Divine needs to be developed in the Christian tradition into a full pneumatology in the person of the Holy Spirit. We could begin by releasing the Holy Spirit from Her institutionalizing by Catholic theology, where She is seen only in relation to ecclesiastical office and ordained ministry, and from Protestant theology, where She is tied to the individual believer.[76] She must be freed to roam the whole Earth, as she does in Wisdom of Solomon 8:1, where She orders all things well. But She is not confined to the Earth but also has a cosmic function, the beginnings of which are seen, for example, in Proverbs 8:27-28. Both of these functions stand in need of further development.[77]

Third, the understanding of Wisdom as the matrix of creation needs to be lived in terms of a spirituality that truly honors the Earth as sacred. [78] While not negating the need we humans have to spend time in the worship of the Divine, this spirituality would see the time spent, for instance, in choosing a means of transportation that least damages the Earth, as an experience that is as holy as our prayer. This is because She is just as present in our moving about as She is in our meditation. She will not force us, but Her invitation is extended to each of us:

> Come, eat my bread and drink of the wine I have mixed,
> Leave foolishness and live, and walk in the way of insight.
> (Prov. 9:5-6)

## A NEW EPILOGUE FOR THIS BOOK

Having read this article on "Divine Wisdom: Her Significance for Today," the reader might be inclined to ask why it has been included in a book on Teilhard's thought when he is not even mentioned once. I can only reply that in my view, it very much reflects the spirit of Teilhard and his writings. I would like to be explicit on this in the three areas the article addresses: the universality of Wisdom as savior; the divine feminine; Wisdom as matrix of creation.

While Teilhard is widely viewed as being very Christocentric in his theologizing, I find two aspects in his thinking that would resonate with my first section on Wisdom as universal savior. The first is in regard to the issue of unity in diversity. Teilhard turns within himself and reflects:

> Indisputably, deep within ourselves, through a rent or tear, an "interior" appears at the heart of beings. This is enough to establish the existence of this interior in some degree or other everywhere forever in nature. Since the stuff of the universe has an internal face at one point in itself, its structure is necessarily bifacial; that is, in every region of time and space, as well, for example, as being granular, coextensive with its outside, everything has an inside.[79]

In other words, from its beginning, all of creation may be said to have an inside, which Teilhard refers to as its consciousness or its spontaneity.[80] His insight is borne out in modern science by the indeterminacy of particles according to quantum theory, as well as by the findings of chaos theory. The second resonance between Teilhard and my section on Wisdom as universal savior may be found in his openness to other religious traditions. Despite, or more likely because of his Christocentricity, Teilhard displayed a real interest in other faith traditions. Looking back, he viewed his invitation to go to China as the decisive event of his life. Ursula King states that the importance of his being in contact with the East refers not only to his scientific undertakings but also to his vision of convergent unity and synthesis as it applied to religion and mysticism. For Teilhard, the Christian mystical act par excellence, that of love, had both to grow further and to become more universalized. He understood that the new mysticism of action, convergence, and transformation depended on the insights of the Eastern religions as well as those of the West. This is evidenced, for example, by his association in the founding, in 1947, of the French branch of the World Congress of Faiths. In the different religious traditions, he looked for the active and animating elements. He evaluated these faith traditions according to their ability to supply the energy needed for human action in society's most urgent task—that of building the Earth and of creating a just, peaceful, and harmonious world for all.[81] In the second section of my study, on Wisdom as the feminine divine, I find two resonances with Teilhard's thinking. The first is in the *Hymn of the Universe* in his description of mystical experience, where he describes the majestic reality—the flood of energy—as feminine. He writes:

> He felt pity for those who take fright at the span of a century or whose love is bounded by the frontiers of a nation. So many things which once had distressed or revolted him—the speeches and pronouncements of the learned, their assertions and their prohibitions, their refusal to allow the universe to move—all seemed to him now merely ridiculous, nonexistent, compared with the majestic reality, the flood of energy, which now revealed itself to him: omnipresent, unalterable in its truth, relentless in its development, untouchable in its serenity, maternal and unfailing in its protectiveness.[82]

Second, in King's description of Teilhard's new mysticism, my findings of Wisdom's biblical transcendence and immanence are echoed. King refers to the three orientations in Teilhard's mysticism which she calls the *Via prima,* or communion with Earth (immanence); the *Via secunda,* or communion with God (transcendence); and the *Via tertia,* or communion with God through Earth. The first two ways—either immanence or transcendence alone—Teilhard found to be incomplete and deficient. It is only through the coming together of immanence and transcendence into the mysticism of action that completion is found, which is also the way of Lady Wisdom, who may be found in the public places (e.g., Prov. 1:20f.).[83]

The third section of my study addresses Wisdom as the matrix of creation. In this regard, I find three issues where Teilhard's thought may be said to be grounded in the Wisdom tradition. First, Wisdom literature sees all of creation as possessing intrinsic worth. Teilhard would also share this thinking, as may be seen, for example, in his understanding that "[f]rom the biosphere to species, everything therefore is but one immense ramification of psyche seeking itself through forms."[84] Second, the Wisdom tradition, for example in Job, recognizes that to see the world is to see the Creator. Teilhard likewise acknowledges that to have mastered matter means to be able to attain and submit to the light of God.[85] Third is the issue of evil. According to the Wisdom tradition, all—both good and evil—is somehow the work of the Divinity. Everything has its place and right time, including fire, hail, famine, and disease. Teilhard was often criticized for not giving the issue of evil its due. He responded by saying that the human phenomenon was not a human idyll but a cosmic drama. For Teilhard, evil was only too self-evident in disorder and failure, decomposition, solitude, anguish, and growth.[86] He poignantly recognizes the power of evil when he states that "even in the eyes of a mere biologist, it is still true that nothing resembles the way of the Cross as much as the human epic."[87] However, ultimately, Teilhard was able to celebrate the gift of life, which is the same gift that Lady Wisdom claims as Her own and offers here and now to those who seek and find Her.

# 15

# The Creative Union
# of Person and Community

## A Geo-Humanist Ethic

### Joseph A. Grau

### Introduction

#### A Global Agenda

Political economist Robert B. Reich, as he charts the course for his 1987 book *Tales of a New America,* lays out the fundamental challenge he sees before him:

> to define jointly promising endeavors and to forge durable ties of mutual obligation and responsibility. To a greater extent and for subtler reasons than either modern conservatism or modern liberalism appreciate, life on this planet has become less a set of contexts in which one party can be victorious, and more an intricate set of relationships which either succeed or fail—we win or we lose together.[1]

Over half a century ago, on board ship en route to China from San Francisco, Pierre Teilhard de Chardin, S.J., stimulated by the vitality and tensions of the world he saw emerging, wrote in his essay "The Spirit of the Earth,"

> The resources at our disposal today, the powers that we have released, *could not possibly be absorbed* by the narrow system of individual or national units which the architects of the human earth have hitherto used. . . . *The age of nations has passed. Now, unless we wish to perish, we must shake off our old prejudices and build the earth.*[2]

In the following study I respond to the challenges both Reich and Teilhard describe. The response is Teilhardian, in that it is drawn from research and reflec-

---

First published in *Teilhard Studies* no. 22 (fall/winter 1989).

tion on his thought. But it is not intended as just an exposition of his original views or what I think he would have said at this time. Rather I have tried, in the spirit of Teilhard, to explore implications of his thought for the current human and environmental concerns.

In my development of a Teilhardian approach to person and community and to ecology and technology, I try to reflect his thought as accurately as I can, indicate some reservations, and then proceed to formulate a position that I judge helpful in the world today. In my reading of Teilhard's views in this regard, I reach a more positive assessment than the one found by Thomas Berry in his 1982 essay in *Teilhard Studies* entitled "Teilhard in the Ecological Age."[3] My own approach is, I believe, confirmed by the views of P. Pierre Noir, S.J., and P. Christian d'Armagnac, S.J., who knew Teilhard, although it was derived prior to my consultation with them at Chantilly, France, in April 1989.[4] By "geo-humanism" I mean the human person set in an Earth-centered reality, a view long advocated by Berry.

The principal issues I will address include the communitarian concerns of Reich and Teilhard as they involve the relations of the human person in community to both the Earth and technology. Teilhard provides an ethical dimension for us, drawn especially from his christological vision as found mainly in *The Divine Milieu*. My own research into the Teilhardian corpus has focused on how, over many years, he worked out an understanding of ethics and morals that could help reveal the paths one might travel in union with Christ and the best of scientific humanist aspirations as one works to further human evolution in a planetary context.[5]

### *The Present Inquiry*

#### *Key Questions*

At the outset, I assume three specific questions as central for establishing a meaningful and comprehensive approach to an economic ethic by which to understand the person in the Earth community and to make sensible use of technological research and development. (1) How can we resolve the tensions between religious values stressing collaboration out of a motive of charity and current economic theory, which stresses vigorous competition in a relatively free market system? (2) How can a balanced geo-humanist approach to human–Earth relations be formulated that will avoid both the depersonalization of merging with nature and irresponsible human exploitation of nature? (3) How can technology be utilized so as to avoid destroying not only the environment but also the integrity of the creative person? Positively, how can it provide support for actualizing human potential for dynamic, constructive love?

These issues are closely connected. The first highlights human awareness of solidarity with other persons in a setting where independence and conflict are recognizably present. The second looks to the significance of the physical and biological environment in which people act together in search of fulfillment. The third is a corollary of the first two and an integral part of the total picture—we must arrive at an appropriate technology that is respectful of the larger Earth–human relations.

### Teilhardian Concepts Pertinent to the Questions

In order to come to grips with these questions, I will examine Teilhard's thought in these areas: (a) his vision of how a personalized Christic universe evolves by means of organized dynamic love energy; and (b) his vision of the organization of this divinized love energy in human life as it involves: collaborative organization of economic activity; constructive geo-humanist interdisciplinary research; and geo-humanized technology as supportive and extensive of the person, the community, and the biosphere.

## THE NATURE AND VALUE OF A TEILHARDIAN PERSPECTIVE

### Personalizing a Christic Universe through Love Energy

### The Overall Vision

In Teilhard's view of the evolutionary process a critical threshold to intelligent consciousness and freedom of decision was crossed with the appearance of *homo sapiens.* The interplay of energies operative for billions of years would no longer propel the development of the universe alone. As the universe, through the human phase, began to move toward higher personal consciousness—"personalization" —a new kind of creative agency would be significant: that of human choice. The personalized cosmos would be built, according to Teilhard, through the organization of ethically informed human energy, and through its highest and most important form, love energy.

For a picture of what this means, drawn in broad strokes, one can consult his major work, *The Phenomenon of Man,* notably the section on survival, where he conveys the significance of personalization and love.[6] For our present purposes, we will examine some of his other writings where he spoke in more detail of three essential kinds of love and how he understood them to fit into the complex task of building an Earth actualized by divine-human energy.

### Three Types of Love

Teilhard's tripartite approach to experiencing the reality of love is best stated in his "Sketch of a Personalistic Universe," written in Beijing in 1936, although one finds pertinent observations scattered throughout his writings from his earliest efforts.[7] The three kinds of love are sexual, generalized human, and cosmic.

*Sexual Love,* as Teilhard saw it, during most of the evolution of life, was approached primarily as reproductive. With the establishment of personality in the human species, sexuality now applies not just to reproduction but also to mutual spiritual energizing. Within marriage, this spiritual reciprocity, in keeping with the principle of creative or differentiating union whereby increased union heightens individual liberty, enables couples to avoid merging into a single ego. Instead, it serves to bring out in a complementary way the unique distinctiveness of the partners. It could also lead to a celibate arrangement. For Teilhard, as a celibate religious, his own experience of the power of the feminine in his life brought him to affirm strongly this catalytic energizing aspect, apart from and independent of physical sexual union.[8] The "affective dyad," man and woman together, however, must in turn look beyond themselves for further completion, to collaborative work in the context of generalized human love, and ultimately to loving communion with the cosmos personalized in Christ-Omega.

*Generalized Human Love,* Teilhard's *le sens humain*, or love of humanity, was considered by him to be essential for the relation between person and community to fully participate in the growth of a numinous universe. Again, in his "Sketch of a Personalistic Universe," after he states that the love of man and woman for each other is in itself not adequate for full personal development, he goes on to say:

> The personalizing energy displayed by passionate love must therefore be completed by another form of attraction which will draw the totality of the human molecules together. It is this particular form of cohesion, spread throughout the whole noosphere, that we call here "the sense of humanity."[9]

Having said that, he immediately calls attention to a difficulty: there seems to be little in the world resembling this particular mode of attraction. Competition with a repulsive "other" seems to be a more common reaction of people who do not know each other well—and, often enough, of those who do. "The other" is someone in the way, a nuisance, an obstacle. Teilhard, however, discovers a basis for attraction in the perception of this "other" as a partner in the greater task of building the Earth. It must be noted, though, that he remarks, "In contrast to the sexual sense, the sense of humanity does not directly touch the persons as such, but is something that surrounds them."[10]

A further complication arises at this point. What kind of love do we have when it does not touch the person, but, it would seem, is something extrinsic to the person? However, five years earlier he had formulated a solution to the problem arising from attraction to this extrinsic aura. In "The Spirit of the Earth," he addressed the same basic issue, in the context of human unity:

> Instinctively and in principle, man normally keeps his distance from man. But on the other hand, how his powers increase if, in research or combat he feels the breath of affection or comradeship. What fulfillment when, at certain moments of enthusiasm or danger, he finds himself suddenly admitted to the *miracle of a common soul.* . . . The sense of the earth is the irresistible pressure which comes at a given moment to unite them in a common enthusiasm. . . . They cannot love millions of strangers. By revealing to each one that a part of himself exists in all the rest, the sense of the

earth is now bringing into sight a new principle of universal affection among the mass of living beings: the devoted liking of one element for another within a single world in progress.[11]

Teilhard drew on his own extensive life experience, in peace and war, to reach these affirmations. He is quite clearly drawing on his knowledge of two kinds of teamwork: the research team, which was part of his experience as a working scientist, and the combat team, which he had known through four years as a stretcher-bearer in the trenches of World War I. In his own mind he was able to extrapolate from these to perceive all humanity as a sphere of evolution, a noospheric constructive team developing around the Earth. The extent to which such an insight is likely to form in other people would, of course, be contingent on their own team, group, or staff situations, and their capacity and willingness to project these to a larger human dimension. While the possibility of what he describes can be acknowledged, it would seem that an argument could be made against his predictive enthusiasm despite an admitted desire and need for a common love of humankind and the Earth. How to foster and develop this type of human understanding remains, in my opinion, a major psychological, intellectual, and ethical challenge, one we are facing in this study.

*Cosmic Love,* for which our source is his "Sketch of a Personalistic Universe," finds Teilhard saying:

I give the name of cosmic sense to the more or less confused affinity that binds us psychologically to the All which envelops us. . . . The cosmic sense must have been born as soon as man found himself facing the forest, the sea, and the stars. And since then we find evidence of it in all our experience of the great and unbounded: in art, in poetry, in religion. Through it we react to the world "as a whole" as with our eyes to light.[12]

As Teilhard proceeds with an explanation of what this involves, he ultimately distinguishes it from pantheism by invoking the reality of personal love toward a personal center of the universe, and once more the principle of creative union, this time in the context of the divine–human relationship.[13] Toward the end of his exposition, he remarks: "One single thing is loved in the end, the loving centre of all convergence. But we can only reach it by completely attaching ourselves to the reality and to the understanding of the particular beings in whose depths it shines."[14]

In *The Divine Milieu,* his theological position, expressed in terms of attachment and detachment, becomes quite clear: "It is God alone whom he [the Christian] pursues through the reality of created things. For him, interest lies truly in things, but in absolute dependence upon God's presence in them."[15] The personalization of the universe, then, in the end leads one to the Personhood of God, at once immanent and transcendent, within and yet behind and distinct from what we see.

### The Christic Personalization of Love in The Divine Milieu

Our considerations up to this point have been drawn, for the most part, from writings by Teilhard that were done with a scientific humanist mentality in mind. The types of love examined—sexual, generalized human, cosmic—should also be seen as capable of "divinization," of being vitalized, through the gift of God's life in grace, with divine energy and power. When Teilhard, in *The Divine Milieu,* writes of the "divinization of activities" (communion with God in what one does) and the "divinization of passivities" (communion with God in what one is given and in what one suffers) he includes all that is authentically human in the ambit of divinization.[16]

The cosmos is thus seen, as Robert Faricy would put it, as "Christic"—alive with the loving presence of divine personality.[17] All human relations— man–woman and generalized human—become divine–human and vitalized in and through charity in Christ. Teilhard's hypothetical Omega Point receives, as the divine focus of cosmic and human evolution, a heart and face in Christ.[18] Men and women become Christ to each other in a special way in marriage. Those not married become capable of a special relationship, finding ultimate fulfillment in Christ, whose life they share. Moreover, all persons, through the charity of Christ, become far more than members of the same humanity uniting in a common effort to continue evolution. They become co-workers and co-redeemers in the mission of continuing to bring the whole Christ to completion in the universe, as they consciously work toward achieving a better world for all life. Generalized human love, as the compassionate, collaborative understanding of people, becomes the love of members of the Mystical Body of Christ for each other as they strive to complete the creation of His Body and His Earth.

### The Activation and Organization of Love Energy in Economic Life

It is important to remember here what we saw earlier about the meaning of love energy in Teilhard's theory regarding the growth of person and community. As we contemplate the rising appreciation of women's equal role in society, the positive catalytic import of Teilhard's thinking on the "affective dyad"—man and woman together—should be kept in mind. His *le sens humain* concept of "generalized human love," emphasizing people as co-workers on the edge of planetary evolution, is clearly of fundamental significance for enhancing collaboration if we are to survive and flourish. As we deepen our realization of our rootedness in the Earth and cosmos, as we grow in sensitivity to our global ecological responsibilities, Teilhard's vision of "cosmic love" has profound implications.

With these ideas on love energy as a constructive power to guide us, we can now explore the use of its creative force. In our introduction we cited three principal challenge areas: (1) economic organization, (2) research, and (3) technology. We now wish to consider them in the light of Teilhard's evolutionary perspectives.

### Collaborative Organization of Economic Life

A basic understanding of Teilhard's approach can be found in his retreat notes of June 1952, where he speaks of the principle of differentiating union as the second of the five "grand illuminations" in his life. I have already touched on it, and here we will explore it in more detail. After he lists the Divine Milieu as the first illumination, he speaks of the principle "Union Differentiates" (personalizes).[19]

Also known as his law of "creative union," this principle means that wherever a genuine love union in human relations exists, persons do not merge into a homogeneous collective, but, rather, each enables the others to develop their distinctive uniqueness. This applies across the spectrum of human bonding: to husband and wife, to members of a research team or social group, and to larger international societies, as well as to communion with God, Christ-Omega (with due adjustments in the latter instance, to avoid pantheism, as has been noted).[20] Creative union is his ultimate concept for resolving the historic individual–community tension. Fulfillment of the person is found in love bonding one with others, yet in a manner so as to respect, encourage, and freely develop the particular varied potentialities of each.

His theory of human community, then, rests on an understanding of the complementarity of constructive love as it strongly emphasizes an awareness of solidarity along with respect for and encouragement of diversity.

We are now prepared to view the workings of economic society in this context. The implications seem quite clear: a Teilhardian spirit of collaboration can enhance human economic survival and advancement, since such mutual cooperation provides great scope and encouragement for individuality and creativity in the cause of evolutionary progress.

Let us turn now to some of Teilhard's specific observations on economic activity, keeping these ideas in mind. In his personal notes of 1947 we find: "The aim of political economy is no longer the chicken in the pot, but the liberation (through organization and mechanization) of the immense store of human energy up to now absorbed in the work of material production."[21]

What kind of liberation of human energy through organization did he envision? His thought here, as can be seen, makes him vulnerable to attack from both socialist and capitalist camps. Earlier, in "Human Energy" (1937), he had written:

Seemingly, no less urgent than the question of sources of energy is the world wide installation of a general economy of production and labor, reinforced by the establishment of a rational gold policy. Financial and social crises are at pains to remind us how confused our theories are in these matters and how barbarous our conduct. But when will men decide to recognize that no serious progress can be made in these directions except under two conditions: first that the proposed organization must be international . . . and secondly, that it must be conceived on a very large scale. More lethal still is their stubborn conservation of a static form and ideal: reciprocal ideas of exchange whose perfection would seem to consist in a private short circuit.[22]

There is emerging in this economic thinking a definite affirmation that some sort of global ethos and organization are needed to break down the fragmenting and isolating barriers, yet at the same time allow for democratic freedom, initiative, and creativity.[23]

In line with his fundamentally democratic political sympathies, he sought to maximize liberty and innovation, but within boundaries called for by the evolving needs of the larger society.[24] While he recognized the incentive aspects of wealth, private ownership, and profit, as well as the rewarding experience of making a business succeed, he was strong in his condemnation of those who looked to possession of wealth as an end in itself, without concern for the welfare of others. Prosperity is a base and source of energy for human personal development. But to hoard it for oneself rather than to use it for humanity was unacceptable. The bourgeois, for him, sadly, was one who chose *to have* rather than *to be,* someone locked in by possessions, cut off from others—unloving and therefore depersonalized.[25]

Teilhard, moreover, actually addressed this matter of ethos in American organizations in his 1950 remarks to Robert Barat:

What dominates with Americans is a passionate interest in the present. They live for the moment—something which leads to astonishing technological developments. . . . But they lack "vision"; the future explicitly counts for little with them. Their current philosophy is a paganism in the classical sense: seek immediate enjoyment of the goods of the earth. Hence, as with all pagans, they experience a certain melancholy. One of the conditions for joy is hope, which is based on thought of the future.[26]

How then might we learn to personalize our business organizations? Not only must there be work toward a form and style of economic culture which achieves balance between planning and free initiatives, again a unity with diversity, but their objectives should respect and foster the priority of the person over possessions and material wealth. The stage of personalizing love energy that needs to be operative here would be generalized human love. In addition, the mutually supportive differentiation of the man–woman dyad should be a model in these times of increasing numbers of women entering the workplace outside the home. Finally, it is important to recall the way in which the spirit and ambiance of the divine milieu would effect spiritualization and divinization of cooperative economic life, infusing it with the dynamic, creative-redemptive charity of co-workers with Christ.[27]

Teilhard's ideas on freedom, initiative, and democratic process can serve as a good base for affirming the value of a certain type of free-market situation, provided fundamental criteria of justice and compassionate concern are maintained. His thought can stimulate the search for a viable option—sorely needed today—to the solipsistic brutality of a capitalism that lacks compassion and to the stifling centralization of a socialism devoid of sensitivity.

It would be noteworthy, in this context, to see how the collaborative concepts we have found in Teilhard resonate with much of what has emerged in recent years under the heading of "participative management." Likewise it will help to keep them in mind in the ongoing dialogue stimulated by the U.S. Bishops' 1986 Pastoral Letter, *Economic Justice for All,* particularly chapter 4, "A New American Experiment: Partnership for the Public Good."[28]

### Constructive Interdisciplinary Research

As industrial technology continues to expand, it generates increasing problems of air and water pollution which disrupt all plant, animal, and human life systems, and inevitably diminish unrenewable natural resources. Meeting these challenges brings a spectrum of responses that typically polarize at opposite extremes. One position tends to downplay the impact on the environment, looking to trade-offs if standards of living are to rise. It trusts in science and technology to save the day, concerned more about the advantages of a technological fix than about the destruction of air, water, and Earth. The other response takes a more jaundiced view of high-tech gadgetry and stresses the primacy of the Earth as a living organism whose very life is threatened by calloused and/or myopic exploitation. These responses range from arrogant or ignorant dominance and irresponsibility to a quasi-mystical submission, an immersion in a benign nature, vast and unfathomable, yet somehow alive. The latter, in my judgment, risks the loss of the person and ultimately individual dignity in a romantic but impersonal pantheism.[29]

To help strike a balance here, I suggest the use of a new term, "geo-humanism." The thrust of its meaning, as influenced by Teilhard's evolutionary vision, would be to call specific attention to the Earth-rootedness of human reality. The term could, I believe, rightly understood, convey simultaneously our emerging awareness of our home in the biosphere that sustains us and at the same time be open to the distinctiveness of the *personal* human in this Earth setting. I say "open to," since it is clear enough from the history of ideas that understanding the human as uniquely personal or as an impersonal speck in the Absolute depends on the specific philosophical/theological premises of whoever uses the word.

With regard to these difficult issues, Teilhard's thought on the meaning and purpose of research and its organization is, I believe, well worth considering. It embodies both a healthy reverence for the Earth and a dynamic, balanced approach to the use of science and technology in the service of a spiritually oriented—"geo-humanist"—evolution.

First, his thought on the meaning and purpose of research: "No longer only to know out of curiosity, to know for knowing's sake, but to know out of faith in a universal development which was becoming conscious of itself as a means of extending and completing in man a world still incompletely formed."[30] He was aware, it should be noted, that this was not the goal universally accepted among scientists, since he had written not long before to a friend concerning the need for a "new psychology and ethics of research," because "so far, research is still egoistic, meaningless."[31]

His scientific ideal was not an ivory tower, but rather a special combination of applied research and development, with a specific motivational factor "to achieve the world as a faithful servant of evolution."[32] Viewed within his Christ-centered divine milieu, research becomes a critically significant way of divinizing the progressive task of achieving a Christic cosmos. Without it, human consciousness would not creatively expand in its evolutionary development to form the noosphere, within the biosphere, grounded in the geosphere.[33]

When the purpose of research is understood this way, the direction of its organization follows a certain logic and looks to the inclusion of several elements: (1) interdisciplinary scientific study, (2) integration of research with technological development for improving human society as a geo-human reality, and (3) integrating these with a faith in a Christ-centered creation—a Christic cosmos. Although Teilhard did not put all of these together in one comprehensive design, he pointed the way to their synthesis. His own contributions involve two main areas: geobiology and anthropology.

First, geobiology. In the midst of being confined to Beijing during World War II, Teilhard founded, with Pierre Leroy, a fellow Jesuit and biologist, the Institute of Geobiology, which ran from 1940 to 1945, when he left for France after the war. Geobiology was conceived to be an independent discipline with a double object: the study of the organic ties among living beings which make up overall a single system closed in on itself and the study of the physico-chemical bonds tying the origin and growth of this living layer to planetary history.[34] If one interjects the impact of the technological phase of noospheric evolution on this nested planetary life system, one finds a fertile matrix for comprehensive ecological research and practice.

With regard to anthropology, in the early 1950s, responding to some ideas of Sir Julian Huxley about an association to study human development on a global scale, he wrote a memo recommending a multifaceted Institute for Human Studies, with theoretical and applied branches.[35] If one were to combine Teilhard's thinking on geobiology with his approach to the suggested institute noted in his 1951 memo "A Major Problem for Anthropology," one could generate, I believe, a scientific geo-humanist philosophical outlook that would both respect the Earth and promote the development of a sustainable human economy on a global scale.[36] We are in much need of such a viable philosophy today.

Moreover, if at this point religious values enter a researcher's consciousness, then applied interdisciplinary research for further human evolution becomes collaborative divine-human action for ongoing co-creation and co-redemption of a Christic cosmos. With Christ-Omega as the ultimate attractive motive force, the entire process emerges as an eminently personal response to a supremely personal ultimate divinity, alive in yet also beyond the visible world.

### The Geo-Humanization of Technology

Close to sixty years ago, in his "hominization" essay, Teilhard laid the groundwork for his thought about technology. Here again, in working with his ideas in this frame, I am concerned with the vision of what *can* be if constructive love energy informs the process. I do not find Teilhard's optimistic claim that technology is being used for human personalization presented with convincing evidence, nor do I see as valid his claim that it will with evolutionary necessity be used in that direction. My purpose is to gather from his material what is quite helpful for indicating what *could* and *should* be done if evolution is to succeed. I am using his thought in a moral, not a predictive, context.

What, then, can be found in his ideas about technology? As he begins his explanation of "The Tool-making Phase of Life," he refers to M. L. Cuénot's remark that zoological phyla in some ways represent the transformation of a limb or a whole body into an instrument. He then goes on:

> The mole is a digging instrument and the horse a running instrument; the porpoise is a swimming instrument and the bird is a flying instrument . . . in every case, the tool is one with the body, the living being passes into its invention.
>
> With man everything changes. The instrument becomes external to the limb that uses it. . . . To appreciate man at his true zoological value, we should not separate "natural" from "artificial" as absolutely as we do in our perspectives, that is to say, ignore the profound connections between the ship, the submarine, the aeroplane and the animal reconstitutions which produced the wing and the fin. . . . The same individual may be a mole, a bird, or a fish, alternately. Alone among the animals, man has the faculty of diversifying his efforts without becoming their out-and-out slave.[37]

How does this perspective serve "The Organic Unity of Humanity?" For Teilhard, scientific technological inventions provide "the creation of a true nervous system for humanity; the elaboration of a common consciousness, on a mass scale in the psychological domain and without the suppression of individuals for the whole of humanity."[38]

He sees all this as "quite simply continuing on a higher plane and by other means, the uninterrupted work of biological evolution."[39] As its source, he speaks of two psychic factors, reflection and conspiration. Of reflection he says it is that "from which has arisen the discovery of the artificial instrument and, consequently, the invasion of the world by the human species."[40]

With conspiration we come to a critical link with key concepts previously seen bearing on personalization:

> "Conspiration," from which is born the entirely new form of connection that distinguishes the human layer from all other departments of earthly life, is the aptitude of different consciousnesses taken in a group, to unite (by language and countless other, more obscure links) so as to constitute a single All, in which, by way of reflection, each element is conscious of its aggregation to all the rest.[41]

With respect to these ideas of Teilhard, we can see the potential of technology for opening up the range and intensity of evolution through human personal activity. That it can also lead to a subhuman, depersonalized, anthill type of existence, he would not deny.[42] But when it is used cooperatively to develop the human person in a united community, and when these activities are infused with the vision of *The Divine Milieu,* we gain vitally supportive and extensive tools through which human personality can effectively express creative divinized love, on all three levels, man–woman, generalized human, and cosmic, and in so doing move evolution forward and upward.

Moreover, when we bring into this picture his later writings on "The Evolution of Responsibility in the World" we have not only an expression of what can be done but a strong statement of urgency regarding ethical imperatives as to what should be done. In this 1950 essay he speaks of how advances in transportation and communication have extended the range of human activity, of how scientific methods have enabled a greater depth of psychological study, and of how various technologies have enlarged the volume and magnitude of human impact. When he asks whether these developments do not point to the need for "a new Ethic of the Earth," he concludes: "At no moment in history has man been found, as he is today, so bound, actively and passively, in the depths of his being, to the value and perfection of everyone around him."[43]

## SUMMARY AND CONCLUDING OBSERVATIONS

To summarize I would like to propose a set of theses that present the basic Teilhardian response of this study to the challenges of collaboration, environmental responsibility, and the geo-humanization of technology—the restoration and regeneration of organic Earth–human relations in the process of noospheric advancement.

1. Human persons reach their ultimate fulfillment as co-workers with each other and with Christ, striving to bring evolution to completion.

2. Human persons live out their solidarity with Christ and others through the development of their unique personal potential and through constructive research, utilizing human and natural resources with concern and respect for the dynamics of Earth processes.

3. In this collaborative effort, research for the employment of technology should be supportive and expressive of dynamic creative-redemptive love energy.

4. In striving to build a more perfect Earth–human community energized within and by the divine milieu, human persons can become the architects of a new Christic geo-humanism.

It is my hope that reflection on the material presented here will show that Teilhard's thought can help significantly in the search for the answer to Reich's—and many others'—concerns about the need for reaching more clearly defined and understood bonds of human solidarity on a local, regional, and global basis. The special value of Teilhard's vision, I would argue, is that he provides for us an evolutionary matrix and mission that reveal crucial guidelines we have not had. From him we can derive a practical philosophy for reconciling in a dynamic reciprocity, in a creative union, the tensions of the economic process as persons and communities interrelate with each other and the Earth. We can also find a religious vision capable of permeating and activating the scientific humanist ideal.

I would hold in closing, therefore, that a Teilhardian vision as outlined above integrates the radical core values of the Christian tradition with the best aspirations of a scientifically informed, ecologically responsible human economy. The task before us, if we would grow and not perish, is to become persons working together in community to bring Christic healing and fulfillment to the whole Earth.

# Notes

### INTRODUCTION

1. Pierre Teilhard de Chardin, "My Fundamental Vision," in *Toward the Future* (London: Collins, 1974), p. 205.
2. Pierre Teilhard de Chardin, *Science and Christ* (New York: Harper & Row, 1969), p. 193.
3. Pierre Teilhard de Chardin, *The Human Phenomenon* (Bristol: Sussex Academic Press, 1999), p. 3. This work is a new translation by Sarah Appleton Weber of the original French manuscript of *The Phenomenon of Man.*
4. See Henri de Lubac, *Teilhard de Chardin: The Man and His Meaning* (New York: New American Library, 1967), pp. 129-43.
5. Pierre Teilhard de Chardin, "How I Believe," in *Christianity and Evolution* (New York: Harcourt Brace Jovanovich, 1971), p. 99.
6. Teilhard coined the term "christic" as an expression of his experience of the Cosmic Christ of evolution, that is, the "omnipresence of transformation" that is centrated in complexity-consciousness drawing it forward. See Pierre Teilhard de Chardin, "The Christic," in *The Heart of Matter* (New York: Harcourt Brace Jovanovich, 1978), p. 94.
7. "Christ is he," Teilhard writes in *Christianity and Evolution,* "who structurally in himself, and for all of us, overcomes the resistance to unification offered by the multiple, resistance to the rise of spirit inherent in matter" (p. 85).
8. See the discussion in chapter 8 of Mary and Ellen Lukas, *Teilhard: The Man, The Priest, The Scientist* (Garden City, N.Y.: Doubleday, 1977), pp. 87-96.
9. Teilhard, *The Human Phenomenon,* p. 12.
10. This holistic view of evolution is now being documented in the new sciences of complex systems. See in particular the annotated bibliography of these sciences compiled by Arthur Fabel available on the Forum on Religion and Ecology web site http://environment.harvard.edu/religion.
11. Teilhard, *The Human Phenomenon,* p. 24.
12. Teilhard, *The Human Phenomenon,* p. 30.
13. Pierre Teilhard de Chardin, *The Appearance of Man* (New York: Harper & Row, 1965), p. 139.
14. Teilhard, *The Human Phenomenon,* p. 27.
15. See the interview with Brian Swimme in the journal *What Is Enlightenment?* no. 19 (spring/summer 2001).
16. Teilhard, *Toward the Future,* p. 175.
17. Teilhard, "My Fundamental Vision," p. 192.
18. Teilhard, *Toward the Future,* p. 193.
19. Teilhard describes this point as a pole of consciousness that is both immanent and transcendent. He sees the Omega point as "an ultimate and self subsistent pole of consciousness, so involved in the world as to be able to gather into itself, by union, the cosmic elements that have been brought to the extreme limit of their centration—and yet by reason of its supraevolutive (that is to say, transcendent) nature enabled to be immune from that fatal regression which is, structurally, a threat to every edifice whose stuff exists in space and time" (*Toward the Future,* p. 185).
20. Teilhard, *Toward the Future,* p. 187.

21. Teilhard, *Toward the Future,* p. 193.

22. Teilhard regards his metaphysics as being linked with the essential Christian mysteries. That is, "There is no God without creature union. There is no creation without incarnational immersion. There is no incarnation without redemption" (*Toward the Future,* p. 198). See also Thomas M. King, "Teilhard, Evil, and Providence," *Teilhard Studies* no. 21 (Chambersburg, Pa.: ANIMA Books for the American Teilhard Association, 1989).

23. Pierre Teilhard de Chardin, *Writings in Time of War* (New York: Harper & Row, 1968), p. 14.

24. Teilhard, *The Heart of Matter,* p. 54.

25. Teilhard, "My Fundamental Vision," p. 12.

26. Pierre Teilhard de Chardin, *Human Energy* (New York: Harcourt Brace Jovanovich, 1971), p. 82.

27. Teilhard, *Science and Christ,* p. 167; and *Let Me Explain* (New York: Harper & Row, 1970), p. 120.

28. Teilhard, *Science and Christ,* p. 168.

29. Teilhard, *Science and Christ,* p. 171.

30. This perspective of Teilhard is developed in Brian Swimme and Thomas Berry, *The Universe Story* (San Francisco: HarperSanFrancisco, 1992).

31. This last sentence reflects the ideas of Thomas Berry drawing on Teilhard as expressed in *The Dream of the Earth* (San Francisco: Sierra Club Books, 1988).

32. See especially John Haught, "In Search of a God for Evolution: Paul Tillich and Pierre Teilhard de Chardin," *Teilhard Studies* no. 45.

33. Thomas Berry takes these up in greater detail in his article in this volume, "Teilhard in the Ecological Age."

34. See Teilhard, "Spirit of the Earth," in *Human Energy,* p. 25.

## 1. TEILHARD DE CHARDIN: A SHORT BIOGRAPHY

1. Pierre Teilhard de Chardin, *Writings in Time of War* (New York: Harper & Row, 1968), p. 14.

2. From Claude Cuenot, *Teilhard de Chardin: A Biographical Study* (Baltimore: Helicon, 1965), p. 3.

3. Ibid., p. 3.

4. Pierre Teilhard de Chardin, *The Heart of Matter* (New York: Harcourt Brace Jovanovich, 1978), p. 41.

5. From Robert Speaight, *The Life of Teilhard de Chardin* (New York: Harper & Row, 1967), p. 45.

6. Pierre Teilhard de Chardin, *The Making of a Mind* (New York: Harper & Row, 1965), pp. 119-20.

7. Ibid., p. 205.

8. Ibid., pp. 267-68.

9. Ibid., p. 277.

10. Ibid., p. 281.

11. Pierre Teilhard de Chardin, *The Phenomenon of Man* (New York: Harper & Row, 1965), p. 137.

## 2. A NEW CREATION STORY

1. Ellen and Mary Lukas, *Teilhard: The Man, the Priest, the Scientist* (Garden City, N.Y.: Doubleday, 1976), p. 14.

2. On the importance of seeing for Teilhard, see the foreword of *The Phenomenon of Man* (New York: Harper Torchbooks, 1965), pp. 31-36.

3. Pierre Teilhard de Chardin, *The Divine Milieu* (New York: Harper Torchbooks, 1965), p. 66.

4. Pierre Teilhard de Chardin, *Activation of Energy* (New York: Harcourt, Brace, Jovanovich, 1971), p. 376. The expression may well be an echo of John 1:39.

5. See Pierre Teilhard de Chardin, "The Death-Barrier and Co-Reflection," in *Activation of Energy*, pp. 395-406. The essay was written in 1955, just a few months before his death.

6. Quoted in Claude Cuenot, *Teilhard de Chardin: A Biographical Study* (Baltimore: Helicon Press, 1965), p. 158. The letter is dated March 18, 1934.

7. While the amount of energy in the universe remains constant (the law of the conservation of energy), the amount of usable energy is on the decline because of continual energy loss (the law of the dissipation of energy—the principle of entropy). The issue is discussed in *The Phenomenon of Man*, pp. 50-52.

8. Teilhard, *The Phenomenon of Man*, p. 52.

9. See the "Epilogue" of *The Divine Milieu*, pp. 150-55.

10. The text was a favorite of Teilhard's and is frequently cited in his writings.

11. For a discussion of this formula, see Donald P. Gray, *The One and the Many: Teilhard de Chardin's Vision of Unity* (New York: Herder & Herder, 1969), p. 121.

12. See Teilhard, *The Phenomenon of Man*, pp. 257-72.

13. The title of a work by Elisabeth Kubler-Ross, *Death: The Final Stage of Growth* (Englewood Cliffs, N.J.: Prentice-Hall, 1975).

14. For Teilhard's most thorough treatment of the passivities, see part 2 of *The Divine Milieu*.

15. Teilhard, *The Divine Milieu*, p. 44.

16. Teilhard's spirituality is poles apart from that "cheap grace" which Dietrich Bonhoeffer railed against in *The Cost of Discipleship* (New York: Macmillan, 1959).

17. Teilhard, *The Phenomenon of Man*, p. 313; see also Robert Faricy, "Teilhard de Chardin's Spirituality of the Cross," *Horizons* (spring 1976), pp. 1-15.

18. See *Teilhard de Chardin: Re-Mythologization* (Waco: Word Books, 1970)—papers by Robert Speaight, Robert Wilshine, J. V. Langmead Casserly.

19. Teilhard, *Activation of Energy*, p. 376.

### 3. Teilhard's Unity of Knowledge

1. The Symposium papers have been published as *Teilhard and the Unity of Knowledge*, ed. Thomas King, S.J., and James Salmon, S.J. (New York: Seabury, 1981). It includes talks by Frederick Copleston, Ilya Prigogine, Richard Leakey, Kenneth Boulding, Paulo Soleri, Raimundo Panikkar, and Monika Hellwig.

2. Pierre Teilhard de Chardin, *The Heart of Matter* (New York: Harcourt Brace Jovanovich, 1979), p. 25.

3. Pierre Teilhard de Chardin, *The Appearance of Man* (New York: Harper & Row, 1965), p. 25.

4. Pierre Teilhard de Chardin, *The Phenomenon of Man* (New York: Harper & Row, 1969), p. 219.

5. Pierre Teilhard de Chardin, *The Vision of the Past* (New York: Harper & Row, 1968), p. 246.

6. Pierre Teilhard de Chardin, *Activation of Energy* (New York: Harcourt Brace Jovanovich, 1970), p. 213.

7. Pierre Teilhard de Chardin, *The Future of Man* (New York: Harper & Row, 1964), p. 222.

8. Teilhard, *The Heart of Matter*, p. 48.

9. Pierre Teilhard de Chardin, *Christianity and Evolution* (New York: Harcourt Brace Jovanovich, 1971), p. 103.

10. Ibid., p. 63.

11. Ibid., p. 62.

12. This basic intuition of elements-in-a-whole rather than things-in-an-ensemble is the

starting point of many of Teilhard's essays. In *The Phenomenon of Man* the first two subheads of chapter 1 tell of *Elemental* Matter and of *Total* (Whole) Matter. There Teilhard insists in several ways that "each element of the cosmos is positively woven from all the others." Perhaps Teilhard's general reluctance to speak of causality could be traced to this sense of the organic connectedness of all things. A causal bond is between separate "things." (It would thus be less intrinsic than the organic bond Teilhard proposes.) For Teilhard, there are no separate things.

13. Teilhard, *The Phenomenon of Man,* p. 35.

14. Teilhard, *The Future of Man,* p. 61.

15. Teilhard, *Christianity and Evolution,* p. 105; idem, *Human Energy* (New York: Harcourt Brace Jovanovich, 1969), pp. 23-24.

16. Teilhard, *Christianity and Evolution,* p. 62.

17. Teilhard, *The Future of Man,* p. 61.

18. Teilhard, *The Heart of Matter,* p. 34.

19. Teilhard, *Human Energy,* p. 23.

20. Ibid., p. 23.

21. Teilhard, *The Heart of Matter,* p. 34.

22. Pierre Teilhard de Chardin, *Man's Place in Nature* (New York: Harper & Row, 1966), p. 18; idem, *The Future of Man,* p. 223.

23. Teilhard, *Man's Place in Nature,* p. 26.

24. Teilhard, *Human Energy,* p. 22; idem, *Writings in Time of War* (New York: Harper & Row, 1968), p. 23.

25. Teilhard, *The Phenomenon of Man,* p. 69.

26. Ibid., p. 70.

27. Teilhard, *Man's Place in Nature,* p. 18; idem, *The Future of Man,* p. 223.

28. Teilhard, *Writings in Time of War,* p. 22.

29. Teilhard, *Man's Place in Nature,* p. 26.

30. Teilhard, *The Phenomenon of Man,* p. 30.

31. Ibid., p. 266.

32. Teilhard, *The Future of Man,* p. 167.

33. Teilhard, *Human Energy,* p. 137.

34. Teilhard, *The Phenomenon of Man,* p. 223.

35. Ibid., p. 247.

36. Teilhard, *Activation of Energy,* p. 153.

37. Teilhard, *The Phenomenon of Man,* p. 240.

38. Teilhard, *The Future of Man,* p. 161.

39. Ibid., p. 178.

40. Teilhard, *The Phenomenon of Man,* p. 264.

41. Teilhard, *Human Energy,* p. 34.

42. Teilhard, *The Future of Man,* p. 82.

43. Teilhard, *The Phenomenon of Man,* p. 295.

44. Teilhard, *Christianity and Evolution,* p. 69.

45. Teilhard, *The Phenomenon of Man,* p. 295.

46. Teilhard, *The Future of Man,* p. 232.

47. Teilhard, *Christianity and Evolution,* p. 69.

48. Teilhard, *The Phenomenon of Man,* p. 293.

49. Teilhard, *Writings in Time of War,* p. 61.

50. Teilhard, *Human Energy,* p. 56.

51. Teilhard, *The Future of Man,* p. 224.

52. Teilhard, *Human Energy,* p. 56.

53. Ibid., p. 73.

54. Teilhard, *The Future of Man,* p. 69.

55. Teilhard, *Activation of Energy,* p. 167; idem, *The Heart of Matter,* p. 37.

56. Teilhard, *The Heart of Matter,* p. 37.

57. Teilhard, *Human Energy,* p. 28; idem, *Christianity and Evolution,* pp. 50, 134, 192.

58. Teilhard, *The Future of Man,* p. 98.

59. Teilhard, *Human Energy,* p. 44.

60. Teilhard, *The Heart of Matter,* p. 52; idem, *Writings in Time of War,* p. 168; idem, *Christianity and Evolution,* p. 125.

61. Teilhard, *The Heart of Matter,* pp. 49, 50, 58; idem, *Christianity and Evolution,* p. 128.

62. Teilhard, *The Heart of Matter,* p. 56.

63. Teilhard, *Human Energy,* pp. 69, 81; idem, *Christianity and Evolution,* pp. 138ff.

64. Teilhard, *Human Energy,* p. 80.

65. Ibid., p. 32.

66. Jean-Paul Sartre, *Being and Nothingness* (New York: Washington Square Press, 1966), p. lxxvii.

67. Teilhard, *Human Energy,* p. 173.

68. Teilhard, *The Phenomenon of Man,* p. 53.

69. Teilhard offers a complex terminology of radial and tangential energy as part of his explanation. I do not find this terminology significant here; I have explained it in detail in *Teilhard and the Mysticism of Knowing* (New York: Seabury, 1981), pp. 120ff.

70. Teilhard, *Human Energy,* p. 113.

71. Teilhard, *The Phenomenon of Man,* p. 32.

72. Teilhard, *Human Energy,* p. 114.

73. Teilhard, *The Phenomenon of Man,* p. 32.

74. Teilhard, *The Heart of Matter,* p. 28.

75. Ibid., p. 26.

76. Ibid., p. 27.

77. Teilhard, *The Vision of the Past,* p. 169.

78. Teilhard, *The Phenomenon of Man,* p. 33.

79. Teilhard, *The Future of Man,* p. 221.

80. Teilhard, *The Phenomenon of Man,* p. 249.

81. Unpublished letter to M. Gignoux, June 19, 1950.

82. Pierre Teilhard de Chardin, *Toward the Future* (New York: Harcourt Brace Jovanovich, 1975), p. 165; idem, *The Vision of the Past,* p. 102.

83. Teilhard, *Human Energy,* p. 171.

84. Teilhard, *The Vision of the Past,* p. 69.

85. Teilhard, *The Phenomenon of Man,* p. 224.

86. Ibid., p. 251.

87. Ibid., p. 221.

88. Unpublished notebook of Teilhard, March 22, 1952.

89. Pierre Teilhard de Chardin, *Letters to Two Friends* (New York: Meridian Books, 1969), p. 73.

90. Pierre Teilhard de Chardin, *Science and Christ* (New York: Harper & Row, 1965), p. 95.

91. Teilhard, *The Phenomenon of Man,* p. 294.

92. Pierre Teilhard de Chardin, *The Hymn of the Universe* (New York: Harper & Row, 1965); idem, *The Prayer of the Universe* (New York: Harper Colophon, 1969).

93. Teilhard, *The Phenomenon of Man,* p. 297; idem, *Human Energy,* p. 159.

94. Teilhard, *The Heart of Matter,* p. 43.

95. Ibid., p. 39.

96. There is an interesting collection of essays that deals with these two understandings of God: *The Other Side of God,* ed. Peter Berger (New York: Doubleday, 1981). These essays were developed in the course of an extended symposium that set out to contrast two understandings of religious experience: "confrontation" and "interiority." The editor writes that in the course of the symposium the difficulties in maintaining the division became evident, and all the participants seemed willing to abandon the distinction. The difficulty they experienced could be seen as an original acceptance of the Cartesian dualism—which in the end did not seem valid in practice.

97. Jean-Paul Sartre, *Nausea* (New York: New Directions, 1969), p. 24.

98. Jean-Paul Sartre, *Baudelaire* (New York: New Directions, 1967), p. 106; idem, *Nausea,* p. 128.

99. Thomas King, S.J., *Sartre and the Sacred* (Chicago: University of Chicago Press, 1974).

100. Henri de Lubac, *Teilhard: The Man and the Meaning* (New York: Mentor, 1967), p. 108.

101. Teilhard, *The Phenomenon of Man,* p. 311.

102. Teilhard, *Christianity and Evolution,* p. 131.

103. Teilhard, *Human Energy,* p. 22; idem, *The Phenomenon of Man,* p. 39; idem, *Science and Christ,* p. 46.

104. Teilhard, *Christianity and Evolution,* p. 57. Matter is the pure multiple, so Teilhard would identify it as "positive non-being" located at "the opposite pole from being" (*Writings in Time of War,* pp. 61, 163, 164). It is "without legitimate existence" (*Christianity and Evolution,* pp. 57, 105). In a similar way, entropy, the anti-evolution movement in the universe, the movement to multiplicity, is repeatedly acknowledged, but it too has a questionable existence "in so far as it exists" (*Human Energy,* p. 53).

## 4. THE LETTERS OF TEILHARD DE CHARDIN AND LUCILE SWAN

1. Thomas M. King, S.J., and Mary Wood Gilbert, eds., *The Letters of Teilhard de Chardin and Lucile Swan* (Washington, D.C.: Georgetown University Press, 1994). Henceforth LTLS.

2. The editors have arranged the letters according to three periods: The Letters of the China Years: from 1932 to 1941; The Letters of the Long Separation: from 1941 to 1948; The Letters of the Last Years: from 1949 to 1955.

3. Pierre Teilhard de Chardin, *The Making of a Mind: Letters from a Soldier-Priest 1914-1919* (London: Collins, 1965).

4. See the account of these excavations by Jia Lanpo and Huang Weiwen, *The Story of Peking Man* (Oxford/New York: Oxford University Press, 1990). The book contains an article by Jia Lampo entitled "Father Pierre Teilhard de Chardin and I," which was written for the one-hundredth anniversary of Teilhard's birthday in 1981.

5. Lucile Swan, "With Teilhard de Chardin in Peking," *The Month* 1/5 (1962). This article summarizes what she wrote about at much greater length in an unpublished autobiographical manuscript available in typescript (henceforth LMS). [Editor's Note: Regrettably, Ursula King has been denied the right to quote from this manuscript, to which she had access as a researcher and scholar. Reluctantly, the editor (Donald St. John) has had to paraphrase her direct quotations. Needless to say, a sense for the sensitivity and passion found in both Teilhard's and Ms. Swan's own words has been denied the reader.]

6. LMS, pp. 13f.

7. LTLS, p. 9.

8. LTLS, p. 156 (May 31, 1942).

9. LMS, p. 1.

10. LTLS, p. 7 (November 14, 1933).

11. LTLS, p. 17 (May 27, 1934).

12. LTLS, p. 19 (July 18, 1934).

13. LTLS, p. 20. In the typewritten version of the letters which I read some years ago this note finishes on the sentence "Oh God, please give me strength to go on and wisdom to see the right path."

14. LMS, pp. 46-47.

15. Dated February 1934, this essay is found in Pierre Teilhard de Chardin, *Toward the Future* (London: Collins, 1975), pp. 60-87.

16. Ibid., pp. 86f. Compare the passage in his letter of July 18, 1934, where in referring to their love, he writes: "we can find some kind of happiness in thinking that what we have to suffer or to miss expresses (and pays for) the work of discovering something which is grand and new—the new 'discovery of the Fire'" (LTLS, p. 19).

17. LMS, p. 69.

18. LTLS, p. 38 (June 16, 1935).

19. LTLS, p. 83 (April 24, 1937).

20. LTLS, p. 112 (March 12, 1938).

21. LTLS, p. 116 (August 15, 1938).

22. LTLS, p. 143 (August 8, 1941).

23. LTLS, p. 148 (September 27, 1941).

24. LTLS, p. 272 (April 3, 1951).

25. See "Letters II," in Pierre Teilhard de Chardin, *Letters to Two Friends 1926-52* (London: Collins Fontana, 1972), pp. 119-227.

26. LTLS, p. 280.

27. LTLS, p. 286 (December 20, 1953).

28. LTLS, p. 290 (April 24, 1954).

29. LTLS, p. 290 (May 7, 1954).

30. LTLS, p. 293.

31. This passage is found in Pierre Leroy, *Lettres familieres de Pierre Teilhard de Chardin* (Paris: Le Centurion, 1976), p. 130 (my translation).

32. LTLS, p. 272 (April 3, 1951).

33. LTLS, p. 139 (October 1939).

34. LMS, p. 39.

35. LMS, p. 46.

36. LMS, p. 11.

37. Dated October 30, 1950, this was published much later in the essay collection of the same title; see Pierre Teilhard de Chardin, *The Heart of Matter* (London: Collins, 1978), pp. 15-79.

38. LTLS, pp. 265, 266 (December 15, 1950).

39. LTLS, p. 95 (June 27, 1937).

40. LTLS, p. 267 (December 22, 1950).

41. Taken from unpublished notes in Lucile's "Blue Book." The passage paraphrases (or is perhaps her own translation) of a very similar passage in Teilhard's "Notes de Retraite 1944-55," of which an excerpt was published as "Pensée 26" in the collection *Hymn of the Universe* (London: Collins Fount Paperbacks, 1970), p. 91. The original French edition appeared in 1961, and one wonders how Lucile had access to this text in 1955.

42. LTLS, p. 58 (May 7, 1936).

43. LTLS, p. 118 (October 28, 1938).

44. LTLS, p. 96 (June 27, 1937).

45. LMS, p. 69.

46. This is a quotation from Lucile Swan's shorter unpublished biographical essay written in 1951, p. 1.

47. Perhaps one can describe their relationship as an example of spiritual friendship for our times. The richness of these letters invites serious study and reflection, perhaps a fuller biography of Lucile Swan, but certainly a new interpretation of Teilhard's writings on "the Feminine," which places such a central role in his thought on love as a unitive force in the world. For a comprehensive study of the theme of love, see Mathias Trennert-Heliwig, *Die Urkraft des Kosmos: Dimensionen der Liebe im Werk Teilhard de Chardins* (Freiburg: Herder, 1993).

### 5. TEILHARD IN THE ECOLOGICAL AGE

1. Pierre Teilhard de Chardin, *The Phenomenon of Man* (New York: Harper Torchbooks, 1965), p. 217.

2. Pierre Teilhard de Chardin, *Activation of Energy* (New York: Harcourt Brace Jovanovich, 1971), p. 172.

3. Erich Jantsch, *The Self-Organizing Universe* (Oxford: Pergamon, 1980).

4. Ibid., p. 159.

5. *New York Times,* August 24, 1981.

6. Pierre Teilhard de Chardin, *Toward the Future* (New York: Harcourt Brace Jovanovich, 1975), pp. 29, 32.

7. Teilhard, *Activation of Energy,* pp. 194-95.

8. Edward Hyams, *Soil and Civilization* (New York: Harper Colophon, 1976).

9. Rachel Carson, *Silent Spring* (Boston: Houghton Mifflin, 1962).

## 7. EDUCATION AND ECOLOGY

1. This is the thesis of Thomas Berry's book *The Dream of the Earth* (San Francisco: Sierra Club Books, 1988).

2. See Pierre Teilhard de Chardin, *The Human Phenomenon* (Brighton: Sussex Academic Press, 1999) (new English translation by Sarah Appleton Weber). See also Brian Swimme and Thomas Berry, *The Universe Story* (San Francisco: HarperSanFrancisco, 1992).

3. Ruth Leger Sivard, *World Military and Social Expenditures* (Washington, D.C.: World Priorities, Inc., 1987), p. 5.

4. From the position paper on "Disarmament and Development" by the New Manhattan Project of the American Friends Service Committee.

5. Center for Defense Information (www.globalissues.org).

6. Sivard, *World Military and Social Expenditures.*

7. See Michael Rennet, "Assessing the Military's War on the Environment," in *State of the World,* ed. Lester Brown et al. (New York: Norton, 1991), pp. 132-52.

8. Barry Commoner, *The Closing Circle* (New York: Alfred A. Knopf, 1972), pp. 143-54.

9. *The State of the World* reports have been published yearly since 1984 by Norton; see also Gerald Barney, *Global 2000 Report* (New York: Pergamon Press, 1980).

10. *State of the World* (1987), pp. 4-5.

11. *State of the World* (1987), pp. 4-5.

12. *State of the World* (1990), pp. 7-9; and 1991, pp. 5-11.

13. *State of the World* (1991), p. 6.

14. Barney, *Global 2000 Report,* p. 39.

15. Ibid., p. 40.

16. Bill McKibben, *The End of Nature* (New York: Random House, 1989; rpt., 1999).

17. See his essay "Technology and the Healing of the Earth," in *The Dream of the Earth.*

18. Lester Brown, *State of the World* (1991), p. 4.

19. Barry Commoner, *Making Peace with the Planet* (New York: New Press, 1992).

20. Amory Lovins, *Soft Energy Paths* (New York: Harper & Row, 1979).

21. Wes Jackson has organized the Land Institute in Salina, Kansas; Wendell Berry lives as a farmer and poet in Port Royal, Kentucky; and Miriam MacGillis has run Genesis Farm in Blairstown, New Jersey, for more than two decades.

22. Teilhard, *The Human Phenomenon,* p. 3.

23. This term was used by the historian of religion Mircea Eliade and more recently has been used by the Confucian scholar Tu Weiming to describe the interaction of heaven, Earth, and humans in Confucianism. See Tu Weiming's book *Confucian Thought: Selfhood as Creative Transformation* (Albany: State University of New York Press, 1985); also Mary Evelyn Tucker and John Berthrong, eds., *Confucianism and Ecology* (Cambridge, Mass.: Center for the Study of World Religions and Harvard University Press, 1998).

24. Pierre Teilhard de Chardin, *Activation of Energy* (New York: Harcourt Brace Jovanovich, 1970), p. 256.

25. Pierre Teilhard de Chardin, *Science and Christ* (New York: Harper & Row, 1968), p. 193.

26. See Thomas Berry's essay "The New Story," chapter 10 in *The Dream of the Earth* and chapter 6 in the present volume; originally published as *Teilhard Studies* no. 1 (winter 1978).

27. Pierre Teilhard de Chardin, *The Heart of Matter* (New York: Harcourt Brace Jovanovich, 1978), p. 85.

28. Pierre Teilhard de Chardin, *The Future of Man* (New York: Harper & Row, 1964), p. 87.

29. This perspective may be outlined for students as a calendar, a clock, or a time line. See Sidney Liebes, Brian Swimme, and Elisabet Sahtouris, *A Walk Through Time* (New York: Wiley, 1998).

30. James Lovelock, *Gaia: A New Look at Life on Earth* (New York: Oxford University Press, 1979).

31. An example of the social ecology movement is the work of Murray Bookchin in *The Ecology of Freedom: The Emergence and Dissolution of Hierarchy* (Palo Alto: Cheshire Books, 1982). The term "deep ecology" was coined by Arne Naess and is developed by Bill Duvall and George Sessions in *Deep Ecology* (Layton, Utah: Peregrine Smith, 1985).

32. Thomas Berry's essay "The American College in the Ecological Age" elaborates on these points for a college curriculum and is published in *The Dream of the Earth*.

33. David Orr, *Ecological Literacy: Education and the Transition to a Postmodern World* (Albany: State University of New York Press, 1992); Mary Clark, *Ariadne's Thread: The Search for New Modes of Thinking* (New York: St. Martin's Press, 1989); Robert Costanza, *Ecological Economics: The Science and Management of Sustainability* (New York: Columbia University Press, 1991).

34. These include centers such as Genesis Farm in Blairstown, New Jersey, the Earth Ethics Institute at Miami Dade Community College, the Earth Literacy Program at St. Mary of the Woods in Indiana, the University of Creation Spirituality in Oakland, Sophia Institute in Oakland, and the program in Philosophy, Cosmology, and Consciousness at the California Institute of Integral Studies. See also http://www.EarthLiteracy.com.

35. Roderick Nash, *The Rights of Nature: A History of the Environmental Movement* (Madison: University of Wisconsin Press, 1989). Aldo Leopold's essay is in *A Sand County Almanac* (New York: Oxford University Press, 1966). See also Holmes Rolston, *Environmental Ethics: Duties to and Values in the Natural World* (Philadelphia: Temple University Press, 1989).

36. Loren Eiseley, *The Immense Journey* (New York: Random House, 1960).

37. Ibid., pp. 63-64.

38. Ibid., pp. 26-27.

39. Wendell Berry, *Recollected Essays* (Berkeley: North Point Press, 1981), pp. 110–12.

## 8. SUSTAINABLE DEVELOPMENT AND THE ECOSPHERE

1. The Brundtland Commission, World Commission on Environment and Development (henceforth WCED), 1987.

2. See, e.g., James Robertson, *The Sane Alternative* (St. Paul: River Basin Publishing, 1978).

3. B. Kneen, "The Contradiction of Sustainable Development," *Canadian Dimension* 23/1 (1989): pp. 12-15.

4. WCED 1987, p. 89.

5. WCED 1987, p. 213.

6. Alan Drengson, "Protecting the Environment, Protecting Ourselves: Reflections on the Philosophical Dimension," in *Environmental Ethics,* vol. 2, ed. R. Bradley and S. Duguid (Vancouver: Simon Fraser University, 1989).

7. Stafford Beer, *Teilhard Review* 15/3 (1981): pp. 1-33.

8. Morris Berman, *The Reenchantment of the World* (New York: Bantam Books, 1984), p. 21.

9. This follows from Galileo's division of reality into the subjective (unmeasurable and therefore unreal) and the objective (accessible to science through measurement and mathematical analysis).

10. Berman, *The Reenchantment of the World,* p. 20.

11. Fritjof Capra, *The Turning Point* (New York: Simon & Schuster, 1982), p. 56.

12. A. Jones, "From Fragmentation to Wholeness: A Green Approach to Science and Society," *The Ecologist* 17/6 (1987): pp. 236-40, here 236.

13. Jeremy Rifkin, *Entropy: A New World View* (New York: Bantam Books, 1981), p. 22.

14. John Locke, "Second Treatise," in *Two Treatises of Government,* ed. P. Laslett (Cambridge: Cambridge University Press, 1967), p. 312.

15. Ibid., p. 315.

16. Adam Smith, *An Inquiry into the Nature and Causes of the Wealth of Nations* (London: Methuen, 1961), vol. 1, p. 475.

17. Rifkin, *Entropy: A New World View,* pp. 26-27.

18. W. Jevons, *The Theory of Political Economy* (London: Macmillan, 1879), cited in N. Georgescu-Roegen, "Energy and Economic Myths," *Southern Economic Journal* 41/3 (1975): pp. 347-81.

19. Ibid., p. 348.

20. N. Georgescu-Roegen, "The Steady State and Ecological Salvation: A Thermodynamic Analysis," *BioScience* 27/4 (1977): pp. 266-70. Also see Julian Simon and Herman Kahn, eds., *The Resourceful Earth: A Response to Global 2000* (Oxford: Oxford University Press, 1984) for an expression of this perspective.

21. Robert Heilbroner, "The Triumph of Capitalism," *New Yorker,* January 23, 1989, p. 102.

22. S. Rowe, "Implications of the Brundtland Commission Report for Canadian Forest Management," *The Forestry Chronicle,* February 5-7, 1989.

23. D. Rapport, "The Interface of Economics and Ecology," in A.-M. Jansson, ed. *Integration of Economy and Ecology—An Outlook for the Eighties,* 1984.

24. Georgescu-Roegen, "Energy and Economic Myths"; idem, "Steady State and Ecological Salvation."

25. Self-producing (renewable) resources used by the economy are, like nonrenewable resources, degraded and dissipated back into the ecosphere. However, this "waste" can be reconstituted and recycled by photosynthesis using an off-planet source of energy (see the following section The Special Case of Ecosystems). In contrast, while it can reduce total resource throughput, recycling and remanufacturing by the economy generally consume additional energy and material imported from the ecosphere.

26. D. Perry et al., "Bootstrapping in Ecosystems," *BioScience* 39/4 (1989): pp. 230-37.

27. Humberto Maturana and Francisco Varela, *The Tree of Knowledge* (Boston: New Science Library, 1988), p. 43.

28. This is a mild form of the Gaia hypothesis originally proposed by James Lovelock (*Gaia: A New Look at Life on Earth* [Oxford: Oxford University Press, 1979]) that "the physical and chemical condition of the surface of the Earth . . . has been, and is, actively made fit and comfortable by the presence of life itself. . . ." Long viewed with skepticism by scientists, the idea of a homeostatic Gaia has begun to attract more adherents from the mainstream for the strength of the testable hypotheses on global feedback mechanisms it has begun to produce. See in this regard O. Sattaur, "Cuckoo in the Nest," *New Scientist,* December 24/31, 1987; and R. Kerr, "No Longer Willful, Gaia Becomes Respectable," *Science* 240 (1988): pp. 393-95.

29. James Lovelock, "Man and Gaia," in *The Earth Report,* ed. Edward Goldsmith and Nicholas Hildyard (London: Mitchell Beazsley, 1988); William E. Rees, "Atmospheric Change: Human Ecology in Disequilibrium" *International Journal of Environmental Studies* 36 (1990): pp. 103-24.

30. For examples, see Rees, "Atmospheric Change."

31. P. Vitousek et al., "Human Appropriation of the Products of Photosynthesis," *BioScience* 36 (1986): pp. 368-74.

32. The field of environmental economics is an exception but has focused almost exclusively on policies and legal instruments available to "internalize" pollution damage and pollution avoidance costs (this reflects the principle of "polluter should pay"). In short, environmental economics was conceived largely as an extension of market economics and pays no attention to biophysical processes and the primacy of the second law. Under this approach, economic prescriptions regarded "environmental policy" largely as a matter of pollution control subject to variable "environmental conditions and local tastes" among jurisdictions (W.

Baumol and W. Oates, *The Theory of Environmental Policy* [New York: Cambridge University Press, 1988]). (With the emergence in the 1990s of a new discipline, ecological economics, we can hope that economic models and analysis will eventually come better to reflect biophysical reality.)

33. See, e.g., Julian Simon and Heman Kahn, eds., *The Resourceful Earth: A Response to Global 2000.*

34. *Economics and the Environment: A Reconciliation,* ed. W. Block (Vancouver: Fraser Institute, 1990); *Blueprint for a Green Economy,* ed. D. Pearce et al. (London: Earthscan Publications, 1989).

35. See J. Gosselink et al., *The Value of the Tidal Marsh,* Publication LSU-SG-74-03 (Baton Rouge: Center for Wetland Resources, Louisiana State University, 1974); and W. Westman, "How Much Are Nature Services Worth?" *Science* 197 (1977): pp. 960-64, for early valuation efforts.

36. C. Clarke, "The Economics of Overexploitation," *Science* 181 (1973): pp. 630-34.

37. E.g., David Ehrenfeld, "The Conservation Dilemma," in *The Arrogance of Humanism* (New York: Oxford University Press, 1978).

38. John Stuart Mill, *Principles of Political Economy* (Toronto: University of Toronto Press, 1965).

39. The need to reflect the depreciation of ecological capital in national income accounts is increasingly being recognized. See D. Pearce et al., "Blueprint for a Green Economy," UNEP/ World Bank, *Report of the Joint UNEP/World Bank Expert Meeting on Environmental Accounting and the System of National Accounts,* Paris, November 21-22, 1988.

40. Robert Heilbroner, *The Nature and Logic of Capitalism* (New York: Norton, 1976), p. 75.

41. For opposing views of the utility of this concept, see World Bank, *Rapid Population Growth and Human Carrying Capacity,* Staff Working Papers 690 (Population and Development Series 15) (Washington, D.C.: World Bank, 1985).

42. Reid Bryson, "Environmental Opportunities and Limits for Development" (Leopold Centennial Lecture, June 1986) (Madison: Center for Climate Research, University of Wisconsin, 1986). (And recall the metaphor that if a pond has a lily pad that doubles daily and completely covers the pond in one hundred days, the pond is only half covered on the ninety-ninth day. The question is, Have we seen the dawn of the one-hundredth day for humankind on Earth?)

43. Lester Brown, *The Changing World Food Prospect: The Nineties and Beyond,* Worldwatch Paper 85 (Washington, D.C.: Worldwatch Institute, 1988).

44. Ilya Prigogine and Isabelle Stengers, *Order out of Chaos: Man's New Dialogue with Nature* (Toronto: Bantam Books, 1984); James Crutchfield et al., "Chaos," *Scientific American* 255 (1989): pp. 46-57; T. Palmer, "A Weather Eye on Unpredictability," *New Scientist* 124/1690 (1989): pp. 56-59.

45. Rees, "Atmospheric Change."

46. I originally applied these concepts to environmental assessment in "A Role for Sustainable Development in Achieving Sustainable Development," *Environmental Impact Assessment Review* 8 (1988): pp. 273-91.

47. Ecological trade is a zero-sum game that can relieve imbalance but not overall scarcity.

48. C. Clarke, "The Economics of Overexploitation," pp. 630-34.

49. William E. Rees, "Energy Policy and the Second Law: Time to Ante Up," *Proceedings, Seventh Canadian Bioenergy Research and Development Seminar, 24-26 April* (Ottawa: Department of Energy, Mines, and Resources, 1989).

50. *State of the World 1984,* ed. Lester Brown et al. (Washington, D.C.: Worldwatch Institute, 1984).

51. *The Living Economy,* ed. P. Ekins (New York: Routledge & Kegan Paul, 1986), p. 129; Pearce et al., *Blueprint for a Green Economy.*

52. WCED, 1987.

53. Ibid., p. 297.

54. Norman Meyers, "Environment and Security," *Foreign Policy* 74 (1989): pp. 23-41.

55. J. Tainter, "Sustainability of Complex Societies," *Futures* 27 (1995): pp. 397-404.

56. William E. Rees, "Globalization and Sustainability: Conflict or Convergence?" *Bulletin of Science, Technology, and Society* 22/4 (2002): pp. 249-68; idem, "An Ecological Economics Perspective on Sustainability and Prospects for Ending Poverty," *Population and Environment* 24/1 (2002): pp. 15-46.

## 9. THE NEW NATURAL SELECTION

1. Thomas Berry, "The New Story," *Teilhard Studies* no. 1 (winter 1978).

2. Gregory Bateson, *Mind and Nature* (New York: Dutton, 1979).

3. Erich Jantsch, *The Self-Organizing Universe* (New York: Pergamon, 1981).

## 10. THE TEXTURE OF THE EVOLUTIONARY COSMOS

1. Pierre Teilhard de Chardin, *Science and Christ* (New York: Harper & Row, 1968), p. 25.

2. Pierre Teilhard de Chardin, *Activation of Energy* (New York: Harcourt Brace Jovanovich, 1970), p. 24.

3. Pierre Teilhard de Chardin, *Writings in Time of War* (New York: Harper & Row, 1967), p. 162.

4. For a brief but beautiful allusion to this theme, see Pierre Teilhard de Chardin, *The Human Phenomenon*, trans. Sarah Appleton-Weber (Portland, Ore.: Sussex Academic Press, 1999), p. xxvii. Sarah Appleton-Weber's translation seems to capture Teilhard's energy more fully than the earlier translation, *The Phenomenon of Man*.

5. Pierre Teilhard de Chardin, *The Heart of Matter* (New York: Harcourt Brace Jovanovich, 1978), p. 21.

6. Ibid., pp. 42, 78.

7. Ibid., p. 20.

8. Ibid., p. 46.

9. According to those who knew him, Teilhard had a marvelous talent for observation. He was "never without his geologist's hammer, his magnifying glass, and his notebook" (Claude Cuenot, *Teilhard de Chardin: A Biographical Study* [London: Burns & Oates, 1965], p. 129). "His quick eye would catch any chipped or chiselled stone that lay on the ground. George Le Febre, for example, noted . . . that 'His downcast eyes would spot the smallest bit of cut stone betraying itself by its redness on the bare greyness of the wind-swept soil'" (Cuenot, p. 91). His co-worker George Barbour describes him as "gifted with very sharp sight. He could spot a single Palaeolithic implement in a bed of gravel three meters away without dismounting" (Cuenot, p. 156). His friend Helmut de Terra says that he "recognized Palaeolithic artifacts with an uncanny sort of instinct. Often he would pick one of these from the ground, look at it briefly from all sides, and hand it to me, saying: 'It is suspicious; we must find more to be absolutely sure'" (Cuenot, p. 190).

10. J. A. Lyons, *The Cosmic Christ in Origen and Teilhard de Chardin* (New York: Oxford University Press, 1982).

11. Teilhard, *The Heart of Matter*, p. 20.

12. Pierre Teilhard de Chardin, *Letters to Two Friends 1926-1952* (New York: New American Library, 1967), pp. 24, 39, 27.

13. Teilhard, *Writings in Time of War*, p. 32.

14. Teilhard, *The Heart of Matter*, p. 16.

15. Teilhard, *Letters to Two Friends 1926-1952*, p. 24.

16. Teilhard, *The Human Phenomenon*, p. 14.

17. Ibid., p. 17.

18. Teilhard, *Writings in Time of War*, p. 155.

19. Teilhard, *The Human Phenomenon*, pp. 15, 16.

20. Ibid., p. 92.

21. A. G. Ward, *The Quest for Theseus* (New York: Praeger Publishers, 1970), pp. 15-16.

22. Teilhard, *The Heart of Matter*, p. 24.

23. Pierre Teilhard de Chardin, *Christianity and Evolution* (New York: Harcourt Brace Jovanovich, 1969), p. 105.

24. Pierre Teilhard de Chardin, *The Divine Milieu* (New York: Harper & Row, 1960), p. 78.

25. Teilhard, *Writings in Time of War*, p. 157.

26. Ibid., p. 228.

27. Teilhard, *Activation of Energy*, p. 188.

28. Teilhard, *The Human Phenomenon*, p. 198.

29. Teilhard, *The Heart of Matter*, pp. 28, 35.

30. Teilhard, *The Human Phenomenon*, p. 99.

31. Teilhard, *Writings in Time of War*, p. 162.

32. Teilhard, *The Human Phenomenon*, p. 7.

33. Teilhard, *The Heart of Matter*, p. 28.

34. Teilhard, *Writings in Time of War*, pp. 125, 123, 157.

35. Teilhard, *Activation of Energy*, p. 55.

36. Teilhard, *Science and Christ*, p. 48.

37. Teilhard, *Letters to Two Friends 1926-1952*, p. 107.

38. Teilhard, *The Heart of Matter*, pp. 54-55.

39. Ibid., p. 16.

40. Ibid., p. 50.

41. Teilhard, *The Human Phenomenon*, p. 213.

42. Ibid., p. 15.

43. Teilhard, *Science and Christ*, p. 79.

44. John R. Albright, "Order, Disorder, and the Image of a Complex God," paper presented at European Society for the Study of Science and Theology (ESSSAT), April 2000, pp. 2-3.

45. M. Mitchell Waldrop, *Complexity: The Emerging Science at the Edge of Order and Chaos* (New York: Simon & Schuster, 1992), pp. 11-12.

46. Emergent phenomena are regularities of behavior that somehow seem to transcend their own ingredients. For instance, the color of a chemical does not reside in the individual atoms or molecules that make it up but emerges only because of the complex interaction of one element with the other (Jack Cohen and Ian Stewart, *The Collapse of Chaos: Discovering Simplicity in a Complex World* [New York: Penguin, 1994], p. 232). Life is also an emergent property, since it is present only in the whole.

47. Ilya Prigogine and Isabelle Stengers, *Order out of Chaos: Man's New Dialogue with Nature* (New York: Bantam Books, 1984), p. 142.

48. Gregoire Nicolis and Ilya Prigogine, *Exploring Complexity: An Introduction* (New York: Freeman, 1989), pp. 13, 15.

49. Stuart Kauffman, *At Home in the Universe: The Search for the Laws of Self-Organization and Complexity* (New York: Oxford University Press, 1995), p. 78.

50. Clifford A. Pickover, *The Loom of God: Mathematical Tapestries at the Edge of Time* (New York: Plenum, 1997), pp. 120-21.

51. Kauffman, *At Home in the Universe*, pp. 8, 112.

52. Brian Goodwin, *How the Leopard Changed Its Spots: The Evolution of Complexity* (New York: Simon & Schuster, 1994), p. 45.

53. James Gleick, *Chaos: Making a New Science* (New York: Viking Penguin, 1987), pp. 128-31.

54. Kauffman, *At Home in the Universe*, p. 10.

55. Roger Lewin, *Complexity: Life at the Edge of Chaos* (New York: Macmillan, 1992), p. 43.

56. Teilhard, *Science and Christ*, pp. 39, 41.

57. Pierre Teilhard de Chardin, *Toward the Future* (New York: Harcourt Brace Jovanovich, 1975), p. 166.

58. Albright, "Order, Disorder," p. 2.

59. Teilhard, *Toward the Future,* p. 167.

60. Teilhard, *The Heart of Matter,* p. 33.

61. Teilhard, *The Human Phenomenon,* p. 15.

62. Teilhard, *Writings in Time of War,* p. 49.

63. Teilhard, *The Human Phenomenon,* p. 15.

64. Teilhard, *The Heart of Matter,* p. 28.

65. Teilhard, *Writings in Time of War,* p. 154.

66. Ibid., p. 157.

67. Thomas M. King, *Teilhard's Mysticism of Knowing* (New York: Seabury Press, 1981), p. 18.

68. Teilhard, *The Heart of Matter,* pp. 84, 83.

69. Ibid., pp. 167-180; quotation from pp. 167-68.

70. Teilhard, *The Divine Milieu,* p. 108.

71. Teilhard, *Toward the Future,* pp. 14-15.

72. Teilhard, *The Human Phenomenon,* p. 12.

73. Teilhard, *Science and Christ,* p. 88.

74. Ibid., p. 89.

75. Teilhard, *The Heart of Matter,* p. 87; idem, *Writings in Time of War,* p. 22.

76. Teilhard, *Science and Christ,* p. 89.

77. Teilhard, *Writings in Time of War,* p. 158.

78. Ibid., p. 154.

79. Ibid., p. 162.

80. Teilhard, *The Heart of Matter,* p. 33.

81. Pierre Teilhard de Chardin, *The Vision of the Past* (New York: Harper & Row, 1966), p. 272.

82. Teilhard, *Activation of Energy,* p. 28.

83. Teilhard, *Writings in Time of War,* p. 175.

84. Ibid., p. 175.

85. Teilhard, *Toward the Future,* p. 38.

## 11. TEILHARD 2000

1. John Horgan, *The End of Science* (Reading, Mass.: Addison-Wesley, 1996).

2. Pierre Teilhard de Chardin, *Man's Place in Nature* (New York: Harper & Row, 1966), p. 15.

3. Arthur Fabel, "Cosmic Genesis," *Teilhard Studies* no. 5 (summer 1981).

4. Harold Morowitz, "Teilhard, Complexity and Complexification," *Complexity* 2/4 (1997), p. 8.

5. Pierre Teilhard de Chardin, *Christianity and Evolution* (New York: Harcourt Brace Javonovich, 1971), p. 184.

6. Jennifer Cobb, "A Globe, Clothing Itself with a Brain," *Wired* (June 1995): pp. 108, 110, 113; quotation from p. 108.

7. G. Mayer-Kress and C. Barczys, "The Global Brain as an Emergent Structure from the Worldwide Computing Network," *The Information Society* 11/1 (1995): pp. 1-27.

8. Francis Heylighen and John Bollen, "The World-Wide Web as a Super-Brain," in *Cybernetics and Systems '96,* ed. Robert Trappl (Singapore: World Scientific, 1996).

9. W. Norris Clarke, S.J., "Living on the Edge: The Human Person as 'Frontier Being' and Microcosm," *International Philosophical Quarterly* 36/2 (1996): pp. 183-99.

10. Sally Goerner, *Chaos and the Evolving, Ecological Universe* (New York: Gordon & Breach, 1994), p. ix.

11. Christian de Duve, *Vital Dust* (New York: Basic Books, 1995).

12. Lee Smolin, *The Life of the Cosmos* (New York: Oxford University Press, 1997), p. 160.

13. For Smolin and Kauffman, see www.edge.org; Kauffman posts new work at www.santafe.edu.

14. George Smoot, *Wrinkles in Time* (New York: Morrow, 1993).

15. Paul Davies, "The Intelligibility of Nature," in *Quantum Cosmology and the Laws of Nature,* ed. Robert Russell et al. (Vatican City: Vatican Observatory Pub., 1993).

16. Stuart Kauffman, *The Origins of Order* (New York: Oxford University Press, 1993).

17. Peter Schuster, "How Does Complexity Arise in Evolution?" *Complexity* 2/1 (1996): pp. 22-30.

18. Brian Goodwin, *How the Leopard Changed Its Spots: The Evolution of Complexity* (New York: Touchstone, 1996).

19. Barbara Finlay and Richard Darlington, "Linked Regularities in the Development and Evolution of Mammalian Brains," *Science* 268/1578 (1995): pp. 1578-84.

20. Pierre Teilhard de Chardin, "Centrology," in *Activation of Energy* (New York: Harcourt Brace Jovanovich, 1971).

21. Benoit Mandelbrot, *The Fractal Geometry of Nature* (San Francisco: Freeman, 1982).

22. D. Green, "Fractal Geometry Gets the Measure of Life's Scales," *Science* 276/34 (1997): p. 34.

23. Stephen Jay Gould, "The Evolution of Life on the Earth," *Scientific American,* October 1994, pp. 84-91.

24. Lynn Margulis and Dorion Sagan, *What Is Life?* (New York: Simon & Schuster, 1995), p. 178.

25. Jean Houston, *A Mythic Life* (San Francisco: HarperSanFrancisco, 1996), pp. 6-7.

26. Pierre Teilhard de Chardin, "Life and the Planets," in *The Future of Man* (New York: Harper Torchbook, 1969), p. 116.

27. *Toward a Science of Consciousness,* ed. Stuart Hameroff et al. (Cambridge: MIT Press, 1996).

28. *Fractals of Brain, Fractals of Mind,* ed. Earl MacCormac and Maxim Stamenov (Philadelphia: John Benjamin, 1996), p. 31.

29. Franz Wuketits, *Evolutionary Epistemology and Its Implications for Humankind* (Albany: State University of New York Press, 1990), p. 8.

30. Peter Arhem and Hans Liljenstrom, "On the Coevolution of Cognition and Consciousness," *Journal of Theoretical Biology* 187/601 (1997): pp. 601-12.

31. Francisco Varela, "Organism: A Meshwork of Selfless Selves," *Organism and the Origins of Self,* ed. Albert Tauber (Norwell, Mass.: Kluwer, 1991).

32. Eva Jablonka, "Inheritance Systems and the Evolution of New Levels of Individuality," *Journal of Theoretical Biology* 170/301 (1994): pp. 301-9.

33. Stanley Salthe, *Development and Evolution* (Cambridge: MIT Press, 1993).

34. Freya Mathews, *The Ecological Self* (London: Routledge, 1991).

35. Connie Barlow, *Green Space, Green Time* (New York: Copernicus, 1997).

36. David Sloan Wilson, "Multilevel Selection Theory Comes of Age," *American Naturalist* 150/Supplement 1 (July 1997): pp. 51-54.

37. Peter Corning, *Nature's Magic: Synergy in Evolution and the Fate of Humankind* (Cambridge: Cambridge University Press, 2003).

38. Michael Batty, *Fractal Cities* (New York: Academic Press, 1994).

39. Robin Vallacher and Andrzej Nowak, "The Emergence of Dynamical Social Psychology," *Psychological Inquiry* 8/2 (1997): pp. 73-99.

40. Daniel Dennett, *Darwin's Dangerous Idea* (New York: Simon & Schuster, 1995), p. 320.

41. Karl Schmitz-Moormann, "Teilhard de Chardin's View on Evolution," in *Evolution and Creation,* ed. S. Andersen and A. Peacocke (Aarhus: Aarhus University Press, 1987), p. 164.

42. Theodore Roszak, *The Voice of the Earth* (New York: Simon & Schuster, 1992).

43. Denis Edwards, "The Discovery of Chaos and the Retrieval of the Trinity," in *Chaos and Complexity,* ed. Robert Russell et al. (Vatican City: Vatican Observatory Pub., 1995).

44. Barlow, *Green Space, Green Time.*

45. Richard Tarnas, *The Passion of the Western Mind* (New York: Harmony Books, 1991).

46. Richard Tarnas, "Commencement Address," Dominican School of Philosophy and Theology, May 20, 1995. (Thanks to Sr. Adrian Hofstetter for this reference.)

47. Catherine O'Connor, C.S.J., *Woman and Cosmos* (New York: Wiley, 1974).

48. Ursula King, *Christ in All Things* (Maryknoll, N.Y.: Orbis Books, 1997).

49. Sanford Drob, "The Sefirot: Kabbalistic Archetypes of Mind and Creation," *Cross Currents* 47/1 (spring 1997): pp. 5-29, quotation from p. 23.

## 12. LIBERATION THEOLOGY AND TEILHARD DE CHARDIN

1. See *Instruction* on Certain Aspects of the "Theology of Liberation" by the Sacred Congregation for the Doctrine of the Faith, August 6, 1984 (Washington, D.C.: United States Catholic Conference), IX, 3; X, 6 (immanentism); X, 6 (humanism and secularism); IX, 6; X, 5, X, 12 (politicization of the Faith); VI, 4 and 5 (reductionism).

2. Deane Williams Ferm, *Third World Liberation Theologies* (Maryknoll, N.Y.: Orbis Books, 1986), p. 103.

3. *Instruction* by the Sacred Congregation for the Doctrine of the Faith, VII, nos. 1-13.

4. Gustavo Gutiérrez, "Theology from the Underside of History," in *The Power of the Poor in History* (Maryknoll, N.Y.: Orbis Books, 1983), pp. 178-85. See also Raul Vidales, "Methodological Issues in Liberation Theology," in *Frontiers of Theology in Latin America,* ed. Rossino Gebellini (Maryknoll, N.Y.: Orbis Books, 1979), p. 39.

5. Gutiérrez, *The Power of the Poor in History,* p. 193.

6. Gustavo Gutiérrez, *A Theology of Liberation* (Maryknoll, N.Y.: Orbis Books, 1973).

7. Leonardo and Clodovis Boff, *Salvation and Liberation* (Maryknoll, N.Y.: Orbis Books, 1984), p. 18.

8. Gutiérrez, *A Theology of Liberation,* p. 13.

9. Ibid., p. 87.

10. Cited from Alfred Hennelly, "Red-Hot Issue: Liberation Theology," *America,* May 24, 1986, p. 428.

11. Gutiérrez, *A Theology of Liberation,* p. 76 n. 35.

12. Ibid., p. 173.

13. Gustavo Gutiérrez, *The Theology for a Nomad Church* (Maryknoll, N.Y.: Orbis Books, 1975), p. 52.

14. Pierre Teilhard de Chardin, "My Universe," in *Science and Christ* (New York: Harper and Row, 1965), p. 48.

15. Pierre Teilhard de Chardin, *The Phenomenon of Man* (New York: Harper Brothers, 1959), p. 262.

16. Pierre Teilhard de Chardin, "Creative Union," in *Writings in Time of War* (New York: Harper & Row, 1968), p. 171.

17. *Gaudium et Spes,* no. 39, *The Documents of Vatican II,* ed. Walter M. Abbott, S.J. (New York: America Press, 1966), pp. 237-38.

18. Medellín, Education, 9 (cited from Leonardo and Clodovis Boff, *Salvation and Liberation,* p. 20).

19. *Evangelii Nuntiandi,* no. 30 (cited from Boff, *Salvation and Liberation,* p. 21).

20. *Evangelii Nuntiandi,* no. 31, in Boff, *Salvation and Liberation,* pp. 21-22.

21. *Evangelii Nuntiandi,* no. 31, in Boff, *Salvation and Liberation,* pp. 21-22.

22. *Evangelii Nuntiandi,* no. 27, in Boff, *Salvation and Liberation,* p. 22.

23. *Gaudium et Spes* distinguishes between earthly progress and the growth of Christ's kingdom and adds that "on earth that kingdom is already present in mystery" (no. 39), but it does not say whether there is any causal relationship between earthly progress and the growth of the kingdom.

24. Gutiérrez, *A Theology of Liberation,* p. 177.

25. Ibid.

26. Juan Luis Segundo, "Capitalism vs. Socialism: Crux Theologica," in *Frontiers of Theology in Latin America,* ed. Gebellini, pp. 247ff.

27. Gutiérrez, *A Theology of Liberation,* p. 178.

28. See the book he co-authored with Clodovis Boff (*Salvation and Liberation*).

29. *Salvation and Liberation,* p. 23.

30. Ibid., pp. 51, 45, 47.

31. Ibid., p. 56.

32. Ibid., p. 58.

33. Schubert Ogden, *Faith and Freedom: Toward a Theology of Liberation* (Nashville: Abingdon Press, 1979), p. 35. Ogden praises Juan Luis Segundo's book *Our Idea of God* (Maryknoll, N.Y.: Orbis Books, 1974), for touching on the metaphysical question of the being and action of God but says that the work suffers because it has not transcended classical theism (pp. 71-73).

34. For example, Leonardo Boff in *Salvation and Liberation:* "God penetrates, permeates, all aspects of reality" (p. 51). Or Gutiérrez, *A Theology of Liberation:* God is present in humanity as his temple and is present in history as the incarnate Christ (chap. 10). Or Segundo in *Our Idea of God:* "God before us" or "God of the covenant" or "the God who becomes acquainted and related through history" (p. 23). All these statements are merely descriptions but not explanations of God's immanence. It is not explained how God is incarnate in Christ or how God is related to history.

35. Segundo, *Our Idea of God,* p. 270.

36. Teilhard's felicitous phrase in *The Phenomenon of Man,* p. 220.

37. Oscar Cullmann, *Christ and Time* (Philadelphia: Westminster, 1950), p. 63.

38. See *Vocabulary of the Bible,* ed. J. J. Von Allman (London: Lutterworth Press, 1958), p. 424.

39. "Esquisse d'un univers personnel," 1936, OE 6, 106. Cited from Robert L. Faricy, S.J., *Teilhard de Chardin's Theology of the Christian in the World* (New York: Sheed & Ward, 1967), p. 146.

40. For an extended treatment of God's immanence in an evolving world, see my *God Within Process* (New York: Newman Press, 1970).

41. Teilhard, *The Phenomenon of Man,* p. 189. Creative union implies creative change, internal and external. In no way does it mean preserving the status quo, which is divisive and oppressive.

42. Ibid., p. 71. For an extended explanation of the evolution of the human soul, see my article "Evolution of the Human Soul," in *The Dynamic in Christian Thought,* ed. Joseph Papin (Villanova, Pa.: Villanova University Press, 1970), vol. 1, pp. 223-51.

43. Teilhard, *The Phenomenon of Man,* p. 88.

44. Pierre Teilhard de Chardin, *Human Energy* (London: Collins, 1969), p. 20.

45. Pierre Benoit, "Resurrection: At the End of Time or Immediately After Death?" in *Concilium: Immortality and Resurrection,* ed. P. Benoit and R. Murphy (New York: Herder & Herder, 1970), p. 113.

46. J. Pedersen, *Israel* (London: Oxford University Press, 1926), vol. 1, p. 170.

47. Anton Grabner-Haider, "The Biblical Understanding of 'Resurrection' and 'Glorification,'" in *Concilium: Immortality and Resurrection,* ed. Benoit and Murphy, vol. 41, p. 76.

48. Benoit, "Resurrection," p. 113.

49. Teilhard, "My Universe," in *Science and Christ,* p. 63.

50. Clodovis Boff, co-author with his brother Leonardo Boff of *Salvation and Liberation,* describes the immanence of the kingdom in the world as "salvation in liberation," which manner of discourse he calls the language of topical realization. He goes on to show the *topos* of the place of the kingdom in society by the use of analogies he borrows elsewhere, thus speaking of society as the chrysalis or cocoon or that the kingdom is gestated in the womb of history. These analogies fit well within an evolutionary framework, but in our view are not as helpful and illuminating as the noetic model of history as a seed or tree and the kingdom as its fruit. This model is not only evolutionary but also corresponds aptly to the scriptural metaphor of

Christ as the first fruit of the growth of the kingdom. It is able to illuminate God's role in the salvific process as the Ground of evolution and history.

## 13. CHAOS, COMPLEXITY, AND THEOLOGY

1. Jürgen Moltmann, *God in Creation* (New York: Harper & Row, 1985), p. 54: "Creation is the universal horizon of Israel's experience of God in history."

2. James Gleick, *Chaos: The Making of a New Science* (New York: Viking, 1987); and Stephen H. Kellert, *In the Wake of Chaos* (Chicago: University of Chicago Press, 1993).

3. Kellert, *In the Wake of Chaos*, p. 2.

4. The new science of "complexity" is summarized in Roger Lewin, *Complexity: Life at the Edge of Chaos* (New York: Macmillan, 1992); and M. Mitchell Waldrop, *Complexity: The Emerging Science at the Edge of Order and Chaos* (New York: Simon & Schuster, 1992).

5. The general ideal of prediction still underlies much recent "scientific" thinking, such as the sociobiological dream of "explaining" human cultural phenomena, including ethics and religion, in terms of biological principles, which in turn are said to be reducible to chemistry and physics.

6. John T. Houghton, "A Note on Chaotic Dynamics," *Science and Christian Belief* 1/2 (1989): p. 50.

7. These questions, or ones like them, are raised repeatedly by the scientists interviewed by Lewin and Waldrop in their books cited earlier.

8. Paraphrase of a quotation given in Gleick, *Chaos: The Making of a New Science*, p. 308.

9. See especially Ilya Prigogine and Isabelle Stengers, *Order Out of Chaos: Man's New Dialogue with Nature* (New York: Bantam Books, 1984); and Louise Young, *The Unfinished Universe* (New York: Simon & Schuster, 1986).

10. This is implied in Whitehead's discussion of the notion of value, which in his thought is equivalent to actuality. To be actual is to be a value, and vice versa. See, e.g., Alfred North Whitehead, *Science and the Modern World* (New York: Free Press, 1967), p. 94.

11. From another point of view, however, modern science needs a contingent universe—if it is to justify the empirical imperative it allegedly follows. For if the world's actual properties could be deduced from necessary first principles, it would not be absolutely necessary to make actual observation of the natural world a requirement of scientific method. As we shall see later on, one of the ways in which chaos and complexity confirm nature's contingency is in their requirement that we cannot predict accurately how most physical processes will actually turn out. We have to follow close behind them, empirically observing their specific features.

12. Of course, an absurdist interpretation of contingency is also possible. It maintains that the universe "just happened" to come into existence, without any reason. Some contemporary scientists who have been persuaded by big bang physics to drop the idea of an eternal necessary universe still fall back on this option. However, their implicit denial of universal intelligibility to the cosmos is problematic for the whole enterprise of science and the human quest for understanding. But it is important to note that this viewpoint is not uncommon among scientific skeptics today. Indeed it is perhaps the only option available to them once they reject the notion of divine creation and at the same time find compelling the new scientific consensus that the universe is not eternal or necessary.

13. See Stanley Jaki, *Cosmos and Creator* (Edinburgh: Scottish Academic Press, 1980). Robert Russell has argued on the basis of the Hartle-Hawking hypothesis that even if the universe did not originate in a temporal singularity it might still be a "finite" universe. See his "Finite Creation without a Beginning: The Doctrine of Creation in Relation to Big Bang and Quantum Cosmologies," in *Quantum Cosmology and the Laws of Nature*, ed. Robert John Russell, Nancey Murphy, and C. J. Isham (Vatican City: Vatican Observatory, and Berkeley, Calif.: Center for Theology and the Natural Sciences, 1993), pp. 293-330.

14. See Brian Swimme, "The Cosmic Creation Story," in *The Reenchantment of Science*, ed. David Ray Griffin (Albany: State University of New York Press, 1988), pp. 47-56.

15. For a useful discussion of the "in principle" unpredictability of chaotic systems, see Kellert, *In the Wake of Chaos,* pp. 29-35, 38-40, 62-67.

16. See Paul Davies, *The Cosmic Blueprint* (New York: Simon & Schuster, 1988), pp. 112-15.

17. Waldrop, *Complexity,* p. 146.

18. Wolfhart Pannenberg, *Toward a Theology of Nature* (Louisville: Westminster John Knox Press, 1993), pp. 83-85.

19. Pierre Teilhard de Chardin, *Activation of Energy* (New York: Harcourt, Brace, Jovanovich, 1970), p. 239.

20. See, e.g., Stephen Hawking, *A Brief History of Time* (New York: Bantam Books, 1988), p. 175; and Steven Weinberg, *Dreams of Final Theory* (New York: Pantheon Books, 1992), p. 6.

21. John T. Houghton, "A Note on Chaotic Dynamics," *Science and Christian Belief* 1 (1989): p. 50. However, John Polkinghorne has expressed some doubts about the significance of such quantum effects in the macro world in his *Reason and Reality: The Relationship between Science and Theology* (London: SPCK; Philadelphia: Trinity Press International, 1991), pp. 89-92.

22. The now classic example of such skepticism is Jacques Monod's book *Chance and Necessity* (New York: Vintage Books, 1971).

23. Stephen Jay Gould, *Ever Since Darwin* (New York: Norton, 1977), p. 12.

24. Stuart Kauffman, *The Origins of Order* (New York: Oxford University Press, 1993), pp. 15-26.

25. Speculation surrounding the so-called "anthropic principle" also possibly points to the way in which physical reality is inherently biased toward the emergence of complexity, life, and mind.

26. See Karl Rahner, *Foundations of Christian Faith* (New York: Crossroad, 1984), pp. 116ff.

27. See John Macquarrie, *The Humility of God* (Philadelphia: Westminster Press, 1978).

28. The theme of divine humility, self-contraction, or self-withdrawal—as the condition for creation—is now widely discussed in Jewish and Christian theology. It is especially prominent in the theology of Jürgen Moltmann. See his *God in Creation,* pp. 86-93.

29. Pierre Teilhard de Chardin, *The Prayer of the Universe* (New York: Harper & Row, 1968), p. 121.

## 14. DIVINE WISDOM

1. This criticism of Wisdom for taking one attribute (emanation) of the divine and making of it the whole, dates back at least to the great Russian Orthodox sophiologists such as Sergius Bulgakov (1870-1944). See Eleanor Rae and Bernice Marie-Daly, *Created in Her Image: Models of the Feminine Divine* (New York: Crossroad, 1990), pp. 22-23.

2. See Rae and Marie-Daly, *Created in Her Image,* pp. 87-89, for a critique of the primacy given to Abba in the Christian tradition.

3. Thomas Berry and Brian Swimme, *The Universe Story* (San Francisco: Harper Collins, 1992), for a telling of this story from the primordial flaring forth to the present and into the next millennium.

4. Sallie McFague, *The Body of God: An Eschatological Theology* (Minneapolis: Fortress Press, 1993), p. 159. McFague goes on to state that perhaps the scandal of uniqueness is not Christianity's central claim.

5. Leo G. Perdue, *Wisdom and Creation: The Theology of Wisdom Literature* (Nashville: Abingdon Press, 1994), pp. 326-27. This claim by Perdue is even wider than that addressed in this section of my study, which is examining Wisdom as universal savior.

6. Patrick John Hartin, "Yet Wisdom Is Justified by Her Children: A Rhetorical and Compositional Analysis of Divine Sophia in Q," paper presented at the annual meeting of the Society of Biblical Literature, November 22, 1992.

7. Roland E. Murphy, *The Tree of Life: An Exploration of Biblical Wisdom Literature* (New York: Doubleday, 1990), pp. 89-90.

8. Elizabeth A. Johnson, *She Who Is: The Mystery of God in Feminist Theological Discourse* (New York: Crossroad, 1992), p. 89.

9. Murphy, *The Tree of Life*, pp. 28-29.

10. Roland E. Murphy, "Wisdom and Salvation," in *Sin, Salvation and the Spirit*, ed. Daniel Durken (Collegeville, Minn.: Liturgical Press, 1979), p. 178.

11. Murphy, *The Tree of Life*, p. 94.

12. Samuel Terrien, *The Elusive Presence: Toward a New Biblical Theology* (New York: Harper & Row, 1978), p. 359.

13. Murphy, *The Tree of Life*, p. ix.

14. Terrien, *The Elusive Presence*, p. 380.

15. Murphy, *The Tree of Life*, pp. 139-42.

16. *Sayings of the Fathers*, ed. R. Travers Herford (New York: Schocken Books, 1962), pp. 158-59. The saying referred to is chapter 6, saying 7.

17. Asphodel P. Long, *In a Chariot Drawn by Lions: The Search for the Female in Deity* (London: Women's Press, 1992), pp. 20-36; quotation from p. 36.

18. See Rae and Marie-Daly, *Created in Her Image*, pp. 16-20, for a more detailed discussion of the loss of the feminine Divine in the Christian tradition.

19. Johnson, *She Who Is*, p. 166.

20. Raimundo Panikkar, *A Dwelling Place for Wisdom* (Louisville: Westminster John Knox Press, 1993), p. 12. The quotation is from the *Ramayana* II, 109, 13.

21. Merlin Stone, *Ancient Mirrors of Womanhood: A Treasury of Goddess and Heroine Lore from Around the World* (Boston: Beacon Press, 1979), p. 214.

22. Joanna Macy, "Perfection of Wisdom: Mother of All Buddhas," in *Beyond Androcentrism: New Essays on Women and Religion*, ed. Rita Gross (Missoula, Mont.: Scholars Press, 1977), p. 315.

23. Ibid., p. 318. The quotation is taken by Macy from the verse summary of the *Perfection of Wisdom in Eight Thousand Lines*, XII, 1, 2.

24. C. N. Tay, "Kuan-Yin: The Cult of Half Asia," *History of Religions* 16/2 (1976): pp. 147-74.

25. Leila Ahmed, *Women and Gender in Islam: Historical Roots of a Modern Debate* (New Haven: Yale University Press, 1992), pp. 99-100.

26. My need to experience the Divine as feminine is a need that I did not realize I had until I was well into my adult years. It first surfaced in 1980, when I was traveling to the north shore of Taiwan to explore some rock formations. Upon turning a corner, a huge magnificent statue of a woman overlooking the sea unexpectedly came into view. I asked our guide who she was and he told me it was Kuan Yin, the Goddess of Mercy. Also, because of my interest, he said we would stop and spend time with her on our return journey, which we did. From that time on, for an extended period of time, the image of Kuan Yin, though not invited, came regularly into my prayer life.

27. G. B. Harrison, annotator, *Lectionary for Mass*, C Cycle (New York: Pueblo Publishing, 1973), p. 336.

28. Macy, "Perfection of Wisdom," pp. 315-16.

29. Claudia V. Camp, *Wisdom and the Feminine in the Book of Proverbs* (Decatur, Ga.: Almond Press, 1985), p. 49.

30. Ibid., p. 71. Camp's choice of this methodology does not lead her to deny the presence of borrowed goddess language in Proverbs (p. 69).

31. Ibid., p. 74.

32. Ibid., pp. 286-87. Camp finds the audacity of this claim to be validated by the love language of Proverbs.

33. See Kathleen M. O'Connor, "Wisdom Literature and Experience of the Divine," in *Biblical Theology: Problems and Perspectives: In Honor of J. Christiaan Beker*, ed. B. C. Ollenburger and Steven J. Kraftchick (Nashville: Abingdon, 1995), pp. 183-99. Examining the

poems about Wisdom in Proverbs, O'Connor concludes: "Although occasionally they distinguish her from the deity, most often they identify her with God. They grant her divine powers and prerogatives, and provide her with transcendent origins, portray her as worthy of absolute loyalty, imply that she herself is Creator, and declare explicitly that she gives and withholds life and wealth" (p. 195).

34. Murphy, *The Tree of Life,* pp. 135-39.

35. Ibid., pp. 142-45.

36. Elaine Pagels, *The Gnostic Gospels* (New York: Random House, 1979), pp. 48-53.

37. *The Other Gospels: Non-Canonical Texts,* ed. Ron Cameron (Philadelphia: Westminster Press, 1982), p. 85.

38. Pagels, *The Gnostic Gospels,* pp. 53-56.

39. Ibid., pp. 59-61.

40. Yves Congar, *I Believe in the Holy Spirit* (New York: Seabury Press, 1983), vol. 3, p. 157.

41. Robert Murray, *Symbols of Church and Kingdom: A Study in Early Syriac Tradition* (London: Cambridge University Press, 1975), pp. 21-22.

42. Congar, *I Believe in the Holy Spirit,* vol. 3, p. 157.

43. Murray, *Symbols of Church and Kingdom,* p. 318.

44. Pagels, *The Gnostic Gospels,* pp. 67-68. Pagels points out, however, that it was not the thinking of the orthodox Clement that prevailed in the church during the coming centuries. Rather it was that of Tertullian, who forbade women to speak in church, to teach, to baptize, or to celebrate the Eucharist.

45. Congar, *I Believe in the Holy Spirit,* p. 157.

46. Ibid., p. 163.

47. Murray, *Symbols of Church and Kingdom,* p. 318.

48. Congar, *I Believe in the Holy Spirit,* vol. 1, p. 13.

49. Donald L. Gelpi, *The Divine Mother: A Trinitarian Theology of the Holy Spirit* (Lanham, Md.: University Press of America, 1984), p. 45.

50. See Rae and Marie-Daly, *Created in Her Image,* pp. 16-20, for a historical exposition of the loss of tradition of the Holy Spirit as the feminine divine.

51. Bernhard Lang, *Wisdom and the Book of Proverbs: An Israelite Goddess Redefined* (New York: Pilgrim Press, 1986), pp. 151-52.

52. Joseph A. Fitzmyer, *The Gospel According to Luke X-XXIV,* Anchor Bible 28A (Garden City, N.Y.: Doubleday, 1985), p. 950.

53. Murphy, *The Tree of Life,* p. 135.

54. Gerhard von Rad, *Wisdom in Israel* (Nashville: Abingdon Press, 1972), pp. 97-106.

55. Murphy, *The Tree of Life,* p. 147.

56. Ibid., p. 145.

57. Samuel Terrien, "The Play of Wisdom: Turning Point in Biblical Theology," *Horizons in Biblical Theology* 3 (1981): pp. 133-37. For Terrien, Divine Presence is the only force that is common to the four sections of the Bible: the Torah, the Prophets, the Writings, and the New Testament.

58. Johnson, *She Who Is,* p. 91; see pp. 86-90, where the biblical texts on which this statement is based are presented.

59. Walther Zimmerli, "The Place and Limit of the Wisdom in the Framework of the Old Testament Theology," *Scottish Journal of Theology* 17/14 (1964): pp. 146-58.

60. Murphy, *The Tree of Life,* pp. 57-59.

61. Ibid., p. 125.

62. Ibid.

63. Von Rad, *Wisdom in Israel,* p. 71.

64. Ibid., p. 317.

65. Murphy, *The Tree of Life,* p. 126. Israel's ability to see creation as divine revelation may be based on its understanding of history as not only "the recollection of times past, but also the analysis of daily experience in which the variable and the incalculable often appear" (p. 113).

66. Ibid., p. 114.

67. Ibid., pp. 91-92. Murphy notes that this understanding of creation is placed in the context of a condemnation of nature worship.

68. Ibid., pp. 118-20.

69. Ibid., p. 43.

70. Richard J. Clifford, *Creation Accounts in the Ancient Near East and in the Bible* (Washington, D.C.: Catholic Biblical Association, 1994), pp. 193-97.

71. Roland E. Murphy, "Wisdom and Creation," *Journal of Biblical Literature* 104/1 (1985): p. 6. A personal experience that fulfills these criteria occurred during a lenten meditation on death. While I planned to meditate on my own personal death, what I experienced instead was the raging of the Earth's molten core, a rage provoked by what we humans are doing to the Earth. I seemed to be being asked how I could place significance on my own death when all around me creation is in the process of being ravaged and destroyed.

72. Murphy, *The Tree of Life*, pp. 71-72.

73. Von Rad, *Wisdom in Israel*, pp. 88-106.

74. Ibid., p. 318.

75. Lang, *Wisdom and the Book of Proverbs*, p. 31.

76. Johnson, *She Who Is*, pp. 124-29.

77. See Eleanor Rae, *Women, the Earth, the Divine* (Maryknoll, N.Y.: Orbis Books, 1994), p. 83, for a beginning discussion of the cosmic function of the Holy Spirit.

78. See Sallie McFague, *Super, Natural Christians: How We Should Love Nature* (Minneapolis: Augsburg Fortress, 1997), as a possible model.

79. Pierre Teilhard de Chardin, *The Human Phenomenon*, trans. Sarah Appleton-Weber (Portland, Ore.: Sussex Academic Press, 1999), p. 24.

80. Ibid., p. 25.

81. Ursula King, "Mysticism and Contemporary Society: Some Teilhardian Reflections," *Teilhard Studies* no. 44 (spring 2002), pp. 5-14.

82. Pierre Teilhard de Chardin, *Hymn of the Universe* (New York: Harper & Row, 1972), p. 63.

83. King, "Mysticism and Contemporary Society," p. 8.

84. Teilhard, *The Human Phenomenon*, p. 99.

85. Teilhard, *Hymn of the Universe*, p. 21.

86. Teilhard, *The Human Phenomenon*, pp. 224-26.

87. Ibid., p. 226.

## 15. The Creative Union of Person and Community

1. Robert B. Reich, *Tales of a New America* (New York: Times Books, 1987); see especially Prologue: The American Story, and chap. 3: The New Context, quotation from p. 50.

2. Pierre Teilhard de Chardin, *Human Energy* (New York: Harcourt, Brace, Jovanovich, 1969), p. 37 ("The Spirit of the Earth").

3. Thomas Berry, "Teilhard in the Ecological Age," *Teilhard Studies* no. 7 (fall 1982).

4. In a personal note, February 15, 1989, prior to my April meeting with P. Noir and P. d'Armagnac, P. Noir expressed his conviction that Teilhard as a "fils de la terre" should not be allied with the enemies of Nature, and that he was fully aware of human responsibility for the planet. In my consultation with P. d'Armagnac on April 7, 1989, he recalled a specific conversation with Teilhard in the 1950s when he asked Teilhard about his understanding of "hominization." In that conversation Teilhard expressed his own concern about the fragility of the biosphere and the dependence of the noosphere on it. P. d'Armagnac readily admitted that the ecological issue had not surfaced with pressing urgency in Teilhard's consciousness at the time. But, arguing from what he knew of his mentality and his respect for the earth, he affirmed that if Teilhard were alive today he would be among those pleading to "Save the earth!"

5. Joseph A. Grau, *Morality and the Human Future in the Thought of Teilhard de Chardin: A Critical Study* (Rutherford, N.J.: Fairleigh Dickinson University Press, 1976).

6. Pierre Teilhard de Chardin, *The Phenomenon of Man* (New York: Harper & Row, 1965), book 4: "Survival." Note especially chap. 11, "Beyond the Collective: The Hyperpersonal," pp. 257-72.

7. Pierre Teilhard de Chardin, "Sketch of a Personalistic Universe," *in Human Energy,* pp. 53-92. The three types of love are described in section 5, "The Energy of Personalization" (pp. 71-84). For a more extensive examination of his thought on love, its development and ramifications, see Grau, *Morality and the Human Future,* chap. 4, "Love the Highest Form of Spiritualized Energy" (pp. 123-79). For a significant study of Teilhard's thought on love from the point of view of a scientist involved in scientific and church affairs, see R. Wayne Kraft, "Love as Energy," in *Teilhard Studies* no. 19 (spring/summer 1988).

8. Pierre Teilhard de Chardin, *The Heart of Matter* (New York: Harcourt Brace Jovanovich, 1976), pp. 58-61 ("The Heart of Matter," Conclusion, The Feminine or the Unitive). See in chap. 1, "The Heart of Matter," the section "Conclusion: The Feminine or the Unitive."

9. Teilhard, "Sketch of a Personalistic Universe," p. 78.

10. Ibid.

11. Teilhard, "The Spirit of the Earth," in *Human Energy,* p. 35.

12. Teilhard, "Sketch of a Personalistic Universe," p. 82.

13. Ibid., p. 83.

14. Ibid., p. 84.

15. Pierre Teilhard de Chardin, *The Divine Milieu* (New York: Harper Torchbook, 1965), p. 73.

16. For other important texts conveying Teilhard's sense of the divine immanent in creation, see *The Hymn of the Universe* (New York: Harper & Row, 1961), pp. 13-37 ("The Mass on the World"), pp. 41-54 ("Christ in the World of Matter"), and pp. 59-71 ("The Spiritual Power of Matter"). See also *The Heart of Matter,* pp. 14-60; and "The Christic," pp. 80-104.

17. Robert Faricy, S.J., *Building God's World* (Denville, N.J.: Dimension Books, 1976), chap. 2, "Christ and the World" (pp. 36-71).

18. Teilhard, *The Heart of Matter,* pp. 40-44.

19. Unpublished retreat notes, June 25, 1952. For Teilhard's best explanation of what he means, see "The Phenomenon of Spirituality," in *Human Energy,* pp. 103-4, and "Centrology," in *The Activation of Energy* (New York: Harcourt Brace Jovanovich, 1970), pp. 116-17.

20. See p. 213 of this study.

21. Grau, *Morality and the Human Future,* p. 288. The text referred to is cited by Pierre-Louis Mathieu, *La pense politique et economique de Teilhard de Chardin* (Paris: Editions du Seuil, 1969), p. 193.

22. Teilhard, *Human Energy,* pp. 133-34.

23. Pierre-Louis Mathieu does not see Teilhard looking to world government structures, but rather to international economic, scientific, and cultural collaboration, without such a framework. But his thought is open to other interpretation. See my *Morality and the Human Future,* pp. 246-49 ("Teilhard and World Government").

24. Pierre Teilhard de Chardin, "The Essence of the Democratic Idea," in *The Future of Man* (New York: Harper & Row, 1964), pp. 238-43.

25. Grau, *Morality and the Human Future,* pp. 275-77 ("The Orientation of Economic Organization").

26. Mathieu, *La pense politique,* p. 190.

27. For development of Teilhard's ideas on "The Divinization of Activities," note especially *The Divine Milieu,* pp. 62-64 ("Communion through Action"). Also important regarding implications for a Teilhardian understanding of struggle to change unjust and unloving economic patterns would be "Our Struggle with God against Evil," in the section dealing with "The Divinization of Our Passivities."

28. Works that look into participative management include Lawrence M. Miller, *American Spirit: Visions of a New Corporate Culture* (New York: Warner Books, 1984), chap. 3 ("The

Consensus Principle"); Charles S. McCoy, *The Management of Values* (Marshfield, Mass.: Pitman, 1985), chap. 9 ("Communication, Participation, and Commitment"); and Max De Pree, *Leadership Is an Art* (New York: Doubleday, 1989). For the U.S. Catholic Bishops' report, see *Economic Justice for All: Pastoral Letter on Catholic Social Teaching and the U. S. Economy* (Washington, D.C.: USCC Publishing Services, 1986), chap. 4 ("A New American Experiment: Partnership for the Public Good").

29. One of the most important reflective works confronting the human devastation of the earth is Thomas Berry's *The Dream of the Earth* (San Francisco: Sierra Club Books, 1988). Also significant in this context is *Thomas Berry and the New Cosmology*, ed. Anne Lonergan and Caroline Richard (Mystic, Conn.: Twenty-Third Publications, 1987). The latter work, with response essays by Donald Senior, Gregory Baum, Stephen Dunn, and others, explores, among other matters, important theological, biblical, social, and moral issues.

30. Teilhard, "The Mysticism of Science," in *Human Energy*, p. 171.

31. Pierre Teilhard de Chardin, *Letters to Two Friends* (New York: New American Library, 1968), p. 125.

32. Ibid. Also significant here would be implications from Teilhard's "Research, Work, and Worship." In this short 1955 paper, he recommends specialized training for young religious who would be going into scientific or priest-worker careers. His emphasis, as expressed in *The Divine Milieu* thirty years before, is on making it clear that work in the world can, through faith and love, be seen as contributing to the fullness of Christ's life in the world. See also his *Science and Christ* (New York: Harper & Row, 1968), pp. 214-20.

33. For Teilhard's best extended treatment of the "noosphere," the "thinking envelope" surrounding the earth, see *Man's Place in Nature* (New York: Harper & Row, 1966), chap. 4 ("The Formation of the Noosphere").

34. Claude Cuenot, "L'apport scientifique de Pierre Teilhard de Chardin," in *Cahiers Pierre Teilhard de Chardin*, 4, *La parole attendue* (Paris: Editions du Seuil, 1963), pp. 64-65. Cuenot quotes from Teilhard's "Geobologie et Geobiologia," in *Geobiologia: Revue de l'Institute de Geobiologie* [Beijing] (1943): pp. 1-2. The complete English text of Teilhard's paper can be found in Nicole and Karl Schmitz-Moormann, *Pierre Teilhard de Chardin: L'oeuvre Scientifique* (Olten and Freiburg im Breisgau: Walter-Verlag, 1971), vol. 9, pp. 3753-59.

35. Claude Cuenot, *Teilhard de Chardin: A Biographical Study* (Baltimore: Helicon Press, 1967), p. 305.

36. Teilhard, *The Activation of Energy*, pp. 313-18.

37. Pierre Teilhard de Chardin, *The Vision of the Past* (New York: Harper & Row, 1966), pp. 56-58.

38. Ibid., pp. 59-60.

39. Ibid., p. 60.

40. Ibid.

41. Ibid.

42. Teilhard speaks of discouraging aspects of modern organized life: "So we get the crystal instead of the cell, the ant-hill instead of brotherhood" (*The Phenomenon of Man*, p. 257).

43. Teilhard, *The Activation of Energy*, pp. 207-14.

# A Bibliography of
# Teilhard's Published Works in English

## COLLECTED WORKS

*The Human Phenomenon.* New translation by Sarah Appleton-Weber. Brighton: Sussex Academic Press, 1999. Original translation: *The Phenomenon of Man.* New York: Harper & Row, 1959. Teilhard's only comprehensive presentation of his major theme of cosmic evolution and the emergence of life.

*The Appearance of Man.* New York: Harper & Row, 1965. Teilhard's theory of human origins.

*The Vision of the Past.* New York: Harper & Row, 1967. A development of the themes of *The Human Phenomenon.*

*The Divine Milieu.* New York: Harper & Row, 1960. A classic essay on the interior life; a spirituality "for those who love the world."

*The Future of Man.* New York: Harper & Row, 1964. Very important to an understanding of Teilhard's vision. Sets forth the challenges that modern humanity must confront in facing the evolutionary future.

*Human Energy.* New York: Harcourt Brace Jovanovich, 1971. Six of Teilhard's major essays in which the theme of love energy is treated extensively.

*The Activation of Energy.* New York: Harcourt Brace Jovanovich, 1971. These essays follow chronologically those in *Human Energy* and are important to an understanding of the inner coherence of Teilhard's vision.

*Man's Place in Nature.* New York: Harper & Row, 1966. Teilhard's concept of the human place in the whole cosmic process.

*Science and Christ.* New York: Harper & Row, 1969. Rich and stimulating reflections on the nature of science in relation to religious ideas.

*Christianity and Evolution.* New York: Harcourt Brace Jovanovich, 1971. These essays, which set forth Teilhard's vision of Christianity and the evolving cosmos, include an early essay on original sin.

*Toward the Future.* New York: Harcourt Brace Jovanovich, 1975. Teilhard suggests that human fulfillment consists in personal communion with the divine center of the evolutionary process, culminating in the spiritualization of matter. Includes the essay entitled "The Evolution of Chastity."

*Writings in Time of War.* New York: Harper & Row, 1968. The seeds of much of Teilhard's later thought are in these essays; they are his "intellectual testament." Written in the trenches in the midst of war, they reflect an impassioned vision of the Earth along with a love of the divine.

*The Heart of Matter.* New York: Harcourt Brace Jovanovich, 1979. This book contains in the title essay a spiritual autobiography and in the essay "The Christic" a further development of his ideas in *The Divine Milieu.*

## OTHER BOOKS

*Building the Earth.* Wilkes-Barre, Pa.: Dimension Books, 1965. Selected excerpts from *Human Energy.* A good introduction to his thought.

*Building the Earth.* New York: Avon Books, 1969. An expanded version that includes John Kobler's "The Priest who Haunts the Catholic World" and Teilhard's essay "The Psychological Conditions of Human Unification."

*Hymn of the Universe.* New York: Harper & Row, 1965. Contains Teilhard's seminal meditation "Mass on the World."

*How I Believe.* New York: Harper & Row, 1969. Teilhard wrote this essay in Peking in 1934 to set forth the rationale for his faith.

*Let Me Explain.* New York: Harper & Row, 1970. Teilhard's thought is skillfully assembled by Jean-Pierre Demoulin from the first nine volumes of the Collected Works and from some unpublished manuscripts. A valuable introduction to his basic ideas.

*The Prayer of the Universe.* New York: Harper & Row, 1973. Selections from *Writings in Time of War.*


## LETTERS

*Letters from Egypt 1905-1908.* New York: Herder & Herder, 1965. Letters to his parents while he was teaching in Cairo as a Jesuit scholastic.

*Letters from Hastings 1908-1914.* New York: Herder & Herder, 1968. Letters to his parents during his years at the Jesuit scholasticate in England.

*Letters from Paris 1912-1914.* New York: Herder & Herder, 1967. Letters to his parents while he was at the Musée de l'Homme.

*Pierre Teilhard de Chardin–Maurice Blondel Correspondence.* New York: Herder & Herder, 1967. A brief exchange of letters in 1919 concerning some essays Teilhard had sent to Blondel for his response.

*Making of a Mind: Letters from a Soldier Priest 1914-1919.* New York: Harper, 1965. An invaluable collection of letters to his cousin Marguerite. This book should be read along with *Writings in Time of War,* for he often refers to those essays.

*Letters from a Traveler 1923-1939.* New York: Harper & Row, 1962. This gives Teilhard's vivid impressions of China, the Gobi Desert, Java, and India.

*Letters to Two Friends 1926-1952.* New York: New American Library, 1968. This rich collection of 170 letters, many written from Peking, is an intimate record of Teilhard's life during his mature years.

*Letters to Leontine Zanta 1923-1939.* New York: Harper & Row, 1969. In letters to this intellectually distinguished friend, Teilhard unburdens his mind of his troubles with the Jesuits and with the church. He also gives spiritual direction and reveals the growth of his thought during these important years.

*Letters from My Friend—Correspondence between Teilhard de Chardin and Pierre Leroy 1948-1955.* New York: Paulist/Newman, 1979. In these letters to one of his closest confidants, Teilhard presents his unmasked face most clearly, infinitely human and attractive. Here his vision is set forth in its full maturity.

# An Annotated Teilhardian Bibliography
# for the 21st Century

Berry, Thomas. *The Great Work*. New York: Bell Tower, 1999. A collection of essays on subjects such as evolution, wilderness, the university, and reinventing the human. Berry
   suggests that the path ahead must involve the fourfold wisdom of indigenous peoples,
   women, traditional religions, and science. "History is governed by those overarching
   movements that give shape and meaning to life by relating the human venture to the
   larger destinies of the universe. Creating such a movement might be called the Great
   Work of a people" (p. 1). "The Great Work now, as we move into a new millennium, is
   to carry out the transition from a period of human devastation of the Earth to a period
   when humans would be present to the planet in a mutually beneficial manner" (p. 3).

Boff, Leonardo. *Cry of the Earth, Cry of the Poor.* Maryknoll, N.Y.: Orbis Books, 1997. In the
   pursuit of social justice and liberation, the new science of self-organizing systems can
   teach interdependence, complementarity, interiority, and common good to reveal the
   spiritual depth and destiny of creation.

Bruteau, Beatrice. *God's Ecstasy.* New York: Crossroad, 1997. A philosopher and theologian
   integrates the nonlinear sciences of complexity with the Christian tradition to envision
   an unfolding universe engaged in the emergence of divine providence. As a contemplative, Bruteau concludes that to share in the sacred life one ought to live mindfully in
   this self-creating universe.

Capra, Fritjof. *The Hidden Connections: Integrating the Biological, Cognitive, and Social
   Dimensions of Life into a Science of Sustainability.* New York: Doubleday, 2002. Capra
   suggests that the growing appreciation of systemic relations between component entities or objects, as exemplified in the symbiotic cell, can provide natural, ecological
   principles to guide and self-organize sustainable, humane communities.

Cobb, Jennifer. *Cybergrace.* New York: Crown, 1998. Cobb observes that the Internet as
   noosphere possesses a spiritual quality through its potential for dialogue that can promote a just Earth community.

Coelho, Mary. *Awakening Universe, Emerging Personhood.* Lima, Ohio: Wyndham Hall Press,
   2003. Coelho undertakes an integration of the new universe story of Teilhard, Thomas
   Berry, and Brian Swimme with the contemplative traditions of Christianity. By such an
   appreciation of a self-organizing cosmos a person may gain creative expression as a
   participant in its future unfolding.

Cousins, Ewert. "The Convergence of Cultures and Religions in Light of the Evolution of Consciousness." *Zygon* 34/2 (1999): pp. 209-19. The Fordham University theologian traces
   the global emergence of humanity from its earliest phase to the "First Axial Period" of
   the major world religions. Cousins suggests that after several centuries dominated by a
   mechanistic worldview, our present period may now be culminating in a "Second Axial
   Period" characterized by the meeting of the world's religions.

Forum on Religion and Ecology. www.environment.harvard.edu/religion. This comprehensive
   website founded by Mary Evelyn Tucker, John Grim, and Anne Custer provides
   resources from ten religious traditions including indigenous cultures, along with relevant environmental, economic, and political links.

Goodenough, Ursula. *The Sacred Depths of Nature.* New York: Oxford University Press, 1998.
   A cell biologist conveys a scientific appreciation of a wondrous and intricate evolutionary process through her "religious naturalism."

Haught, John. *God after Darwin.* Boulder, Colo.: Westview, 1999. Haught explores an evolutionary theology rooted in Alfred North Whitehead and Teilhard that finds purpose in an unfinished cosmos moving toward a divine future.

Holmes, Barbara. *Race and the Cosmos.* Harrisburg, Pa.: Trinity Press International, 2002. A theologian, ethicist, activist, and lawyer argues that the seemingly intractable issues of race and social justice can be resolved within the encompassing context of a dynamically interconnected quantum cosmology now being articulated by the holistic sciences. "I am suggesting that we view issues of race and liberation from the perspective of the cosmos, and that we begin to incorporate the languages of science into our discussions of liberation. This is a reasonable choice given the reality that the universe is an integral aspect of any human endeavor, even when it is a taken-for-granted backdrop for our activities. I am challenging all justice seekers to awaken to the vibrant and mysterious worlds of quantum physics and cosmology" (p. 3).

King, Thomas, S.J. *Jung's Four and Some Philosophers.* South Bend, Ind.: University of Notre Dame Press, 1999. The Georgetown University theologian employs Carl Jung's quaternity of thinking, sensation, feeling, and intuition to gain new insights into a dozen philosophers from Socrates to Sartre. The chapter on Teilhard is an especially clear review of his integrating vision of evolution.

King, Ursula. *Spirit of Fire: The Life and Vision of Teilhard de Chardin.* Maryknoll, N.Y.: Orbis Books, 1998. A well-researched, illustrated biography of Teilhard.

King, Ursula, ed. *Pierre Teilhard de Chardin: Writings.* Maryknoll, N.Y.: Orbis Books, 1998. A selection of Teilhard's writings on science and faith with an introduction by King.

Liebes, Sidney, et al. *A Walk through Time.* New York: Wiley, 1998. Jointly written with Brian Swimme and Elisabet Sahtouris, this is an evocative, beautifully illustrated journey through the new creation story of a self-organizing universe.

Malin, Shimon. *Nature Loves to Hide: Quantum Physics and Reality, a Western Perspective.* New York: Oxford University Press, 2001. Malin argues that if quantum physics is properly understood, with roots in Plato and Plotinus and informed by Alfred North Whitehead, it can overturn the machine model of the cosmos to reveal an organic, meaningful universe.

Matthews, Clifford, Mary Evelyn Tucker, and Philip Hefner, eds. *When Worlds Converge: What Science and Religion Tell Us about the Story of the Universe and Our Place in It.* Peterborough, N.H.: Open Court Publishing, 2002. Noted scientists, historians of religion, and theologians explore the new cosmology along with the resources of the world's religions for an environmental ethics. Anthropologist Terrence Deacon proposes an emergent view of consciousness: "From this perspective life and consciousness can be seen to be deeply interrelated, not just because consciousness has evolved in living things, but because they are each manifestations of a common underlying creative dynamic" (p. 152).

McFague, Sallie. *Super, Natural Christians.* Minneapolis: Fortress Press, 1997. The feminist theologian draws on insights from process philosophy, ecological science, and feminist epistemology to evoke a "functional cosmology" of the human affinity with and care for a sacred Earth. "The thesis of this book can be stated simply: Christian practice, loving God and neighbors *as subjects,* as worthy of our love in and for themselves, should be extended to nature" (p. 1).

Morowitz, Harold. *The Emergence of Everything: How the World Became Complex.* New York: Oxford University Press, 2002. Morowitz, a systems biologist, draws on Teilhardian ideas to describe how the new complexity sciences are revealing a universe that evolves sequentially into sentient beings.

O'Murchu, Diarmuid. *Evolutionary Faith.* Maryknoll, N.Y.: Orbis Books, 2002. We are indeed between stories, as Thomas Berry advises. As a contribution to the growing witness and revelation of a creative, nurturing cosmology, O'Murchu evokes a living, relational universe engaged in a self-organizing genesis. "We are an interdependent species within an interdependent universe, endowed uniquely for the release of self-conscious awareness throughout the entire spectrum of the divine-human creative process" (p. 150).

Rolston, Holmes, III. *Genes, Genesis, and God.* Cambridge: Cambridge University Press, 1999. A philosopher of environmental ethics offers a prescient reading of evolution as a self-organized, autopoietic process of intelligent, personified spirit. In this view, cosmic and earthly nature can be seen as a process of giving birth.

Ruether, Rosemary Radford. *Gaia and God: An EcoFeminist Theology of Earth's Healing.* San Francisco: HarperSanFrancisco, 1992. Ruether documents the ecological dimensions of the biblical traditions as well as the ecological potential of the new story of the universe.

Salmon, James, S.J., and Nicole Schmitz-Moormann. "Evolution as Revelation of a Triune God." *Zygon* 37/4 (2002): pp. 855-71. A synthesis of Teilhard's vision of evolution by creative union and the science of thermodynamics as a way to affirm Christian belief in a divinity who is both transcendent and immanent.

Schmitz-Moormann, Karl. *Theology of Creation in an Evolutionary World.* Cleveland: Pilgrim Press, 1997. This German theologian explores Teilhardian and Whiteheadian process thought of an organic universe. Schmitz-Moormann is assisted by the Jesuit scientist James Salmon.

Skehan, James, S.J. *Praying with Teilhard de Chardin.* Winona, Minn.: St. Mary's Press, 2001. Meditations on the essence of Teilhard's spiritual vision with chapters on topics such as Mass on the World, Co-creators of the Earth, Divinization of Our Activities, Finding God in All Things, and Communion Through Action.

Swimme, Brian. *The Hidden Heart of the Cosmos.* Maryknoll, N.Y.: Orbis Books, 1999. An exploration of the quantum vacuum as the fecund heart of reality. Swimme's lyrical celebration of this cosmological perspective provides a basis for a relational resonance with Earth and its myriad forms of life.

Swimme, Brian, and Thomas Berry. *The Universe Story.* San Francisco: HarperCollins, 1992. This unique collaboration of a mathematical cosmologist and a cultural historian conveys an epic sense of a self-organizing creation from its singular origin to a potentially humane, sustainable "Ecozoic" age. "The important thing to appreciate is that the story as told here is not the story of a mechanistic, essentially meaningless universe but the story of a universe that has from the beginning had its mysterious self-organizing power that, if experienced in any serious manner, must evoke an even greater sense of awe than that evoked in earlier times at the experience of the dawn breaking over the horizon, the lightning storms crashing over the hills, or the night sounds of the tropical rainforests, for it is out of this story that all of these phenomena have emerged" (p. 238).

Toolan, David, S.J. *At Home in the Cosmos.* Maryknoll, N.Y.: Orbis Books, 2001. In a book dedicated to Teilhard, the Jesuit theologian Toolan integrates biblical tradition with a self-organizing universe reaching consciousness through its human phenomenon. From this synthesis follows an "Earth ethics" to inspire an ecological sustainability within sacramental creation.

Tucker, Mary Evelyn, and John Grim, eds. *Religions of the World and Ecology.* Cambridge, Mass.: Center for the Study of World Religions and Harvard University Press, 1998-2003. A ten-volume series that arose from conferences held at Harvard to explore the insights of the world religions as a wellspring for environmental ethics and public policy. The edited volumes include: Buddhism, Christianity, Confucianism, Daoism, Hinduism, Indigenous Traditions, Islam, Jainism, Judaism, and Shinto.

Tucker, Mary Evelyn, and John Grim. "Religion and Ecology: Can the Climate Change?" *Daedalus* 130/4 (2001): pp. 1-22. A special issue on the wisdom of the world's religions for a sustainable future drawn from participants in the Harvard Religions of the World and Ecology conferences. Among the authors are Michael McElroy, J. Baird Callicott, Sallie McFague, Tu Weiming, and Bill McKibben.

Wessels, Cletus, O.P. *The Holy Web: Church and the New Universe.* Maryknoll, N.Y.: Orbis Books, 2000. An insightful rethinking of the structure and role of Christianity in light of the new story of an organically self-developing universe. Within an abiding divine creativity, as persons grow in spiritual awareness and relational concern, so the cosmos may come to consciousness. Drawing from its self-organizing patterns, a model for a similarly viable church is offered as a nested "holarchy" of integral communities.

————. *Jesus in the New Universe Story.* Maryknoll, N.Y.: Orbis Books, 2003. In this volume, Wessels goes on to lay out a path by which the Jesus Christ of biblical tradition can be appreciated within a dynamically emerging creation. The presence of God is seen to unfold as the holy web of relationships between all peoples and the encompassing earth. Salvation is thus recast as restoration, transformation, reconciliation, and renewal, facilitated by Jesus' eternal message of love and liberation.

Wright, Robert. *Nonzero.* New York: Pantheon, 2000. A Teilhardian argument for an innate penchant for cooperation in and progressive direction of evolution whence all parties benefit, rather than the prevalent view of zero-sum involving win/lose competition.

# Index

materialists, 39
mathematics: and fractal
complexity, 158-60; and
natural selection, 129-
30, 132-33
Mathews, Freya, 161
matter: complexity-con-
sciousness as emergent
property of, 1; develop-
ment of, 6; and granula-
tion, 6; nonconscious,
and universe, 1; phe-
nomenology of involu-
tion of, 2, 4; plurality of,
3; qualities of, 4; and
spirit, 1-2, 3, 4, 138-53,
142-43; wholeness of, 5;
*see also* proto-matter
McFague, Sallie, 195
McKibben, Bill, 93
Medellín: Conference of
Latin American Bishops
meeting, 168
metaphysics: of union with
spirit, 2, 7-8
military industrial societies,
90-91
Modernist controversy, 2
Monod, Jacques, 156
Muir, John, 64, 70, 72
Murphy, Roland, 200, 202-4
mysticism: of centration of
person, 2, 8-9; Teilhard's
definition of, 9

Naess, Arne, 161
natural resources, use of,
90-91
natural selection: and mathematics, 129-30, 132-33;
new, 127-37; principles
of, 128, 134-37
natural world: objectification of, 107
necessity: of universe, 186-
87; *see also* universe
Neoplatonism: perfected
cosmos in, 3
Newton, Isaac, 79; and
mechanical model of
universe, 105

noogenesis, 6
noosphere, 1, 6, 155-56; the
Earth-layer of thinking
beings, 22

Obermaier, Hugo, 18
O'Connor, Catherine, 163-
64
Ogden, Schubert: criticism
of liberation theologians
of, 173
Omega point, 222n. 19;
Christ as, 143, 169; as
culmination of evolu-
tionary process, 6-7, 29,
30, 143; *see also* Christ,
Cosmic

Pagels, Elaine, 200-201
Pannenberg, Wolfhart, 189
Paul VI (pope): *Evangelii
Nuntiandi,* 171, 175
person: mysticism of centration of, 2; union of, with
community, 209-21
personalization: of universe,
211-14
phenomenology: of involu-
tion of matter, 2; and
significance of complex-
ity-consciousness, 4-7;
*see also* complexity-consciousness
Pius X (pope): anti-Mod-
ernism of, 18, 21
Pius XI (pope): intellectual
climate under, 22
Pius XII (pope): conserva-
tism of, 24
planet Earth: envelopes
encircling, 1
plenitude, principle of, 65
plurality: as one of three
qualities of matter, 4-5
polarity, 8
Prigogine, Ilya, 158
progress: idea of, 58; myth
of, 91-93
proto-matter, 141; *see also*
matter

radial energy, 5
Raven, Peter, 93
reality: cultural roots of,
104-6; ecological, 107-
10
redemption: as orientation
of Western religious
thought, 68-69, 81-82
reductionists, 39
religious thought, Western:
redemption orientation
of, 68-69
research: constructive interdisciplinary, 217-18
Roszak, Theodore, 163

Sagan, Dorion, 159
Saint-Simon, Comte, 79
Salthe, Stanley, 161
salvation: liberation and,
170-71
Santa Fe Institute, 144, 148,
157
Sartre, Jean-Paul, 42, 61
Schmitz-Moormann, Karl,
163
Schuster, Peter, 158
science: and chaos and
complexity, 181-89; con-
structive interdiscipli-
nary research in, 217-18;
mystique of, 71; role of,
61-62, 71; Teilhard's
concern for, 71; *see also*
technology
secularism, 167
seed: metaphor of, 179
"seeing": challenge of, 2-4
Segundo, Juan Luis: on
immanence of God, 173;
on liberation, 171
self, emergent, 151-62
Smith, Adam, 106
Smolin, Lee, 157
Smoot, George, 157
Sober, Elliott, 162
space: and time, 141
spirit: correlation of, with
Wisdom, 200; and mat-
ter, 1-2, 3, 4, 138-53;
metaphysics of union